THE WATERS OF THE NILE

The WATERS of the NILE

Hydropolitics and the Jonglei Canal, 1900-1988

Robert O. Collins

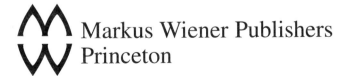

Markus Wiener Publishers
Princeton

First American paperback edition, 1996.

© 1990 by Robert O. Collins and Oxford University Press.

For information write to:
Markus Wiener Publishers
114 Jefferson Road, Princeton, NJ 08540

Library of Congress Cataloging-in-Publication Data

Collins, Robert O.
    The waters of the Nile: hydropolitics and the Jonglei Canal, 1900-1988/by Robert O. Collins.
    Includes bibliographical references and index.
    ISBN 1-55876-099-7
    1. Water resources development—Political aspects—Nile River Watershed—History. 2. Jonglei Canal (Sudan).   I. Title.
    HD1699.N496C65 1994
    338.91'00962—dc20   94-39649
                                              CIP

Printed in The United States of America.

TO THE MEMORY OF MY FATHER,
WILLIAM G. COLLINS
WHO NEVER DRANK OF
THE WATERS OF THE NILE,
BUT HAD THE GOOD SENSE
TO TELL ME TO GO AND DO SO

Preface

M Y first researches into the history of the Jonglei Canal and
Nile control were part of a larger work on the history of
Britain in the southern Sudan. I was attracted to the subject of
the canal because it passed through a remote and romantic
region of the upper Nile basin where I have spent a lifetime in
scholarly abstractions; but perhaps more seductive was the
fact that the investigations concerning Jonglei embraced
virtually every discipline of the human and animal condition
from anthropology to zoology. I foolishly thought to prepare a
modest description of this unique water project, but quickly
learned from my experience as a white-water guide on the
rivers of the American west that any portion of a river is a part
of the whole. One cannot construct a single hydrological
project without affecting the entire river basin. Thus I was
drawn irresistibly downstream and upstream and became
immersed in the complexities of Nile hydrology and Nile
politics. The result has been more years of research than I had
originally contemplated, but in the end, I hope, a better
understanding of the meaning of Jonglei and Nile control for
the reader.

The spelling of place-names in the Nile basin has always
bedevilled the writer, whether journalist, scholar, or administrator.[1] I have employed the *Gazetteer No. 68, Sudan*, of the US
Board of Geographic Names, which overcomes many of the
problems of spelling place-names in the middle Nile basin and
provides a rational standardization. Nevertheless, it is more
convenient for the reader to spell place-names by common
usage rather than to employ a system of transliterated spelling
with proper diacritical marks to conform to an accurate but
rigid standard which in the name of purity often creates
confusion rather than clarity. Consequently, Khartoum is not

[1] See Wright and Janson-Smith (1951).

al-*Kh*artūm, Kosti is not al-Kūsti, nor Rejaf, al-Rajjāf. I have retained the traditional names of Lake Edward and Lake Albert, not as a supporter of imperialism, but rather from a wish to avoid any confusion which might arise from the use of later names which, linked as they are to transitory political periods, are not likely to be long-lasting. These are arbitrary decisions, to be sure, but ones which I believe the reader will welcome in readily recognizing a place or name which pedantic adherence to the rule of transliteration rather than common sense would otherwise obscure.

All of this could not have happened without the personal interest and financial support of numerous individuals and foundations. The people were many, numbering in the hundreds, but some deserve special recognition. In the Sudan, Yahia Abdel Magid, A. M. Ibrahim, Bakheit Makki Hamad, Daniel Deng Yong, Jonathan Jenness, and James Ajith Awuol were of immense help in unravelling Jonglei. I owe a special word of thanks to an old friend without whose help and support Sudan studies would be much the poorer, M. A. I. Abu Salim, Director of the National Records Office in Khartoum. Yusuf Fadl Hasan, Mohamed Omer Beshir, and Sayyid Hurriez have always opened the doors of the Institute of African and Asian Studies, Khartoum University, which has been a second home to me for over two decades. The hospitality and interest of my dear friends Francis Deng, Bona Malwal, and Hilary Logali have contributed more than they know to Jonglei. In Paris, François Lemperiere, Spiro Agius, and Xavier de Savignac helped to sort out the complexities of excavating the longest navigable canal in the world. In Great Britain, Paul Howell and John Winder have graciously made available their experience and knowledge of the environmental effects of Jonglei on the canal zone.

Support for the research has come from numerous sources to whom I am deeply grateful: the Council for the International Exchange of Scholars for a Fulbright Research Grant; the Ford Foundation; the long-suffering research committee of the University of California Santa Barbara; and particularly the Rockefeller Foundation, which provided a month of solitude in the 'Veduta' at the Villa Serbelloni in Bellagio, Italy, where the core of the manuscript was prepared. This burst of activity at Bellagio was made possible by the research and writing carried out while I was the Trevelyan Fellow at the University of Durham, where I was privileged to deliver the Trevelyan Lecture, 'The Jonglei Canal: The Past and Present of a Future', and as Visiting Fellow at Balliol College, Oxford. To the Principal and Fellows of Trevelyan College and the Master and Fellows of Balliol I am most grateful for their generosity, companionship, and encouragement. At Durham, Lesley Forbes, the inspiration of the Sudan Archive, produced materials on Jonglei as if by magic. My wife, Jan Collins, was always at my side supporting me through the rain and snow of Durham, Oxford, and Paris, the heat of Khartoum, the mud of Sobat camp, PK141, and those eternal swamps of the upper Nile.

Finally, and always, yet another manuscript could not have been completed without the support of my dear friend Dorothy Johnson.

Once one has drunk of the waters of the Nile one shall return, and so shall I.

R.O.C.

Santa Barbara
1 January 1988

Contents

Illustrations

MAPS

FIGURES

Technical Abbreviations and Conversion Factors

TECHNICAL ABBREVIATIONS

cm	centimetre(s)	m^3	cubic metre(s)
km	kilometre(s)	Mm^3/d	millions of cubic
km^2	square kilometre(s)		metres per day
m	metre(s)	mm	millimetre(s)
m^2	square metre(s)	kW	kilowatt(s)

CONVERSION FACTORS

1 billion	1,000 million = 1 milliard

Units of length:

1 cm	0.3937 in
1 m	3.28 ft
1 km	0.621 mile

Units of area:

1 m^2	10.76 ft^2
1 km^2	0.386 sq. mile
	248 acres
	238 feddans
1 feddan	4,200 m^2
	1.037 acres
1 hectare	2.381 feddans

Units of volume:

1 m^3	35.31 ft^3
	1.308 yd^3
	220 imperial gallons
	257 US gallons
	0.000811 acre feet

Units of weight:

1 kantar   99.05 lb

Units of flow:

1 million m³ per day   11.6 m³ per second
                        408 ft per second
                        153,000 imperial gallons per minute
                        255,500 US gallons per minute

Units of slope:

1 cm per km   0.0528 ft per mile

Abbreviations

AAAID	Arab Authority for Agricultural Investment and Development
ASCE	American Society of Civil Engineers
AUFS	American Universities Field Staff
BADA	Bor Area Development Activities
BIEA	British Institute of East Africa, Nairobi
CCI	Compagnie de Constructions Internationales
CFE	Compagnie Française d'Enterprise
CIFA	Committee for Inland Fisheries of Africa (FAO)
CILSS	Comité Permanent Inter-États de Luttre contre la Sécheresse dans le Sahel (Inter-State Committee to Fight Drought in the Sahel)
CRED	Centre for Research and Economic Development
DTP	Société Dragages et Travaux Publics (Company for Dredging and Public Works)
DVS	Doctor of Veterinary Science
DVW	Deutscher Verlag für Wissenschaften, Berlin (German Scientific Publishing House)
EGY	Egypt
EIFAC	European Inland Fisheries Advisory Committee (FAO)
ELC	Environmental Liaison Centre, Nairobi
EMWP	Egyptian Master Water Plan
FAO	Food and Agriculture Organization (UN)
FO	Foreign Office
GCMG	Knight Grand Cross of the Order of St Michael and St George
Geo. J.	*Geographical Journal*
GTM	Grands Travaux de Marseille
GTMI	Grands Travaux de Marseille International
HMSO	Her (His) Majesty's Stationery Office, London
IAHR	International Association for Hydraulic Research

IBRD	International Bank for Reconstruction and Development (World Bank)
IJAHS	*International Journal of African Historical Studies*
ILACO	International Land-Use Company, Arnhem, Netherlands
ILCA	International Livestock Center for Africa
ILO	International Labour Office (UN)
IWE	Institute of Water Engineers, London
JAH	*Journal of African History*
JEO	Jonglei Executive Organ (Executive Organ for Development Projects in the Jonglei Area)
JIT	Jonglei Investigation Team
MERIP	Middle East Research and Information Project
MPW	Ministry of Public Works, Egyptian Government, Cairo
NCR	National Council for Research, Khartoum
ODI	Overseas Development Institute, London
ORSTOM	Office de la Recherche Scientifique et Technique d'Outre-Mer
PDU	Project Development Unit, Regional Ministry of Agriculture, Juba
PJTC	Permanent Joint Technical Commission
PRO	Public Records Office, London
Proc. Inst. Civ. Engrs.	*Proceedings of the Institute of Civil Engineers* (UK)
Proc. RGS	*Proceedings of the Royal Geographical Society*
PWM	Public Works Ministry (*see also* MPW)
RAF	Royal Air Force
SA	Société Anonyme (Joint-Stock Company, Limited, France)
SAD	Sudan Archives, Durham University
SGE	Société Générale d'Enterprise Sainrapt et Brice
SIR	*Sudan Intelligence Report*
SNR	*Sudan Notes and Records*
SOGREAH	Société Grenobloise d'Études et d'Applications Hydrauliques, Grenoble
SpA	Società per Azioni (Public Limited Company, Italy)

Srl	Società a Responsibilità Limitata (Private Limited Liability Company, Italy)
SUD	Sudan
UN	United Nations
UNDP	United Nations Development Programme
UNEPTA	United Nations Programme of Technical Assistance
UNESCO	United Nations Educational, Scientific, and Cultural Organization
UNICEF	United Nations Children's Fund
UNIDO	United Nations Industrial Development Organization
UNP	Provincial Records of the Upper Nile Province in the National Records Office, Khartoum
UNSF	United Nations Special Fund
WAPDA	West Pakistan Water and Power Development Authority
WHO	World Health Organization
WMO	World Meteorological Organization

Arabic and Vernacular Terms

dura   sorghum, millet

effendia   upper middle class in Egypt, many of Turkish origins

fallahin   Egyptian peasant

falucca   narrow Nile river boat propelled by lateen sails

hafir   surface storage-tank for water

haria   method of cultivation by which the old grass is burnt to clear the ground and stimulate new growth

jallaba   petty merchants from the northern Sudan, often associated with the Danaqla people of Nubia

khor   natural water-course

luak   large thatched building that houses livestock and people

marissa   locally brewed beer

sa'idi   Egyptian peasant labourers, principally from upper Egypt, noted for their endurance in excavation, e.g. of the Suez Canal

toic   Dinka word for a seasonally inundated flood-plain

tukul   small, mud-walled, thatched home

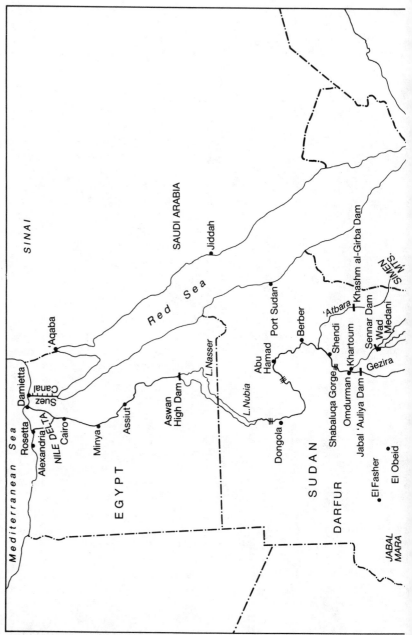

MAP 1. The Nile basin

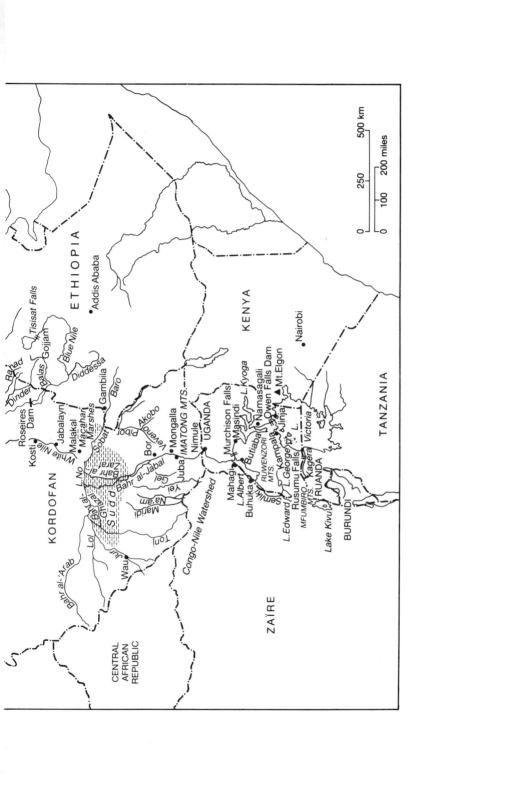

I

The Nile

Father Nile, how can I explain the cause of this,
    Or in what lands you·have hidden your head?
Because of you, your soil begs for no showers,
No dry grasses implore rain-bringing Jove.

Albius Tibullus, *Elegy* I, 7

THE Nile is one of the great natural and romantic wonders of the world. It is the longest river, flowing south to north 6,825 km (4,238 miles) over 35° of latitude through civilizations of great antiquity. Its basin is broad and big, embracing some three million km² (1,196,000 sq. miles) of equatorial and north-east Africa. It flows irresistibly through every natural formation, from mountainous highlands to barren deserts. Today its basin includes nine independent States—Ruanda, Burundi, Zaïre, Tanzania, Kenya, Uganda, Ethiopia, Egypt, and the Sudan.

Although the measurements of land-forms, except perhaps those subjected to volcanic and earthquake activity, remain constant over short periods of geological time, the size and elevation above sea-level of lakes, and the length and course of rivers and streams, will vary according to numerous factors such as rainfall, evaporation, run-off, topography, discharges, and man-made regulators. Thus any measurement of a body of water—lakes, rivers, or cataracts—is only precisely accurate at the moment of calculation. Consequently, the measurements of the Nile system which follow are only approximate. They have been determined by the comparison and contrast of calculations made throughout this century and recorded in government reports, scientific papers, travellers' accounts, private papers, atlases, gazetteers, encyclopaedias, and maps, both standard topographical and of satellite origin. What is striking is not the deviation of measurements of the Nile system between 1900 and 1988, which one would expect, but rather that the percentage of deviation in relation to the total length, area, or height above sea-level of any part of the Nile system is relatively insignificant. The exception is the rise of some 2.5 m in the levels of Lake Victoria and Lake Albert during the heavy rains of 1961–4, and the consequent increase in the permanent swamp of the Sudd. Thus the measurements which follow are designed to provide the reader with an understanding of the hydrology and topography of the Nile system which, while imprecise, is comprehensible. The measurements have been recorded in the metric system, the standard accepted by the international community of hydrologists.[1]

Within this vast area, man from palaeolithic times to the present has watched the rich brown waters of the Nile flow northward to the Mediterranean Sea, anxiously awaiting the life which came with them; and in its northern reaches, without the Nile there would be only sand and rock and wind in Egypt and much of the Sudan. Man cannot survive where there is no water, and cannot multiply where there is no fertile soil. The Nile has provided both these necessities.

This is what distinguishes the Nile from the other great geographical features of the world. At times the river gave too much, resulting in disastrous floods which swept away the human habitations huddled by the river's banks. In other years the waters did not rise, and there was drought and famine. And so from earliest times, when man drifted out of the desiccation of the Sahara to the banks of the Nile, he wondered what forces controlled the flow of life. No one who has ever drunk from the waters of the Nile or who has lived by

[1] Ministry of Irrigation (1975, p. 7). There has in the past been some confusion over the term 'milliard'. In hydrological writing, however, 'milliard' has universally been used to designate 1000 million. In order to simplify terminology, I have substituted billion (1000 million) for milliard to preserve continuity and clarity. There is another and more confusing problem in counting. The total mean annual flow of the Nile is fixed by treaty (1959) at 84 billion m³, as measured at Aswan for 1900–29 and later revised to 1959. Consequently the sum total of the mean annual flow of all the Nile tributaries must add up to the mean annual flow at Aswan. Thus for convenience the contributions of the tributaries have traditionally been counted as 28 billion from the White Nile, 45 billion from the Blue Nile, and 11 billion from the 'Atbara. The accepted flows do not reflect reality in any given year or even the mean annual flow from 1905 to 1980. Despite the below-average flows of the Blue Nile during the 1980s, the total mean annual volume measured at Aswan for the past 75 years is in excess of 84 billion m³.

its fertility, no matter in what age, could have failed to ask this
fundamental question. For thousands of years, man's greatest
fear in Egypt and the Sudan was that the Nile would cease to
flow; and so throughout the centuries it was firmly believed,
by Pharaohs and peasants alike, that interference with the
Nile, and therefore life, was possible when the Nile flood did
not flow. Indeed, if one did not believe the myth, there were
times when the waters did not come, and man was reminded
of his dependence upon gods who could control the river.
Without its flood, unimpeded by men or gods, the people of
Egypt perished.

As they watched the dramatic rise and fall of the Nile, men
also began to measure the flood to determine when to plant
and how much to cultivate. Pharaohs recorded the lean or
bountiful years when the Nile flowed or not. In the eighth
century AD the Arabs erected a nilometer on the island of
Rodah at Cairo to measure the Nile waters. Constructed about
711, the gauge consisted of a white marble column in the
centre of a square well, with a scale measured in cubits of
about 54 cm (approximately 22 in.). There were other
nilometers scattered along the river, and information from
ancient writers resulted in the compilation from 622 to the
present of the longest series of records of any river.[2]

Despite gaps in the recorded flows of the Nile, the measurements indicate the floods which drowned the inhabitants and
the scarcity of water which caused death. There was a disastrous dearth of water from 944 to 953 and from 1059 to 1066.
From 1180 to 1182 extremely low Nile flows are reported to
have produced a catastrophic famine in Egypt, during which
tens of thousands died. In 1201 a third of the population of
Cairo is reputed to have perished. In desperation the sultans
of Egypt were supposedly to have sent ambassadors bearing
tribute to the Ethiopians so that they would not obstruct the
waters. Even the Renaissance poet Lodovico Ariosto wrote in
his *Orlando Furioso*:

> And the Egyptian Sultan, it is said,
> Pays tribute and is subject to the king,
> Who could divert into another bed
> The river Nile, and thus disaster bring

[2] Hurst (1952, pp. 258–60).

On Cairo, and on all that region spread
The blight of famine and great suffering.[3]

The legend became belief. James Bruce of Kinnaird, the
Scottish traveller who lived in Ethiopia from 1769 to 1771,
recounts a letter from the king of Ethiopia to the pasha of
Egypt in 1704 threatening to cut off the water. In 1851
Charles T. Beke, an eminent British geographer and student
of the Nile, sent to Lord Palmerston, the British foreign
secretary, a 'Memoir on the Possibility of Diverting the
Waters of the Nile so as to Prevent the Irrigation of Egypt'.[4]
In the twentieth century, the waters did not flow in 1914, and
in 1984 the failure of rain in Ethiopia would have produced
suffering in Egypt without the high dam reservoir. In 1987 the
dearth of rain will not be able to sustain both the irrigation
and hydroelectric potential of that reservoir.

Dependence upon the Nile led naturally to the question of
whence the waters came. Men speculated. Pharaohs sent out
expeditions to seek the source. Nero ordered his centurions up
the river. All were defeated, and the doubts remained. Like
the timelessness of the Nile itself, the centuries slipped by
without man knowing the source of the life-giving waters. By
the middle of the nineteenth century the Nile quest had
become, in the words of Sir Harry Johnston, 'the greatest
geographical secret, after the discovery of America'.[5] In fact,
after 2,000 years man had not improved upon the description
of the Nile source which the Greek historian Herodotus had
received from the scribe of the sacred treasury of Athene at
Saïs during his travels in Egypt. In 460 BC he told Herodotus
that the Nile flowed from springs of great depth between two
tall mountains. It was to be another 2,400 years before these
elusive fountains were found, and the source of the longest
river in the world discovered.

In 1937 an obscure and eccentric German explorer, Dr
Burkhart Waldekker, wandering impoverished and alone in
the deep green Kangosi hills in the Republic of Burundi,
stumbled upon a spring which bubbled into the Nile basin
further from the Mediterranean Sea than any previously

[3] Canto xxxiii, st. 106, trans. B. Reynolds (London, 1981), ii. 305.
[4] Emily Beke, letter to *The Times*, 25 Oct. 1888.
[5] Johnston (1905, p. vii).

known source. From that spring in Burundi, marked by a modest pyramid perched atop a hill of lush green grass with the succinct inscription 'Caput Nili Meridianissimum' ('southernmost source of the Nile'), the great river begins. Its water flows northward fed by streams until it becomes the Luvironzia, which winds through the hills until reaching the Ruvuvu River rising in the highlands of north-west Burundi. The Ruvuvu is an ample river, free of swamp, which passes steadily north and east into Tanzania to its meeting with the Kagera River just above Rusumu Falls. But the Kagera does not rely only on the Ruvuvu and its origins at the Nile source for its sustenance. To the north in Ruanda two important tributaries, the Nyavarongo and the Akanyaru, flow down from the hill country, collecting the waters of hundreds of streams and rivers from the lush valleys of Ruanda to add to the Kagera flow. Tumbling over the Rusumu Falls the Kagera turns northward along the fault line marking the boundary between Tanzania and Ruanda through swampy lakes before angling abruptly eastward, its placid surface broken by the rapids at Kyansore Island, the traditional home of the sacred drums of the Banyankole, to flow phlegmatically into the vast inland waters of Lake Victoria.

Although the spring above the Luvironzia is the ultimate source, the Nile has others. North of Ruanda the lovely Mfumbiro (Virunga) Mountains in the Republics of Zaïre and Uganda block the great trench of the Rift Valley and determine the northward course of the Nile. The great Rift Valley is one of Africa's most dramatic features. Beginning in the Mozambique channel far to the south, the Rift slices northward across the continent as if the land had been rent by a massive cleaver. Up the Zambezi to Lake Malawi the Rift then bifurcates. The eastern branch runs through the Kenya highlands and Ethiopia to the Red Sea and up the Gulf of 'Aqaba to the valley of the River Jordan. The western branch parallels the eastern Rift through Lakes Tanganyika, Kivu, Edward, and Albert before disappearing into the swamps of the Nile. All the great lakes of central and eastern Africa, except Lakes Kyoga and Victoria, lie at the bottom of these two trenches, confined by steep and imposing escarpments. Formed by parallel faults whereby the valley floor sank or the escarpments on either side were thrust upward by tectonic forces, the rivers and streams of eastern Africa, which had hitherto flowed westward into the Congo basin, were captured in the Rift Valley to pass northward to the Nile. Some time in the geological past volcanic activity threw up the Mfumbiro range, running 100 km east and west across the western Rift to divert the Nile into Lakes Kivu and Tanganyika to the south, while the waters from the northern slopes continued to form a source of the Nile from thousands of streams which coalesce into Lake Edward at the bottom of the Rift. The home for myriads of water-birds—pelicans, flamingoes, egrets, gulls, and Nile geese—and many varieties of fish of which only three kinds are found further down the Nile, Lake Edward is one of the most beautiful lakes in the world. 'Sometimes at sunset when the sun dips behind these mountains the peaks stand out in deep purple masses against a sky flaming in crimson and orange, and again blending into tints of rose and salmon colour'.[6]

Northward from Lake Edward, the Semliki River follows the Rift Valley around the imposing Ruwenzori range to form an important link in the hydrological system of the upper Nile basin. The Semliki is a swift-flowing river, plunging through a deep narrow valley until entering dense papyrus swamps at the southern end of Lake Albert. During its tumultuous course the Semliki receives torrents of water cascading down the precipitous slopes of the Ruwenzori to the east and the uplands of Zaïre to the west. Here is Africa in all its grandeur— immense, wild, and breath-taking. No other region on the continent captures the imagination more than the reality of the Ruwenzori, the Mountains of the Moon, rising precipitously on the equator into the swirling mists of icy crags and snow-capped peaks. The life of the Ruwenzori comes from the west. Originating in the south Atlantic, the monsoon rains sweep across Africa to obscure the mighty summits of the Ruwenzori some 300 days of the year, while on the ground the forbidding tropical rain forest of Zaïre creeps across the Semliki to ascend the flanks of the mountains. Here impenetrable tropical vegetation flourishes in the hot and humid climate;

[6] Garstin (1904, p. 55).

gigantic flowers bloom, and the trees are giants in this land of cliffs and streams hurtling into space to be blown away by the wind. The Mountains of the Moon are Africa in all its majesty.

Lake Albert, now Lake Mobutu Sese Seko, was discovered by Sir Samuel Baker in 1864. Indeed, it was his goal in the Nile quest to find the Luta Nzigé or dead locust lake, but he did not circle it, confining himself to make his way northward along the eastern shore in canoes. In 1876, however, Romolo Gessi Pasha, the Italian administrator and explorer, circumnavigated the lake to find an elliptical body of water filling the Rift Valley below its escarpments, characterized by shallow water and loneliness. Nowhere does the depth of Lake Albert exceed 50 m, allowing the frequent tropical squalls to whip the surface quickly into large, treacherous waves. The other striking feature of Lake Albert is the lack of habitation along the narrow plain between the escarpment and the shore. Except for the forlorn and dilapidated lake port of Butiaba on the eastern shore, there are few villages as far as Buhuka to the south, or on the west bank in Zaïre between Kasengi and Mahagi, which was densely populated in the nineteenth century. Forty km north of Butiaba the waters from the ultimate source, the spring above the Luvironza River in Burundi, reach Lake Albert, having passed through Africa's greatest reservoir, Lake Victoria.

Lake Victoria is the second largest body of fresh water after Lake Superior. A huge, shallow saucer only 80 m deep but with a surface of 67,000 km^2 resting on the Lake Plateau between the two great Rift Valleys, its only significant source is the Kagera River. Unlike Lake Albert, whose monotonous shoreline follows the straight fault lines of the Rift Valley, the coast of Lake Victoria is broken by numerous bays and gulfs— Kavirondo, Napoleon, and Murchison in the north, Emin Pasha and Speke on the southern shore. Clusters of fertile islands of idyllic beauty dot the surface near the shore— the Sesse Islands in the north-west, the Buvuma archipelago in the north, and the Ukerewe group in the south-east, capped by verdant hills and occasional sharp peaks. In sunlight the vast expanse of Lake Victoria sparkles a brilliant blue, deepened when the rays break through the dark

thunder-clouds which frequent the lake. Like the shallow
waters of Lake Albert, those of Victoria are easily lashed into
dangerous turbulence from the squalls, and occasional water
spouts can suddenly appear north and south of the equator to
pose a constant hazard to small craft. Indeed, so vast is Lake
Victoria that it creates its own discrete climate, manufacturing
rainfall from the equatorial evaporation on its surface.

Lake Victoria has only one outlet situated on its northern
shore, at Jinja, 5,611 km from the Mediterranean Sea. Here
on 28 July 1862 John Hanning Speke stood to watch the Nile
flow out of the lake between high cliffs to drop suddenly 5 m
through three separate channels to disintegrate below in a
roar of white, turbulent water. The first European to gaze
upon this wild and beautiful scene, he was convinced, and was
soon to inform the world, that these falls were *the* source of the
Nile which had eluded men for so long. Upon reaching
Khartoum, Speke despatched his famous cryptic telegram to
the Royal Geographical Society: 'The Nile is settled.'[7] Today
John Hanning Speke is all but forgotten, his moment in
history compromised by a bronze plaque at the site bearing
the ambiguous inscription: 'John Hanning Speke on 28th July
1862 FIRST DISCOVERED THIS SOURCE OF THE NILE.' Thereafter,
everyone was too polite to claim that this was *the* source of that
ancient river, and their doubts were accommodated by the
ambiguous bronze plaque at Jinja.

Today the outfall from the lake is partially regulated by the
Owen Falls dam, below which the Nile, usually known here as
the Victoria Nile, runs in a north-westerly direction, tumbling
over a series of rapids between high wooded cliffs to
Namasagali. From there the river flows broad and navigable,
gradually widening into the labyrinth of Lake Kyoga first
discovered in 1874 by Colonel Charles Chaillé-Long, the
insufferable American administrator in Egypt's Equatoria
Province. The lake itself has a number of shallow arms
running roughly east and west, but its open water is surrounded
by marshy inlets and papyrus swamps which penetrate the
low-lying land among the surrounding undulating country.
Some of the passages are navigable; most are choked by

[7] Maitland (1971, p. 177).

aquatic plants. The lake itself is fed from the south by many swampy streams which rise on the height of land not far from the shores of Lake Victoria. In the east Lake Kyoga receives the run-off from Mt. Elgon through a chain of swamps whose open water is barely distinguishable from the mass of papyrus and water weeds which covers their shallow surface.

The Nile current passes along the western edge of Lake Kyoga through open water, avoiding the swampy arms of the lake to Masindi Port, where the Nile turns sharply northward for 88 km before swinging to the west. Here the Victoria Nile plunges over the Karuma rapids, then to flow, stately, between high cliffs and over and around a succession of rapids, reefs, and islands. On either bank forest and parkland fall away from the cliffs as the gradient steepens and the channel narrows, until the Victoria Nile disappears over the edge of the Rift Valley in one of the spectacular sights of Africa—Murchison Falls. The Nile at Murchison Falls, recently renamed Kabarega Falls after the nineteenth-century king of Bunyoro, approaches the lip of the Rift where it is compressed between high cliffs and funnelled through a cleft in the rock walls of less than 6 m to plunge 43 m to the valley floor. Above the falls rock walls rise, festooned with luxuriant vegetation continuously drenched by the mist and spray which is thrown upward amidst a thunderous roar. Below, in the pool and swirling eddies, neither hippopotamuses nor crocodiles are seen. Even the ubiquitous birds of Africa are absent, and the Nile perch and tiger-fish of Lake Albert and the Nile further downstream are not indigenous to Lake Victoria. (The Nile perch was artificially introduced by the Ugandan authorities in 1962, with apparently serious and unsuspected detriment to the lake's environment—the carnivorous perch devouring many species of fish indigenous to the lake, and upon which the other lakeside inhabitants depended for a major portion of their diet.) Instead, in the sunlight a rainbow spans the chasm and illuminates thousands of sparklets of water quivering on the sheen of dark green gneiss, slate-coloured mica, and crystalline quartz.

Beyond Murchison Falls the Nile swirls between wooded highlands and over and around rocks, with flocks of birds flitting from bank to bank and numerous crocodiles basking

on islands and shore. Now at the bottom of the Rift Valley the
river broadens, slows its pace, deposits its sediment, and fans
out into a marshy delta with many channels as the banks give
way to papyrus, swamp reeds, and hippopotamuses. The
current in the main stream is now almost imperceptible as the
Nile enters Lake Albert. The scene at sunset has endured
through the ages.

As the sun sets the nearest hills become a deep purple, whilst the
higher ranges are bathed in a rose-pink glow. The water is full of
opalescent tint and reflects each one of the many hues of the sky.
The broad river channel is framed by lines of feathery papyrus in
dark green borders, and beyond the calm lake stretches a deep shade
line reflecting the distant ranges. As the sun sinks behind the
mountains the rosy tints of the western sky deepen into flame, while
the outlines of the hills are marked in indigo in a strong and gorgeous
contrast.[8]

The outlet from Lake Albert is just north of the entrance of
the Victoria Nile where the shores constrict to form the river
known as the Albert Nile. It is not an auspicious beginning.
The water is green from the algae and smells of decaying
aquatic vegetation. The banks on either side are obscured by
the swamps and lagoons which vary in width as the river
makes its way downstream. The bottom is mud. Occasionally
bluffs come down to the shore to narrow the river, but beyond,
the flood-plain broadens out again, with ambatch and
papyrus swamps, before the land rises into the hill country to
the east and west. When the channel widens islands appear,
and the current disappears as the Albert Nile flows sluggishly
northward until given definition again by the Kuku Mountains
looming precipitously in the west as a continuation of the Rift
escarpment. The river now flows broad and deep in sweeping
curves between well-defined banks. The land on either hand is
high, with well-wooded parkland, to the river port of Nimule,
the end of navigation and the Albert Nile. Here the river turns
dramatically to the left, 120°, plunges in a north-westerly
direction over the reefs which come down from the western
escarpment, and assumes another name, the Bahr al-Jabal,
the 'mountain river'.

[8] Garstin (1904, p. 63).

For the next 160 km the Bahr al-Jabal is indeed the river of the mountains, as it tumbles down a narrow valley strewn with rocky islands whose outcrops are covered with reeds and papyrus dividing the river into more than one channel. Suddenly the banks become cliffs and the valley a narrow gorge, where the river churns like a mill-race, ending in boiling turbulence before breaking out into a wider stream only to cascade yet again over more rapids. The awesome beauty of this wild river is unchanging. The walls are deep black, vertical strata covered by bright green creepers, while mimosa trees bursting with white and pink flowers cling to the narrow banks and rocky islands, all displayed against a brilliant blue sky above and white water below. Throughout its course the Bahr al-Jabal is laced by numerous deep ravines which enter the river from either bank, barren in the dry season but contributing significant flows in flood, known to the hydrologists as torrents. To the west the escarpment towers upward in an unbroken wall; on the east an undulating plateau rises in tiers to the horizon.

As the Bahr al-Jabal continues its northward course, the landscape begins to change. The western escarpment of the Rift recedes from the river to the north-west and begins to break up into a series of low hills. The Rift subsides, and its walls are replaced by ridges and isolated peaks erupting from the levelling plateau which stretches away to the east and west. The river runs straight and full between gradual banks to slide over the Bedden rapids, the last rocks to impede this Nile until it reaches the stones of the Shabaluqa gorge north of Khartoum. Now free of reefs, dykes, and dams, the Bahr al-Jabal flows north through undulating flatlands of forest and bush, its channels multiplied by islands and its banks broken only by dry water-courses which discharge in spates during the rains. Suddenly, Mt. Rejaf juts 114 m into the sky on the west bank of the mountain river, its perfect cone made all the more dramatic by the flat surrounding plain. Like a sentinel guarding the passage south up the Nile, Mt. Rejaf has always marked, not only the end of navigation to those coming up the Bahr al-Jabal, but also the beginning of the high country and the great equatorial lakes of East Africa. North of Mt. Rejaf lies the sprawling city of Juba, situated on a ridge along the west bank where the vital Juba bridge links the west with the east bank, Uganda, and Kenya, the only crossing over the Nile until Kosti 1,436 km downstream.

Beyond Juba the Bahr al-Jabal continues northward around numerous islands in the stream to swing eastward near Mongalla, where the banks are still well defined and the bush and forest come down to the river, interspersed by low-lying swamps. At Bor, perched precariously on the east bank, the Sudd or great swamps of the Nile begin. Here the character of the mountain river changes yet again. The banks disappear into marshland which stretches beyond the horizon, and the current of the Bahr al-Jabal alternates between straight stretches and curves, twists, and bends as it wanders through the labyrinth of the Sudd, a dreary wasteland of desolation where neither trees nor hills appear to break the monotonous scene of endless swamp. On either hand the wall of papyrus and water reeds which grow over 3 m high appears impenetrable, but there are thousands of spill-ways which lead to countless lagoons and lakes beyond the river. To the west are Lakes Fajarial, Shambe, and Nyong; to the east flows the open water of the Atem channel, as large as the Bahr al-Jabal itself. Eight km downstream from Lake Shambe the Bahr al-Zaraf (the 'giraffe river') branches off from the Bahr al-Jabal to the north-east, a listless, sluggish stream meandering some 370 km through the Sudd to the White Nile. In fact, much of the limited water which flows into the Bahr al-Zaraf originates in the swamps which spread north of Bor, and from the rains which create a vast expanse of grassy swamp to the east and whose water eventually creeps into the Bahr al-Zaraf.

Further north, low-lying land gradually emerges from the Sudd between the Bahr al-Jabal and the Bahr al-Zaraf, known as the Zaraf Island, where trees mark the skyline but do not relieve the pervasive oppression of the swamps. The air is close and steamy, and fetid with decomposing vegetation. There are few sounds—the cry of the fish eagle, the unremitting buzz of insects, the occasional splash of fish. Both crocodiles and hippopotamuses avoid the Sudd, and few birds frequent the swamps except the antediluvian Bogbird (*Balaeniceps rex*) or Shoebill stork which one occasionally sees standing forlorn among the reeds, seeming to brood on life and death in this primordial land. The Nile swamps are the very symbol of the geological depression they represent, a timeless region in which only the rise and fall of the swamp water marks the seasons. Out of this purgatory the Bahr al-Jabal struggles into the open water of Lake No, 1,156 km from Lake Albert. Its course is complete, its strength as the mountain river spent.

Lake No is a shallow lake, but acts as a reservoir for all the rivers rising in the great basin of the Congo–Nile watershed, including those feeding into its western end through the Bahr al-Ghazal river (the 'gazelle river'). The lake itself is surrounded by swamps composed of a plethora of aquatic plants; beyond this the land to the north rises gradually to higher ground where live the Nuer, from whom the lake may have derived its name, Lake Nu. The traders coming up the Nile in the nineteenth century frequently referred to Lake No as the *Mugran al-Buhur*, the meeting of the rivers. As a reservoir it rises and falls with the flood, and its size depends more on the flow of the Bahr al-Jabal than on the Bahr al-Ghazal. Here wildlife is in abundance: as hippopotamuses gambol and waterfowl feed in profusion in the open waters of the lake.

To the west the Bahr al-Ghazal is a much smaller and shorter river than the Bahr al-Jabal. Ironically, however, it drains a basin far larger, an area the size of France spanning 10° of latitude and the most extensive drainage basin in the Nile system. Yet its contribution to the Nile waters is insignificant. From the Congo–Nile watershed northward into Darfur and Kordofan, the tributaries of the Bahr al-Ghazal, when they flow, are consumed by evaporation and transpiration in the swamps which surround the river. In the south, numerous rivers flow from the Congo–Nile divide north-eastwards toward the Bahr al-Ghazal. The divide itself is almost imperceptible, a strip of tableland 600–900 m above sea-level, but the rainfall coming across the great tropical rain forest of Zaïre is sufficient to produce lush parklands and savannah forests. In the ravines where flow the many streams of the upper watershed, thick forests flourish, with giant trees similar to those of the tropical rain forest further south. They tower above the rivulets and streams in triumphant arches to form the striking 'gallery forests' first named by the German

botanist Georg Schweinfurth during his expeditions to the
watershed in the Bahr al-Ghazal and Zaïre between 1868 and
1871. Along the water-course below the trees the ravines are
filled with luxuriant bush, reeds, and bamboo. Above, the
country of the watershed consists of an undulating plateau of
laterite ironstone, which turns the rivers red in flood but
provides a firm bed as the tributaries flow north and east
down the gradual slope of the plateau into the swamps.
Frequently, the ironstone will thrust up from the plateau in
isolated patches of flat, rocky hills. During the rains, which
reach their maximum fall between July and September, the
rivers are in flood and the swamps of the Bahr al-Ghazal
expand over the vast, flat Nilotic plain below the ironstone
plateau. In the dry season from November to March the rivers
fall and the swamp diminishes, leaving rich grasslands known
as the *toic* which reach to the edge of the permanent swamp.
Unlike the laterite gravels of the ironstone plateau, the soils of
the plain are a black clay, impermeable when dry, impassable
when wet.

The Nilotic plain stretches from the Nile watershed in the
west, nearly 1,500 km, to the Ethiopian escarpment in the
east. The northern boundary of this is the Bahr al-'Arab river,
which rises on the watershed and frontier between the Sudan
and the Central African Republic to flow eastward in a great
arc to its confluence with the Bahr al-Ghazal river at Ghabat
al-'Arab. Throughout its course the Bahr al-'Arab is frequently
an intermittent stream of ponds interspersed with bare river-
bed in the dry season, and in its lower reaches the channel is
often choked with aquatic plants. The drainage basin of the
Bahr al-'Arab covers a huge area extending northward into
Kordofan and Darfur, but the dry river-beds or wadis of these
Sahilian plains north of the river contribute virtually nothing
to the flow of the Bahr al-'Arab, which depends for its water
upon the rains and sluggish streams flowing from its head-
waters in the west and the ironstone plateau and the Nilotic
plain to the south. More important than its waters, which are
lost in its lower reaches and contribute little to the Bahr al-
Ghazal, the Bahr al-'Arab represents the volatile frontier
between the Africans of the southern Sudan and the Arab–
Muslim peoples of Darfur and Kordofan. Here on the

borderlands Arabs and Africans compete for the grazing lands north and south of the Bahr al-'Arab, sometimes in peace, often in violence.

What little water arrives at Lake No from the Bahr al-Ghazal is the accumulation of waters which seep through the river's swamps from its tributaries. Beginning as small streams on the Congo–Nile divide, they coalesce into well-defined tributaries flowing down the gradual slope of the plateau over rocks and riffles which can become rapids during the rains in the upper course of these rivers. Further downstream they leave the plateau and proceed in ever-widening curves as they reach the plain. Here the trees give way to savannah grasslands and ultimately the swamp which stretches eastward to the Bahr al-Jabal, broken only by patches of dry land with small trees like the heglig (*Balantis aegyptiaca*). The tributaries are as numerous as they are unpredictable. There are the Gel (Tapari) and the Yei, which in fact make their way northward into the Bahr al-Jabal. To the west are the Na'am, Maridi, Tonj, Jur, and Lol, which all lose their identity in the swamps of the Bahr al-Ghazal. Although these tributaries are mostly intermittent rivers, their total amount of water passing into the Bahr al-Ghazal amounts to 70 per cent of the total discharge of the Bahr al-Jabal at Mongalla just before the mountain river is about to enter the Sudd. Here in the swamps this vital water is lost in such enormous quantities that the contribution of the Bahr al-Ghazal at Lake No is of no significance.[9] What little remains trickles unimpressively into the lake, to the despair of the hydrologists in Khartoum and Cairo.

The Sobat River and its tributaries is the last river basin, in addition to those of the Lake Plateau, the Bahr al-Jabal, and the Bahr al-Ghazal, to complete the formation of one of the two major branches of the Nile—the Bahr al-Abyad or White Nile. The Sobat drains a huge basin, including the plains east of the Bahr al-Jabal and Bahr al-Zaraf, the mountains and hills on the Sudan–Uganda frontier far to the south, and the rivers and streams which pour down from the Ethiopian highlands onto the Nilotic plain. Unlike the Bahr al-Ghazal,

---

[9] The loss is estimated at 20 billion m³, or nearly one-quarter of the total mean annual flow of the Nile (84 billion m³) as measured at Aswan.

with its larger drainage basin but minimal discharge into the White Nile, the Sobat provides from the run-off in Ethiopia one-half of the total mean annual flow of the White Nile.[10] The Sobat itself is formed by two rivers, the Baro and the Pibor, which come together below the Ethiopian escarpment. The Baro is the Sobat's most important tributary, itself formed by numerous streams and rivulets cutting down through the Ethiopian plateau to contribute 72 per cent of the total flow of the Sobat. Thundering in torrent from June to October, the Baro is navigable in these months as far as Gambila at the base of the escarpment, and thereafter diminishes to a stream after the rains. Once on the Nilotic plain the Baro receives virtually no water, and in flood actually loses some into the large swamp to the north and east, known as the Machar Marshes, lying in a shallow basin beneath the Ethiopian highlands. The marshes also receive water coming off the plateau into the Machar depression, where it disappears by evaporation and transpiration.

The other branch of the Sobat, the Pibor, has many tributaries and a larger basin than the Baro, but its contribution to the waters of the Sobat is much less significant, amounting to only 17 per cent of the Sobat flow. Three streams rising far in the south make up the Pibor—the Veveno, Lotilla, and Kangen. All three are shallow depressions in the dreary plains between the Bahr al-Jabal and the Ethiopian escarpment. Their ultimate source lies in the Imatong and Didinga Mountains, where streams like the Kideppo come down from the hills in spate to lose themselves on the plain and then to re-emerge in the three distinct but intermittent river valleys. Once formed, the Pibor flows north to its confluence with the Baro to produce the Sobat, which moves westward to the White Nile in stately fashion across the monotonous Nilotic plain, fed only by a few sluggish streams coming from the south out of their swampy depressions. Here the immensity of the Sobat flatlands overwhelms and reduces the individual to

[10] The total mean annual flow of the White Nile is 28 billion m^3, 14 billion contributed by the Bahr al-Jabal and Bahr al-Zaraf, 14 billion by the Sobat, derived from the total mean annual flow as measured at Aswan of 84 billion m^3, and fixed by the Nile Waters agreements of 1929 and 1959. In fact the mean annual measured outflow from the Bahr al-Jabal, Bahr al-Zaraf, and Bahr al-Ghazal from 1905 to 1980 is 16.06 billion m^3.

his proper proportion in nature, exposing his mortality in a land where there is no place to hide. Yet despite this dismal landscape the Sobat contributes from its Ethiopian sources as much water as that which is lost by the Bahr al-Jabal in the Sudd.

The White Nile begins at Lake No, out of which it flows 1,000 km to Khartoum and its historic confluence with the Blue Nile. From Lake No the White Nile first moves in an easterly direction as a broad river, with swampy banks to separate its flow from lagoons, marshy ponds, and parallel channels like the Khor Lol. Gradually the strip of swamp on either side narrows, and downstream from Tonga the valley becomes more defined and trees line the river on higher ground. The Bahr al-Zaraf meets the White Nile downstream from Tonga, adding perhaps a third of the total mean annual flow of the White Nile before its confluence with the Sobat. Here the White Nile has become a majestic river, 100 m wide, as it swings northward with its greenish-grey hue from the Sudd to intermingle reluctantly with the brick-red waters from the Ethiopian plateau.

From the Sobat to Khartoum the White Nile receives no other significant tributary; the river is complete, contributing one-third of the total mean annual flow of the main Nile. Not far downstream is Malakal, the capital of the Upper Nile province, perched on a high bank which constitutes the busy waterfront, lined by tall, shady trees from which clouds of egrets leave with a clatter at dawn to feed west of the Nile, returning to roost in the evening with their snow-white plumage illuminated against a blood-red setting sun. Along the bank beneath the trees are the offices of the Egyptian irrigation department which in the past maintained a watch on the flow of water from the rivers of the southern Sudan. Old Nile hands will still be heard to say, 'Africa begins at Malakal', far to the north the Nile and its people look to the world of Islam and the Arabs, while to the south live the Africans with their own cultural traditions. Here on the borderlands of two different cultures there has been interaction and borrowing, but as the Nile moves sedately toward the Mediterranean Sea its peoples are drawn ever more definitively into the orbit of the Arab world.

Along the reach of the White Nile the land becomes increasingly arid; the lush green of Africa gradually disappears. The land beyond the river becomes covered in short grass and then turns to sand and stone. Camels and horses now come down to the river, and with them men speaking Arabic and worshipping Allah. The river, broad and slow-moving, is dotted with clusters of water hyacinth and papyrus, bifurcating into islands, while the land from either bank stretches across a great plain. The horizon remains a straight line, broken occasionally by isolated granite hills like Jabalayn. At Kosti two large bridges span the Nile to link the Gezira region south of Khartoum with the western provinces of Kordofan and Darfur. It is the principal river port of the White Nile (named after a Greek merchant who settled there in the early part of the twentieth century), from which goods and supplies are transshipped up the White Nile after coming overland by rail and road from Khartoum, Wad Medani, and Port Sudan. North of Kosti the White Nile divides its channel around Abba Island, the ancestral home of Muhammad Ahmad al-Mahdi, whose followers, the Ansar, destroyed the Egyptian Administration in the Sudan in 1885.

Throughout this reach the White Nile is in fact no longer a river but a vast reservoir behind the Jabal 'Auliya dam 47 km south of Khartoum. The purpose of the dam was to hold back and store the waters of the White Nile while the massive flood from Ethiopia passed Khartoum into the main Nile from July to December. When the Blue Nile waters had spent themselves by December, the sluices of the Jabal 'Auliya dam were opened to provide Egypt and the northern Sudan with water during the winter and spring months, January to June, until the flood comes down the Blue Nile once again from the highlands of Ethiopia. Nevertheless, a very high price continues to be extracted by Jabal 'Auliya, since over 2.5 billion m^3 of precious water are lost annually by evaporation in the shallow reservoir and intense heat behind the dam. To be sure, it has been a barrier against the spread of the water hyacinth and a source of water for the numerous entrepreneurial pump schemes in the Sudan which suck the water from its lake; but for the Egyptians it has become an expensive consumer of water.

Not far below Jabal 'Auliya the waters of the White Nile meet those of the Blue Nile at the historic capital of the Sudan, Khartoum. Surprisingly, Khartoum is a relatively new city, having been established in 1825 as the administrative headquarters of the Egyptian empire in the Sudan. Its name, meaning 'elephant trunk', comes from the long spit of land known as the *Mugran* (the meeting) which is formed by the confluence of the Blue Nile and the White. Across the White Nile sprawls the bustling city of Omdurman. Of even more recent origin than Khartoum, it was a small village of no importance until the Mahdi made it the capital of the Mahdist State after destroying Egyptian rule in the Sudan and levelling the symbol of that oppressive regime, Khartoum. Upon the reconquest of the Sudan by Anglo-Egyptian forces in 1898, Khartoum was rebuilt, and has remained ever since the capital of the Sudan and the centre of its commercial, diplomatic, and government activity. Opposite Khartoum, across the Blue Nile, the former village of Halfaya has rapidly expanded in this century into an important industrial and residential suburb, Khartoum North. Here, at the meeting of the waters these new cities, the Nile of the ancients is born.

The scribe in Egypt who informed Herodotus in 460 BC that the Nile flowed from springs of great depth at the base of tall mountains was, in fact, not far wrong. Just as the White Nile begins at Waldekker's spring in far-off Burundi, so too does the origin of the Blue Nile begin at the holy spring of Sakala at the foot of the mountain of Gish in the highlands of Ethiopia. The spring is small but filled with clear water of no measured depth. It is enclosed by a palisade of bamboo, situated in a marshy bay on a shelf of high ground which drops steeply to the floor of the valley of Gish. In every direction mountains rise to the horizon, as they do at the spring in Burundi. Nearby is the Church of St Michael and Zarabruk, whose priests are the guardians of the hallowed spring to which come pilgrims to seek its curative and spiritual powers. The first European to see this source of the Nile was the Portuguese Jesuit Pedro Paez, who reached Sakala on 21 April 1613. In November 1770 James Bruce arrived at Sakala, and his description of the then three springs surrounded by marsh not only corroborated that of Father Paez, but varies little from the

site of this source of the Nile today. The stream which flows
out of the marshy bog down the slope from Sakala, the Little
Abbai, gathers strength and tumbles over rapids and waterfalls
through the precipitous valley of Gish to Lake Tana. Lake
Tana lies in the heart of the Ethiopian highlands, a majestic
plateau rising grandly from the surrounding plains of north-
east Africa, characterized by ridges of high hills and mountains
laced by steep ravines and deep valleys which cut down
through the high country. The plateau is normally well-
watered from the moisture-laden clouds which blow across
Africa out of the south Atlantic from March to September.
Having deposited their water upon the tropical rain forest of
Zaïre and the upper Nile, they collide with the Ethiopian
escarpment, rise, and drop their remaining rains on the highlands amid violent thunderstorms and destructive lightning.[11]
During the winter months from October to February, the
winds turn about to blow dry and cool across the arid land
mass of Asia and Arabia.

Lake Tana itself nestles on the plateau, almost a perfect
saucer, its water soft green with a brownish turbidity. Like
Lakes Victoria and Albert it is shallow, with only one outlet
near Bahar Dar at its southernmost extremity, where a lava
flow has dammed the Blue Nile valley to form the lake.
Numerous islands are scattered on its surface, mostly close to
shore with the exception of Dek Island and its satellites which
emerge in the south central portion of open water. Monasteries,
churches, and the tombs of kings and emperors are to be
found on many of these islands. The shores of the lake are a
low-lying grassy plain from which the land rises to the high
country. Despite its height and size Lake Tana does not have
the hydrological significance of the lakes of equatorial Africa:
the discharge at its outlet amounts to only 7 per cent of the
total flow of the Blue Nile, whose volume is supplied not from
the lake but from the many tributaries pouring out of the
ravines and valleys of the highlands.

Twenty-six km from Lake Tana the Blue Nile, known to the
Ethiopians as the Abbai, suddenly disappears over the lip of
Tisisat Falls to plunge into a narrow gorge which, like

---

[11] Brooks and Mirrlees (1932).

Victoria Falls on the Zambezi, runs at right angles to the river and parallel to the cliff over which the water drops in a burst of foam and a cloud of spray. Tisisat in Amharic means 'smoke of fire', derived from the mists which rise up out of the gorge and can be seen long before the falls themselves. Like the outlet of Lake Tana, the Tisisat Falls are formed by a dam of lava running across the river, divided into four separate falls by bush-covered islands of basalt, which create an awesome spectacle when the Blue Nile is in full flood. Immediately below the falls the river careens through a narrow rocky spillway only 6 m wide, where a masonry bridge, probably built in the seventeenth century by the Portuguese, spans the circumscribed channel.

Beyond the bridge the Blue Nile cuts a great zigzag groove through the plateau, in some places no more than 4 m wide, between perpendicular walls. Frequently the narrow gap opens at the deltas of tributaries coming down the steep valleys from the highlands, or intermittently broadens to form cultivatable flats between the canyon walls and the steep banks covered with loose, basaltic rocks and tall trees through which giant, colourful butterflies flutter. The second Blue Nile bridge, known as Sabera Dildi, the 'broken bridge', with its main double arch and its three smaller arches to accommodate the river in flood, was probably also built by the Portuguese in their characteristic rock and mortar style, but was largely rebuilt by the Italians during their occupation of Ethiopia from 1936 to 1941. Just below the bridge at Sabera Dildi, the Blue Nile emerges from its lava gorge to cut down into the softer underlying sedimentary rocks where it now can erode more rapidly in a wider bed, but still flowing in a south-east direction. Here the river is a slow placid stream in the dry season and easily fordable in selected places, but in the rains it is transformed into a chocolate-brown, raging torrent fed by steep-flowing tributaries such as the Giamma, Muger, Guder, Finchaa, Diddessa, and Balas.

At the bottom of the Blue Nile gorge the temperature becomes tropical in contrast to the cool climate and temperate breezes of the high plateau. The banks of the river are virtually uninhabited, for the Ethiopians avoid the malarial lowlands of the canyon and find no solace in its walls, which

tower above in ascending terraces. As the Blue Nile cuts
through the sedimentary rock the steep cliffs, which have
hitherto come down sheer to the water, fall away, and the
flood-plain broadens despite the river eating ever more deeply
into the Ethiopian plateau. Above Shafartak the Blue Nile
swings to the west as it begins its great bend around the high
plateau and mountains of Gojjam, where the main all-weather
motor road from Addis Ababa to Gojjam winds down from
the high plateau and crosses the river on a modern steel
bridge. Beyond the bridge the Blue Nile collects yet more
tributaries from the Gojjam highlands, now to the north, and
from the mountains to the south-east which rise above Addis
Ababa. Shallow streams in the dry season, they become
torrents in the rains, draining large basins and depositing
immense quantities of water into the Blue Nile. There is no
stretch of the White Nile system from the Lake Plateau to
Khartoum that can rival this fall through the grand canyon of
the Blue Nile.

Beyond the western headland of the plateau, the Blue Nile
leaves the highlands to pass northward in a great bend
through the rich coffee-growing country of the borderlands
between the Sudan and Ethiopia. Its gradient is constant and
heavily loaded with silt in flood as it drops to its confluence
with the Balas River, a long and important tributary which
comes in on the right bank from its origins only a few
kilometres from the western shore of Lake Tana. The Blue
Nile enters the Sudan at the Bumbode river and thence flows
downstream into the reservoir of the Roseires dam at Damazin
in the Sudan. The dam is 1,000 km from Lake Tana, but at
Damazin the Blue Nile has yet to flow another 3,736 km to the
Mediterranean Sea. The Roseires dam was completed in 1966
for the extension of the irrigation in the Gezira, known as the
Managil scheme, and to provide hydroelectric power for
Khartoum, Omdurman, and Khartoum North. Since its
construction, however, the dam has been subjected to very
heavy silting; deforestation in Ethiopia has sharply increased
erosion throughout the Blue Nile watershed, which has
diminished the capacity of the reservoir and interrupted
hydroelectric power.

Released from Roseires, the Blue Nile flows through a flat

plain tilted slightly to the north. Two important seasonal tributaries, the Dinder and the Rahad, reach the Blue Nile in flood, adding 10 per cent to its total annual flow. Rising in the Ethiopian borderlands, these two spate rivers cross the plains of the Sudan, but their substantial catchment basins are mostly in Ethiopia. Nevertheless, after the rains they dry up into pools in their sandy river-beds. The country of the Blue Nile in the Sudan is an unbroken plain covered with bush and small trees, punctuated by semi-arid grass pastures, in the clay soils deposited from Ethiopia by the Blue Nile over the millenniums. The combination of fertile soil and water from the Nile has created large-scale irrigation schemes between the White Nile and the Blue—the Kenena (Funj) Sugar scheme, the Managil–Gezira cotton schemes, and the Rahad project on that tributary of the Blue Nile.

The original Gezira scheme was first proposed by Sir William Garstin and C. E. Dupuis, inspector-general of irrigation in the Sudan for the Egyptian irrigation service, as early as 1904, although the idea had been suggested by General Kitchener in 1898 after the Anglo-Egyptian forces under his command had defeated the Mahdists at the battle of Omdurman. The dam essential to irrigate the Gezira (island) plain between the two Niles was completed at Sennar in July 1925, and the growing of irrigated cotton and crops begun shortly thereafter. Below the dam the Blue Nile moves sedately across the plains (carrying an average mean annual flow of 45 billion m³ or 54 per cent of the Nile flow) to its confrontation with the waters of the White Nile at Khartoum; it is still over 3,000 km from the Mediterranean Sea, with no other potential tributaries as the Nile passes through a formidable environment characterized by intense heat and absence of precipitation. No other river in the world makes such an extraordinary journey, which in itself would render the Nile unique; but the total dependence, therefore, of man on the waters of the river gives the Nile a unique place in the history of civilization.

Some 320 km north of Khartoum, the large and important spate river, the 'Atbara, thunders down from the highlands of Ethiopia, during its flood contributing 13 per cent of the total annual flow of the Nile (11 billion m³) but from January to

TABLE 1. *The contributions to the total mean annual flow of the Nile (as measured at Aswan) from the Ethiopian plateau and the Upper Nile basin*

Catchment	River	%
Ethiopian	Sobat	14
	Blue Nile	59
	'Atbara	13
East African	Bahr al-Jabal	14

June the 'Atbara bed is dry, broken only by pools and ponds. The river rises as the Setit (Takkaze) River during the rains in the Simen Mountains just to the north of Lake Tana, entering the Sudan near Qallabat on the Sudan–Ethiopia border. After its confluence with the 'Atbara the Nile is at last whole, yet 86 per cent of its water coming down to Egypt originates in Ethiopia—the Sobat, the Blue Nile and its tributaries, and the 'Atbara—while only 14 per cent comes from the Lake Plateau via the Bahr al-Jabal, the Bahr al-Zaraf, and the Bahr al-Ghazal, winding their tortuous way through the Sudd (see Table 1). Ethiopia therefore appears to be the natural place to regulate the Nile flow; and the construction of dams and barrages in the Ethiopian highlands would increase the total annual amount of water deposited on the doorstep of Egypt, since the losses by evaporation in Ethiopia are much less than those experienced at Aswan. Nevertheless, any regulation of the Blue Nile appears far in the future, and Ethiopia cannot be regarded as a likely source of additional water for irrigation downstream. At the same time that this fact becomes increasingly apparent, made all the more self-evident by the past eight years of below-average rainfall in Ethiopia, the great reservoirs of the equatorial lakes have risen by heavy rains beginning in 1961, slackening in the late 1960s and then increasing again in the 1970s to raise the level of the lakes by 2.5 m, producing an enormous volume of additional water (170 billion m^3). Here in the equatorial lakes lies the water to irrigate the arid wastes of Egypt and the Sudan, both countries rapidly running out of water, the impact of which has been made all the more ominous by the acute drought in

Ethiopia and the Sudan in 1984 and 1987. Today the Nile waters cannot support the burgeoning population of an Egypt of some 52 million people expected to increase to 70 millions by the end of the twentieth century. Yet the water to make the desert bloom lies in the equatorial lakes, trapped by the Sudd, whereby the wealth of water in the lakes is dissipated. The partial solution is Jonglei, the canal to pass the waters of the Lake Plateau down to Egypt, without which the construction of any regulators at the lakes is useless even if the many riparian powers agreed. By itself the Jonglei Canal will not resolve Egypt's long-term water requirements, but at the present it remains the only viable hydrological project to provide additional water to the millions of people living north of the enervating swamps of the Nile.

From its confluence with the 'Atbara the Nile makes its great S-bend, rolling over three cataracts to flow placidly into the enormous reservoir behind the high dam at Aswan. Here the Nile bed is only 87 m above sea-level, yet has to flow 1,180 km through a myriad of irrigation works and a labyrinth of canals in the delta of the Nile to deposit a drop of water into the Mediterranean Sea. To all intents and purposes, however, the course of the Nile stops at Aswan.[12]

[12] See Waterbury (1979, p. 116).

2
European Imperialism and the Nile

All the advantages which we have hitherto derived from our insular position will be at an end if we remain in Egypt. We deliberately adopt a land frontier, constantly liable to attack which will inevitably carry us further and further into the heart of Africa. We are doomed forever to be a great fighting empire, dependent on the support of subject races who may turn against us any day when they have learned their strength.

Louis Mallet, 9 April 1884

UNTIL the third quarter of the nineteenth century the importance of the Nile had been confined to continental Africa, and specifically to the people living by its banks, particularly the Sudanese of Nubia and the Egyptians inhabiting the barren deserts of its northern reaches. To be sure, men had pondered over the sources of the life-giving Nile waters, but these speculations were those of geographers, poets, and kings, whose curiosity may be the foundation of civilization but was the ethereal fascination with the unknown, devoid of the reality of daily life and death by the Nile. Within twenty years, between 1862 and 1876, three events expanded the crucial significance of the Nile valley beyond its banks in north-east Africa to the world—the discovery of the Nile source flowing from Lake Victoria in 1862, the opening of the Suez Canal in 1869, and the financial collapse of Egypt in 1876.

On 28 July 1862 John Hanning Speke stood on the banks of the Nile at its only outlet, *the* source of the Nile. From that moment in 1862, the attention of Europe was riveted on the equatorial lakes of Africa as the source of the waters that flowed down to Egypt. This fascination with the Lake Plateau was to absorb the attention of geographers, explorers, and prime ministers alike, and thereby to mislead them into making the equatorial lakes the focus of a world-wide political strategy far beyond the African continent, not knowing that 86 per cent of the Nile Waters rose in Ethiopia.

The second event occurred only a few years before Stanley's confirmation of Speke. In 1869 the khedive Isma'il Pasha opened the Suez Canal which had at last been completed by the persistence and conviction of Count Ferdinand de Lesseps. The opening on 17 November 1869 was a grand display, complete with an army of European aristocracy, including the Empress Eugénie of France and the Emperor of Austria, massed bands, banquets, fireworks, and the blessing of the waters by representatives of all the world's major religions. Pomp and circumstance, however, could not disguise the enormous political and strategic importance of the canal. As the last spadeful of sand was dug, the way to India and the Orient ceased to involve the circumnavigation of the African continent and the traverse of the treacherous waters of the Cape of Good Hope. The journey from Europe to the East was reduced by half in time and distance, and no maritime nation or imperial power could ignore this. The Nile suddenly assumed a global importance which the Victorians immediately recognized. The *New York Herald* summed up the relationship between the canal at Suez and the lakes of equatorial Africa: 'The ... Suez Canal brings all these late discoveries around the equatorial sources of Speke, Grant, Baker, Burton, Livingstone within a convenient distance for English colonization.'[1]

The third event was neither as dramatic nor as sudden as the discovery of the source of the Nile at Lake Victoria or the opening of the Suez Canal: it was instead the pervasive and subtle sinking of Egypt into bankruptcy. When Isma'il Pasha had succeeded his uncle Muhammad Sa'id in 1863, Egypt was enjoying a financial bonanza from the sharp rise in the price of cotton created by the shortages produced by the American Civil War. With the Egyptian treasury overflowing with cash, Isma'il was determined to spend it for the modernization of Egypt and his own comfort and glory. With singular abandon he constructed canals, rebuilt the army, expanded the Egyptian empire toward the equatorial lakes, reformed the

---

[1] Editorial, *New York Herald*, 17 Nov. 1869.

post office, and for his own pleasure erected the great Abdın Palace, bought the title of khedive from the sultan at Constantinople, and lavished vast sums on women, jewels, and *objets d'art*. By 1875 Isma'il was £100 million in debt (about half a billion in today's currency and prices), and Isma'il the Magnificent was now Isma'il the Impecunious. Even the purchase of the khedive's shares in the Suez Canal Company (Compagnie Universelle du Canal Maritime de Suez) in 1875 by Great Britain was but a palliative. By 1876 Egypt was destitute, its revenues barely equal to the interest on the debt. The bankers of Europe quickly turned a deaf ear to Isma'il's pleas for additional credit at any rate of interest. The financial collapse of Egypt was inevitably followed by foreign fiscal control, which was soon translated into foreign political intervention to protect not only the European bond-holders and the industrial interests of British manufacturers but the strategic interests of the imperial powers which in Egypt were inexorably dependent upon the Nile waters.

The discovery of the great lakes of equatorial Africa and the assumption that these vast reservoirs were the true source of the Nile soon drew the attention of the nineteenth-century public to the interior of Africa. Attracted by the many editions of the explorers' books filled with graphic accounts of daring exploits among hitherto unknown peoples and exotic fauna and flora in their Nile quest, the British public in particular accepted without question that the ultimate source lay in the equatorial lakes of Africa. And if anyone was so churlish as to doubt the word of the world's greatest explorers, they need only look at the unfolding map of Africa to see the lakes from which the Nile flowed majestically northward to the Mediterranean Sea.

In fact, the opening of the upper Nile was accomplished more by the efforts of Muhammad 'Ali and tough Turkish captains like Salim Qapudan, who was the first to pass through the Sudd to the verdant lands beyond the swamps, than by the heroes of European exploration. Salim was followed first by European merchants and missionaries and then by traders from the Levant, Egypt, and the northern Sudan, whose slave-raiding evoked the opprobrium of Britain but who in fact opened the upper Nile basin to the world far more than the wanderings of individual (intrepid, to be sure) European explorers who knew little of the inhabitants whom they encountered and not much more about the territory they traversed. Indeed, the distasteful memory of the Turko-Egyptian presence remained well into the twentieth century, and was not erased by the arrival of British administrators, who were regarded as just more Turks. In the nineteenth century, however, while it was the slave trade and its depredations throughout the upper Nile which aroused the humanitarians in Britain, it was the Nile waters and their strategic significance that preoccupied the officials in Whitehall and in Downing Street.

The politicians were equally susceptible to the seemingly obvious deduction of the men who had risked their lives to find the source of the Nile on the Equator. Irresistibly, as in a trance, even the most hard-headed of Victorian statesmen found themselves following the course of the Nile southward from the Mediterranean thousands of miles into the very heart of the African continent. Who could doubt that these waters rising in the mountains and plateaux of east central Africa were the waters which made the deserts of Egypt bloom and Cairo a great city? Suddenly, vast areas of a hitherto unknown continent took on a strategic significance which no one had previously considered. The Nile waters, from their source to the Mediterranean were essential to the very existence of Egypt. And Egypt was now the homeland not only of the ruins of an ancient civilization and the city of Cairo but of the Suez Canal, whose global importance directly affected Egypt because it passed through Egyptian territory.

The opening of the Suez Canal had dramatically changed Britain's imperial strategy. Suez was now the high road to Britain's Indian and Oriental empire. Once Prime Minister Disraeli had bought control of the canal in 1875, Britain had to ensure its security. No other power could be allowed to occupy Egypt or the canal without threatening the route to Britain's empire east of Suez. This profoundly important strategic consideration was not threatened so long as Egypt remained independent under British influence exercised by Khedive Isma'il, who was to contain any national aspirations from within and foreign powers from without.

Indeed, there was no desire on the part of the British government to occupy Egypt so long as Britain controlled Suez and its influence at Cairo was respected by the profligate khedive.

Moreover, there were increasingly important economic reasons for British concern over Egyptian affairs besides the Suez Canal and the interests of the bond-holders. The profitable cotton trade, which had been given an impetus by the American Civil War, continued after 1865. By 1880 Britain consumed 80 per cent of Egypt's exports and sold in return nearly half of all Egyptian imports. This commercial expansion was overshadowed by the fiscal and strategic questions which so perturbed British statesmen and politicians; but it certainly did not go unnoticed by British manufacturers and private British investors, who were quietly putting considerable sums into financing industrial and agricultural schemes in Egypt, schemes which were separate from the question of the public debt but equally susceptible to annihilation if Egypt declared bankruptcy. And the close ties between the financiers of the City of London and the politicians at Westminster need no elucidation.

Unfortunately, Khedive Isma'il did not co-operate by placing as his first priority the pecuniary, economic, and strategic interests of the British empire. His concern was to modernize Egypt and have a good time doing so. The result was bankruptcy and the imposition of foreign fiscal control through a commission, the Caisse de la Dette Publique, dominated by the representatives of Britain and France to reform Egyptian finances to protect the bond-holders and thereby the security of the Suez Canal. The attempt proved futile. So deep had Egypt sunk into the fiscal quagmire of massive loans at exorbitant rates of interest that not even the skills of British and French financial wizards could resolve the question of the debt, despite heavier taxation on the peasants and ever more constrictive supervision of the wealth of Egypt, all of which aroused the resentment of Khedive Isma'il and embittered the incipient Egyptian nationalists. By 1878 the British and the French were demanding that the khedive co-operate by relinquishing some of his autocratic powers in return for a new loan temporarily to retain his solvency.

Isma'il would have none of this. He was not prepared to hand over control of Egypt to foreign powers, and indeed had become a symbol of defiance for the privileged classes of Egypt and the Egyptian army, whose wealth and position would be severely curtailed by the foreign demands for fiscal reform. With their support Isma'il struck at the growing influence of his foreign advisers. In April 1879 he fired his European supervisors and rescinded all the financial restrictions imposed upon him by the debt commission. Britain and the European powers swiftly retaliated. They demanded that the khedive's suzerain, the Ottoman sultan at Constantinople, depose Isma'il. The sultan complied and Isma'il went on one last spending spree, cleaned out the cash in the Abdin Palace, and sailed away on his yacht, the *Mahrousa*, to a glorious exile on the Bosphorus.

Isma'il's successor, Tawfiq, was a timid man devoid of charisma or character, content to play the puppet to his European masters. To the Egyptians he was a Christian lackey, to the peasants a debt-collector for the privileged classes, to the landlords the symbol of European fiscal control when he raised taxes and abolished their cherished exemptions, to the army the symbol of the retrenchment of the military budget. In fact, through Tawfiq British and French financial controllers soon managed, by fiscal manipulation, every level of Egyptian life from that of the lowliest peasant to that of the most exalted pasha. Squeezed first by Isma'il and then the debt commissioners, the peasants were near revolt. The landlords were deeply discontented at the loss of their privileges, the Muslim hierarchy angered by the intervention of Christian controllers. The army, totally disaffected, provided the leadership to mould together these rival and disparate elements into a nationalist reaction against the penetration of European authority into their lives as well as their pocket. The result was anarchy, out of which emerged the Egyptian military under 'Urabi Pasha to lead a national revolution.

The more Europe, and particularly Britain, intervened the more national opposition was generated. Matters came to a head during the winter of 1881–2, when the Egyptian army under Colonel 'Urabi Pasha seized control of government and threatened the Suez Canal, which had become the very life-line of the British empire. It has been argued that it was Cairo, not Suez, which was the focus of the Egyptian crisis and Alexandria, not Port Said, which was ultimately bombarded; but Suez can no longer be insulated from Cairo and who would bombard Port Said when the object was to protect it?[2] Cairo controls Suez and the Nile waters control Cairo. Certainly none of the European powers, and least of all Prime Minister Gladstone and his Liberal ministers in Britain, wanted to challenge the Egyptian nationalists directly by the occupation of Egypt; the Colonel 'Urabi and the army forced Gladstone's hand in the irreconcilable dilemma of Britain and France having undermined the authority of the khedive in their efforts to impose fiscal reforms. In September 1881 the army surrounded the khedivial palace and forced Tawfiq to dismiss his European advisers and restore cuts in the army budget, but at the same time to reaffirm Egypt's international financial obligations. By the winter of 1881–2 the crisis had worsened.

Gladstone's response was typically British: he sent the Mediterranean fleet to show the flag by lying off Alexandria in force. This, however, did nothing to restore the khedive's authority in Cairo. On 11 and 12 June 1882, riots erupted in Alexandria against the impending threat of foreign intervention, and Europeans were killed in the streets. 'Urabi was immediately blamed for the outrages, but in fact he sought to intervene and quell the rioters. Whoever was to blame, the wanton massacre of British subjects sealed Britain's fate in Egypt and with it the defence of Suez, the Nile waters, and ultimately the European partition of much of Africa. On 11 July British power was unleashed, and Admiral Beauchamp Seymour, commander of the British Mediterranean fleet, was ordered to destroy the Egyptian forts at Alexandria and restore order. No sooner were the Egyptian fortifications levelled than anti-European riots swept throughout Egypt, and 'Urabi reacted by declaring a jihad or holy war against the Christian infidels and vowed to destroy the Suez Canal. Alarmed by the British assaults on Alexandria, 'Urabi was taken at his word. There was now apparently no way of

---

[2] Hopkins (1986, pp. 363–90).

protecting the British life-line to the East except by armed intervention dressed in the rhetoric of law and order.

Originally the occupation of Egypt was to be carried out by a joint Anglo-French military expedition. But French political paralysis and heavy military commitments in Tunis at that crucial moment of decision in the summer of 1882 left no government in Paris to act, and the British were in no mood to wait on the vagaries of French political life. On 16 August the British army, under the command of General Sir Garnet Wolseley, landed at the canal; having massed his forces, Wolseley assaulted the entrenchments of the Egyptian army at the village of At-Tal al-Kabir at first light on the morning of 13 September 1882. Spearheaded by the Scots of the highland brigade, the British soldiers carried the Egyptian fortifications in twenty minutes and within the hour had routed the Egyptian troops. Long on rhetoric, 'Urabi Pasha was short on military talent. Suddenly, and not a little surprised, a somewhat muddled British government found itself absent-mindedly not only the masters of Suez and Cairo but the guardians of the Nile upon whose waters their security depended. British statesmen intended the occupation to be temporary, at best a few short months, at worst a few short years. In the end they stayed almost half a century. Most certainly, only a few prescient men in Britain foresaw in 1882 where this seemingly effortless conquest of Egypt would lead the course of empire.

The unilateral occupation of Egypt by Great Britain profoundly embittered the French, their embarrassment as a great power made all the more infuriating by their political impotence at the time of the crisis. But French fury at the British conquest of Egypt ran much deeper in the French psyche than the political peccadillo of the ministerial crisis in the summer of 1882. Ever since Napoleon had conquered Egypt in 1799, France had possessed a greater influence in Cairo equal to, if not greater than, that of Great Britain. The bevy of scholars who had accompanied the French expeditionary force under Napoleon had begun the monumental task of investigating the mass of Egyptian antiquities, and the results of their research are to be found in the volumes of the famous *Description de l'Égypte* which remain today the foundation of all modern studies into the Egyptian past. French commerce was increasingly active throughout the nineteenth century, surpassing that of Britain. French investors flocked in large numbers to invest in Isma'il's bonds. For their part the privileged classes of Egypt looked to Paris, not London, for their education and spiritual regeneration. Isma'il himself was educated in France. French, not English, was the second language of Egypt, and it was Ferdinand de Lesseps, the famous French engineer, who had built the Suez Canal against almost insurmountable obstacles. All these cultural, commercial, and diplomatic ties forged a subtle but powerful alliance against British administrative and military influence, and a bond between Egypt and France which remains to this day. Consequently, throughout the last twenty years of the nineteenth century Egypt remained the great stumbling-block between close and amicable relations between the two great liberal powers of the West who, under any other circumstances, would have been natural allies against the autocracies of central Europe and Russia. The co-operation which had brought the French and the British together in the Crimea against Russian designs against the Ottoman empire and ambitions in the Mediterranean disappeared at At-Tal al-Kabir. The French relentlessly pressed the British to honour their declaration, made in 1882, that their occupation was only temporary until law and order had been established in Egypt. The polite but contemptuous rejection of their repeated requests only infuriated the French further and inspired their passionate desire to free Egypt from British occupation or, at worst, to force the British to accept a joint administration of the country with France.

The fall of Gladstone's Liberal Government in June 1885 did not dramatically alter the official view that the British occupation of Egypt was but a temporary intervention. It is true that after three years it was no longer in good taste to predict a short sojourn for the British forces, but Lord Salisbury and his Conservatives appeared to have 'no specifically Egyptian policy at all'.[3] Germany, Turkey, Ireland, and Gladstone absorbed Salisbury's energies more than

[3] Robinson et al. (1961, pp. 257–8).

Egypt, and whenever the Egyptian question was raised in the Cabinet the division among his own ministers permitted him the luxury of reaching no decision at all. His shrewd and sceptical mind preferred an indefinite situation, where a variety of alternatives remained open, to a decisive policy that narrowed choice and eliminated preference. Thus by the beginning of 1887 Salisbury still preferred quiet drift to the perils of evacuation or the responsibilities of empire, at least until conditions in Europe should not only make his decision imperative but invest it with the mantle of success. Within two years Salisbury's patience was rewarded. Events in Europe and conditions in the Mediterranean made uncertainty increasingly dangerous. He thus abandoned his ambiguity: Britain would remain on the Nile.

Salisbury's decision to stay in Egypt rested not so much on any fundamental change in his own mind as on his reaction to events. Since 1885 his attitude toward Egypt had been one of watchful waiting, depending on the actions of his allies and his enemies in the eastern Mediterranean and the administrative success or failure of his officials in Cairo. The abortive Drummond Wolff Convention in 1887, which failed to effect a British withdrawal from Egypt, general mistrust of the Turks, increasing chauvinism in France, and even Russian pressure at Constantinople could all have been ignored by Salisbury if the naval balance in the Mediterranean had continued in Britain's favour. By 1888 it had not. In the late 1880s both France and Russia were busily constructing swarms of fast cruisers and torpedo boats which could out-steam and outmanœuvre the ponderous battleships of the British fleet and challenge Britannia's rule of the Mediterranean waves. The Naval Defence Act of 1889 was designed to bolster the thin grey line, but not until 1894 at the earliest. Until that time British power could hardly defend Constantinople. It could not afford to lose Cairo. Even more decisive were events in Egypt. By 1889 Sir Evelyn Baring had convinced Salisbury that a stable government in Egypt could be built only on Western lines, and that such a transformation would require British occupation for many years to come. But the Western-ization of Egypt cost money, and it was not until 1889 that favourable balances became habitual and dependence on the

financial control of the European powers correspondingly
weaker. At Cairo, Salisbury no longer found himself so
glaringly exposed by the floodlights of diplomatic pressure to
withdraw from Egypt, and consequently slipped into the
comforting shadows of a more permanent occupation. On 9
November 1889 he publicly declared at the Guildhall that the
British government intended 'whether it were assisted or
obstructed by the Powers to pursue to the end the task which
it had undertaken' in Egypt.[4]

Once Salisbury had decided to prolong the British occupation
of Egypt indefinitely, he now had to consider the defence of
the country as much for Egyptian interests as for British. And
the security of Egypt traditionally depended on control of the
upper Nile, whence came the water to make the desert bloom.
And if British statesmen ever forgot for a moment the
consequences for their occupation of Egypt if the Nile waters
were prevented from reaching the Mediterranean, they were
given no opportunity to ignore so unpleasant a prospect. Sir
Samuel Baker, the greatest Victorian authority on the Nile,
was convinced that the water might be diverted, and the Nile
flood of 1888, the lowest on record, dramatized that possibility.
Baker quoted biblical texts to prove that the seven years of
famine in Egypt were caused by a diversion of the river. Now
this might not be very scientific, but when he thundered, in a
series of letters to *The Times* in October 1888, that any civilized
power could dam the Nile, obstruct the waters, and cause 'the
utter ruin and complete destruction of Egypt proper', he was
believed.[5] But if Baker's warning reminded the British
Foreign Office of a danger they had long preferred to ignore,
no one regarded the threat as imminent. Since the fall of
Khartoum in 1885, the Sudan was controlled by the Sudanese,
Mahdists whose primitive technology precluded any possibility of their diverting the Nile. The loss of the nilometer
at Khartoum was an inconvenience, to be sure, but so long as
no European power moved into the Sudan or established
a position astride the Nile, Egypt would have water and
the British domination of Egyptian affairs would remain
secure.

[4] Cecil (1921–32, iv. 137–8).   [5] *The Times*, 9, 17, 25 Oct. 1888.

Suddenly in 1889 British complacency was shaken. The first threat to the Nile by a European power loomed menacingly in the east from the lofty heights of the Ethiopian plateau. The Italians had long wished to establish a protectorate in Ethiopia, and after 1885 the British had even encouraged Italian forward moves into the highlands. At first the Foreign Office calculated that Italian penetration would not only occupy the Ethiopians and keep them out of the Sudan but would also act as a counterweight to the French who were strengthening their position at Djibouti. Then in 1889 the Italians seized the first real opportunity to enlarge their prospective sphere of influence. On 9 March the forces of the Mahdist State defeated the Ethiopians at Qallabat, killing King John and routing his army. The new emperor, Menelik, in order to consolidate his internal position among the traditional warring feudal factions, welcomed Italian support and signed the treaty of Ucciali in May. The treaty was an outright piece of skulduggery in which the Italian version reduced Ethiopia to an Italian protectorate, while in the Amharic translation Menelik merely agreed to seek the advice of the Italian government. Although Menelik was furious, such semantic difficulties did not bother the British until the Italians translated the treaty into action and laid claim to Kassala, situated below the escarpment in the Nile basin. British statesmen from Cairo to London were at once alarmed. Sir Evelyn Baring, the British agent in Egypt, warned that 'whatever power holds the Upper Nile must by the mere force of its geographical situation, dominate Egypt'.[6] Lord Dufferin, the British ambassador in Rome, complained that the Italians were 'a little too enterprising on the shores of the Red Sea' and feared that they might attempt 'to tap the Upper Nile and Soudan'.[7] By March 1890 Lord Salisbury had made up his mind to stop the Italians, and for that matter to defend the 'Nile Valley against the dominion of any outside Power'.[8] He officially warned Italy to stay away from the Nile, and the Italians, already discredited over the treaty of Ucciali

[6] Sir Evelyn Baring to Lord Salisbury, 15 Dec. 1889, FO 78/4243.
[7] Marquis of Dufferin to Knutsford, 26 Feb. 1890, and Dufferin to Salisbury, 9 Mar. 1890, quoted in Lyall (1905, ii. 231, 233).
[8] Salisbury to Baring, 28 Mar. 1890, quoted in Cecil (1921–32), iv. 328.

and at odds with Menelik, were only too glad to agree. In March 1891 the Italians signed the Anglo-Italian Treaty, in which they officially consented to remain out of the Nile valley in return for British recognition of an Italian sphere of influence in the Ethiopian highlands.

Ironically, the Italians were a greater threat to the Nile waters than the British ever realized. Until hydrological studies were carried out along both the Blue Nile and the White in the first decade of the twentieth century, the British and everyone else assumed that the Nile flow was composed predominantly of water carried northward by the White Nile from the great reservoirs of the equatorial lakes. A cursory glance at the map of Africa appears to confirm this assumption. In fact, most of the Nile waters come from Ethiopia by the Blue Nile and the 'Atbara river. In Ethiopia, however, the Italians, not the British, had carved out a sphere of influence; but, confident in the presumption that the upper Nile was the source of the waters which made Egypt flourish, Salisbury was content to leave the Italians alone in Ethiopia so long as they remained outside the southern Sudan. Indeed, British interest in the security of the Blue Nile water was not officially registered until the signing of the Anglo-Ethiopian treaty of 1902, in which Ethiopia agreed not to obstruct the flow of the Blue Nile unilaterally. But by then control of the upper Nile was securely in British hands.

The Italian threat to the Nile valley was nevertheless a great watershed in the evolution of Salisbury's Nile policy in particular and his imperial strategy in general. Hitherto British statesmen had intuitively understood the relationship between the upper Nile and Egypt, but this understanding was never transformed into action. The Sudan lay securely in the hands of the Mahdists, isolated from the moves of any power with the means to interfere in the life-giving waters. The British position in Egypt was thereby preserved, the Suez Canal secure, and the seaway to India safe. Although it never assumed serious proportions, the Italian threat challenged this complacency. It forced Salisbury to crystallize his upper-Nile policy and to consider for the first time the eventualities of further attempts by other powers to seize control of the upper Nile reaches. Diplomacy succeeded in keeping the

Italians off the Nile, and although diplomacy could not be expected to keep rival European powers out of the Nile valley forever, it could do so long enough to allow Egypt, with British assistance, to conquer, occupy, and administer the Sudan.

Having protected his eastern flank in Ethiopia, Salisbury set out to prevent European encroachment from East Africa. The problem centred around the curious figure of Emin Pasha, one of the strangest individuals to wander down the tortuous paths of African history. Emin Pasha was born Eduard Schnitzer at Oppeln in Silesia in 1840. A German Jew of Protestant Christian parentage, he studied medicine in Germany, practised his profession in the Ottoman service, and promptly turned Muslim. He arrived penniless in Khartoum in 1875 with the intention of setting up in private practice, but soon joined the service of Colonel 'Chinese' Gordon and accompanied him to the equatorial province as a medical officer. Here, on the wild reaches of the upper Nile, Emin found himself at home. He took on administrative duties as well as his medical work, and in 1878 was appointed governor of the province, a position he happily retained until 1889. Emin Pasha was an intrepid if bizarre figure. His short, spare frame was accentuated by his trim and punctilious attire. He wore a beard and thick, round spectacles to compensate for extreme short-sightedness. His badge of office was a bright red fez tilted at a respectable angle. He looked the perfect parody of a baffled and bumbling eastern functionary in Africa. Yet he was an accomplished musician and a competent scientist, with a favourable reputation among those European scholars who frequently and without warning received from Emin crates and boxes of specimens from the heart of Africa. His record as an administrator, though inconsistent, remains that of a clever and sensitive man.

After the fall of Khartoum in 1885, Emin and his people subsisted in Equatoria isolated from Europe by the forces of the Mahdist State. Emin appealed for help, and he was not disappointed. The idea of this strange little man holding high the torch of civilization, while surrounded by barbarian hordes in darkest Africa, captured the imagination of Europeans and, in particular, the British. The interest in Emin, of course, was not all philanthropic. MacKay in Uganda and Consul Holmwood at Zanzibar were urging assistance for Emin, the former to forestall the Germans, the latter to acquire a base of operations for the retention of the upper Nile; but in London the sympathy for Emin was aroused more by a genuine and benevolent desire to aid a beleaguered representative of civilization than by any visions of imperial adventure. When news reached the British Foreign Office in October 1886 that Emin Pasha's equatorial province had survived the Mahdist upheaval, even a bureaucratic and hardened sceptic like Sir Percy Anderson, the head of the African Department, initially regarded the proposals to relieve Emin as basically humanitarian.

Above all, Emin must not be allowed to perish by such tardy action as had caused the death of Gordon. 'If the expedition goes,' wrote Sir Percy, 'it should start *at once*.'[9] Everyone agreed, but with the political consequences of the failure to relieve Gordon still a fresh and unpleasant memory, Salisbury and his Cabinet refused to commit the government to the rescue of Emin. The task would have to be left to private philanthropy, to which Anderson's encouragement would have to remain unofficial; and there was no dearth of greedy benefactors anxious to take up where Salisbury's altruism ended. In November 1886 the 'Emin Pasha relief committee' was speedily organized by Sir William Mackinnon and his friends. Mackinnon was a tough, able, pious Scot. Born in poverty in Lanarkshire in 1823, he had gone out in 1847 to India where, by a combination of luck and business acumen, he prospered and established the British India Steam Navigation Company. The company grew and with it Mackinnon's wealth, which he generously used to assist his friends, geographical exploration, and Christian missions. Like other Victorians he was drawn to Africa by the happy combination of exercising Christian humanity against the slave trade with the opportunity to share and profit in African development.

When the news of Emin Pasha's plight in Equatoria reached England in October 1886, Mackinnon at once set

[9] Minute by Anderson, 18 Oct. 1886, FO 84/1775; quoted in Sanderson (1965, p. 30).

about organizing a relief expedition. He contributed heavily himself while enlisting the financial support of his rich business friends, and summoned the Napoleon of African exploration, Henry Morton Stanley, from a successful American lecture tour to lead it. Unlike Sir Percy Anderson, however, Mackinnon was not motivated purely by a humanitarian concern for Emin. His own avowed purpose in sponsoring the relief expedition was to 'establish British commerce and influence in East Africa, and for relieving Emin Bey'—in that order.[10] Mackinnon, and practically everyone else, had initially regarded the east coast as the obvious and easiest approach to the southern Sudan, and he looked to Stanley 'to open a direct route to Victoria Nyanza and the Soudan and thereby establish stations and commerce in the interior of Africa'.[11] But a few weeks later, in December, Stanley was telling Anderson that the Congo, not East Africa, afforded the 'quicker [sic] easiest and safest' route to reach the beleaguered Pasha.[12] Someone had upset the original scheme to rescue Emin Pasha. It was Leopold II, King of the Belgians and sovereign of the Congo Free State.

Leopold's interest in the Nile valley was first aroused by Gordon, who as early as 1880 appears to have urged the king, in the name of humanity, to suppress the slave trade there. But Leopold was not interested so much in suppressing the slave trade as in penetrating into the Nile valley, and the king's humanitarian motives were certainly more than matched by his desire to acquire, through military conquest or diplomatic manœuvre, as much as possible of the southern Sudan. It cannot be doubted that Leopold, with his determination and megalomania, took such grandiose plans seriously, and he now sought to use the Emin Pasha relief expedition to extend his Congo empire just as his friend Mackinnon sought to use it to extend British influence and commerce into East Africa.

Theoretically the Congo route had advantages over the ones from the east coast. Many assumed that it would be quicker to ascend the Congo River than to go overland

[10] Memorandum by Mackinnon, Private and Confidential, 1886, Mackinnon Papers, School of Oriental and African Studies, University of London.
[11] Ibid.
[12] Sir Percy Anderson to Sir Julian Pauncefote, 24 Dec. 1886, FO 84/1795.

through East Africa. Salisbury was relieved: the Congo route raised no question of 'war with Uganda', while Anderson helpfully added that 'we should escape German jealousy'.[13] From Leopold's point of view the Congo route was ideal. Stanley's expedition would blaze the way through the unexplored territory of the eastern Congo at the expense of Mackinnon and his charitable friends and open a passage through the Congo which might eventually link up with the trade routes Mackinnon hoped to establish across East Africa. Like King Leopold, Sir William Mackinnon had an imagination the size of Africa. As Salisbury put it, 'he is rather unreal.'[14] Although his interest in East Africa had lain dormant during the early 1880s while he dabbled in Leopold's Congo schemes, his enthusiasm for eastern Africa had returned with the mission to rescue Emin Pasha. He now dreamed of a British East African empire developing in harmony with the Congo Free State, the latter providing an outlet for British trade on the west coast. In the Emin Pasha relief expedition he saw the beginning of a British chartered company in East Africa, and by January 1887 he had decided to go ahead and form the commercial organization that later became the Imperial British East Africa Company. He conceived of British trade flowing across the African continent—back and forth and up and down—co-operating with Leopold's Congo on the one hand, merging with Cecil Rhodes's empire on the other.

To Sir Percy Anderson and Lord Salisbury, in 1886, such grandiose schemes would have apeared little more than flights of fancy by an ageing Scot. To them at that time Equatoria was devoid of any economic or strategic importance. Their bemused interest in the plight of Emin Pasha sprang from Victorian charity, not from unscrupulous designs of empire. Yet three years later Equatoria had become the linchpin of Salisbury's Nile policy. This transformation was not the result of events in Equatoria, for Emin Pasha did little but continue Egyptian administration on his dwindling resources. Rather, Equatoria's location astride the upper Nile altered dramatically from a remote and wild remnant of the Egyptian empire in

[13] Minute by Salisbury on memorandum by Anderson, 15 Oct. 1885, FO 84/1775; memorandum by Anderson, 5 Jan. 1887, FO 84/1830; and Stanley (1891, i. 44–5).
[14] Minute by Salisbury, 22 Dec. 1887, FO 84/1837.

1886 to a strategic position in British imperial policy in 1889, when Salisbury reached his decision to keep Britain in Egypt and the European powers out of the Nile valley. Once having determined not to evacuate Egypt, the British Administration, as well as the Egyptians themselves, believed they could be secure only when the Nile waters were safe. By 1890 Salisbury had cautioned the Italians to stay out of the Nile valley, and Rome had heeded his warning. But no sooner had the Italian threat from the east been contained in Ethiopia than a more serious menace loomed to the south in Equatoria. Before Europe knew that Stanley had reached Equatoria and, at that very moment, was intrepidly leading the shattered remnants of his expedition and Emin Pasha out of Africa, the German explorer Carl Peters was racing toward the southern Sudan at the head of a rival expedition to rescue his fellow countryman.

Carl Peters was Germany's leading and most unsavoury imperialist. In 1884 he had founded the Gesellschaft für Deutsche Kolonisation and with three companions had travelled in disguise to East Africa, where he concluded twelve treaties with African headmen which he used to assert his claim to a large area inland from Dar es-Salaam. Although Bismarck had previously warned Peters against such a move, the Iron Chancellor was now only too pleased, for reasons of European diplomacy, to make use of Peters's work. On 3 March 1885 a German *schutzbrief* was granted over the territories acquired by Peters, and Germany had its first possession in East Africa. A few months later the enclave of Witu at the mouth of the Tana River was added to the German protectorate, and was extended up the coast to the Juba River in November 1889. In 1888 Peters sought to repeat his earlier triumph in Tanganyika with an even more splendid contribution to German empire-building in the Witu hinterland. Supported by the influential Admiral Livonius and Rudolf von Bennigsen, Peters organized a German Emin Pasha expedition in June 1888. Under the pretext of rescuing Emin, who after all was a German, Peters hoped to strike inland from Witu, enlist Emin in the German service, and acquire Equatoria and the land stretching southward to Lake Victoria and the German sphere, thereby encircling the British sphere with German possessions. It was a brilliant scheme, and quite

feasible, for the Anglo-German agreement of 1886 had never
defined the western limits of the respective British and
German spheres, nor had subsequent undertakings effectively
prevented the possibility of rival annexations in the interior.
The African hinterland was open to whomever first claimed it.
Bismarck, of course, would neither support nor approve of a
project so calculated to create anti-German feeling in Britain;
but then he had not approved of Peters's treaty-making
expedition in 1885 yet had utilized its results. And even
Salisbury had seemed to acquiesce in a German expedition to
the interior when the news reached London in 1886 of Emin's
difficulties in Equatoria. In fact, the prime minister had
encouraged the Foreign Office to pass on information about
Emin to the Germans, for 'it is really their business if Emin is
a German'.[15] By 1888, however, certainly Anderson and
perhaps even Salisbury were thoroughly alive to the dangers
of a German expedition racing to Uganda and beyond to
Emin Pasha and the Nile. In June, the plans for the German
Emin Pasha expedition were made known. In September,
Mackinnon's Imperial British East Africa Company received
its charter on the understanding that the company would
press on to Uganda before the Germans. As in other regions of
Africa, the British government had called upon private
enterprise to block the imperial designs of other nations.
Mackinnon would checkmate Peters, while Salisbury would
rely on Bismarck's good sense not to commit the German
government to an aggressive policy toward the Nile. As for
Peters, he made no attempt to conceal the fact that the relief of
Emin was nothing but an excuse to expand the German
empire in East Africa. 'The German Emin Pasha expedition',
he later wrote, 'was no pleasure trip, but a large-scale
colonial, political enterprise.'[16]

Although Lord Salisbury could distinguish between the
schemes of an adventurer like Peters and the repeated
disavowal of him by a responsible statesman like Bismarck,
Sir William Mackinnon could not. If Leopold was his ally, he
regarded all Germans as his enemies, and when Peters
belatedly started out from Witu in 1889, Mackinnon raised

[15] Minute by Salisbury, Oct. 1886, FO 84/1775.
[16] Peters (1891, p. 298); Müller (1959, pp. 463-4).

the hue and cry after the German 'felon'. By August 1889 Mackinnon's fears had turned to frenzy. He wrote to Stanley, somewhere in the interior, that the Germans were seeking a delimitation which would exclude the Imperial British East Africa Company from the future development of British territorial influence at the source of the Nile discovered by British explorers and essential to the protection of the Nile waters in British-occupied Egypt.

At the time Stanley was already on his way back from Equatoria. Having opened the eastern Congo for Leopold, where his expedition nearly met disaster, and rescued Emin Pasha, who did not particularly wish to be saved, Stanley, as he marched through East Africa to the coast, tried to do something for Mackinnon by concluding treaties for the Imperial British East Africa Company. Ironically, they later proved to be fraudulent. On 4 December 1889 the expedition straggled into Bagamoyo. Bagamoyo means 'lay down the burden of your heart', an appropriate terminus for such an epic journey, the heroic character of which was marred only by Emin's reluctance to be rescued.

Unfortunately, Emin's rescue only intensified the problem of the upper Nile. On the one hand he had refused Leopold's offer to undertake the rule of Equatoria as a Congolese province, yet on the other he had turned down Mackinnon's offer to take over the territory between Equatoria and Lake Victoria for the Imperial British East Africa Company. In fact Emin's rescue had left Equatoria a no man's land, a vacuum irresistibly drawing the European powers; Carl Peters, too late to save Emin, appeared the most likely to fill it. Salisbury at first was not alarmed. Count Hatzfeldt, the German ambassador in London, had assured him in June 1889 that 'Uganda, Wadelai, and other places to the east and north of Lake Victoria Nyanza are outside the sphere of German colonization'.[17] Moreover, Bismarck had refused to support Peters's designs on that region, and had even ordered German naval units in East African waters to assist the British in preventing Peters from landing in Africa. In 1884–5 Britain had encouraged German colonial adventures, and at Zanzibar

[17] Salisbury to Sir Edward Malet, 25 June 1889, Africa No. 266, FO 84/1954.

had even sought to smooth the way for the German empire in
those parts of East Africa where no vital British interests were
at stake. After the decision to remain in Egypt, Britain did not
appear to have a large strategic stake in the upper Nile, and
Salisbury could calculate that Bismarck's prudence would not
permit him to jeopardize his European alignments for a
wilderness in central Africa or the schemes of a freebooter like
Peters.

Salisbury thus counted on Bismarck's caution. In fact the
prime minister required it, for in 1889–90 he did not possess
the parliamentary strength to ignore the ever-growing influence
of the British colonial groups, precisely those people who
became most excited about the activities of German nationals
in Africa. Throughout the autumn of 1889 and the spring of
1890 the Conservatives were losing ground, and in the House
of Commons they were increasingly dependent upon the
Liberal Unionists to maintain their majority. The Irish
question had obstructed the march of Tory democracy, and the
electorate's frustration with the Conservatives was reflected
by the party's dismal showing at the by-elections. On 17 June
1890 the government majority actually plunged to a perilous
four votes. Even if Salisbury did not approve of Mackinnon,
Rhodes, and their wealthy followers, and was constantly
annoyed by the importunities of the missionary groups, he
would have to be prepared to keep them all satisfied in Africa
in order to keep their powerful support at home.

Moreover, in spite of Bismarck's assurances of co-operation
and Salisbury's scepticism about any German design to seize
the Nile, both British and German nationals were exacerbating
potential difficulties in East Africa to the point where a
settlement was desirable before the repercussions of their
quarrels damaged Anglo-German relations in general. Zanzibar,
the Tana–Juba hinterland behind Witu, and the regions west
of Lake Victoria and Lake Nyasa were all, more or less,
disputed ground which both Bismarck and Salisbury would
have liked to have settled—each on his own terms. Then
suddenly, in March 1890, Bismarck ceased to guide the
destinies of Germany. The dismissal of Bismarck and the
emergence of Emperor Wilhelm II at the head of German
affairs had a profound impact on Salisbury. Wilhelm II had

sympathized with Peters's plan for German expansion, but Bismarck had been able to keep the emperor's 'equatorial enthusiasm' in check. Now Bismarck was gone, and German policy in Africa, as elsewhere, increasingly reflected the Kaiser's erratic and frequently imprudent views.

Certainly, German words and deeds following Bismarck's fall were hardly calculated to reassure Salisbury, who had grounds for disquiet even if, in fact, the Germans had no intentions of a forward policy. Already by the first week in May the German secretary of state, Baron von Marschall, was insisting that there was no understanding over the hinterland west of Lake Victoria which the British regarded as part of Uganda. Moreover, Emin Pasha, now in the German service, had left Bagamoyo on 26 April 1890 with a hastily organized expedition for the interior—rumour had it, Equatoria and the upper Nile. Here was another Peters expedition but without Bismarckian repudiation—grounds enough for British distrust. Then there was Carl Peters, wherever he might be. Finally, on 12 May, the German chancellor, Georg Leo von Caprivi, requested four and a half million marks 'for the suppression of the Slave Trade and the protection of German interests in East Africa'. The chancellor perhaps had no intention of altering Germany's African policy, but the impression created by his strong speech and the large resources suddenly requested for German East Africa could not but have caused concern in London. Indeed, only the most insensitive of British officials could have ignored the implications of German words and deeds in the spring of 1890, particularly when they suddenly appeared one after the other and their ends were by no means made clear.

On 18 April 1890 Salisbury returned to London after a bout of influenza. Many months before, he had decided that the European powers must be kept out of the Nile valley for the security of Egypt and the British position in that country. Before his illness in March, he had even warned the Italians to remain in Ethiopia and not to venture into the Nile valley. Thus during the first weeks of May his uneasiness over German activities in East Africa were now fused with his principle of the inviolability of the Nile valley. Only a comprehensive settlement with Germany could resolve the

nagging East African disputes with Germany, thereby preventing any German threat, real or imaginary, to the upper
Nile.

Salisbury moved decisively. On 13 May 1890 he presented
a comprehensive programme to the German ambassador in
London to resolve Anglo-German rivalry in the hinterland of
East Africa, and after less than three weeks of negotiations the
principal terms of the Anglo-German agreement were settled
on 5 June and signed on 1 July 1890. In return for the British-
owned island of Heligoland just off the German coast in the
North Sea, long an irritating symbol to German nationalists,
and full possession of the East African coastal strip which the
sultan of Zanzibar had leased to the Germans, Britain would
receive Witu and its hinterland, the upper Nile. The boundary
between the British and the German spheres west of Lake
Victoria was fixed at latitude 1° south. Salisbury had not only
removed the many potential danger spots in East Africa where
the activities of his more exuberant nationals would clash with
the Germans, but he had also sealed off the upper Nile from
possible German encroachment. He wrote triumphantly to
the British ambassador in Berlin, Sir Edward Malet: 'The
effect of this arrangement will be that, except so far as the
Congo State is concerned, there will be no European
competitor to British influence between the first degree of
south latitude and the borders of Egypt, along the whole of the
country which lies to the south and west of the Italian
Protectorate in Abyssinia and Gallaland.'[18] Having settled
with the Germans, Salisbury turned to tidy up his previous
threats to the Italians to remain out of the Nile valley by the
signing of the Anglo-Italian Treaty of March 1891. To him
the Nile was securely British, or so he thought.

In 1893 two seemingly innocuous events occurred which
were ultimately to present Great Britain with its most
formidable challenge at the time for control of the Nile waters.
In January 1893 the new khedive, 'Abbas Hilmi, who loathed
the British, sought to reassert his authority by appointing
his own ministers more sympathetic to Egyptian national
aspirations than the sycophants of British choice. Lord

[18] Salisbury to Malet, 14 June 1890, FO 84/2030.

Cromer, the British agent and consul-general in Egypt, did not hesitate. He demanded and received immediate reinforcements of British troops. Not only did their presence, to the dismay of Prime Minister Gladstone, appear to make more permanent the British occupation of Egypt, but it also thereby logically assured the retention of Uganda at the Nile source as a British protectorate, which was being passionately debated at the time. Cromer's high-handed tactics in the humiliation of the khedive were commensurate with his style as one of Britain's foremost proconsuls, but they infuriated the French, whose reaction was to demand that Great Britain officially open discussions with the French Government with a view to British withdrawal from Egypt. They were summarily rebuffed.

The khedivial crisis of January coincided with a lecture by the French hydrologist Victor Prompt, entitled 'Soudan Nilotique', delivered before the Institut d'Égypte on 20 January, in which he proposed the construction of a dam on the White Nile below its confluence with the Sobat which could be so regulated in order to ruin Egypt by drought or flood. In the atmosphere of the day his lecture, despite its highly speculative assumptions, was received with considerable interest, which extended beyond the scientific and intellectual circles of the Egyptian Institute. Circulated throughout the principal government ministries, it was brought to the attention of the new minister at the colonial department, Théophile Delcassé, who saw in Victor Prompt's proposal a means to exert pressure on Great Britain to reopen the Egyptian question. Despite his junior status in the government, Delcassé sought to enlist the support of Sidi Carnot, president of the republic and an old schoolfriend of Victor Prompt. Carnot met with Delcassé and the highly acclaimed French African explorer, Commandant P. L. Monteil, at the Elysée palace on 3 May 1893 and there the great French Fashoda expedition was born.

The French ultimately chose Fashoda as their goal, not only because it was the capital of the Shilluk kingdom located just north of Malakal on the west bank of the Nile, but because anyone at that time, or even today, casually looking at the configuration of the upper Nile basin without any specific knowledge of its hydrology would observe that all of the many tributaries of the White Nile come together to form a single mighty river at Fashoda. No one at the time appears to have given any thought as to the feasibility of a dam at Fashoda, but its location alone made it seem perfectly obvious that any regulator at Fashoda would be able to control all of the waters rising in the equatorial regions of central and eastern Africa, thereby making the British position in Cairo completely untenable. With a French force at Fashoda, how could the British refuse to negotiate the evacuation of Egypt once they had lost control of the irreplaceable water supply?

Not only did the French Fashoda expedition possess that grand cartographic sweep so appealing to the French, but it fell perfectly into place with other equally heroic schemes for securing African territory envisaged by French imperialists. Not that there was any great popular demand for French expansion in Africa, but the work of French explorers had aroused great interest in the dark continent among a host of influential organizations which had evolved over the past quarter-century to further French colonization. There were the chambers of commerce, the geographical societies, the imperialists, the army, and, perhaps most important, a hard core of imperial-minded civil servants within the heart of the French government who saw the course of empire as a means to advance their own personal ambitions. All of these various groups sought French overseas expansion, not only as a revival of the greatness lost to the Germans on the battlefield of Sedan in 1870, but a tangible commercial and strategic benefit to the metropolis and a visible means of enhancing that elusive but eminently satisfying attribute known as prestige. The French had already carved out a large empire in the western Sudan while at the same time they were moving inexorably northward into the great basin of Lake Chad and the kingdoms of Bornu and Wadai. The one overwhelming problem facing the president of France and the minister of the marine on that wintry day in Paris 1893 was how to place a French force astride the upper Nile in the remote village of Fashoda.

The vision of a great trans-African empire extending from Dakar on the Atlantic to Djibouti on the Red Sea with its centre at Fashoda engendered overwhelming enthusiasm; the great risk which the achievement of this vision entailed was summarily dismissed by the cartographic elegance of the Tricolour stretching across Africa from west to east. The French imperialists did not seem too concerned by—or even to consider—the equal enthusiasm of the British imperialists for an 'all-red' route of British territory sweeping up the backbone of the continent from Cape Town to Cairo, with its pivot also at Fashoda. Both were grandiose schemes appealing to the imperialists and the patriotic imagination of an influential segment of the public in both countries. Yet in those halcyon days of the early 1890s few seemed to contemplate the repercussions of an Anglo-French confrontation at the cross-roads of these two imperial ambitions at the thatched huts of Fashoda, where the fantasies of empire were reduced to the realities of who would control the Nile waters and, thereby, Cairo, Egypt, and Suez. The French, however, had first to reckon with the Italians.

The Italian imperialists, led by the prime minister, Francesco Crispi, bewailed the fact that the new Italy had entered the partition of Africa late in the game. He declared: 'Colonies are a necessity of modern life. We cannot remain inactive and allow other powers to occupy all the unexplored parts of the world.'[19] Indeed, upon surveying the African continent at the end of the nineteenth century Italy saw the pervasive influence of powers greater than herself in virtually every sphere but Ethiopia, which in the declining decades of the nineteenth century appeared much as it had to the historian Edward Gibbon in the eighteenth: 'Encompased on all sides by the enemies of their religion, the Aethiopians slept near a thousand years, forgetful of the world by whom they were forgotten.'[20] Here in the fertile highlands of the Ethiopian plateau Italy could revive the grandeur that once was Rome and thrust the new nation into the front ranks of the imperial powers at the expense of Menelik, Lion of Judah and Emperor of Ethiopia. Given the blessing of the British government in 1891 to move aggressively into Ethiopia, and thereby forestall the French, the Italians could occupy Ethiopia by military force—diplomacy having previously failed them at Ucciali—

---

[19] Quoted in Langer (1956, p. 272).   [20] Gibbon (1946, ii. 1601).

so long as they stayed out of the Nile valley. Ever since that
diplomatic débâcle in 1889, Menelik II, the Lion of Judah,
King of Kings, and Emperor of Ethiopia had thundered that
'Italy will never win an empire by mistranslating Amharic',
and prepared for war.[21] The French were only too happy to
help, in the hope of expanding their influence at Addis Ababa
by military and diplomatic support; but since the Italians
were determined on a forward course in Ethiopia, the way to
Fashoda for the French in 1893 did not lie directly through the
highlands of north-east Africa but in the longer and more
tortuous journey from Loango on the Atlantic coast of the
French Congo, up the Rivers Congo, Ubangi, and M'Bomu,
over the watershed into the Nile basin, down the tributaries of
the Bahr al-Ghazal, and thus through the swamps of the Nile
to Fashoda.

Such an expedition was fraught with every conceivable kind
of natural disaster and human calamity. In scope it can only
be compared with Henry Morton Stanley's trans-African
journey between 1874 and 1877 or with his Emin Pasha relief
expedition of 1887–9. Although preparations began in 1893,
the project was temporarily suspended by political complica-
tions in Europe (and France in particular) and by the
vacillation of Monteil himself. Nevertheless, the idea of the
Fashoda expedition did not die, and in November 1895 it was
revived by Captain Jean-Baptiste Marchand who, at thirty-
one, was already a veteran of active service in Africa, where he
had established a brilliant reputation as a military explorer
and soldier. He had been deeply interested in the Fashoda
expedition since the summer of 1893, actively supported the
project, and even drafted a detailed proposal by which a
French expedition could reach Fashoda from the Atlantic
coast. He was encouraged by Monteil himself, by the colonial
lobby in Paris, and particularly by the bureaucrats of the
ministry of colonies at the Pavillon de Flore. In November
1895 the Fashoda expedition was brought to the attention of
the new foreign minister, Marcellin Berthelot, who was
particularly struck by the plan of Captain Marchand reaching
the Nile through the Bahr al-Ghazal and promptly approved

---

[21] Quoted in Woolf (1968, p. 172).

his striking for the Nile. In February 1896 Marchand's instructions were drafted, and in June he left for Africa and the long march to Fashoda.

The British government, through its intelligence services in Paris and Cairo, were quite aware of these French activities and, although not particularly alarmed, were prepared to formulate contingency plans to protect the Nile waters. South of the Egyptian frontier the entire middle Nile from Wadi Halfa to Equatoria was firmly in control of Khalifa 'Abd Allahi, the successor to the Mahdi. He and his followers were no threat to the flow of the Nile waters, but the presence of thousands of formidable Sudanese warriors did not inspire the British government, whether Conservative or Liberal, to launch an expensive and dangerous military campaign to fight its way through the barren wastes of the Sudan to Fashoda.

In June 1895 Lord Salisbury and his government returned to power. He immediately sought alternatives, other than the unwanted reconquest of the Sudan, to protect the Nile waters. At the time the British were unable to determine the exact goal of the Marchand expedition, but any simpleton would have realized that a French expedition moving up the tributaries of the Congo in a north-east direction could only terminate at Fashoda. Salisbury reacted by playing the Ugandan card. Unwilling to expend British and Egyptian money and men in the conquest of the Sudan, he sought a more expedient route to the Nile source by pushing through parliament an expedition to extend the Uganda railway to Lake Victoria as fast as possible. But the race for the Nile was not solely a two-nation competition. There was a third member, King Leopold II of the Belgians, the uncontested proprietor of the Congo Free State.

King Leopold's interest in the upper Nile was usually cloaked in the rhetoric of suppressing the slave trade. Regrettably, humanitarianism was not the driving force of Leopold's imperialism, and although he flaunted his philanthropy, it was usually to disguise more sinister schemes for commercial and economic exploitation and to satisfy his insatiable lust for African territory. To him, 'striking at the slave trade' and penetrating the Nile valley were one and the same problem. Although Leopold never possessed a large national population eager for imperial adventures nor could command the military and economic resources of Britain or France, as sovereign of the Congo Free State he exercised unchallenged rule over a large and wealthy African territory, unhindered by popular demands or constitutional limitations. In Europe Leopold was a restricted monarch; in Africa he was his own master. As the sovereign of the Congo he was answerable to no one, although he may have had some ill-defined obligations to the signatories of the Berlin Act who had created the Congo Free State in 1885. As its enlightened despot he could marshal and manœuvre the Congo's resources to carry out his schemes, untrammelled by interference from within, alert only to intervention from without. This enormous advantage helped offset the superior power of his rivals. When it was combined with the astute and venturesome diplomacy he practised with such flair, the king was indeed a dangerous opponent. Leopold thought big in Africa. His designs were always breath-taking in scope if frequently unrealistic in practice, and their sheer magnitude made their consequences all the more alarming. Thus Leopold obstinately pursued his goal of controlling the upper Nile and, caught in the web of his own megalomaniac ambition, he lavishly expended the resources of the Congo on the Nile quest. From the founding of the Congo Free State in 1885 until his death in 1909 he never abandoned his search for the elusive fountains of the Nile, and in that quest he challenged Britain on the upper Nile and threatened her position in Egypt, the Mediterranean, and the Indian Ocean.

Although Lord Salisbury's Heligoland treaty with Germany in 1890 kept the Germans off the Nile, it unwittingly left the way to the Nile open to a more tenacious rival—King Leopold. Although Leopold had originally sought to extend his Congo empire by using the expedition to relieve Emin Pasha in Equatoria, his first diplomatic success came as a result of the Heligoland treaty, which did not prevent his advance to the Nile. Four months after the signing of the Anglo-German agreement ceding the island of Heligoland in return for the Nile, the king sent Captain van Kerckhoven to the Congo in the greatest secrecy to prepare an expedition to march to Wadelai and claim the upper Nile by effective occupation. By 1892 the forces of the Congo Free State had reached the Nile, and the following year they established garrisons on the river. The occupation, however, was not permanent. On the upper Nile the Congolese faced a strong Mahdist drive up the river and consequently retired to less exposed posts in the interior. In Europe Leopold's diplomatic position in the upper Nile valley began to crumble as well. When reports reached Europe in February 1892 that the van Kerckhoven expedition was pressing on toward the Nile, the British demanded that the Congo Free State stay off the river. Having fended the Italians and the Germans off the Nile, Salisbury was not prepared to cede the Nilotic provinces to Leopold. Moreover, since his Congolese troops had been forced by the Mahdists to retire, Leopold's threat to the upper Nile seemed to have quietly disappeared.

Nothing, however, seemed to stop the irrepressible Leopold. His advance to the Nile momentarily checked by the Mahdists, he proposed that Great Britain lease to him the Bahr al-Ghazal, thereby blocking the French designs to march through the southern Sudan to Fashoda. In 1894 the British government hastily signed an agreement with King Leopold by which they leased to the king the vast province of the Bahr al-Ghazal in the uneasy hope that Leopold's presence would frustrate any advance by the French. The Anglo-Congolese agreement backfired. Not only did it fail to frustrate the French, but it gave to King Leopold an enclave at Lado on the upper Nile and claims to the Bahr al-Ghazal which were later to challenge British policy and position in Egypt. Leopold remained a troublesome factor in Britain's Nile policy.

While Marchand was making his preparations to march to Fashoda in the spring of 1896, French fortunes were suddenly and dramatically advanced by the overwhelming defeat of the Italian army at Adua on 1 March 1896. Although the idea of rebuilding the Roman empire in Ethiopia did not appeal to the mass of Italians, it was regarded as a fundamental prerequisite by the Italian imperialists for Italy to take its place among the great powers of Europe. By 1895 the Italians had assumed control of the plains of Eritrea along the Red Sea coast below the Ethiopian highlands. Here an Italian army of some 18,000 men under the command of General Oreste

Baratiere was ordered by the prime minister, Francesco Crispi, in February 1896 to advance into the highlands and begin its conquest for the greater glory of Italy. Having assiduously carried out his preparations for the past six years, the Emperor Menelik was ready to meet the advancing Italians. He had acquired large quantities of rifles and artillery, which he deployed among his army of over 100,000 men concentrated around the strategic town of Adua. Advancing into the highlands, the Italian army became divided among the precipitous valleys and mountain passes, whereupon Menelik launched his overwhelming force upon the scattered Italian units, destroying the Italian army and ending for the nineteenth century Italian imperial designs in Africa.

The importance of Menelik's victory cannot be over-emphasized. It was a stunning victory of a technologically less developed people against the armies of the European invaders which has left a profound impact on Africans to this day. Of greater concern to the self-appointed defenders of the Nile waters, the British, was the fact that the collapse of the Italian position in Ethiopia opened the way for French encroachment into the Nile valley from the east at precisely the same time that Marchand was making his final preparation to march to Fashoda from the west. The Italian defeat realized all the British fears about the security of the Nile valley. The Germans had been bought off by the island of Heligoland; the Italians by threats and a treaty. The Nile valley itself was safely in the hands of the Mahdist State under Khalifa 'Abd Allahi, whose formidable army of fighting Sudanese was more than capable of protecting their territory and the Nile unless threatened by a European power with the technological superiority to destroy them. The British were quite content to let the Mahdists remain in control of the Sudan, for it precluded its conquest, and the savings thereby realized could be used by Lord Cromer for the reorganization and modernization of Egypt without wasting them on what would be an expensive campaign in the wasteland south of Aswan. Adua changed all this and presented the British government and its prime minister, Lord Salisbury, with an unwanted dilemma. Salisbury first used an appeal from the Italians for assistance after their defeat at Adua to move an Anglo-Egyptian expeditionary force to Dunqula, 322 km south of the Egyptian frontier with the Sudan, but Dunqula was still 1,835 km from Fashoda. The way to Fashoda was still clear from the east and west, and the French were pursuing it by mounting two expeditions within the year after the Ethiopian victory at Adua, while Marchand was pressing up the Ubangi toward the Congo–Nile watershed and the Bahr al-Ghazal.

Lord Salisbury first tried diplomacy to stop the French. In April 1897 the prime minister sent Rennell Rodd, one of Lord Cromer's 'amiable giants,' accompanied by Reginald Wingate, the director of military intelligence for the Anglo-Egyptian army, to Addis Ababa in the hope of scuttling the French expeditions which were preparing to march to Fashoda from the east. The British, however, had nothing to offer Menelik compared with the French promise of military and diplomatic support, including the recognition of the emperor's claims to the east bank of the Nile valley virtually from Khartoum to Lake Albert. Rennell Rodd returned to Cairo with a treaty whose terms were meaningless in defence of the Nile. When Salisbury learned of the failure of the Rodd mission he was presented with a dilemma. Diplomacy having failed, Salisbury had to contemplate securing the Nile by military force. On the one hand there was the British military establishment in Cairo, who were convinced that one day they would have to march into the Sudan and destroy the Mahdist forces. To enhance this objective they regularly produced intelligence reports and popular books which portrayed the rule of the khalifa as one of unmitigated tyranny, a portrait which had enormous appeal for a British public thirsting for revenge for the death of Gordon at the hands of the Mahdists during their destruction of Khartoum in 1885. On the other hand, Salisbury was not about to be moved by such propaganda, particularly when he was constantly aware of the dispassionate assessment of the hard-headed proconsul of Egypt, Lord Cromer, who was reluctant to expend the money necessary for the regeneration of Egypt on an expensive and dangerous mission to defeat the Mahdists before the gates of Omdurman. Salisbury consequently sought other expedients.

In order to frustrate the French attempts to reach Fashoda he therefore looked to an advance from the south, through eastern Africa. The problem was to move large numbers of troops from the British Indian army from Mombasa to Uganda and down the Nile. This was a long, arduous march through extreme deserts and highlands, and could only be accomplished in the nineteenth century by a railway. It was for this strategic purpose that the idea of the Uganda railway was born. Surveys had been undertaken as early as 1891, and Salisbury had consistently pushed funding through the House of Commons to advance this scheme. By 1895 Salisbury was pursuing the construction of the Uganda railway with all deliberate speed, its construction supervised by the extra-ordinary expedient of the Uganda railway committee sitting in the Foreign Office and under the immediate responsibility of the prime minister. A month after Marchand had left France for Loango and four months after the Italian débâcle at Adua, the Commons voted the necessary appropriations for the line amidst a cloud of rhetoric about combating the slave trade and developing the commercial potential of Uganda. These were indeed thin arguments, and precipitated embar-rassing questions from the opposition about the 'Lunatic Express', inspired by that stormy petrel of British politics, Henry Labouchere:

> What it will cost no words can express;
> What is its object no brains can suppose;
> Where it will start from no one can guess;
> Where it is going to nobody knows.[22]

In most continents railways do not run on time, and Africa is no exception. As British intelligence reports streamed in, from Cairo and Paris, of Marchand's progress toward the upper Nile and the advance of French expeditions across Ethiopia, Salisbury received equally dismal news about the construction of the Uganda railway. The lions were uncooperative, their predatory instincts provoking work stoppage by the Indian labourers enticed from their homeland to construct the line. The Rift Valley and the highlands required engineering feats unforeseen in the initial surveys. Clearly, the construction could not keep pace with Captain Marchand or with the

[22] Quoted in Robinson et al. (1981, p. 362).

French expeditions from Addis Ababa, and yet Salisbury had to do something. He fell back on the idea of sending a 'flying column' to the upper Nile under Captain J. R. L. Macdonald, formerly of the Uganda railway survey. The column of troops consisted of the former Sudanese troops of the Egyptian garrison under Emin Pasha, who were recruited as mercenaries by Captain Frederick D. Lugard to assert British authority in Uganda in 1891. These 'Nubies', as they were known in Uganda, however, were chafing under numerous grievances, mutinied against the British officials in Uganda, and virtually ended any hope of their once again coming to the defence of the British empire. When it appeared that the Macdonald expedition was a complete failure, the British commissioner in Uganda, E. J. L. Berkeley, improvised an expedition on his own under Major Martyr, which marched down the Bahr al-Jubal to Bor, where any further progress was blocked by the Sudd.

Frustrated at every turn in his efforts to reach the upper Nile from East Africa and Uganda, Lord Salisbury was besieged by a steady stream of intelligence reports and alarming newspaper accounts that the French were 'going in' to Fashoda. Diplomacy having failed in Ethiopia, flying columns aborted in Uganda, the prime minister had in the end to rely upon the big battalions to defend the Nile waters. On 26 January 1898 the British Cabinet authorized General Sir Horatio Herbert Kitchener, in command of the Anglo-Egyptian army, to go to Khartoum to destroy the Mahdist army of the Khalifa 'Abd Allahi and, if necessary, to confront the French at Fashoda. Salisbury's orders came none too soon.

The Marchand expedition can only be described either as comic opera or as heroic tragedy. Delayed by disturbances in Loango, quarrels with de Brazza, governor of the French Congo, and acrimonious negotiations with the agents of King Leopold for steamers to carry his expedition up the Ubangi and the M'Bomu, Marchand prevailed over all difficulties. Africans hauled his steamer, the *Faidherbe*, over the watershed into the Nile basin to Wau on the Jur River by the end of November 1897. November, however, is at the end of the rains; the Nile tributaries collapsed, leaving Captain Marchand and

120 Senegalese marooned in the Bahr al-Ghazal waiting for
the spring floods to float them through the Sudd. At 5 p.m. on
10 July 1898 Marchand walked ashore at Fashoda. Two days
later he raised the Tricolour in the presence of the reth (king)
of the Shilluk, with whom he later signed a formal treaty of
protection in which he claimed possession of the Bahr al-
Ghazal and the land of the Shilluk in the name of France, with
a panache that belied his beleaguered position over 1610 km
from the nearest French outpost.

While the French were intrepidly making their way through
the swamps of the Nile, King Leopold was assiduously
pursuing his impassioned goal of linking the two great
waterways of Africa—the Congo and the Nile. In 1896 he
launched a large expedition in two parts. The first, under
Baron Dhanis, was to march through the great rain forest of
the Aruwimi valley, in the footsteps of Stanley, to the head-
waters of the Nile. The second and smaller expedition, under
the command of Captain L. N. Chaltin, proceeded up the
River Uele toward the Congo–Nile watershed. Baron Dhanis
never completed his rendezvous with Captain Chaltin. His
troops mutinied from the terrors and hardships of marching
through the tropical rain forest which had almost destroyed
Stanley's expedition to rescue Emin Pasha a decade earlier.
Chaltin had better luck. He reached the Nile at Bedden in
February 1897, defeated the Mahdists at the battle of Rejaf,
and consolidated Leopold's claim to the upper Nile. As
isolated as the French at Fashoda, Chaltin's presence had
legal precedents but no power to support it.

With Marchand in the Bahr al-Ghazal moving relentlessly
toward Fashoda, there could no longer be any other choice
but confrontation. To be sure, there was no way that France
could supply Marchand at Fashoda, let alone build a
regulator across the Nile at that location. Ignorant of the
hydrology of the Nile, Lord Salisbury and his ministers were
unaware of the modest role of the White Nile in contributing
to the waters to irrigate Egypt. Emotionally the martyrdom of
Gordon at Khartoum in 1885 still remained unavenged in the
soul of the British public. And if there was any doubt, the
bronzed and spurred young British officers of the Anglo-
Egyptian army were ready to test their years of determined

preparation against the massed armies of the Mahdist State. It was now time for Kitchener to go to Khartoum.

Although a plodding engineer and pedantic soldier, General Kitchener was obsessed by a personal ambition which revealed moments of creativity if not inspiration. He rightly perceived that the defeat of the Mahdist forces was a matter of logistics and technology. Logistically, he had to transport and supply a large army up the Nile through some of the most inhospitable terrain in the world. Technologically, he had to bring to bear the terrifying force of modern artillery, and paticularly the machine-gun, to destroy the massed charges of the indomitable Sudanese before they overwhelmed his outnumbered British, Egyptian, and Sudanese battalions. The first problem he resolved by building a railway from Wadi Halfa to Abu Hamad across the Nubian desert, rather than following the traditional route into the Sudan from Al-Dabba at the bottom of the great bend of the Nile to Al-Matamma downstream from the confluence of the White Nile and the Blue. From Abu Ḥamad the railroad was extended parallel to the Nile to feed the troops and supply the ammunition. Technologically, Kitchener depended upon the dramatic innovations in weaponry which had characterized the latter half of the nineteenth century. The repeating rifle, the Maxim gun, and the gunboats more than compensated for the superior numbers of the brave Sudanese.

The Khalifa 'Abd Allahi believed in Armegeddon, one titanic battle between the invading infidels and the massed forces of Islam before the gates of Omdurman. To forestall the advancing Anglo-Egyptian forces he sent his foremost general, Mahmud Ahmad, north to the 'Atbara, where he was decisively defeated on 8 April 1898. Always cautious, the engineer mentality prevailed. Kitchener settled down to regroup during the long hot summer of the Sudan rather than advance immediately on Omdurman. He brought up the Nile additional British units with their weaponry to ensure a victory at Omdurman and to confront the French, which British intelligence confirmed were in the Bahr al-Ghazal, with an overwhelming force.

The battle of Omdurman took place on the plains of Karari, north of the city. Here at 'Iqayqa Kitchener embarked his forces under the shield of his gunboats while the khalifa was massing his forces behind the hills which dot the plains. His forces numbered between 50,000 and 60,000 men but were overwhelmed by the technological superiority of the Anglo-Egyptian army. Early on the morning of 2 September the Sudanese assaulted the crescent of armed forces which Kitchener had drawn up with their back to the Nile, supported by the firepower of his gunboats. The Sudanese flung themselves upon the invaders with incomparable courage, only to be destroyed by Kitchener's Maxim guns. The final display of the old order was the charge of the 21st Lancers, with Winston Churchill riding in the pack. It was the machine-guns, not the courage of the Lancers, that won the day, an important military lesson which was lost upon the British high command sixteen years later, in Flanders. By noon the battle was over; 11,000 Mahdist warriors lay dead on the plains of Karari, another 16,000 wounded limped back to Omdurman, many to die. Kitchener lost 48 killed and 382 wounded.

Three days later, on 5 September 1898, two Mahdist steamers arrived from the south, riddled with bullets of French manufacture. Marchand had beaten Kitchener to Fashoda. Kitchener promptly opened the sealed and hand-written instructions from Lord Salisbury and immediately steamed up the White Nile with a flotilla of gunboats, two battalions of British troops, and a sizeable number of Maxim guns. He arrived at Fashoda on 19 September to see the Tricolour flying in the breeze. The atmosphere was tense, symbolized by the thunderheads and lightning which roll over Shillukland every afternoon during the rainy season; but the representatives of the two great Western powers treated one another with a civility that has disappeared in great international confrontations. After a sumptuous lunch on the steamer *Dal*, Kitchener and Marchand retired to a small table on the after-deck to discuss the situation over coffee and liqueurs. Kitchener flatly stated that Marchand's presence was a direct violation of the rights of Egypt and Great Britain which had been regained by his victory at Omdurman. Marchand replied that his orders were precise. He had

established French authority at Fashoda, which was acknowledged by his treaty with the reth of the Shilluk. Kitchener
suggested that they refer the matter to their respective
governments. He would leave the French flag undisturbed but
would hoist the British and Egyptian flags at Fashoda without
delay, surrounded by a substantial garrison.

When the news reached London and Paris there was
immediate hysteria. Crowds filled the streets crying for
Fashoda or war. Lord Salisbury's position was simple and
strong. Kitchener had a battle-hardened army of 25,000
troops fully equipped and supplied. Marchand had seven
lonely French officers and 120 *tirailleurs sénégalais* marooned on
the banks of the Nile. Salisbury had a united government and
public behind him. The French government was divided. So
too were their military chiefs. The British were prepared to
fight. The reserves were called up and the fleet put to sea. The
French military were impotent. The army had only begun to
heal the deep wounds of the Dreyfus affair and was in no
condition to fight a major war. The French navy was in worse
condition, its ships rotting, its crews near mutiny. Marchand
was ordered to withdraw and, to save face, returned to Paris
via Ethiopia, where he received a hero's welcome. The
Fashoda crisis was over. Except for a small enclave at Lado
where King Leopold tenaciously clung to his dream of linking
the Congo with the Nile until his death in 1909, the Nile from
its presumed source at Lake Victoria to the Mediterranean
was securely British. Or was it?

Within five months of the collapse of Mahdist rule in the
Sudan, the Anglo-Egyptian condominium agreement was
signed on 19 January 1899. This arrangement resolved,
temporarily at least, the curious imperial relationship between
Britain, Egypt, and the Sudan by investing all civil and military
powers in the hands of a governor-general of the Sudan
'appointed by Khedivial Decree on the recommendation of
her Britannic Majesty's Government'. On the same day
Kitchener was appointed the first governor-general of the
Anglo-Egyptian Sudan. But though Kitchener was to have
supreme civil and military powers, he was by no means free
and unrestrained. Lord Cromer in Cairo, creator of the

condominium and virtual ruler of Egypt, was not inclined to
let affairs in the Sudan slip from his control. He wrote to
Kitchener with unmistakable candour:

Generally what I want is to control the big questions, but to leave all
the detail and execution to be managed locally. In the 'big' I of
course include all such measures, for instance, as involve any serious
interference with the water-supply of the Nile, or any large concession
to Europeans or others.[23]

Kitchener appears to have given little heed to these instructions. He plunged into the complex problem of creating a
functioning administration and rebuilding the Sudan without
consulting Cromer or keeping him fully informed. Not only did
Kitchener cast aside his former passion for economy and
frugality, but he employed methods which Cromer wryly
observed were 'perhaps a little more masterful and peremptory
than is usual in dealing with civil affairs'.[24] No detail was too
small, no problem too insignificant for Kitchener to handle
personally, and very few of these problems ever found their
way north to Cairo for answer or advice. Cromer complained
that if Kitchener 'tries to manage not only the public affairs
but also the private business of all his new subjects—after the
Napoleon and Frederick the Great system—he will find
he has far more to do than he can ever get through'; and on
another occasion the proconsul bitterly lamented that the
sirdar did not 'see with sufficient clearness the difference
between forming a country and commanding a regiment'.[25]
Control of even the 'big questions' in the Sudan was fast
slipping from Cromer's hands, and since knowledge and
understanding of such questions, among them the Nile waters,
were necessary to the formulation of policy in Egypt, Cromer
sent Sir William Garstin, the affable under-secretary of state
for public works in Egypt, engineer, hydrologist, and friend of
both Cromer and Kitchener, to the Sudan in February 1899 to
observe and report at first hand on the Nile.

Accompanied by Colonel W. S. Sparkes Bey, then governor
of Fashoda, Garstin travelled throughout the northern Sudan

[23] Quoted in Arthur (1920, i. 261).
[24] Cromer to Salisbury, 14 Jan. 1899, FO 633/6/307.
[25] Cromer to Salisbury, 10 Feb. and 22 Apr. 1899.

and personally steamed up the White Nile to test the navigability and hydrological significance of the Bahr al-Jabal and the Bahr al-Zaraf. Garstin found the Bahr al-Jabal completely impassable and, except for short stretches of open water, nearly obscured by sudd. Nor was the Bahr al-Zaraf much better. Despite the fact that the channel was now free of sudd obstructions for 300 km south of its juncture with the White Nile, the river beyond was tightly blocked. Only the Bahr al-Ghazal appeared open to navigation, but even the last kilometres to Mashra' al-Raqq were found to be closed. There could be no question of effective occupation of the southern Sudan until the Nile and its tributaries were cleared. Without free passage up the rivers, the region would remain unknown, the possibility of draining the swamps to increase the amount of Nile water would remain remote, and the question of preventing large concessions to Europeans would be unresolved.

The Nile waters and their defence had been the driving force of British imperial policy in north-east and east central Africa. The time had now come to determine the validity upon which so many monumental decision had been made. The facts of Nile hydrology were soon to prove that assumptions which have their own mysterious ways of becoming reality are not always the best foundations for the formulation of a great power's foreign policy.

3
The Sudd

No-one who has not seen this country can have any real
idea of its supreme dreariness and its utter desolation. To
my mind, the most barren desert that I have ever crossed
is a bright and cheerful locality compared with the White
Nile marshland.

Sir William Garstin, 1909

ALTHOUGH the difficulties of navigation through the Nile
swamps had long been known, the exact character of the
obstructions, called sudd, remained obscure until the British
began methodically to clear the rivers at the beginning of this
century. Sudd is derived from the Arabic word *sadd* (سَدّ)
meaning barrier or obstacle, and came into general use among
the European and Arab merchants and traders whose passage
through the swamps in the nineteenth century was impeded
by large dams of aquatic vegetation blocking the channels.
Today the term is used to describe the permanent swamp of
the Nile or, more loosely, to refer to the whole of the Nile
flood-plain, including the seasonal wetlands as well as the
permanent swamp.[1]

Sudd itself is formed in the large, shallow lagoons situated
on either side of the rivers. These lagoons are ringed, if not
covered, by reeds and water plants which bed their roots in
the soil and matter just below the surface. The strong gales
which sweep through the swamps buffet the plants and loosen
the roots. Then, during a rise in the level of the lagoon, the
plants break away to float freely on the surface, their roots a
tangled web of earth and humus whose weight acts as ballast
to keep the tall reeds upright. In this way large islands of

[1] For purposes of clarity I have referred to the flood-plain of the upper Nile,
including both the permanent and seasonal swamps, as the 'Sudd'. The individual
blocks of vegetation which created so many obstructions to navigation are 'sudd'
without capitalization.

aquatic plants drift aimlessly over the lagoon, constantly changing their position until wind and current and chance propel them into the river channel through one of the numerous spillways. Floating downstream, the sudd is soon caught at one of the sharp bends of the channel. Quickly the roots of the reeds strike down into the muddy river bottom, anchoring the island of sudd. Once secured, the reedy clump catches and entangles other floating islands until the whole surface of the river is obscured. Then the river is forced beneath the barrier, and as its velocity quickens with every constriction of the aperture, each fresh mass of sudd is relentlessly sucked beneath the original until the hole is plugged by a solid block of earth, roots, and reeds, broken up and then solidified by the pressure of the river. So great is the force of the Nile that the whole barrier is frequently pushed well above the water-level, and its surface serrated into alternate ridges and furrows. Soon the river is completely closed; its water is forced to spill into the lagoons, where a new channel is cut around the obstruction until it too is blocked by fresh masses of floating islands broken loose by the sudden rise in the water-level of the nearby lagoons. Frequently, the pressure of wind and water is so great that the dam will burst, carrying away the obstacle and precipitating a flood which, sweeping all before it, roars down the river until its force is spent in the twisting channels and sluggish lakes of the Nile swamps.

The lagoons themselves are found in the swamp, permanently flooded around the banks of the rivers, and not on the grasslands beyond, in which the extent of inundation will vary with the seasonal rainfall and the flow of the Nile. They change, of course, with the local rainfall and the amount of water emerging into the Sudd from the equatorial lakes, Victoria, Kyoga, and Albert, whose discharge is augmented by the torrents below Lake Albert. The lagoons themselves are no more than 4 m deep, and their distribution has changed dramatically throughout this century. Many of the lagoons north of Adok disappeared between 1904 and 1930, while those south of Shambe have increased in size from 1930 to the present day, particularly in recent times from the increased discharge from the equatorial lakes in the 1960s, when large quantities of water would first spill at the beginning of the Sudd rather than further downstream. Every lagoon has its own character. Some are part of a flowing river channel, others are separated from the river flow by walls of papyrus, to rise and fall with the rains and seepage from the surrounding swamp. Other lakes are more isolated from the regime of the river but, like the others, will have an exchange of water depending upon the river flow. There are, of course, large lagoons, like Lake Shambe and Lake Nyong, which have their own channels with the river but whose size has remained relatively unchanged, containing a considerable volume of dead water.[2]

From time immemorial the sudd blocks diverted, impeded, and even eclipsed the flow of the Nile, but only within the last century and a half have they played any significant role in the affairs of men except the inhabitants of the upper Nile. In November 1839 Salim Qapudan, a Turkish frigate captain, set out from Khartoum in command of ten boats with instructions from the viceroy of Egypt, Muhammad ʿAli, to seek the source of the White Nile. The expedition followed the course of the river upstream past the mouth of the Sobat River, across Lake No, and then south up the Bahr al-Jabal to Bor. Here the expedition was blocked by a large sudd obstruction and forced to return. In the following year, 1840, and again in 1841, Salim sailed for the upper Nile, and although hampered by sudd he was able to navigate through the great swamps all the way to Gondokoro. There are no records of any previous expeditions having passed through the sudd-choked channels of the Bahr al-Jabal. The Sudd surely must have checked the spread of Pharaonic Egyptian influence southward to the central African lakes and the hills and plains of East Africa. In AD 61 the Emperor Nero, an avid geographer, sent two centurions up the Nile, who ventured as far south as the Sobat where they reported an impenetrable swamp hardly of any interest to the Roman empire.[3] During the many centuries which followed, men satisfied their curiosity by accepting the account of Herodotus that the Nile

---

[2] Mefit-Babtie (Oct. 1983, i. 35–6).
[3] Kirwan (1957, pp. 13–19).

sprang from coy fountains of great depth at the foot of tall mountains in the heart of Africa.

Salim never found the source of the White Nile, but he did succeed in opening a river route to equatorial Africa. Merchants and missionaries soon followed, to exploit the natural and human resources of the southern Sudan, while geographers and explorers were stimulated by the accounts of Salim and his European companions, G. Thibaut, J. P. D'Arnaud, and Ferdinand Werne, to begin a systematic search for the Nile source. The merchants were the first on the river. Led by the Savoyard Brun Rollett, a small group of tough-minded European traders organized regular commercial expeditions in spite of the official disapproval of the Egyptian administration in the Sudan and the difficulties of navigation through the swamps. They traded cloth, beads, and wire for ivory, and their profits were substantial. In 1852 a dozen boats sailed for Gondokoro. Four years later the number had increased to over forty a year. In 1859 eighty boats set out from Khartoum for the southern Sudan, and by 1863 the number had reached 120 annually. Missionaries soon joined the merchants in an unholy alliance. As early as 1846 Pope Gregory XVI had created the Vicariate Apostolic of Central Africa, and the Congregatio de Propaganda Fide sent out four priests to pioneer a route to the pagans living in the wild land of the upper Nile basin. Led by Knoblecher, a Slovene, the first band of missionaries made a reconnaissance to the upper Nile in 1849, and just over a year later Angelo Vinco settled near Gondokoro to proselytize among the Bari. Although the missionaries were decimated by fever and the mission was eventually abandoned in 1860, Knoblecher had purchased a *dhahabiyah* which during the life of the mission plied laboriously between Khartoum and Gondokoro, adding to the increasing number of trading vessels.

At first all the river traffic went up the White Nile, across Lake No, and then through the meandering channel of the Bahr al-Jabal. In 1855, however, a Copt called Habashi discovered the mouth of the Bahr al-Ghazal in a boat owned by John Petherick, the British trader and consul at Khartoum. The following year Petherick himself sailed through the serpentine channel of the Bahr al-Ghazal to Mashra' al-Raqq.

A month later Brun Rollet followed Petherick, and soon the Bahr al-Ghazal formed a second and even more important waterway to the land beyond the rivers that stretched south and west to the Congo. All these early traders and missionaries on the Bahr al-Jabal and the Bahr al-Ghazal encountered great difficulties with sudd obstructions in the hazardous channels of the two rivers. Frequently a path had to be cut through the sudd, and the boats dragged through the passage. At times the sudd was sufficiently pliable for vessels to be pulled, pushed, and poled over the barrier. Not infrequently boats would fail to break through an obstruction and become entrapped as fresh sudd closed behind them. If unable to work their boats free, the crew had to await rescue, for to abandon ship meant certain death in the swamps. Often a relief expedition would fail to reach the stranded vessel in time to save the crew from starvation or the boat itself from being crushed by the pressure of the sudd. Then, as today, the passage south from Lake No was enveloped by the pervasive smell of nature so implacable and unremitting in the fetid swamps.

Sudd conditions beyond Lake No throughout the nineteenth century appear to have remained surprisingly consistent; but the size, depth, and compactness of the obstructions varied considerably from one year to the next and from one decade to another. During the twenty years following Salim's pioneering voyage the blocks of sudd do not seem to have seriously thwarted the traders, but in the 1860s and 1870s the numerous European travellers and officials of the Egyptian government experienced many delays, hardships, and even death in the swamps. When Sir Samuel Baker made his first journey up the White Nile in 1862–3, he passed to Gondokoro without serious difficulty in forty days. A few months later, however, the beautiful Dutch heiress, Alexandrina Tinné, encountered numerous sudd obstructions when she and her party set out from Khartoum in a fleet consisting of a steamer and some smaller boats to explore both the Bahr al-Jabal and the Bahr al-Ghazal. Although she was hindered by the sudd, the size of the expedition enabled her to overcome the obstructions and reach Gondokoro and later Mashra' al-Raqq. In succeeding years the sudd obstacles met by the

Tinné expedition grew into formidable barriers. In the spring of 1865, during his return journey from equatorial Africa, Baker and his men had to cut a passage through a large sudd block east of Lake No on the White Nile. Five years later Baker returned to the upper Nile at the head of an enormous expedition sent by Isma'il, khedive of Egypt, to suppress the slave trade and occupy Equatoria as an Egyptian province. This same sudd block had now grown so large that Baker found that the White Nile had disappeared beneath the solid, compressed vegetation. Unable to break through to the Bahr al-Jabal, Baker entered the Bahr al-Zaraf, an alternative route to the south formerly utilized by the traders when they could no longer force a passage up the Bahr al-Jabal. For nearly two months Baker directed the assault on the sudd obstructions in the Bahr al-Zaraf. The boats were dragged through the narrow channels of the river, which were regularly blotted out by the interminable marsh. Baker's men died from fever, sunstroke, and depression as the sudd closed to prevent any advance. Temporarily beaten, Baker ordered the expedition to retreat to the White Nile, where a camp was established at Tawfiqiyah. After nine months he decided to try again, and on 1 December 1870 the first section of his fleet headed south up the Bahr al-Zaraf. After three months of unremitting toil the expedition broke through the barrier to reach the confluence and the open water of the Bahr al-Jabal. Baker's journey through the swamps was a triumph of his will and determination, which were fully matched by the patient and herculean efforts of his men. It convinced Baker, and dramatically demonstrated to officials in Cairo and Khartoum, that Egypt could not hope to establish, let alone maintain, her supremacy over the equatorial regions if the authorities in the Sudan delayed clearing the sudd obstructions from the main channel of the White Nile and the Bahr al-Jabal. In the southern Sudan communications were, and remain today, the prerequisites for control.

Stirred to action by Baker's experience, the governor-general of the Sudan, Isma'il Pasha Ayyub, personally led a sudd-cutting party of several hundred soldiers upstream in 1872, where they toiled for several months to clear the river. By the end of 1873 the White Nile and the Bahr al-Jabal were

open, and Colonel Gordon, then governor of Equatoria,
reported in March 1874 that one could now reach Gondokoro
in three weeks. But the mysteries of the river did not favour
the Egyptian administration in the Sudan, and when the sudd
patrols and proper maintenance parties were not initiated,
the river was blocked again within a few years. In 1878 Emin
Pasha, the governor of Equatoria, reported that the Bahr
al-Jabal was obstructed by sudd after an unusually high flood
and that all efforts to pass through the barrier had failed.
During the next two years Gordon, now governor-general of
the Sudan, sent several steamers up-river to open the Nile,
but none of these feeble expeditions was successful. River
communications between Equatoria and Khartoum remained
completely severed. The isolation of Equatoria from the
northern Sudan seriously undermined Egyptian authority in
the province and checked the attempts of Emin Pasha to
broaden and develop the economy. Without effective transport,
Emin's schemes to grow cash crops—cotton, coffee, and
sugar—were stillborn. Moreover, Emin could hardly extend
Egyptian rule beyond the river stations nor hope to expand
Egyptian sovereignty south into Bunyoro without regular
consignments of supplies and the periodic arrival of reinforcements from the north for his garrisons.

The unpredictable and indiscriminate formation of sudd
certainly discouraged the government from sending troops
and supplies up the Nile, and between 1878 and 1883 only
nine steamers reached Lado from Khartoum and these
brought no merchandise. The interests of northern merchants
in the southern Sudan trade had sharply diminished with the
decline of the slave trade and with the more rigorous supervision
of the traders' activities by the European governors in the
south. Declining profits did not encourage merchants to risk,
even for legitimate trade, the hazards of a river route
frequently impassable and always dangerous. As the river
traffic decreased the sudd formations remained undisturbed,
to compress and enlarge into impenetrable barriers. The cycle
was complete when the few remaining merchants ceased to
trade, and by 1878 the commercial community at Lado was
reduced to three indigent traders. The khedive could hardly
hope to retain his equatorial empire by such a slender thread,

and no merchant could be expected to trade in a land that was fast slipping from Egyptian control.

To open the river and restore communications with Emin Pasha in Equatoria, a large expedition was organized in 1879 under the leadership of Ernst Marno. Like many administrators employed by the Egyptian government for service in the southern Sudan, Marno was a European who had come to Africa to travel, explore, and seek adventure. Born and reared in Vienna, he arrived at Khartoum in 1867, and after ten years of wanderings, during which he sojourned with Baker at Gondokoro and later with Gordon at Lado, he entered the Egyptian service and was ordered to take command of the sudd-cutting expedition to clear the Bahr al-Jabal. Proceeding upstream with a fleet of steamers, the cutting party managed to open the river after months of exhausting work. Then, his task completed, Marno and his men returned downstream, pausing only long enough to explore the Bahr al-Ghazal river. Here he fortuitously came upon the steamer of Romolo Gessi Pasha immobilized by the sudd. Gessi was a European like Marno who had come to Africa for adventure, served under Gordon, and in 1878 had been appointed governor of the Bahr al-Ghazal province. Here he had carried out Gordon's anti-slave trade policy with determination and success, but upon Gordon's resignation Gessi left Mashra' al-Raqq for Khartoum in September 1880 to confer with the new governor-general, Muhammad Ra'uf Pasha. From the start Gessi's men had to cut through large sudd barriers. By October the flotilla was virtually immured. Soon the fuel and supplies were exhausted; starvation and disease decimated Gessi's crew and turned the desperate to cannibalism. All would have perished if Marno had not suddenly appeared on 5 January 1881 to rescue the stranded ships and starving men. For over three months Gessi and his men had struggled to open the Bahr al-Ghazal river, but from the beginning they were doomed to failure. No expedition, no matter how large or well-equipped, could hope to cut through the sudd from the upstream side of the obstruction, for chunks hacked from the barrier and dragged free would only float back into place or wedge themselves behind the boats and steamers of the cutting party. All the great Nilotic sudd-clearing expeditions have attacked the

sudd dams from the downstream side where the cut blocks
could be carried away by the Nile current. Gessi lost over 100
men, and he himself died at Suez on his way home to Italy
from fever contracted in the Sudd.

Except for temporary obstructions in 1881 and 1884, the
Bahr al-Jabal remained precariously open until 1895. Only
the inscrutable vagaries of the Sudd can account for nearly
fifteen years of free passage, for after Marno's expedition no
cutting parties patrolled the swamps and the traffic in
steamers was hardly sufficient to keep the river open. During
these years the Sudan was convulsed by the violent upheaval
of Mahdism. Led by Muhammad Ahmad, al-Mahdi, whose
puritanical and mystical interpretations of Islam were soon
translated into direct political action, the Mahdists had driven
the Egyptians from the northern Sudan by 1885. Three years
later the Khalifa 'Abd Allahi, who in June 1885 had assumed
the temporal powers of the deceased Mahdi, dispatched a
strong flotilla under the command of 'Umar Salih up the
White Nile with orders to occupy Equatoria. For seven years
thereafter the Mahdists were able to supply and support their
forces in Equatoria by a fleet of river steamers plying between
Omdurman and Rejaf. When the Bahr al-Jabal became
hopelessly blocked again in 1895, the Mahdist position in the
southern Sudan soon collapsed.

The first obstruction of the river was met by 'Umar Salih on
his return to the northern Sudan to procure reinforcements
and supplies. After several months spent cutting a passage
through the sudd, 'Umar was able to drag two steamers
through to Lake No and on to Omdurman. He returned to the
south, but upon his next journey north he encountered heavy
sudd and was only able to pass the small steamer *Muhammad
'Ali* through the barriers after much difficulty. To extricate the
remaining vessels a large sudd-cutting party was organized at
Rejaf by Sa'id Sughaiyar, but his men had little hope of
success so long as they attempted to force a passage from the
upstream side of the sudd. Throughout May and June 1896
the Mahdists toiled frantically to hack a channel out of the
sudd blocks. Suffering from hunger, exhaustion, and fever, the
men quickly became ill and many died. By July so few able-
bodied men remained that the attempt had to be abandoned.

Ivory and loot from Equatoria were then laboriously carried across the sudd to steamers waiting beyond the obstructions, which were then turned about and headed northward to Omdurman. But the Mahdists had not seen the last of the Sudd. Further downstream the steamers were stopped by yet other obstructions so large that even after six hours of marching the men could not reach the end of them. For twenty-four days Sa'id Sughaiyar and his subordinates searched the swamps before an alternative channel was discovered. Abandoning one steamer which had become trapped from behind by floating sudd, Sa'id successfully guided the remaining steamer and boats down the White Nile to Omdurman. Impressed by Sa'id's descriptions of the formidable Sudd and threatened from the north by the invading Anglo-Egyptian army under Kitchener, the khalifa decided not to expend further effort on opening the Bahr al-Jabal. The Mahdists in Equatoria would have to defend themselves against the advancing forces of the Congo Free State and the hostile raids of the southern Sudanese without additional support from him.

Early in 1898 the river mysteriously opened a channel to the north. The Mahdists in Equatoria had nothing to do with this phenomenon, for although they had worked diligently to clear the sudd, they had made little progress cutting from the upstream side of the obstructions. The new channel, however, opened too late. Scarcely a month after a Dinka messenger had left Rejaf to report that the river was clear, the khalifa had been decisively defeated at the battle of Omdurman in September 1898. In December the messenger himself was captured near the Sobat River by Egyptian troops under the command of Colonel J. F. Maxwell.

Although the Mahdists had been unable to force a passage through the sudd of the Bahr al-Jabal, Captain Marchand's expedition made its way successfully through the sudd of the Jur and the Bahr al-Ghazal Rivers in June 1898. The preceding February, Captain A. E. A. Baratier had reconnoitred this route accompanied by twenty-five Senegalese troops of the Marchand expedition. They were forced to cut a passage through sudd blocks and drag their canoes over marshy channels shrunk by the dry season. His report convinced Marchand that he would have to await the advent of the rains

before he could hope to lead the main body of his expedition
through the swamps of the Bahr al-Ghazal. Thus the
Marchand mission remained at Fort Desaix, near the former
Egyptian station of Wau, before proceeding downstream in
June in canoes, followed six weeks later by the small steamer
Faidherbe which had been hauled over the Congo–Nile
watershed and launched on the Jur River. After a difficult
passage through the Sudd, the French reached Fashoda in
July to await the dramatic confrontation with the Anglo-
Egyptian forces. Even to such an optimistic and forceful
officer as Marchand, the Jur and the Bahr al-Ghazal Rivers
could never have become a practical route by which to sustain
the French outpost at Fashoda in the face of effective British
railway and steamer connections with supply bases in Egypt.
The Sudd was the African counterpart of the French military
weakness in Europe, and it contributed to the failure of
Marchand's heroic attempt to seize control of the upper
Nile.

Kitchener did not have to be reminded by Lord Salisbury's
personal instructions to him of the importance of the Nile
waters. Within a month after his meeting with Captain
Marchand, Kitchener established a post at the confluence of
the Sobat and the White Nile, to which, ironically, the French
were to return eighty years later to excavate the Jonglei Canal,
but from which in 1898 the steamer *Tamai* continued
upstream in October under the command of Major Malcolm
Peake Bey 'to get in touch with the Belgians at Rejaf' and to
verify reports brought back by the *Faidherbe* that the Bahr al-
Ghazal was solidly blocked by sudd. Peake first ascended the
Bahr al-Jabal, only to find the river completely clogged. Retiring
to Lake No, he then steamed up the Bahr al-Ghazal River
nearly to Mashra' al-Raqq before being stopped again by sudd
obstructions. Peake then returned to the Sobat, replenished
his supplies and, accompanied by Major E. A. Stanton Bey,
continued up the Bahr al-Zaraf for 252 km before shallow
water prevented further progress. Clearly the British could
not confront the forces of King Leopold at Rejaf or control the
Nile waters until the channels were free to carry a force
sufficient to establish British presence throughout the basin of
the upper Nile.

While Peake was reconnoitring the rivers of the swamp in October 1898, Major C. G. Martyr had led a small column of Sudanese troops from Uganda down the Bahr al-Jabal to the Congo Free State post at Rejaf with the intention of dislodging the Mahdists. Reinforced by a contingent of Congolese troops, Martyr pushed north in November 1898 to Bor, from which the Mahdist garrison had fled to make their way across the plains of the Bahr al-Ghazal to southern Darfur. Martyr had hoped to continue down the Nile to join Kitchener's forces, but like the Sudanese he was unable to penetrate the sudd. For the first time the British learned the futility of attempting to clear a passage from the upstream side of a sudd barrier. All three of the river routes to the southern Sudan, the Bahr al-Jabal, the Bahr al-Ghazal, and the Bahr al-Zaraf, had been proved closed to navigation. Until the rivers were opened and efficient communications established, the British could hardly assert their claims to the upper Nile basin, the occupation of which had so absorbed the energies of British statesmen, set in motion vast armies, and brought the two great liberal powers of Europe, Britain and France, to the brink of war. In 1898 Britain stood victorious on the Nile. The time had clearly come to forge the last link in her continental chain of imperial possessions by opening a way to the south and securely binding the upper Nile and its waters to the British empire.

These doleful reports from the upper Nile and Kitchener's peremptory behaviour at Khartoum galvanized Lord Cromer into action. As Britain's proconsul in Egypt he was not about to abdicate the 'big questions' in favour of Kitchener, and he sent Sir William Garstin to the upper Nile in February 1899. Garstin's tour of the upper Nile simply confirmed the reports of Majors Peake and Martyr. The channels of the Nile were closed, but the larger implications as to the availability of Nile water and its security could only be ascertained after further study which was quite impossible until the Nile channels were cleared of the sudd. These were, however, matters for the future, considerations to be based upon hydrological observation and measurements. For the moment, a greater and more immediate political danger threatened Britain's position in the Nile valley. The forces of the Congo Free State were at Rejaf, poised to expand northward into the Bahr al-Ghazal and to turn Leopold's temporary claims to the Lado enclave into permanent riparian rights further down the Nile. Only effective British occupation of the southern Sudan could forestall the sovereign of the Congo Free State, but first the Nile and its tributaries must be cleared of sudd and opened to navigation.

Upon his return to Cairo in the spring of 1899 Garstin advised Lord Cromer to send an expedition at once 'to clear the Bahr al-Jabal of sudd, commencing from its northern end at Lake No and work southward until its whole channel was free from obstruction, as far as the upper reaches of the river above Shambe'.[4] A credit of £E10 000 was at once opened for sudd removal, £E1 000 for materials and £E9 000 for the pay and care of the Mahdist prisoners employed as labourers. The primary object was, of course, to open the river to navigation, but Cromer argued persuasively that the £E10 000 was fully justified by the expectation alone that the summer supply of water from the White Nile would be increased.

In the autumn of 1899 a large sudd-cutting party began to assemble at Omdurman to proceed up-river at the end of the rainy season in the southern Sudan. The need to open the Bahr al-Jabal became every day more urgent as the blistering heat of the central Sudan in summer was cooled by the north winds of autumn. Rumours had reached Omdurman that the Congolese had occupied portions of the Nile valley downstream from the Lado enclave, and British officials in Cairo and Khartoum were determined to contest any such occupation before it assumed a more permanent character. On 16 December 1899 the sudd-cutting party embarked from Omdurman under the command of Peake Bey. An artillery officer, Peake had fought in the river war and had made the first reconnaissance of the upper Nile the year before. He had a reputation for being a 'lucky' man which was later to be justified in the Sudd. His flotilla consisted of five steamers, five British officers (three of whom were lieutenants in the Royal Navy especially assigned to the party), twelve Egyptian and Sudanese officers, five British Royal Marine Artillery sergeants, 100 Sudanese troops, and over 800 Mahdist prisoners

[4] Despatch from HM Agent and Consul-General at Cairo, Egypt No. 5, C. 9332, 1899, p. 19.

accompanied by 100 women. Unhappily the size of the expedition was no indication of the efficiency of its organization. Kitchener had ordered a sudd-cutting party to be assembled with 'a few sweeps of the arm', had added several consoling phrases about how everything 'would be all right', and had then characteristically turned his attention to other matters.[5] In fact Kitchener's solution was to 'telephone over to the Governor of Umdurman and tell him to hand over to Peake Bey anyone he has in the jails of Umdurman!' Even the prisons of Omdurman could not provide more than 500 men, so Kitchener resolved the inadequacy by summoning his ADC and ordering him to 'telephone to the Governor of Umdurman and tell him to arrest 500 suspicious characters, and hand them over to Peake Bey!'[6] Such were the days of the British imperium on the Nile.

The expedition's equipment was inadequate, its supplies quite insufficient. Only a small ration of dura was available for the prisoners, many of whom suffered from smallpox. The British officers were concerned about the amount of work such a crew could accomplish in a day and feared that, because of high-sounding but ill-informed press reports, much more was expected from the expedition than in fact was possible. A base camp and field hospital were established on the right bank of the White Nile, some 15 km upstream from the mouth of the Sobat. Then, advancing to Lake No and the Bahr al-Jabal, the cutting party began to hack a passage through the Nile swamps on the last day of 1899.[7] After nearly three weeks two large blocks of sudd, each over 900 m long, had been broken up and the channel cleared. But this was just the beginning. Each day from sunrise to sunset the men, tormented by mosquitoes, bitten by flies, and frequently overcome by heat and exhaustion, laboured to free the obstruction. To clear the blocks, a party of men with swords, hoes, and axes first cut and then burned the surface vegetation. Clearing the papyrus and reeds not only facilitated later

[5] Col. J. G. Maxwell to Sir Reginald Wingate, 19 Jan. 1900, SAD 270/1/2.

[6] Quoted in Stewart (1927, pp. 159–60).

[7] *SIR*, 66, Dec. 1899. The sudd-cutting party lost 35 dead, 207 disabled. Nearly a quarter of the work force was hospitalized at any one time. Half of the deaths were caused by dysentery; the most common complaints were ulcers of the skin and heat exhaustion. *SIR*, 77, Dec. 1901.

operations, but often large blocks of sudd would smoulder for days and then abruptly turn completely over, making it easy to dislodge them.

After the vegetation had been burned off, cutting parties armed with axes, shovels, picks, and saws would trench the sudd into pieces four yards square. It was desirable, of course, to dig until the tangled, matted vegetation was cut through, but infiltration of water into the trench seldom permitted this, making it quite impossible to excavate deeper than 2 m. Once the trench had been completed on three sides of the square, a steamer would ram the sudd at full speed, in an effort to jar the piece loose. If this failed, telegraph poles were then driven as far as they would go around the edge of the cutting. A 1.5-in. steel hawser was then passed around the square and sunk deep into the trench by means of pronged pikes. The hawser was secured to the steamer, which would churn backward and forward, backward and forward, backward and forward, belching smoke and filling the fetid air with the screams of straining winches and taut cables. Suddenly the sudd would rip away, the steamer would lurch violently and then, panting, slowly pull the torn block into open water. Sometimes as much as two hours were required to tear out a piece from the main obstruction, but in other places where the sudd was very thin a simple grapnel anchor attached to the steamer was sufficient to detach the cut section.[8]

As Peake's men chopped their way through block after block of sudd, the river released the tremendous pressure built up behind the sudd dams. On 13 January Peake recorded a sudden rise in the river of 1 m after a particularly stubborn barrier had been removed. On 2 March a huge block on which the party had been working for days suddenly gave way, carrying steamers, barges, and men downstream. Fortunately the boats survived unharmed, and the expedition was able to extricate itself to watch in awe as the sudd moved majestically down the Nile. So gigantic was this obstruction that the sudd

[8] There is a curious though highly speculative story one still hears on the upper Nile that the sudd obstructions were created intentionally by the Nilotic inhabitants to impede the boats of the Khartoum slavers. It is alleged that the Nilotes would stretch cables of hippopotamus hide across the channel which would catch floating vegetation to block the river. There is no substantiation of this tale except the fact that it still exists after nearly 100 years.

took over thirty hours to pass Peake's steamer, and its sudden release precipitated a dramatic rise of six feet in the river. This was not an uncommon danger to sudd-cutting parties. Gordon reported that when Isma'il Pasha Ayyub was clearing the White Nile in 1873 the pressure of the river broke the sudd dam and

swept down on the vessels, dragged the steamers down some four miles, and cleared the passage. The Governor says the scene was terrible. The hippopotamuses were carried down, screaming and snorting; crocodiles were whirled round and round, and the river was covered with dead and dying hippopotamuses, crocodiles, and fish who had been crushed by the mass.[9]

Throughout the whole of the sudd-cutting operations, Peake always kept a steamer at Lake No which could come immediately to the rescue if sudd ripped from the blocks reformed downstream to isolate the cutting party which could not remove it from their position upstream.

By 27 March Peake and his men had cleared fourteen blocks of sudd, opening eighty-two miles of river (see Map 2). There remained just five dams to break, but these were the largest and the most difficult yet encountered by the expedition. Block 15 alone was over 35 km long. Depressed at the prospect of tackling so formidable a barrier just before the rains, Peake sought to bypass the obstruction by seeking a passage through the side-channels which meandered through the swamp on either side of the river. Accompanied by Lieutenant W. B. Drury, a tough and very determined Australian officer of the Royal Navy, and the ubiquitous Garstin, who was making his second tour of the upper Nile, Peake pushed southward through shallow lagoons and a maze of tortuous channels in two steamers, the *Tamai* and the *Abu Klea*. On 8 April both steamers ran aground, and having only sufficient fuel to maintain steam for a few days, the party reluctantly returned to the flotilla.

In April 1900 the rains returned to the southern Sudan, making sudd-cutting operations even more difficult and unhealthy. Any day the expedition would be recalled to Omdurman to recuperate and refit. If no channel were

[9] Gleichen (1905, i. 304).

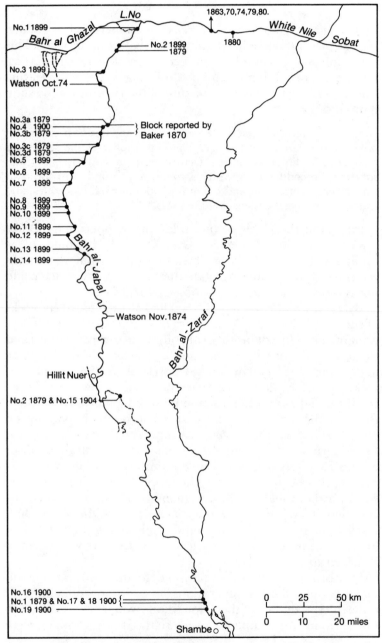

MAP 2. Bahr al-Jabal and Bahr al-Zaraf, showing sudd blocks
Source: Lyons (1906)

discovered before that time, the Anglo-Egyptian occupation of the southern Sudan would be delayed another year. Peake remained unconvinced, however, that an alternative channel could not be found, and relying on his good fortune and intuition, he set out again on 19 April to seek a passage south. Lieutenant Drury was there as Peake threaded his way through side-channels and lagoons. For six days the *Tamai* forced its way through reeds and papyrus, up culs-de-sac, down false channels and then, as much by luck as design, struck the main channel of the Bahr al-Jabal near Shambe. Once in open water Peake steamed freely up-river to Kiro, the headquarters of Congolese forces in the Lado Enclave.

After visiting the Congolese posts on the west bank of the Bahr al-Jabal, Peake crossed over to Fort Berkeley on the east bank, established by Major Martyr as a remnant of his attempt to reach Fashoda from the Uganda Protectorate, where on 5 May he picked up the American explorer Dr Arthur Donaldson Smith, who was the first non-African to travel overland from Lake Rudolf to the Nile. With Smith, Peake and the *Tamai* returned downstream through the tortuous channels of the Peake passage, past the advanced part of sudd-cutters stationed at the desolate and lonely spot named Godelphus ('God help us'), and reached the White Nile base camp on 14 May. Peake had discovered a channel to the south none too soon. Two days after his arrival at camp, orders came from Khartoum recalling the expedition. Unknown to the authorities a way to Equatoria had been found, but once a passable route had been discovered up the Bahr al-Jabal, the primary task was to keep the river free, improve the channel, and open additional tributaries. This difficult work has never ceased to this day. The job of clearing the river of vegetation has been seriously complicated in recent years by the appearance in the Nile and its tributaries of the water hyacinth, which has long been a hazard to navigation on the river Congo, and by the outbreak of the civil war in the southern Sudan in May 1983, which has brought river traffic to a halt on the Bahr al-Jabal reach from Lake No to Juba.

The importance of clearing a way south to the source of the Nile and thereby ensuring British domination of the Nile waters was beyond doubt; but the presence of the perceptive

Sir William Garstin demonstrated the importance attached by all authorities, political as well as scientific, to understanding the hydrology of the Nile basin. Little was known of the Nile and how it functioned south of Khartoum. Everyone knew of the Nile flood and that it came from Ethiopia, but what of the great lakes of equatorial Africa, which explorers for the past half century had claimed were *the* source of the Nile? And what was their relationship to the Sudd, the White Nile, and beyond? Already in his report of 1901 Garstin had dwelt at some length on utilizing the supply of water in the upper Nile despite his very limited observations. There was no doubt that from this moment the efforts of British hydrologists who dominated the Egyptian ministry of public works and their British political supporters were concentrated on unravelling the regime of the Nile from its source to the Mediterranean Sea.[10]

In January 1901 a second sudd-cutting party was sent south from Omdurman to complete the work begun the previous year. Peake did not lead this expedition. His health undermined by fever, he was awarded a CMG but never returned to the Nile swamps. His place was taken by the tenacious Lieutenant Drury, who knew the Nile and its sudd. He had immense prestige among the Sudanese river men, and legendary tales of his exploits in the swamps are still remembered as part of the river lore by those crews which used to work on the Bahr al-Jabal before the outbreak of civil war in 1983. Before its recall to Khartoum his expedition succeeded in breaking all the barriers except block 15.

The following November a third sudd-clearing party, consisting again of convicts, began to struggle with block 15 under the direction of Major G. E. Matthews. Garstin had predicted in the spring that block 15 could be removed in three months, but Lieutenant Drury was not so optimistic. Covering the river from bank to bank, the sudd had taken root deep in the soft mud of the river bed, and even after being cut, the blocks had to be towed several miles downstream before there was sufficient current to carry them off. As the distance increased over which the blocks had to be dragged, water

---

[10] Garstin (1901; 1904).

flowing back upstream into the cuttings became so swift that
the chunks ripped from the obstruction could not be pulled
against the current by even the most powerful steamer. In
desperation Matthews ordered his men to pry the sudd loose
and anchor the cut blocks to the banks of the channel until the
current slackened and reversed itself. This was slow and
unrewarding work, not only complicated by the stagnant and
unhealthy water but made ever more difficult by the steady,
strong wind which blows up the Nile during the winter season.
In spite of the men having 'worked unflaggingly under the
highest possible pressure', the expedition failed once again to
open a channel through block 15 by the end of April 1902.[11]
Soon the rains came, the work was abandoned, and the
cutting party was recalled.

Nothing was done during the winter season of 1902–3, for
the Peake channel, bypassing block 15, continued to be
navigable, and the Sudan government's men and money were
required elsewhere than in the swamps of the upper Nile. In
October 1903, however, Drury was again on the Bahr al-Jabal
to lead the assault on block 15. Although most of Matthew's
work had been undone by the accumulation of fresh sudd,
Drury nearly succeeded in clearing the obstruction after six
months of 'dogged perseverance' before operations were again
abandoned at the onset of the rains. Determined not to lose
the advantage of Drury's work, yet another expedition went
up-river the following winter, 1904–5, and finally managed to
clear the remaining sudd of block 15. The channel of the Bahr
al-Jabal was at last opened.

Although the most extensive sudd obstructions had been
encountered on the main channel of the Nile, over the years
the Bahr al-Ghazal and its tributaries proved more difficult to
keep clear for river traffic than the Bahr al-Jabal. Fortunately,
at the time of the Anglo-Egyptian occupation of the southern
Sudan, the Bahr al-Ghazal was virtually free of sudd. Major
Peake in October 1898, and later Sir William Garstin in
March 1900, had found the Bahr al-Ghazal open to within a
few miles of Mashra' al-Raqq. Reassured by this information,
British officials in Khartoum hoped to use the river as far as

[11] Maj. G. E. Matthews, Governor, Fashoda to Wingate, 9 Apr. 1902, *SIR*, 93,
App. A, Apr. 1902.

Mashra' al-Raqq to transport their troops to that traditional gateway to the hinterland of the Bahr al-Ghazal province.

The most important tributary of the Bahr al-Ghazal is the Jur River. Shallower, narrower, and more sluggish than either the Bahr al-Jabal or the Bahr al-Ghazal, the Jur traverses the very heart of the province and connects the strategic station of Wau with the Ghazal River and the White Nile. To reach Wau by water, and thereby avoid the long and difficult overland journey from Mashra', the Jur River was the only alternative. Consequently, Lieutenant H. H. Fell of the Royal Navy was given command of a sudd-cutting party, and dispatched from Omdurman in November 1900 to widen the channel of the Bahr al-Ghazal and to clear the Jur River which 'must become the principal line of communications between Khartoum and Wau in the heart of the Bahr al-Ghazal'.[12] Arriving at Mashra' al-Raqq on 8 November, the sudd-cutting party quickly expanded the channel of the Bahr al-Ghazal and set to work clearing the Jur. Labouring from dawn to dusk throughout the winter and spring of 1901, the expedition made rapid progress. In June Fell reported optimistically that the Jur River would be open to Wau by the end of July. This view was premature; the sudd on the Jur turned into soft soil and mud, necessitating dredging operations. In fact a regular canal had to be excavated, and as the Sudan Intelligence Report of September 1901 laconically observed: 'This new development precludes all possibility of steamers reaching Wau for probably some months to come.'[13] Again in August 1902 another sudd-cutting party returned to the Jur, led by the veteran Lieutenant Drury and Captain Sanders of the Fifteenth Sudanese battalion. By the end of September the expedition had cleared all but one enormous sudd block on the Jur. Impressed by the size of the obstruction, Sanders wagered a case of whisky that Drury could not clear the river within three weeks. Ten days later a crumpled piece of paper was found wedged in a clump of reeds floating at the mouth of the Jur on which Drury announced that the river was free and open to Wau. Sanders lost not only his whisky but his hope of relief; he replaced Drury to complete the dredging of the Jur

---

[12] *SIR*, 77, Dec. 1900.   [13] *SIR*, 86, Sept. 1901.

River channel. Nevertheless the Jur remained unnavigable to steamers during the months of low water from November to July, and required annual sudd-cutting parties to rid the channel of aquatic plants. Throughout the months of navigability all the supplies needed by the administration, as well as trade goods and other stores, had to be transported up the Jur to Wau. When the river again fell after the rains, steamers only went as far as Mashra' al-Raqq, where their cargoes were carried overland to Wau.

Annual sudd-cutting parties were also sent to remove obstructions from the Ghazal River. Usually the sudd on the Bahr al-Ghazal consisted mostly of small blocks easily broken up, but on not a few occasions a well-equipped expedition was necessary to open the river. Ingenious wire traps were used to collect the floating water plants and explosives were even employed to dislodge large blocks of sunken vegetation hidden below the water-line. Particularly bad years were recorded on the Bahr al-Ghazal in 1906, 1907, and 1908. The heavy annual expenditure to keep the Bahr al-Ghazal and the Jur Rivers open during these years so discouraged the Sudan Government that in 1908 it considered diverting available funds from river clearance to construct a system of roads for porterage and wheeled traffic from Shambe on the Bahr al-Jabal westward into the Bahr al-Ghazal Province. The difficulties of building roads and bridges through the marshlands of the southern Sudan appeared more insurmountable, however, than keeping open the rivers; and although several officials continued to press for road construction, river transport remained the principal link between Khartoum and the upper Nile for another half-century. After 1909 conditions on the Bahr al-Ghazal and its tributaries improved, but in 1912 large sudd barriers 'caused many serious delays in transit, in many cases for over forty days', and the year was 'said to have been one of the most arduous on record'.[14] Throughout succeeding years sudd obstructions, low water, and narrow channels continued to hinder river traffic, but after the First World War the introduction of mechanical

[14] *SIR*, 220, Dec. 1912.

dredgers greatly facilitated clearing operations and reduced many of the interruptions of river transport.

Historically, sudd blockages on the Bahr al-Jabal have been associated with high rather than low flows, and most have been found in the last 150 km upstream from Lake No, where the river meanders in a labyrinthine course with sharp bends which entrap floating masses of sudd.[15] In the years of heavy rains in western Ethiopia, the Sobat undoubtedly contributes to sudd formation on the Bahr al-Jabal by blocking the White Nile flows. High flows on the Bahr al-Jabal during 1872 and 1878–80 were accompanied by the formidable obstructions encountered by Sir Samuel Baker and Emin Pasha. The lower mean annual flows of the twentieth century, an average of 84 billion m³, have produced obstructions on the Bahr al-Jabal only during those years of higher flows, 1926 for instance, when an 8 km sudd block appeared above Shambe and another of 7 km collected near Lake Papiu; but the regular passage of steamer service during the Condominium was probably as decisive in keeping the Bahr al-Jabal clear as was the level of the river, since the wash from the wake of steamers dislodged the accumulation of aquatic plants along the banks before they could form in sudd dams.[16] The dramatic rise in the level of the equatorial lakes in the 1960s with the concomitant high flows down the Bahr al-Jabal precipitated serious blockages between Bor and Shambe in 1969, closing the Bahr al-Jabal and forcing navigation into a new channel known to river-men as the Bahr al-Jadid, the 'new river'; but the infrequency of steamers plying the Bahr al-Jabal during the civil war in the southern Sudan during those years undoubtedly contributed to its closure.

The sudd-clearing expeditions of the first decade of the twentieth century not only made possible travel to the upper Nile and its consolidation within the bosom of the British empire but permitted the investigation of the basin and particularly the Sudd. No study of this great swamp can begin without reference to Sir William Garstin's magisterial reports on the upper Nile in 1901 and 1904, or to Captain Lyons's

[15] Lyons (1906, pp. 132–3).
[16] Howell *et al.* (1988, pp. 185–6, 388).

topographical and historical analysis of the physiography of the Nile in 1906.[17] For sheer breadth of observation, lucidity, and perspicuity they have never been equalled in the history of Nile hydrology. The work of those who followed Garstin and Lyons in Sudd studies—A. D. Butcher, H. G. Bambridge, H. A. W. Morrice, and J. V. Sutcliffe—has surpassed them in their investigations and ingenuity by the accumulation of data, its manipulation, and incisive mathematical computations; but their singular talents have neither diminished the achievements of Garstin's foresight or Lyons's methodical technology, tempered the Olympian sweep of Garstin's imperial imagination, nor reduced the importance of the gauges invented by Lyons which made the consistent measurement of the Nile possible. Garstin exploded the long-held myth that the Sudd was 'a more or less continuous expanse of vegetation floating on the surface' when in fact it consists of what Lyons delimited—a labyrinth of lagoons and lakes surrounded and choked by a formidable array of aquatic plants.[18]

The total area of the great Sudd flood-plain can never be measured with precision since its size varies with the day, the month, the season, and the year, all governed by the fluctuations of the outflow from the equatorial lakes, the annual increment from the torrents which flow violently or remain passive between Lake Albert and Mongalla, and the amount of rainfall. Extending from the ironstone plateau of the Bahr al-Ghazal in the west to the Duk ridge in the east, the Sudd flood-plain nestles in the heart of the Nilotic plain, tilting almost imperceptibly south to north at an average slope of 10 cm/km. The extent of the Sudd flood-plain can, however, be estimated by the use of aerial photography, satellite imagery, and vegetation maps. The Sudd itself consists of two principal zones, the permanent and the seasonal swamps.

Maps based on air photography in 1930–31 were planimetred to give a mean flooded area of 8,300 km^2 at that period; a map based on satellite imagery of February 1973 gave a flooded area of 22,000 km^2 on that date, reflecting the increased Mongalla flows after 1961. The area of permanent and seasonal swamp may be deduced from

[17] Garstin (1901; 1904); Lyons (1906, pp. 132–8).
[18] Garstin (1901, pp. 117–18; 1904); Lyons (1906, pp. 132–8).

vegetation, which responds to flooding over a few years. A vegetation map based on aerial survey, satellite imagery of 1979–80 and field observation gave estimates of permanent swamp of 16,600 km^2 and seasonal swamp of 14,000 km^2 [a total of 30,600 square kilometres, 12,000 square miles or an area of the size of Belgium].[19]

Another way to view the extent of the Sudd is to measure the annual mean size of both the permanent and seasonal swamps during this century, 1905–80, which is 16,931 km^2 (the size of Yorkshire), or approximately half the area inundated during the great floods of the 1960s (see Fig. 1).[20]

The size of the Sudd is principally dependent upon the outflow from the equatorial lakes and the torrents which sweep into the Bahr al-Jabal between Lake Albert and Mongalla. During the years of the great rains over the lakes, 1961–4, they received 20 per cent more water than the average; this led to a rise of 2.5 m in Lake Victoria alone, which increased her outflow from a 55-year mean average discharge of 27 billion m^3 to 50 billion for 1961–80, with the consequent dramatic expansion of the Sudd[21] (see Table 2). North from Juba the Bahr al-Jabal is broken by islands into more than one channel, from which there is modest spillage in high water into successive lagoons; these, however, are confined within a trough approximately 15 km wide as the Rift disappears into the Nilotic plain. At Bor the Sudd begins as the banks fade away and the river divides into three channels, the Bahr al-Jabal, the Aliab to the west, and the Atem to the east.

Between Bor and Jonglei the Bahr al-Jabal and the Aliab merge to make their way north to Shambe, but not before the

TABLE 2. *The Bahr al-Jabal flood-plain from Bor to Malakal (km²)*

	1952	1980	Increase
Permanent swamp	2,700	16,200	13,500
Seasonally river-flooded grassland	10,400	13,600	3,200
Total	13,100	29,800	16,700

Source: Howell et al. (1988, p. 104).

[19] Sutcliffe and Parks (1987, p. 148).
[20] Sutcliffe and Parks (1982b, fig. 1).   [21] Howell et al. (1988, p. 104).

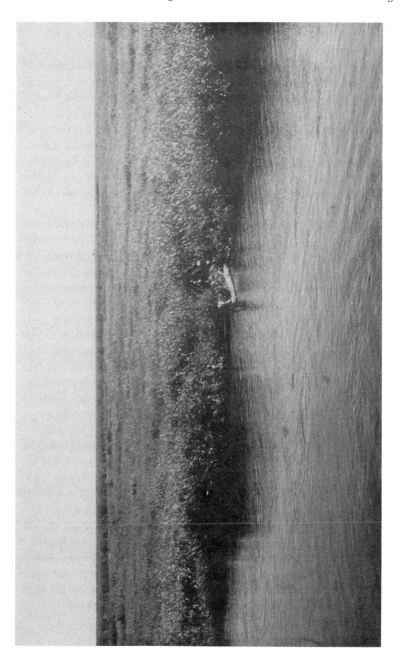

Fig. 1. The Sudd

main navigation channel bifurcates from the Bahr al-Jabal
after 1961 to form the Bahr al-Jadid, the 'new river', which in
turn is joined at Jonglei by the Atem after it flows through a
series of aquatic lakes. North of Jonglei the main channel
continues to meander, interacting with an extensive chain of
lakes spilling eastward and receiving water in return, in a
complex and ever-changing pattern within the seasonal rise
and fall of flow from the equatorial lakes and the torrents. To
the west, the now unnavigable channel of the Bahr al-Jabal
winds northward through the Sudd to Shambe and Adok
where the permanent swamp attains its greatest width, 'with
vast, largely inaccessible swamps, and fewer lakes and side
channels than further south'.[22]

Here, at the outflow from Lake Shambe, the Bahr al-Jabal
reforms with the Bahr al-Jadid to carry much of the river flow
north to Adok. At Gayom, south of Adok, the artificial Zaraf
Cuts dredged in 1910 and 1913 drain off water from the Bahr
al-Jabal to merge with water coming from an unapproachable
lagoon and river complex known as the Southern Zaraf
System to form the Bahr al-Zaraf River, whose sluggish and
sudd-choked channel drains in a north-easterly direction to its
confluence with the White Nile. Some 50 km to the west the
Bahr al-Jabal makes its way to Lake No, where the Bahr
al-Ghazal enters from the great catchment basin of that province
but with no meaningful contribution to White Nile water.
From Lake No to the Sobat confluence more lakes, lagoons,
and parallel channels dot the landscape beyond either bank of
the White Nile before they become well defined at Malakal.[23]

Between Juba and Bor the lagoons function as reservoirs in
a manner which both Garstin and Sir William Willcocks had
thought was applicable for the Sudd as a whole—storing
water from a rising river; returning water to a falling channel.
The Sudd begins at Bor, and from there northward its
character is determined by the diminished carrying capacity
of the channel, so that spilling is continuous into the lakes,
lagoons, and grasslands along an eastward-flowing gradient
with no barriers. The greater the flow, the more extensive the
flood; most of this water returns to the Nile, and the rest is lost

[22] Howell et al. (1988, p. 110).
[23] Ibid. 106–10; Mefit-Babtie (Oct. 1983, i. 8–19).

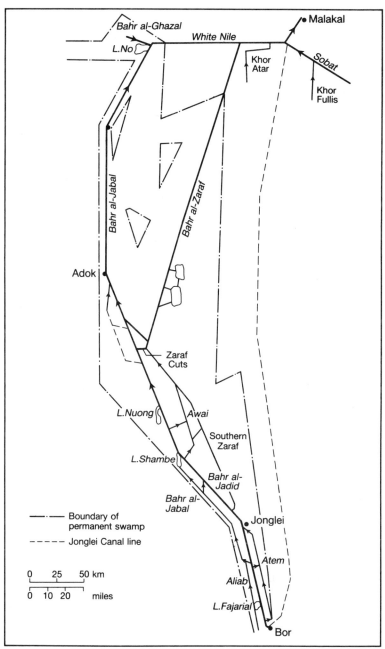

MAP 3. Water flow through the Sudd
Source: Howell *et al.* (1988)

by evaporation. 'The net result of these successions of spills is that the seasonal succession of rises and falls of inflow is damped down to a fairly steady outflow. . . . Within the swamps the processes of spilling and water flow are so complex that nobody has been able to investigate or describe them over the whole area'.[24] When the Bahr al-Jabal flows are modest, the river spill seeks out channels; when the Bahr al-Jabal flows are high, the water simply pours over the ill-defined banks into the lagoons and onto the Nilotic plain. Thus when the great rains of 1961–4 resulted in the dramatic rise of Lake Victoria, the increased volumes being passed down into the Sudd produced an equally dramatic increase in the permanently flooded swamps, while the size of the seasonal flood-plain remained dependent upon the amount of water added to the flow from the equatorial lakes by the torrents of the Bahr al-Jabal above Mongalla.

Since the depth and range of flooding determine the species of the swamp and grassland pasture, their composition has varied with the river flows, and indeed the size of the Sudd can be measured by the changing patterns of the vegetation. Within the Sudd flood-plain there are four zones, each of which will expand and contract in the annual life cycle of the upper Sudd. In the east lies the famous Duk ridge, a fragile spine extending south to north through the heart of the Upper Nile province from Bor and Kongor to Mogogh. Here there is permeable soil for cultivation, drainage, and a vegetation of thorn bushes and trees, acacias (*Acacia seyal* and *Acacia polyacantha*), and the heglig tree (*Balanites aegyptiaca*), below which there is a ground-cover or limited grass and, in the rains, a dense population of human and animal refugees from the advancing flood. Here the Nilotes dwell in permanent villages throughout the rainy season, the trees providing firewood, charcoal, and poles for their animal shelters, *luaks*, where the cattle grow lean on the inadequate grazing while the inhabitants patiently wait with their diminishing food supplies for the flood-waters to recede. The floods of the 1960s did much to destroy the woodlands near Fanjak, on the Zaraf Island, and along the Duk ridge, where the acacias and heglig

[24] Howell *et al.* (1988, p. 112).

trees succumbed to the waters. With the flood-waters destroying the roots of these trees, the demands of an expanding population for firewood, charcoal, and building timber took its ominous toll on the dying trees, whose vulnerable trunks were soon burnt to ash by the range fires ignited to regenerate pastures.

Below the narrow ridge the land slopes away imperceptibly stretching to the horizon, an expanse of open grassland broken by the occasional sentinel of a single tree, clusters of forest, or pockets of woodland. These are the intermediate wetlands of the impermeable clays, the 'cotton soils', heavily used by livestock from the *luaks* for its nutritional value during the rains. These plains accommodate different types of grass, according to the amount of rainfall, of which *Hyparrhenia rufa* predominates. Here on the intermediate lands the old growth is burned in October and November, the horizon ablaze with long lines of fire sweeping across the earth to regenerate the land. With the high floods of the 1960s, *Hyparrhenia rufa* has given way to grasses (*Oryza longistaminata* and *Echinochloa pyramidalis*) which can withstand heavy seasonal flooding.[25]

Beyond the intermediate lands lies the *toic*, a Dinka word meaning land which is seasonally flooded—lush green meadows rich in nutrients which spring up after the retreating river-waters and which provides the grazing during the dry season. Unlike the intermediate lands, the soil of the *toic* retains sufficient moisture during the dry season to support the sweet grass upon which the cattle grow fat and productive. Here are located the great cattle camps of the Nilotic peoples from February and May, where the living is full and, in normal times, easy, the remembrance of which sustains them through the harsher months of rain and flood in the *tukuls* and *luaks* on the Duk ridge and high grounds scattered around the permanent swamp. Here the pastures are dominated by the grasses *Oryza longistaminata* and *Echinochloa pyramidalis*. The *Oryza* reaches its maximum crop after several months of deep flooding to provide grazing of high quality, rich in protein. *Echinochloa pyramidalis* grasslands are situated further from the

25 Ibid. 180.

river, and are flooded only in years of high flows, which produces some regrowth in the dry season.[26]

In the heart of the Sudd rests the permanent swamp, to many the true Sudd, the mean size of which in this century has been measured at some 9,520 km², but whose actual extent varies from one year to the next depending upon rainfall, the torrents above Mongalla, and the quantities of water in the equatorial lakes. The permanent swamp is continuously flooded land and the principal breeding nursery in the lagoons and lakes for the myriad aquatic plants such as papyrus (*Cyperus papyrus*) accompanied by climbers, macrophytes, ferns, and the most sinister of all, the ubiquitous water hyacinth (*Eichhornia crassipes*). These lakes and lagoons have shifted with every passing flow or sudd blockage, which either drain off or impound water, and their numbers dramatically increased during the high flows of the 1960s. Since then papyrus has moved southward to Bor and beyond, displacing the swamp grass (*Vossia cuspidata*).[27]

Here in the permanent swamps the lakes and lagoons vary enormously in size, some being elongated extensions of the river channels, others being more isolated but clear; and then there are the dark lagoons surrounded by swamp vegetation, with little oxygen remaining from the demands of its fauna and fish consumers. The bodies of open water are dominated, however, by the water hyacinth, which has spread with relentless rapidity since 1957 to replace the Nile cabbage (*Pistia stratiotes*) which had prevailed in the open water of the Sudd for a century after the first arrival of explorers, merchants, and missionaries. The water hyacinth is not alone in the heat and humidity of the Sudd, being colonized by *Vossia cuspidata*, which encircles it in a symbiotic relationship and is in turn surrounded by *Cyperus papyrus*.[28]

Beyond the lagoons and lakes in which the hyacinth proliferates lie the marshlands distinguished best by the giant swamps they support—*Vossia cuspidata*, *Cyperus papyrus*, and *Typha domingensis*. The *Vossia* swamps are the least significant, occurring in the southern reaches of the Sudd or in patches as far north as Adok in its association with the water hyacinth.

---

[26] Howell *et al.* (1988, pp. 150–6).   [27] Ibid. 187–8.   [28] Ibid. 47–8.

Papyrus has historically been almost synonymous with the Sudd, from the papyri of the Pharaohs to the manufacture of suddite briquets in this century. Today the *Cyperus papyrus* swamps form a wall along the Bahr al-Jabal about 5 m high and 30 km broad, presenting to the steamer passengers an endless vista of desolation. In fact the swamps of greatest extent in the Sudd are the *Typha*, which flourish away from the main river channels, rooted in shallow lagoons inaccessible to man or even to the water hyacinth. More water-resistant than *Vossia*, *Typha domingensis* expanded enormously after the floods of the 1960s, and the area of *Typha* was estimated in 1980 at 13,750 km².[29]

Despite their profusion and the transmission of water vapour by transpiration, the aquatic plants of the Sudd are not primarily responsible for the massive loss of water.[30] Evaporation, not transpiration, is the principal cause of the disappearance of billions of cubic metres of water from the Sudd.[31] This conclusion is fundamental to an understanding of the hydraulics of the Sudd and consequently of Nile water development. A. D. Butcher, director-general, southern White Nile, determined that the loss of water in the Sudd could not be explained by evaporation alone, but he could offer no explanation for the mysterious loss of such an enormous quantity of Sudd water.[32] His investigations between 1927 and 1936 were undertaken at a time of steady Nile flows, when he could not observe the effect of evaporation on an enlarged flood-plain such as occurred after 1961. Moreover, he measured the losses only in a much reduced permanent swamp on the Bahr al-Jabal, without taking into account losses on the seasonal flood-plain. His principal failure to explain the loss must, however, be attributed to his gross underestimation of the rate of evaporation (1,533 mm/yr as against 2,150 mm/yr). Nevertheless, Butcher's influence dominated Sudd studies for over a generation, and the primary role of evaporation to explain Sudd water loss had to await the work of J. V. Sutcliffe and Y. P. Parks half a century later.

The chief characteristics of evaporation in the Sudd are twofold. First, the rate of evaporation over the past fifty years

[29] Ibid. 187.   [30] Penman (1963); Rijks (1969, pp. 643–9).
[31] Sutcliffe and Parks (1982b, p. 19).   [32] Butcher (1938d, pp. 1, 7–8).

has been virtually constant, averaging 179 mm per month, 2,150 mm per year. Second, the rate of evaporation does not vary significantly between that over open water and that in the permanent or seasonal swamps covered by aquatic vegetation.[33] The volume of water lost by evaporation is determined, therefore, not by the rate of evaporation, which is constant, but by the area of flooding over which the evaporation takes place. On a plain of such insignificant slope the rise of flood waters by a few centimetres can inundate hundreds of square kilometres, exposing them to evaporation at a proportionately greater loss not offset by the rainfall, which averages 871 mm per year.[34]

Thus when the flow of the Bahr al-Jabal at Mongalla registers 30 Mm³/d, the loss in the Sudd is of the order of 17 per cent, the channels of the Bahr al-Jabal and the Bahr al-Zaraf being able to accommodate the flow without vast flooding, thereby containing the total loss of water by evaporation. When the discharge at Mongalla increases to 40 Mm³/d the rivers can no longer carry the flow, which spills on to the surrounding flood-plain; and depending upon the extent of the flood, the volume of water lost by evaporation will increase proportionately (see Table 3). Therefore, although the rate of evaporation may remain constant, the volume of

TABLE 3. *Discharge into Sudd at Mongalla: proportionate loss*

Mm³/d	Loss (%)
40	22.5
60	40.0
80	50.6
100	57.0
120	61.2

Source: JEO (1975, pp. 48–9).

[33] Sutcliffe and Parks (1982b, pp. 20–2); ILACO (1981, vol. i).
[34] Sudan Meteorological Department (1973).

water exposed to and thereby lost by evaporation 'depends directly on the area flooded'.[35] Between 1905 and 1980 the mean annual flow of the Bahr al-Jabal at Mongalla has fluctuated from 15 billion to 66 billion m³, the mean annual inflow being 33 billion, 39 per cent of the total mean annual flow measured at Aswan over the same period. The mean annual outflow at Malakal remains, however, 16 billion m³ or approximately half of that measured at Mongalla. Seventeen billion m³ of water represent the mean annual loss over the past seventy-five years. This enormous quantity of water is the equivalent of 20 per cent or one-fifth of the total mean annual flow of the river Nile at Aswan.[36] It could irrigate between two and two and a half million feddans in Egypt and the northern Sudan.

The Sudd was not only a profligate waster of water but also a regulator of it. Garstin was the first to recognize this characteristic.

The swamps have a powerful regulating influence upon the supply at all seasons, but more particularly in flood. They retain water in an immense reservoir, returning it gradually back into the river channel minus the quantity lost by evaporation and absorbed by the swamps vegetation. This is the real cause of the constancy of the White Nile supply throughout the winter and summer months.'[37]

There was, however, a major difference between the Sudd as a reservoir for regulation, which it was, and a conserving mechanism, which it was not. Sir William Willcocks, in his lectures before the Egyptian Institute in February 1919, regarded the Sudd as a storage reservoir, never bothering to reconcile the fact that the Sudd returned only half of the water

[35] Sutcliffe and Parks (1982b, p. 1).
[36] If one combines the average of the mean permanent swamp from 1905 to 1980 (9520 km²) and the mean permanent and seasonal swamp during the same period (16 931 km²), the average area exposed to evaporation for those 75 years equals 13 225 km². If this area is exposed to a constant rate of evaporation minus average rainfall (2,150 mm − 871 mm = 1,279 mm), the loss attributed to evaporation results in an astonishing 17 billion m³ or half the mean annual inflow into the Sudd of the Bahr al-Jabal as measured at Mongalla (33.014 billion m³). If one takes a single year of above-average flood, 1979–80, when the average area of the permanent swamp (16 600 km²) and seasonal swamp (14 000 km²) was 15 300 km², the loss of water by evaporation equalled 20 billion m³ or 24%, nearly a quarter of the total annual Nile flow as measured at Aswan. See Sutcliffe and Parks (1987).
[37] Garstin (1904, p. 134).

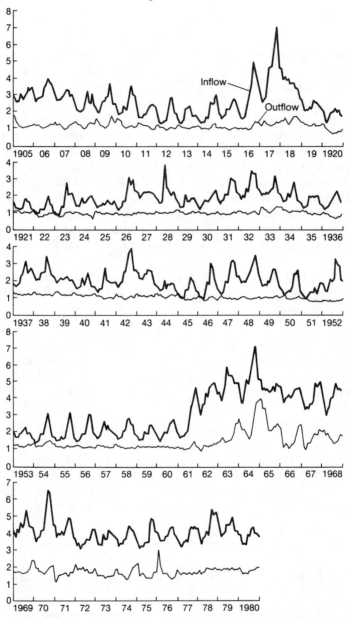

FIG. 2. Measured monthly inflows and outflows from the Sudd at Mongalla (Mm³/month), 1905–1980. This dramatic diagram demonstrates that, whatever the inflow of the Nile at Mongalla, the outflow at Malakal remains relatively constant. This represents not only the loss of water but the dynamics of Sudd hydraulics.
Source: Sutcliffe and Parks (1982*a*)

discharged at Mongalla into its care. Dr H. E. Hurst, the long-time director of the physical department of the Egyptian ministry of public works, refused to accept the concept of the Sudd as a reservoir: 'The swamp itself over its whole length falls away from the Bahr al-Jabal and nowhere acts as a reservoir in direct connection [with] the river alternately receiving water and returning water at the same point.'[38] More recently, the work of Sutcliffe and Parks has returned to Garstin's original view of the Sudd as a great reservoir, in which huge amounts of water are lost but in which water is also stored 'when the river rises and [is returned] to the river downstream when it falls'.[39]

Whether the Sudd is a regulator or a reservoir, the fact remains that it disposes of an extraordinary amount of water desperately needed in the desiccated regions between Malakal and the Mediterranean Sea. To reduce this forfeiture, Garstin recommended a canal to bypass the Sudd in order to bring down the water to Egypt without wastage in the swamps. In his report of 1901 he had proposed to embank the Bahr al-Jabal or the Bahr al-Zaraf. This idea remained the genesis of the embankment projects which became so popular with British engineers during the years between the First and Second World Wars. In 1902 J. S. Beresford had suggested to Garstin that he bypass the Sudd with a direct-line canal, and Garstin in turn adopted this proposal in his report of 1904. His canal, known as the Garstin Cut, would follow a straight line from Bor to the Sobat River at its confluence with the White Nile. The Garstin Cut was to be a monumental excavation capable of carrying 1000 m^3/sec, 86 Mm^3/d, or 28 billion m^3 per year. To carry such a huge volume of water, nearly four times the capacity of the partially completed canal today, the Garstin Cut would have had radically to affect the way of life of the Nilotic peoples of the upper Nile; but no one eighty years ago could possibly measure these effects upon a people unknown and ungoverned. The sole concern was water for Egypt, with no regard for those whose livelihood had been regulated by the Sudd for centuries. The Jonglei canal was born.

[38] Hurst and Phillips (1938, p. 116).
[39] Sutcliffe and Parks (1987, p. 145).

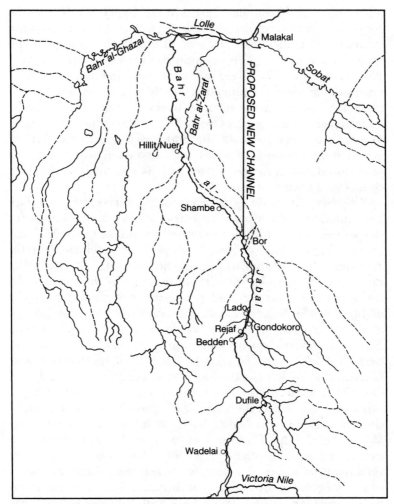

MAP 4. The Garstin Cut
Source: Garstin (1904)

4
British on the Nile

I desire to point out that in my opinion there is a good
danger of the Sudan losing now a good opportunity of
further development in the near future without prejudice
to Egypt, unless an agreement is made between the two
Governments admitting the right of the Sudan to use
Gebel Aulia water not required by Egypt when able to
pay for it.

H. T. Cory, 1920

No river in the world has been measured over so long a time
as the Nile. Its vital statistics formally begin with the erection
of the Rodah nilometer in the eighth century, but the flows of
the Nile have been the constant concern of the inhabitants
since Pharaonic times. Moreover, the Rodah nilometer was
only the principal source of measurement, to which were
added throughout subsequent centuries information from
numerous gauges upstream, as well as the observations of the
Arab chroniclers of medieval and modern Egypt. The purpose
of this obsession with the flow of the Nile, which continues
unabated to this day, was as obvious as it was understandable,
since the prosperity of Egypt has always been dependent upon
the waters of that great river flowing out of Africa. These
measurements, no matter how massive or how long in time,
have never explained, however, the hydrology of the Nile or
the characteristics of its huge basin. The search for understanding of the vagaries of the river, its tributaries, and the
nature of the lands whence came the water was unproductive,
its frustration symbolized by the lengthy and fruitless quest
for the source.

In order to appreciate why these massive quantities of
records collected through the centuries contributed little to
the understanding of Nile hydrology, the tabulation of Nile
flows must be placed in perspective. Despite the work of

Kamal Ghaleb Pasha[1] in reconstructing and translating the old statistics and records of the Rodah nilometer into the metric scale, this vast accumulation of data has failed to produce any accurate history of the relative or absolute discharges of the Nile waters. Rodah and its subsidiary nilometers alone cannot measure the amount of water diverted from the Nile south of Cairo for irrigation. Moreover, the channel of the Nile itself from Cairo to the Mediterranean has been subjected to countless changes which would modify the gauge readings at Rodah, eroding over time any significance concerning relative discharges. Indeed, since the rate of taxation traditionally levied in Egypt has depended upon the official reading of the Rodah gauge, any recorded readings may be suspect. In fact, no reliable readings exist before 1873 to verify those at Rodah.[2]

It was, in fact, not until the British had come to dominate the Nile basin by conquest at the end of the nineteenth century that hydrologists and engineers, mostly British, could turn to the scientific examination of the Nile basin as a whole in order to understand, not just the quantity of water available to Egypt, but how that water could most effectively be used to meet the needs of an expanding Egyptian population. The Nile quest may have resolved the long search for the source or sources of this enigmatic river, but these explorations, no matter how heroic, were conducted by amateurs whose information created more questions than answers, despite the eagerness with which their discoveries were assimilated by the scientific community in Europe. Yet a complete knowledge of the Nile and its tributaries was so fundamentally important to British control at Cairo and Suez and to the administration of British conquests in the Nile basin itself that no one could disagree that a systematic, scientific, and continuing investigation of this great river should proceed immediately in the wake of the victorious Anglo-Egyptian and British armies in the middle and upper Nile.

---

[1] Kamel Ghaleb Pasha (1951). The oldest record of the Nile flood was recorded on the Palermo Stone during the Fifth Dynasty, 2500 BC, with markings indicating the level of the Nile flood for every year back to the reign of King Zer in the First Dynasty, 3,050 BC. See Bell (1970, pp. 569–73).

[2] Lyons (1906, p. 318).

On the basis of information compiled by nineteenth-century explorers, a host of European geographers—von Klöden in Germany, Lombardini in Italy, Chavanne in Austria, and Chélu in France—were able to construct the general outline of the Nile and its tributaries, but not its hydrology.[3] By 1890 knowledge of the natural flow of the Nile had become crucial to the engineers in Cairo who were responsible for making the desert bloom. The problems facing them in Egypt were twofold. First, the introduction of perennial irrigation in the early nineteenth century by Muhammad 'Ali had transformed the productivity of the irrigated fields of Egypt from the ancient tradition of basin irrigation and one crop to a continuous flow of water via regulators to produce two or even three crops in any given year. Not only did this enable Egypt to produce more food and cash crops, particularly cotton, but it provided a surplus to feed a burgeoning population. By the end of the century, however, the regulators and barrages of the great viceroy and his successors could only sustain the three million feddans under perennial cultivation, at a time when the population of Egypt was increasing beyond the means to feed it.

By 1890 Lord Cromer had convinced Lord Salisbury that Britain's paramountcy in Egypt was not going to be temporary, as was supposed at the time of the conquest in 1882. Thereafter, the primary consideration of Britain's imperium on the Nile and at Suez was the security of its waters. If Britain were to remain in Egypt, however, British engineers must also increase the supply of water available after the Nile flood had passed, impounding it to ensure a continuous flow to the ageing barrages and irrigation works constructed in the nineteenth century. Under the leadership of Sir Colin Scott-Moncrieff, the under-secretary of state for public works in Egypt, a group of hydrologists and engineers were recruited, largely from the Indian irrigation service, to begin the regeneration of the irrigation system in Egypt. Among the scientists assembled at Cairo were three remarkable men—Sir William Willcocks, Sir William Garstin, and Sir Murdoch MacDonald. The modern age belittles the accomplishments of

[3] See von Klöden (1856), Lombardini (1865), Chavanne (1883), Chélu (1891). See also Matronne (1897).

FIG. 3. Sir William Garstin

individuals; but these were men made to tame the river that the most mighty of the Pharaohs feared.

Sir William Willcocks was the most erratic and eccentric of the three. Born and educated in India, he seldom visited England and never exhibited any affection for that far-off land. He was volatile, unpredictable; 'always difficult to agree to differ'. Like many whose personalities have been captivated by the East, he was at heart a romantic who could produce the most outlandish provocations while proposing the most creative and bold engineering projects. Even his intractable opponents, Garstin and MacDonald, would grudgingly concede that he was one of the greatest engineers at the turn of century. He was recruited by Scott-Moncrieff in 1890 from the Indian irrigation service, and his great contribution to Nile hydrology was his *Report on Perennial Irrigation and Flood Protection for Egypt*, published in Cairo in 1894, in which he proposed the construction of a great dam at Aswan, an enormous structure, a symbol of modern technology to control one of the world's most mighty rivers. The Pharaohs would have been proud. Willcocks retired from the irrigation service in 1911, but his long tenure in Egypt and his overwhelming personality remained to dominate younger men and to continue to be a pernicious nuisance to those who succeeded him. He regarded himself as the sole authority on Nile waters, and there were few who would dare to dispute his views. Not surprisingly, his arrogance and eccentricities led him into troubled waters, and after his disgrace in 1921 he was virtually ostracized by the British community in Egypt, where he spent the rest of his life.

Sir William Garstin was a very different sort of man. Rather than flout the Establishment he joined it, complete with black tie, at the British residency (see Fig. 3). Like Willcocks, Garstin was born in India, on 29 January 1849. His father was a bureaucrat in the Bengal civil service, his mother was the daughter of W. Mackenzie of the East India Company. Unlike Willcocks, he was sent to England for his education, at Cheltenham and King's College, London, before returning to India and the ministry of public works in 1872. Like Willcocks, he was recruited by Scott-Moncrieff for Egypt, in 1892, at which time he was appointed inspector-general of irrigation at the Egyptian ministry of public works. Garstin possessed two pre-eminent qualities: an affable personality and one of the most perceptive minds in understanding water and how it flows. For all his brilliance, Willcocks never could match Garstin's grasp of the Nile basin. He was too much an Egyptian. Garstin could transcend this parochialism, an ability which Lord Cromer exploited to develop Britain's Nile and global strategy. Cromer's dictum in the 1890s defined the needs of Egypt as justice and water. Cromer provided justice, though by his definition. Garstin gave Egypt water. It was no exaggeration when Cromer asserted that Garstin 'had raised himself to the rank of the greatest hydrologic engineer in this or any other country'.[4] Remarkably, even the Egyptian nationalists praised him as 'the treasure of Egypt'.[5]

Sir Murdoch MacDonald could not have been more different from Sir William Willcocks and Sir William Garstin. Willcocks was brilliant but erratic. Garstin thought in imperial terms, and possessed an astonishing grasp of the Nile and its basin as a whole. MacDonald was at heart an engineer, a 'construction man'. He was born on 6 May 1866 in Inverness, the seventh of nine children. But here in the highlands of Scotland was his home, not some far-off imperial possession. He was educated at the Farraline Park School in Inverness, known locally as 'Dr Bell's institution'. In the Scottish tradition, he worked his way as an engineer on the Highland Railway, accumulating accolades for his designs for the Black Isle Railway. In 1898 he was appointed as an assistant engineer on the construction of the Aswan dam by Benjamin Baker, who at that time was the official consulting engineer for the Egyptian Government. Here he was instrumental in devising the aprons to prevent scouring below the dam— earning thereby, however, the eternal enmity of Sir William Willcocks. The latter had failed to take into account the massive erosion of the river-bed during periods of heavy discharge; MacDonald resolved this flaw in Willcocks's otherwise brilliant creation.

MacDonald was a builder, a pragmatic and charming Scot, an engineer without the imagination of Willcocks or the vision

---

[4] Weaver (1937, p. 329).   [5] Ibid.

of Garstin. He simply got the job done. He supervised, to Willcocks's fury, the heightening of the Aswan dam, constructed the Esna barrage, and achieved British and Egyptian honours by rebuilding in a few months the three main regulators of the delta barrage in 1910 under the most difficult circumstances. When Lord Kitchener returned to Egypt in 1912 MacDonald became his under-secretary, and later adviser to the Egyptian ministry of public works, with results which were neither to his advantage nor to that of the empire.

While these three strong personalities manœuvred within the cloistered world of Nile hydrology for nearly a quarter of a century, the realities of Egypt's growing population and the need for the water to feed it could not be ignored. The principal problem was to augment the water supply of Egypt, particularly in the months from January to July after the Nile flood had receded. No one was more concerned than Lord Cromer. Acting on Willcocks's recommendation of the building of a high dam at Aswan, he appointed an international commission under the chairmanship of his close personal friend, Sir Benjamin Baker, with M. A. Boulé from France and an Italian, G. Torricelli, to consider the Willcocks proposal and recommend any other projects that might be undertaken in Egypt to increase the number of feddans under perennial irrigation, since the presence of the Mahdist State in the Sudan precluded any hydrological investigations south of Wadi Halfa. Sir Benjamin Baker had established his reputation by extrapolating, from practical experience as an apprentice in the iron industry, a theory to predict the ability of materials to withstand stress. He applied his studies as one of the architects who designed the Firth of Forth bridge and the City and South London line, the original 'tube', which was opened under his scrutiny. He and his fellow commissioners approved the Willcocks report and sanctioned the construction of a dam at Aswan, but to Willcocks's bitter regret it was not to be his 'high' dam. At the insistence of Boulé, Willcocks's original proposal was scaled down by some 20 ft so that the exquisite temple of Philae would not be permanently inundated.

Although Willcocks was the inspiration for Aswan, the first suggestion for a dam at this site had been made as early as 1876 by General F. H. Rundall of the Royal Engineers. At the time Rundall was the deputy secretary for irrigation to the Indian government, and he had come upon this idea, as a means of dramatically increasing perennial irrigation in Egypt, while on a consulting tour in the delta at the request of Khedive Isma'il. Ironically, Rundall proposed a mighty dam at Aswan far greater than even Willcocks envisaged, and one which took another 100 years to build.[6] Sir Benjamin Baker was the consulting engineer, but the Aswan dam was the creation of Willcocks, for which he received his knighthood. Nevertheless, its construction was regarded as a bold risk, and financing proved difficult until Cromer put the problem to his family banking firm, Baring Brothers. Through the financial skill of Sir Ernest Cassel the funds were forthcoming, construction began in 1898, and the Aswan dam was completed in 1902, a year ahead of schedule, helped by successive years of low Nile floods.

The same year that the first stone was laid at Aswan saw the defeat of the Khalifa 'Abd Allahi and his army on the plains of Karari outside Omdurman on 2 September 1898 and the subsequent collapse of the Mahdist State. The occupation of the Sudan now enabled Britain to control, by conquest or treaty, virtually the whole of the Nile basin and to reaffirm the primacy of the Nile in British imperial strategy. Always suspicious of the generals, who were too intolerable, too ambitious, and too expensive, Lord Cromer turned to his friend, Sir William Garstin, to understand more fully the importance of Nile control to Egypt and Britain's position therein. Cromer held the purse-strings; Garstin possessed the technology and vision to make the water flow. Together they made a formidable and progressive pair, determined to develop to its fullest extent the hydrological potential of the Nile valley. Regrettably, they have never been emulated, regardless of their detractors, to the detriment of Egypt and the lands lying south of Wadi Halfa.

In the solitude of their evenings Cromer and Garstin discussed over brandy the control of the Nile waters which, from Cromer's point of view, was one of the principal objectives of the Anglo-Egyptian occupation of the Sudan.

---

[6] Hurst et al. (1951, p. 118).

Cromer cared little for the Sudanese. In fact he was grateful to the Mahdists for their State astride the middle Nile, which excluded interlopers while not possessing itself the technology to interfere in the flow of its waters. Once, however, the French sought to disrupt this sanctuary, Cromer had to call upon the generals and the big battalions to ensure Britain's domination over the Nile basin. Six months after the victory at Karari, and again in 1900 and 1901, he sent Garstin up the river to test the waters, and again in 1903 to the Lake Plateau and the great lakes of equatorial Africa, to assess the hydrological significance of the million square miles which Britain had conquered *not* out of absence of mind.

Garstin's pioneering hydrological surveys between 1899 and 1903 securely established him as the father of Nile hydrology, and his two reports published in 1901 and 1904 remain the foundations for the development of the waters of the Nile basin to this day.[7] Not only did Lord Cromer strongly support Garstin's recommendations for Nile control, but he wrote rather optimistically, in his covering despatch: 'We shall before long have arrived at the conclusion of what may fitly be termed the first and initial stage of dealing with the water of the Nile.'[8] Accompanied by J. I. Craig, Garstin wandered throughout the Nile basin, measuring discharges and collecting sporadic hydrological data to support the shrewd observations on the basis of which his prescient predictions and, more important, his recommendations for Nile water utilization were to be formed and incorporated into his influential reports. Although his proposals have withstood a century of intense scientific scrutiny, Garstin was the first to recognize that his work was preliminary, requiring supporting data either to confirm or to refute his intuitive conclusions. The completion of the Aswan dam in 1902 and the barrages at Assuit and Zifta only emphasized the need for greater information about the river south of Egypt.

Consequently, C. E. Dupuis of the irrigation service was sent on an expedition to Lake Tana, whence flows the Blue Nile. The purpose of Dupuis's reconnaissance was to determine whether Lake Tana could become an alternative reservoir to

[7] Garstin (1901b; 1904).
[8] Earl of Cromer to the Marquess of Lansdowne, 19 June 1901, in Garstin (1901b).

the equatorial lakes, since there were no swamps on the Blue Nile to impede its flow. His observations, included in Garstin's report of 1904, were inconclusive and thus not very helpful to the task of accumulating data, which had to wait the report of G. W. Grabham and R. P. Black of their expedition in 1920–1, published in 1925. At the same time Garstin proposed that a separate Sudan irrigation department be established to oversee the collection of hydrological information from Khartoum; but he found little support from the fragile and impecunious Anglo-Egyptian administration in the Sudan and none whatsoever in Cairo, where the feeling, which later became an obsession, was growing that the study of the Nile basin should be a monopoly of the Egyptian irrigation service. Garstin had to be content with a Sudan branch, organized in 1904 under C. E. Dupuis, who reported directly to Cairo, to the increasing irritation of British officials in the Sudan.

With the creation of the Sudan branch, the scientific study of the Nile basin became the sole responsibility of the Egyptian irrigation service with the 'object of surveying, levelling, and measuring the volume of the rivers throughout the year; erecting gauges; and generally collecting data for the different projects for the improvement of the water supply of Egypt and the development of perennial irrigation in the Sudan'.[9] To carry out this charge Garstin ordered his subordinates in 1905 to seek new sites for reservoirs. This task was assigned to the survey department for mapping. Line levels were run from Wadi Halfa to Khartoum, and Murdoch MacDonald, then residential engineer at the Aswan dam, devised a new and more accurate means to measure Nile discharge through the sluices to meet precisely the irrigation requirements downstream. These were heady days for the band of British hydrologists, E. M. Dowson, Lt.-Col. B. F. R. Keeling, and J. I. Craig, turned loose, under the supervision of Sir Henry Lyons, the director-general of the survey department, to map with precision the Nile.

Sir Henry Lyons was another of those remarkable men who were seduced by the Nile at the turn of the century. A royal engineer from the Royal Military Academy at Woolwich, he

[9] Hurst (1952, pp. 225–6).

was posted to Cairo in 1890, where he established a reputation for the skilful use of instrumentation to resolve problems of Nile hydrology. He was responsible for the systematic study of the Nile later taken up by the mathematician H. E. Hurst. In 1896 the ministry of public works had published Lyons's modest report on *The Island and Temples of Philae*, which was brought to the attention of Cromer. In the following year Cromer asked Lyons to organize the geological survey of Egypt within the ministry of public works. Cromer had wanted only a cadastral survey, but Lyons provided more than that. By 1901 he had assembled a superbly efficient organization which, staffed by young, bright, British hydrologists, broadened the range of the geological survey to embrace geodesy, meteorology, and the measurement of the Nile. Lyons was the first to introduce current-meters to measure velocity in 1908. Current-meters enabled hydrologists to make accurate readings of Nile flow at any given time and place for the first time in the history of Nile hydrological records. He established the official meteorological service of Egypt and the Sudan to calculate the effect of rain on the volume of Nile water, and enlarged the Khedivial Observatory, which was moved to Helwan. In 1902 it was Lyons who organized the first systematic collection of discharges of the Blue and White Niles. He crowned his career before retirement in 1908 by the publication of *The Physiography of the River Nile and Its Basin* in Cairo in 1906.

Neither as magisterial nor as perceptive as Garstin's reports, *The Physiography of the River Nile and Its Basin* was, nevertheless, by far most comprehensive compilation of all that was then known of the characteristics of the river and its basin. It does not confine itself merely to hydrology but provides a general description of the basin's geology and climate. Its main purpose, however, is made clear: 'Hitherto, the source of the Nile supply, its amount, its periodicity, the possibility of increasing it at low stage, and of guarding against the danger of excessive floods have been the special points of the river regimen which have received attention.'[10] Lyons's description of the Nile basin was primarily scientific, but scientific for a utilitarian purpose. He perceived that the

[10] Lyons (1906, p. 2).

objectives of the Egyptian government and its British masters would require 'the results of geographical study [which] can greatly assist the practical development of the resources of the river basin'.[11] Towards this more pragmatic end Lyons, like his counterparts in the USA, was to justify public expenditure on scientific enquiry in the fields of geology, meteorology, and the chemistry of water by the simple but irresistible prospect that such investigations would increase the supply of water available to Egypt and therefore its wealth.

The publication of Lyons's work also marked the end of the Cromer–Garstin era. Lord Cromer retired as British agent and consul-general in 1907, and Garstin, as the under-secretary of state in the ministry, left Egypt the following year. The departure of these two dominating Victorians, with their vast store of experience, vision, and common sense, created a vacuum in the leadership of Nile studies which the younger men recruited in the new century could not fill. Although their enthusiasm for the collection of data and its analysis remained undiminished, the position of adviser to the ministry of public works, to which Garstin had given the responsibility for the overall planning of Nile control, was held for brief and unproductive periods by Sir Arthur Webb and by C. E. Dupuis, who provided little guidance and less inspiration for the younger officials. Nile development languished, devoid of grand schemes, confined to the uninspired accumulation of measured discharges, until the appointment in 1912 of Lord Kitchener as the British agent and consul-general in Egypt and of Sir Murdoch MacDonald as adviser to the ministry revived the Garstin initiatives. But neither Kitchener nor MacDonald could match the experience and knowledge of Cromer and Garstin. The imperious Kitchener succeeded Sir Eldon Gorst with little appreciation for the depth of Egyptian nationalism. MacDonald had little interest in being the adviser to the ministry. He possessed drive, charm, and a gift for discourse, which his detractors dismissed as 'gab', all combined with a determined, combative style. To the British scientists in the ministry he was always regarded as a 'construction' man bereft of any theoretical foundations or

[11] Lyons (1906, p. 3).

education. His appointment deeply divided the Egyptian irrigation service into pro- and anti-MacDonald factions and, of course, confirmed the latent and long-standing hostility of Sir William Willcocks.

Nevertheless, the Kitchener–MacDonald years sputtered into life, seeming to begin a new era of Nile development by the approval of the British and Egyptian Governments in 1914 for the construction of dams on the Blue Nile at Sennar and the White Nile at Jabal 'Auliya. These two conservancy projects owed much to the measurements made after 1906 by the Sudan branch of the irrigation service under the direction of C. E. Dupuis. Until that year, data collection south of Aswan had been the responsibility of the survey department of the Egyptian government, which was in fact attached to the ministry of finance, not the ministry of public works. This anomaly was an historical accident, brought about by the dynamic leadership of Sir Henry Lyons. Upon his retirement in 1906, however, the task of measuring the Nile was shifted more appropriately to the Egyptian irrigation service within the ministry of public works and its Sudan branch.

From its inception the Sudan branch suffered from divided loyalties and disparate objectives. Garstin had foreseen this incongruity in 1904 when he recommended a separate Sudan irrigation department, but neither Cromer, who sought to grant as little independence to British officials in the Sudan as possible, nor the governor-general of the Sudan, Sir Reginald Wingate, who did not wish to incur additional expense which his administration could ill afford, wanted an independent department in the Sudan. Garstin did not press the point, and a unique opportunity was lost, creating deplorable repercussions which remained until the end of the Condominium. Consequently, the Sudan branch, despite its name, became merely an extension of the Egyptian irrigation service, which employed British and Egyptian officials from Egypt to promote Egyptian, not Sudanese, interests. Planning in the Sudan branch focused primarily on the volume of water available from January to July, for it would be stored and reserved for irrigation in Egypt at a time when the Nile flowed in greatly reduced quantities after the flood-waters from Ethiopia had subsided. The importance of a constant supply of water during these months cannot be over-emphasized. Indeed, the purpose of the Aswan dam was to provide stored water at that time, and the difference in views as to the precise amount available during these critical months was largely responsible for the disputes over water which raged throughout Egypt after the low Nile of 1914.

The Sudan branch soon discovered that the problem of finding water for Egypt after the expiration of the Blue Nile flood could not be dissociated from the needs of the Sudanese. Although there are no universally agreed principles for the apportionment of water, hydrologists and politicians alike recognize that one cannot regulate a segment of a river basin without affecting the whole. Consequently, in selecting sites for dams in the Sudan to provide water for Egypt the hydrologists could not ignore Sudanese claims to the water, and the nascent administration in the Sudan was not about to let them forget those claims. Herein lay the divided loyalties of the British officials attached to the Sudan branch of the Egyptian irrigation service. On the one hand they were British and presumably loyal to the Crown and empire. On the other they were employees of a ministry of the Egyptian government, and obliged by professional ethics to carry out loyally the interests of the irrigation service even if those interests conflicted with the requirements of the British empire. From the inception of the Sudan branch, its British officials were faced with this irreconcilable dilemma, which was increasingly exasperated by the tumultuous relations between the British and Egyptian governments throughout this century. This dilemma became more sharply focused when the British hydrologists in the irrigation service were charged with devising a scheme to divert water from the Blue Nile, the historic source of Egypt's water, by the construction of a dam at Sennar to reserve that water to irrigate the Gezira plain lying south of Khartoum, in the heartland of the Sudan.

The very idea of draining off Nile water for the Sudan produced suspicion among British officials, for the whirlpools of emotion and the eddies of fear created by the Sudan's claim to a share of the Nile waters were not confined to Egyptian politicians in Cairo. British administrators in the Sudan became increasingly perturbed, in the years ahead, about the real and imaginary designs of the engineers of the Sudan branch, who appeared to reserve their loyalty for Egyptian water projects while ignoring their fellow countrymen in Khartoum, working independently from them, withholding information, and reporting (as was in fact their duty) directly to the irrigation service in Cairo.

Appearances, however, could be deceptive, particularly, in this case, taking into account unremitting pressure from Sir Reginald Wingate in Khartoum and the staunch support of Kitchener and MacDonald in Cairo for a dam at Sennar to irrigate the Gezira. Wingate and his officials in the Sudan had struggled for years to make the Sudan administratively independent of Egypt, whether ruled by Lord Cromer or by the Egyptians. Administrative freedom, however, was directly proportional to the Sudan's ability to meet not only the costs of government but the expense of development. In a land with few means to produce revenue, the growing of cotton in the Gezira appeared the only financially feasible way out of this imbroglio. Yet the irrigation of the Gezira was economically possible only by means of a dam and storage reservoir at Sennar. Indeed, Kitchener himself, with the eye of an engineer, saw from the ruins of Khartoum in 1898 the possibility of irrigating the natural slope of the Gezira plain south of the city. As for MacDonald, he was quite convinced even before becoming adviser to the ministry that there would be sufficient water for the immediate needs of Egypt and the Sudan. Acting on the measurements collected by the Sudan branch (despite the fact that the records spanned less than a decade) and on the recommendations of P. M. Tottenham, inspector-general for the Sudan branch, Kitchener peremptorily, though characteristically, intervened in 1912 to force the Egyptian government to appoint his hand-picked commission, consisting of Sir Arthur Webb, Sir Murdoch MacDonald, and H. H. McClure, to review the proposals for two dams, one at Jabal 'Auliya on the White Nile south of Khartoum to meet Egyptian needs for an increase in seasonal water and a second at Makwar (Sennar) on the Blue Nile to provide water to irrigate the Gezira. The commission unanimously recommended the construction of both dams. Kitchener speedily endorsed the report of the commission when he forwarded it to the

British and Egyptian governments, who in turn gave their approval in 1914.

While the irrigation service was busy measuring Nile flows and proposing dam sites, the survey department under J. I. Craig had not been idle during the years before the First World War. Its task was to establish with precision the height above sea-level of the great lakes and tributaries throughout the Nile basin, an immense undertaking but one essential for Nile development. So critical was this information that the survey department was transferred to the ministry of public works in 1915, where it was combined with the Nile river studies, then the responsibility of the Egyptian irrigation service, to form a new agency, the physical department, within the ministry. Under a director-general, the mathematician Dr H. E. Hurst, who had begun his long career in Nile hydrology in 1906, the responsibilities of the physical department were far-reaching but simple: the study of the Nile river and its basin. This included 'Hydrology, Meteorology, the Helwan Observatory, the Weights and Measure service and the Scientific Instrumentation Workshops'.[12] The data from which the physical department made its analysis continued to be collected by the Sudan branch of the irrigation service.

The First World War brought Nile development to a virtual halt, although measurements continued to be collected. The two principal personalities, Kitchener at the residency and MacDonald at the ministry, abandoned their interest in the Nile—Kitchener to lead the British military until his death at sea in 1916, MacDonald to Sinai where, as a colonel in the Royal Engineers, he advised General Allenby on various engineering matters, the defence of the Suez Canal, and the means to supply Allied expeditionary forces with fresh water. Upon the conclusion of the war MacDonald returned as adviser to the ministry, and under his leadership Hurst directed the expansion of scientific investigation of the Nile in a more methodically planned programme than had characterized the pre-war years.

The increase in the number of sites as well as measurements had only exacerbated the problems of maintenance, cataloguing,

[12] Hurst (1952, p. 227).

and collation of these hydrological records, which in the ministry had been sloppy at best, incompetent at worst. By 1914 the clerical inadequacy in record-keeping had seriously begun to hamper the analysis of Nile flows, and one of the reasons for the creation of the physical department had been to bring order out of the chaos. The staff was expanded. Two British hydrologists who were to play an important role in Nile basin planning, Dr P. Phillips and R. P. Black, joined Hurst, who also recruited a number of able Egyptian mathematicians and physicists. L. J. Sutton took over the direction of the meteorological service. Before putting the records in order, they first had to collect the hydrological data which had accumulated, for historical reasons, in the various ministries of the Egyptian government. This information was then integrated into that which had already been gathered more systematically by the irrigation service.

No sooner had the war clouds dissipated and the physical department undertaken its work of co-ordination and expansion than a storm of titanic proportions broke over the ministry. In 1914 the Nile recorded one of its lowest floods in many years, and although there was open dispute whether or not it was *the* lowest Nile in a century, the dearth of water convinced Lt.-Col. M. Ralston Kennedy Pasha, the director-general of public works in the Sudan government since 1906, that there was in fact insufficient water to irrigate the Gezira without seriously jeopardizing the supply of water available to Egypt. The issue had simmered as the world turned to war but ultimately came to a boil two years later in 1916 when Kennedy, using measurements taken by his own department in the Sudan, concluded that the discharge figures by which the amount of available water was calculated had been deliberately tampered with by Sir Murdoch MacDonald in 1914 in order to gain the approval of the British and Egyptian governments for the Sennar dam. In November 1916 Kennedy personally confronted MacDonald with the wide discrepancies between his measurements and those of the irrigation service, in some instances differences in excess of 50 per cent, only to be politely dismissed and ignored. Kennedy returned to Khartoum where he sulked at MacDonald's rebuff. Pouting soon turned to fury, however, and in April 1917 he officially informed the governor-general that according to his calculations there was simply not enough water to supply a reservoir at Sennar without detriment to Egypt. He labelled MacDonald's proposal for the Sennar dam as a 'Dead Scheme'.[13]

Kennedy himself was not a popular figure among British officials in Khartoum and was positively disliked by Sir Lee Stack, the acting governor-general, and Sir Reginald Wingate, who had just left the Sudan to become the British high commissioner in Cairo (Wingate officially retained the position of governor-general of the Sudan). Both men had fought hard to secure the support of the British and Egyptian governments for the Sennar dam and the Gezira cotton scheme, despite political opposition in Egypt, where competition from the Gezira for Egyptian cotton was regarded as a serious threat. They had triumphed in 1914 when the dam had been approved, and were not about to have Kennedy undo all their labours to give the Sudan its only scheme capable of generating sufficient revenue. They dismissed Kennedy's charges with even less politeness than MacDonald, and were only too happy to accept his resignation from the Sudan service.

Once uninhibited by his official position, Kennedy now publicly charged in Cairo that Sir Murdoch MacDonald had deliberately falsified the evidence and even quoted MacDonald himself as saying that 'the site [Sennar] however has no real storage capacity'.[14] Alone, Kennedy and his charges might have gone unnoticed, but he was soon joined by a very formidable ally, Sir William Willcocks. Willcocks had never had much use for MacDonald, a feeling that was reciprocated. They had fallen out many years before over alterations for the Aswan dam, which had been designed and carried out under MacDonald's supervision. Thereafter alienation turned to open hostility as Willcocks in retirement fulminated over MacDonald's ideas for the control of the Nile, which he regarded as badly flawed and not in the best interests of his beloved Egypt. If MacDonald had his way, 'the Sudan will take its share of the water high up the course of the river, and

---

[13] Lt.-Col. M. Ralston Kennedy Pasha to private secretary (M. J. Wheatley) to governor-general, Sir Lee Stack, 6 Apr. 1917, SAD 108/14.
[14] Ibid.

Egypt will receive much of its share on paper'.[15] Willcocks argued that the development of the Gezira was an economic chimera, for the rate of evaporation would be greater than in Egypt and the cotton of inferior quality. The water would be used more effectively if it were employed to increase the proven success of cotton cultivation in Egypt.[16] Willcocks enlisted the support of Sir Valentine Chirol, one of the dominant figures in British journalism of his generation, Egyptian nationalists of every persuasion, and the Committee of Egyptian Engineers, who represented the professional and more moderate Egyptian opinion, to launch an attack on MacDonald in the press, on the podium, and within the Egyptian parliament. The uproar over the dams at Sennar and Jabal 'Auliya even penetrated throughout the countryside among the *fallahin*, who required no sophisticated political analysis to understand any threat, real or imagined, to the Nile waters. By 1919 the controversy over the Nile waters had 'quite ousted all other subjects as a topic of conversation throughout the delta and was a potential lever for nationalist appeals to the fallahin'.[17] By the end of the year Willcocks had aroused the most deep-seated fears latent in every class of Egyptian society.

The opposition to both dams was implacable, but for different reasons. Led by the nationalist newspapers, there was a continuous denunciation of British plans for Nile development, the attacks being aimed specifically at MacDonald as the adviser at the ministry and fuelled by the implications by Kennedy and Willcocks of deliberate fraud. Their charges were founded on technical data which were understood by the committee of Egyptian engineers but had little appeal to the Egyptian public. They were aroused more by their deep suspicions of any plans proposed by the British that had to do with water and led by the nationalists, particularly Sa'd Zaghlul and the Wafd, compulsively suspicious of any

[15] Sir William Willcocks to HE high commissioner, Lord Allenby, 18 July 1918, SAD 108/7.
[16] 'Future Development of Cotton Production in Egypt', H. Fountain, Mar. 1918, SAD 156/1/112.
[17] R. S. Stafford, inspector of interior, Tanta, to adviser, ministry of interior, 24 Feb. 1920, FO 141/435/101844.

hydrological schemes that were to be constructed beyond the territorial boundaries of Egypt.[18]

One would have thought that the assault of the nationalists would have been aimed at the Sennar dam, since its reservoir was to be utilized for the Sudanese to grow cotton, presumably in competition with Egypt, while the Jabal 'Auliya dam was solely to provide water for Egypt from January to July. Paradoxically, this was not the case. The nationalists focused their opposition principally against Jabal 'Auliya because it would be built in the Sudan, beyond the sovereignty of Egypt. So too was the dam at Sennar, but the arguments against its construction were of necessity moderated, since the nationalists were already seeking to turn the Sudanese from their acceptance of British administration. Gezira cotton may have represented potential competition for Egypt in the future, but the political struggle to win the Sudanese to Egypt was immediate and paramount. The torrent of articles denouncing MacDonald's plans for Nile water development in the nationalist press quickly accelerated in proportion to the publicity accorded to Kennedy and Willcocks. Intense pressure began to mount on the more moderate Egyptian ministers, particularly the technologically competent but, to the nationalists, all too compliant minister of public works, Husayn Sirry Pasha. Much to British embarrassment he resigned, and although he later gave his support to MacDonald, his blessing remained unheard amid the hue and cry from Egyptian public opinion.

Egyptian suspicions were not confined to Sir Murdoch MacDonald. There had long been growing discontent, sharpened by necessity, at the domination of British officials in the irrigation service. Clearly Egypt did not possess the technically skilled personnel to plan Nile development with scientific rigour, but this frustration was exacerbated by the frequent lack of sensitivity of British technocrats, who saw themselves as in Egypt to do a job, not to pander to the psychoses of ignorant politicians and peasants. Needless to say, this arrogance did nothing to bridge the dramatic difference between British and Egyptian perception of the Nile

[18] 'Memorandum on the Political Aspects of the Egyptian Irrigation Scandals', Lord Allenby to Lord Curzon, 22 Nov. 1919, FO 371/3710; Tignor (1977, p. 195).

waters. Enshrouded by measurements and equations, the British officials of the irrigation service appeared to many Egyptians as a mysterious and consequently devious clique, loyal to Britain and the empire and therefore not working in the best interests of Egypt, a conviction which appeared confirmed when Hurst and other British officials rallied to the defence of MacDonald. Willcocks later publicly accused MacDonald of intimidating his subordinates to secure their support. He was believed.

The charges by Kennedy and Willcocks were fifteen in all, the accusation of criminality consisting in the charge that MacDonald had deliberately falsified measurements of Nile discharges 'to deceive Egypt as to the amount of water at her disposal'.[19] The depth of MacDonald's supposed iniquities was only matched by Willcocks's indignant pronouncements. MacDonald was accused not only of forging the gauge readings but of deliberately 'losing' incriminating public documents which 'have officially disappeared off the face of the earth'.[20] This is a direct reference to the famous 'Blue Nile memorandum' of 19 February 1914 in which were recorded the critical discharges at Sennar for that year. Willcocks was convinced that the measurements of White Nile flow contained in that memorandum would support Kennedy's records, demonstrating that there was insufficient water for both Egypt and the Gezira. Willcocks thundered: 'The Blue and White Nile Projects, independently of their inherent merits or demerits, stand or fall upon the question of whether there is any water to spare in the years of low supply, for use or storage in the Sudan, *without prejudicing Egypt's well established water rights.*'[21] He demanded that MacDonald hand over to him the Blue Nile memorandum. MacDonald refused. In fact, neither he nor his staff could find this crucial memorandum in the files at the ministry. A desperate search ensued. No memorandum was found. It had mysteriously disappeared. Willcocks was now more convinced than ever that MacDonald had deliberately destroyed the critical evidence which would have been detrimental to the Sennar and Jabal 'Auliya dam projects at

[19] MacDonald to Wingate, 14 July 1920, SAD 108/14.
[20] Willcocks to H. P. Harvey, financial adviser, 23 Jan. 1920, SAD 108/8.
[21] Willcocks (1919, intro.).

the time when they were being considered for approval by the British and Egyptian governments. Willcocks moved in for the kill. These criminal charges were serious accusations. They had been brought forward by a major public figure, and would have received massive publicity even if the question of water and the political implications had not existed. Certainly, in Cairo and London British officials took the press campaign against MacDonald seriously, deeply concerned that these public allegations would prejudice the construction of the Sennar dam.[22] Willcocks continued to heap fuel upon the fire of the press campaign when he wrote, in February 1920:

It is new in the experience of civilized countries that the most serious criminal charges can be made against one of the highest officials of a government, that these charges can be supported by evidence supplied under pressure by the official himself, and that they can be unanswered. And in the meanwhile, this official, who ought to be on his trial defending himself, is allowed to dispose of public documents at will, to intimidate his subordinates into silence, and even to represent the Government by the side of the judges who are there to judge him for committing criminal acts. Trials conducted on these principles remind one of the perverted justice which induced Zola to write his book which he rightly called 'J'accuse'.[23]

The immediate reaction of the British government, like most governments in similar situations, was to appoint a commission. In October 1918 the British high commissioner, Sir Reginald Wingate, asked the Egyptian government to establish a six-man committee to consider Willcocks's charges made four months before, in July. When Willcocks learned of the composition of the committee, he unleashed his full fury. Four of the commissioners were former officials of the ministry of public works whom he denounced as personally hostile to him. Two others had indiscreetly let it be known that they were determined to prove Willcocks wrong on the basis of information they had received from MacDonald. Willcocks promptly disowned the committee, refused to testify, and sulked in Cairo. The committee tried to make the best of a bad job, but when its report was published in the Egyptian press,

[22] For a sample of these articles see al-Akhbar, 23, 26 Feb. 1920.
[23] Willcocks to Harvey, 3 Feb. 1920, in Willcocks (1919, p. 19).

the commissioners had pointedly refused to answer five of Willcocks's most serious charges, thereby nullifying the remainder. Undeterred, Willcocks remained on the offensive, determined that his accusations should not be buried. He prevailed. The Egyptian Government, acting, of course, on advice from London, appointed on 10 January 1920 another committee, the Nile projects commission, consisting of three men with impeccable credentials, none of whom had any previous connection with Egypt, but two of whom were British. F. St. John Gebbie, inspector-general of irrigation for the government of India, was appointed president. Dr G. C. Simpson, meteorological reporter to the government of India, was nominated by Cambridge University as a leading authority on rainfall, a colleague of Gebbie in the Indian service; upon the adjournment of the commission he was elevated to the headship of the weather service of Great Britain. The third member was an American, Harry Thomas Cory, who was selected after a thorough investigation by the British embassy in Washington. Born in Indiana, a graduate in civil engineering from Purdue University, he had taught at the universities of Missouri and Cincinnati before becoming a consulting engineer. He was chosen by E. H. Harriman of the Union Pacific railroad to direct operations to repair the devastating diversion of the Colorado River into the Salton Sea in 1906–7 which threatened the rich Imperial valley of California. His success under difficult and dramatic circumstances won him professional acclaim and legendary status in the folklore of the American south-west, where he was portrayed as the engineer hero in Harold Bell Wright's popular novel *The Winning of Barbara Worth* which sold one and a half million copies and was made into a popular movie in 1926 starring Ronald Coleman and Gary Cooper. He appeared just the man to champion the oppressed, and the Egyptians singled him out from his British colleagues on the commission, not realizing that the fierce independence of his Hoosier traditions would direct his sympathies to a people more oppressed than the Egyptians.

The appointment of the Nile projects commission was not without difficulties. There was no Egyptian representative. Suddenly, the press had a fresh grievance which they immediately sought to exploit. Lord Allenby, the British high commissioner in Egypt, at once tried to repair this insensitive omission, but the damage had been done. After the outcry in the press no competent Egyptian, even if acceptable to both the British and the nationalists, would agree to serve. Husayn Sirry's resignation compounded the embarrassment, and Allenby had to employ all his persuasive powers and prestige to prevail upon Muhammad Shafik Pasha to take over temporarily the ministry of public works in addition to his more placid department of agriculture. As for Willcocks, he agreed to testify, but only if the evidence was taken under oath. Reluctantly, Sir Murdoch MacDonald agreed to this condition. He had little choice. Sir Valentine Chirol percept-ively commented that, if the Nile waters question had been 'handled with wisdom and frankness from the beginning it might have always remained an economic question', but that it had 'now passed into the dangerous domain of politics'.[24]

The commission first had to deal with the fifteen charges. They were complex and controversial, but they were all linked by the common themes of falsification on the one hand and the destruction of public documents on the other, with particular reference to the level of discharges and the Blue and White Nile dams. Willcocks, however, could not pass up this opportunity to press upon the commission his views concerning the Sudd, a subject to which he had devoted considerable attention over the years. As early as 1893 he had become aware of the potential value to Egypt of water from the equatorial lakes, which in turn precipitated his interest in the Sudd. He subsequently presented two well-attended lectures, one to the Sultanieh Geographical Society and the other to the Egyptian Institute, about the Sudd.[25] Willcocks had passed through the Sudd in 1907, 1912, and 1918, but he relied principally for his information on the research of E. P. Shakerley of the Egyptian

---

[24] Chirol (1920, pp. 287–8).

[25] 'The Sudd Region of the White Nile and the Harnessing of its Waters', by Sir William Willcocks and John Wells, a lecture delivered at the Sultanieh Geographical Society and published in Willcocks (1919, app. G, pp. 105–41); 'The Sudd Reservoir for the Whole of the Nile Valley', by Sir William Willcocks, a lecture delivered at a meeting of the Institute of Egypt, 7 Feb. 1919 and published in Willcocks (1919, app. H, pp. 142–62).

irrigation service, who was killed shortly after the outbreak of the First World War in 1915.

Willcocks proposed a rather elaborate scheme for recovery of the water now lost in the Sudd. He dismissed the Garstin Cut as much too expensive without adding 'anything to the water supply of the Nile'.[26] He argued that the true drainage line through the Sudd was the Bahr al-Zaraf, not the Bahr al-Jabal. Thus the least expensive, viable method of increasing the volume of the White Nile was to dredge the present channel of the Bahr al-Zaraf with banks 4 m high, and to create two reservoirs beside the river to store flood-waters. Once the channel of the Bahr al-Zaraf had been remodelled, additional water lying in the swamps west of the Bahr al-Jabal in the Bahr al-Ghazal province would drain by gravitation into the Bahr al-Jabal by lowering its level below that of the swamps. Then cuts and regulators could be constructed, at little cost, to divert the flow of the Bahr al-Jabal into the streamlined channel of the Bahr al-Zaraf. This would not only provide additional water flowing down the Bahr al-Zaraf and the White Nile to Egypt but also increase the flow of the Bahr al-Jabal from the waters drained from the western swamps. Where gravity was insufficient to force the swamp-water back into the Bahr al-Jabal, pumps would be powered by Sudd fuel converted into gas, the feasibility of which J. H. Wells had demonstrated at his experimental station at Shubra.[27] Inspired

---

[26] 'The Sudd Regions of the White Nile', p. 119.

[27] In 1920 John Wells revived a previous concession by the Sudan government to the Sudd Fuel Company to process sudd briquets from papyrus. Nothing came of this scheme because of the war, so the concession was transferred to Wells and his Sudan Cotton, Fuel, and Industrial Development Corporation, with Howard Spicer organizing a subscription of some £250,000. Lord Percy joined the board of directors in 1920, and Sir Henry Belfield was retained to advise on land acquisition in the Sudan. Wells envisaged a grandiose scheme of African development which required, however, that the Sudan government concede hundreds of square miles of territory in which fuel production, power plants, mining, fishing, trade, and indentured labour would be used. This scheme was much too ambitious for the cautious administrators in Khartoum who, to Well's fury, limited the concession to 50,000 feddans. Machinery was shipped to Lake No and a site selected for processing the sudd. The economic recession in England in 1921 shrivelled up available capital and the work was abandoned, leaving a pile of rusting machinery. Although Wells was a friend of Sir Lee Stack, the governor-general, the Sudan officials were suspicious of his connection with Willcocks, and were not about to encourage his doubtful cotton scheme when they were fighting to save the Sennar dam for cotton growing in the Gezira.

by Wells, Willcocks envisaged cutting off immense areas of the Sudd and replanting with fuel-producing plants of 'small wood' which were supposedly suited to the swamps. With lyrical confidence in this bizarre project, Willcocks finished his peroration:

The water is there and the fuel is there in quantities beyond the dreams of avarice. We have only to bring them together, and, as with the touch of a magician's wand, all the waters which Egypt and the Sudan will need for many and many a year will be there, renewing themselves as the seasons come round in their courses. Far from there being any waste, there will be nothing but economy. Not one cubic metre will be withdrawn from the existing supplies of the Nile; but these existing supplies will be added to in an ever increasing measure to meet the additional calls of the newly broken up lands.[28]

Three months later Willcocks had more to say about the Sudd in his lecture at the Egyptian Institute. Rather than a waster of water, the Sudd was in fact a beneficent reservoir.

The Sudd region of the White Nile, which has been cursed by hundreds, possibly thousands of travellers, and called by one 'an inhospitable waste of water', by another 'this desperate and forbidding region', and by a third 'a damp hell', is in reality one of the most wonderful reservoirs in the world . . . it is a veritable glacier at the head of the White Nile.

Willcocks claimed that when the Blue Nile flood failed, 'the Sudd reservoir saves the situation'.[29] Garstin had regarded the Sudd as a reservoir, but it was E. P. Shakerley who convinced Willcocks of this view in discussions with him in 1912. It was not, however, until John Wells came along with his Sudd fuel scheme that Willcocks saw how to extract the water of the swamps by gravity feed and pump drainage. By lowering the level of the Bahr al-Jabal and draining the swamps through regulators by gravity and sudd-fuelled pumps, he calculated that the Sudd would increase the flow of the White Nile by 7.5 billion m^3. Conversely, the regulators could be closed to retain the water in the Sudd when not required downstream. Willcocks was emphatic that any such Sudd waters conserved were to be 'reserved' for Egypt.

[28] 'The Sudd Regions of the White Nile', p. 119.
[29] 'The Sudd Reservoir', p. 148.

Willcocks's knowledge and understanding of Sudd hydraulics was superficial if not naïve. He grossly underestimated the amount of water actually in the Sudd, and his description of the effect of evaporation as 'moderate' has proved wrong. Nothing, of course, was mentioned about the effect on the inhabitants of draining the swamps, but in 1918 he can hardly be criticized for not taking their well-being into account. His Sudd scheme, however, had two interesting refinements. The first was a regulator at Tonga on the White Nile, just above its confluence with the Bahr al-Zaraf. The second was the construction of a regulator at Omdurman which, since the Sudd was controlled upstream, could be opened to allow excess water from the Blue Nile to pass off up the White for storage. Certainly he underestimated the expense of all these control projects.

Although Willcocks later fulminated that the Nile projects commission did not even take up the subject of his Sudd proposals during its hearings, his proposal to embank the Bahr al-Zaraf reappears in virtually every proposal for a Sudd canal in the 1920s, and even becomes part of A. D. Butcher's proposal for the Jonglei Diversion Canal in 1938. Of more lasting but wasteful importance was his dismissal of the Garstin cut as 'too expensive'. How much Willcocks was motivated by his personal enmity toward Garstin is impossible to discern, but his blunt rejection of Beresford's direct line was accepted without question by the engineers of the irrigation service during the inter-war years. Although they conducted numerous surveys in the Sudd for some nine other schemes, by the outbreak of the Second World War, astonishingly, no attempt at even a preliminary reconnaissance of the direct line had been undertaken.

While Willcocks marshalled his fifteen charges, orchestrated the nationalist press, and used the lecture platform to discredit MacDonald, the irrigation adviser was not about to let an eccentric old curmudgeon destroy his integrity, reputation, and career. His first line of defence was to prepare a public proposal for his plan for the development of the Nile basin by which he hoped to silence his critics. Using the available information collected by the irrigation service and collated by Hurst, he published *Nile Control* in 1920. His object was

to proclaim and defend his programme. His intention was to
overwhelm Willcocks by supportable evidence contrary to
that supplied by Kennedy. Nile Control was

A Statement of the Necessity for further Control of the Nile to
complete the Development of Egypt and develop a Certain Area in
the Sudan, with Particulars of the Physical Conditions to be considered and a Programme of the Engineering Works involved.[30]

MacDonald sought to defuse the Egyptian press and divert
the fears of politicians that his dams would deny Egypt its
'historic rights' to Nile water. He emphasized that the
prosperity of Egypt was his principal concern. 'How to make
the natural supply of water in the Nile meet the progressive
demands of agriculture at all seasons of the year has always
been the great problem facing Irrigation engineers in Egypt.'[31]
No Egyptian could quarrel with that objective. They could
not, however, accept, the means of achieving it. MacDonald
envisaged a series of regulators or dams throughout the Nile
basin, but not in Egypt, to conserve water in the Sudan and
the equatorial lakes to provide over-year storage or what later,
after the Second World War, became known as 'century
storage'. Although a detailed and complete plan to achieve
over-year storage was not produced until 1946, MacDonald
was the first to propose such a comprehensive concept for
control and the most effective means of achieving it. The
proposal for century storage in 1946 was based on half a
century of recorded measurements, but did not vary significantly
from MacDonald's plan in 1920, based on poorly recorded
readings from gauges in only part of the Nile basin over a
relatively short period of time, haphazardly preserved and just
recently collated by the physical department. Nevertheless,
MacDonald's principle of over-year storage was 'a prescient
and telling one' which remains the foundation of Nile
hydrology today, whether expressed by Hurst as century
storage or by General Rundall as a massive high dam at
Aswan.[32] In fact, MacDonald acknowledged that his concept
of over-year storage owed much to the recommendations of Sir

[30] Subtitle to MacDonald (1920).
[31] Ibid., p. xii.
[32] Tignor (1977, p. 193).

William Garstin, conceived not by flawed statistics but by the perspicacity of an acute observer.

The need to increase the agricultural yield of Egypt by means of more water was the direct result of the uninhibited growth of population. 'This demand is due to the pressure of the rapidly increasing population, which has about doubled itself in the last forty years, while the increase in crop area has by no means kept pace with this growth.'[33] The fact that Egyptian agriculture did not see significant expansion in the inter-war years, and certainly not enough to keep pace with the increase in population, is not because of Nile control but in spite of it. The problem MacDonald faced in 1920 remains today, only in a more acute form. The population of Egypt is conservatively estimated at 52 million and is expected to reach some 70 million by the end of the twentieth century. In 1986 the crop area of Egypt has continued to decline in proportion to the population, and this trend, with the subsequent decrease in per capita income, will remain irreversible without additional water.

As a first step to controlling the Nile, MacDonald argued the need for the speedy construction of dams on the White Nile at Jabal 'Auliya and on the Blue Nile at Sennar, the dams which had already been approved by the British and Egyptian governments. But MacDonald went further. He proposed dams at Lake Tana and Lake Albert in conjunction with the necessary Sudd canal. It was a bold and sweeping plan but it failed to win the approval of his critics. In fact, the publication of *Nile Control* proved a lightning rod in the storm of controversy over which rolled the thunder of Sir William Willcocks. *Nile Control* was MacDonald's defence. It was also, however, an official government document, published at Egyptian expense, which freed the press, politicians, and engineers from their dependence upon the technical and very personal charges levelled at MacDonald by Willcocks. The British government had first sought to defuse the controversy in its early stages by the appointment of the six-man committee in 1918. Willcocks had swiftly destroyed their credibility. The publication of *Nile Control*, however, had

---

[33] MacDonald (1920, p. 1).

refuelled Egyptian fears, which the British now hoped to assuage by the appointment of the Nile Projects Commission. The stage was set for the Nile duel.

Throughout the winter and spring of 1920 tension mounted in Egypt as the Nile duel between Sir William Willcocks and Sir Murdoch MacDonald began in the political arena of Cairo, before the international tribunal of Gebbie, Simpson, and Cory. They were given their charge by the Egyptian council of ministers on 10 January.

The Commission is requested to give to the Egyptian Government its opinion on the projects prepared by the Ministry of Public Works with a view to the further regulation of the Nile supply for the benefit of Egypt and the Sudan. In particular the Commission is requested:

(1) To examine and report upon the physical data on which the projects are based.
(2) To report upon the propriety of the manner in which, as a result of these projects, the increased supply of available water provided by them will be allocated at each stage of development between Egypt and the Sudan.
(3) To advise as to the apportionment of the costs of the proposed works and of this inquiry as between Egypt and the Sudan.[34]

The first item was, of course, to deal with the fifteen charges of Sir William Willcocks; the second and third had to do with the larger and more important question of future Nile development. These issues were, of course, of much greater importance than Willcocks's vendetta, but the very scope which they implied lacked the popular appeal of the spectacle of two of Britain's foremost hydrologists seeking to destroy one another in public. The Egyptians loved it.

Since Willcocks had agreed to appear before the commission only on condition that testimony be taken under oath and in public, a judicial member, G. Arthur W. Booth, was added in an ex officio capacity on 24 March. His report and opinion were deeply to influence the other members during their deliberations. By the end of February the commission with its support staff had assembled in Cairo, and on 2 March it set out for Khartoum with Sir William Willcocks, confident of victory, in tow. MacDonald himself remained sullenly in

[34] *Nile Projects Commission Report* (1920, p. 5).

Cairo, putting the finishing touches to *Nile Control* while plotting his next move to wreak vengeance on Willcocks and Kennedy.

The commission proceeded up the Nile, inspected the Esna barrage and the Aswan dam, and arrived at Khartoum on 8 March to meet the more timorous representatives of the irrigation officials of the Sudan branch. From Khartoum they visited the Nile gauges at Tamanit on the White Nile, at Soba on the Blue, and at the capital itself. Since the charges were based on the methods of measurement of discharges as well as recorded readings, the commission carefully studied both, checking the accuracy of gauges and investigating the records. They spent three days at Sennar, the site of the most controversial measurements. Thereafter they cruised up the White Nile on the steamer *Kassala* and into the Sudd via the Bahr al-Zaraf for 250 km until halted by aquatic vegetation obstructing the channel. They returned to the White Nile and proceeded westward to Lake No and the Bahr al-Ghazal, where again they were halted by sudd blocks. Returning to Lake No, they pressed up the Bahr al-Jabal to the limit of navigation near Rejaf, before making their way back to Khartoum and Cairo in early May.

During their absence the Egyptian government had published, at their request, in the *Official Journal* and the press, invitations to appear before the commission to anyone who wished to give public testimony. Beginning on 15 May, eleven public meetings were held during which evidence was taken under oath, principally from Willcocks and Kennedy. On 22 June a public meeting was held specifically to hear criticisms by the Egyptian committee of engineers led by the well-known Egyptian irrigation engineer, Abdullah Pasha Wahbi, to complement numerous informal meetings between the commissioners and Egyptian engineers. On 24 June the commission submitted an interim report before retiring to London to draft its final observations, which were submitted to the Egyptian council of ministers on 25 August 1920.

Two themes emerge from the months of investigations and the mountains of evidence. The first was the attempt by Willcocks and Kennedy to prove 'a conspiracy on Sir Murdoch MacDonald's part to attribute by fraud exaggerated discharges to the Blue and Main Niles in low years in order to bolster up the Gezira Irrigation Scheme, which was being criticized by Colonel Kennedy on the ground of insufficiency in low years of the Blue Nile water supply'.[35] The second theme was the effort by Willcocks and Kennedy to demonstrate that MacDonald had deliberately falsified and suppressed public documents. Although these two themes were inextricably intertwined, the first was substantive, the second the product of a tawdry vendetta. Of the fifteen charges, six were brought before the commission by Willcocks and seven by Kennedy. Many of the charges were repetitive, others overlapped between those of Willcocks and those of Kennedy. But the commission was not a court of law and did not view itself as such. It had no power to pass sentence, and indeed agreed not to be bound by the strict rules of the English law of evidence, thereby enabling Willcocks and Kennedy to submit evidence of alleged wrongdoing which would not have been admissible in an English court of law. Such evidence, however, was recorded in the official report of the commission, thereby ironically rendering it admissible when it was later used to MacDonald's advantage in the libel proceedings which followed the investigations of the commission.

The public sessions were characterized by acrimony, passion, obstinacy, and sanctimonious tedium. Willcocks stoutly insisted that MacDonald had falsified the records to give the impression that there was ample water in a low Blue Nile flood to meet all the requirements of Egypt with sufficient water remaining to irrigate 300,000 feddans in the Gezira. This judgement was based on the readings of the crucial nilometer at Sennar. Willcocks charged MacDonald with deliberately tampering with that gauge. When the commission arrived at Sennar, Willcocks had demanded that he measure the discharge in its presence. His measurements did not agree with either of the two official discharge tables for the low years of 1919 and 1920 as they had done in the low flood of 1914. He immediately jumped to the conclusion that the Sennar gauge had been intentionally dropped by 35 cm to give a false reading to support MacDonald's contention that there was

---

[35] 'Report and Opinion of Judge Booth', ibid. 19.

ample water for both Egypt and the Gezira even in low flood. The Sennar gauge which Willcocks measured was in fact a new one, erected in 1916 by an engineer of the ministry of public works, Mr Nasce. Willcocks had called for a level to be taken of the masonry steps of the new site and the old gauge a short distance away. To the surprise of the commissioners and the triumph of Willcocks, the level showed that indeed the new gauge was exactly 35 cm below the old—the implication being that the new gauge would show a greater volume of water than was in fact the case. Willcocks returned to Khartoum thoroughly convinced of the proof of MacDonald's fraud. He passed quickly down to Cairo, prepared to claim victory.

Upon returning to Cairo in May, the commission investigated the matter, inspecting the drawings of the new gauge and the sworn testimony of Mr Nasce. It subsequently transpired that the steps of the old nilometer ran from half-metre to half-metre and the marble markers did not come to the bottom of the step as they should. Nasce simply changed the steps from metre to metre and, by placing the marble markers at the bottom of the step, had to lower the gauge by 35 cm to be level with the markings on the old gauge. Willcocks's charge was summarily dismissed.

The second theme was the destruction of evidence by MacDonald. This was in reference to the 'lost' Blue Nile memorandum. This now famous memorandum was prepared by MacDonald on 19 February 1914 at the behest of the governor-general of the Sudan, Sir Reginald Wingate, in response to the request from Kennedy, then director of public works in the Sudan, for precise information as to the quantity of water in the Blue Nile. At that time Kennedy was erecting pumps at Wad al-Nau and expressed concern that, since the Nile flood was the lowest on record, it was questionable whether there would be sufficient water. The two-page memorandum with an accompanying letter was forwarded to Wingate's private secretary, Gilbert Clayton, on 25 February 1914. To MacDonald's embarrassment, neither he nor the ministry could find the original or even a copy. MacDonald had written in desperation to Wingate asking him to ransack his massive correspondence on the off-chance that he might have kept a copy. Wingate found nothing. It was probably the only document that Wingate had not preserved in his private files, which remain to this day an unholy collection of trivia and public documents of great importance. Willcocks, however, could do little better. Kennedy was able to produce only a copy of the second page of the Blue Nile memorandum. Nevertheless, both men thought this was sufficient evidence to condemn MacDonald, particularly when he himself could not produce the original. Since it could not be found, it must have been destroyed—and how but by MacDonald himself?

MacDonald fought back. A frantic staff at the ministry managed to uncover the postcards called 'Nile gauge readings' from Sennar in 1914. Throughout the Nile basin, readers would record the daily measurements of the nilometers on cards which were then posted to the ministry of public works in Cairo. The cards mailed from Sennar during the critical period from late January to mid-February 1914 were the source from which MacDonald compiled the Blue Nile memorandum, and upon which he based his assertion that, even in low years like 1914, there was ample water for the immediate needs of both Egypt and the Gezira. Willcocks branded the cards a forgery, hastily concocted by MacDonald to cover up the supposedly damaging information contained in the Blue Nile memorandum which he presumably had destroyed. MacDonald marshalled a parade of witnesses from the ministry to swear on oath that the cards were genuine. Willcocks retorted that the cards themselves were 'not honest-looking postcards' and dismissed the testimony of the witnesses as 'well-drilled'.[36] This denunciation made little impression on the commissioners or Judge Booth. They simply refused to believe that all of the numerous individuals who had handled or who had seen the postcards would be prepared to perjure themselves, no matter how 'well-drilled'. Willcocks seemed to agree, for despite questions from the commissioners he steadfastly refused to accuse the witnesses as 'liars', only referring to them as 'government officials'. Nowhere does his obsession to 'get' MacDonald and only MacDonald appear more transparent than in his stubborn refusal to implicate anyone else.

[36] 'Report and Opinion of Judge Booth', ibid. 17.

During this exchange Kennedy was less than helpful. He had been able to produce only the second page of the Blue Nile memorandum. Suddenly, the suspicion shifted from MacDonald to Kennedy: could he be the forger, particularly when he arrogantly told the commission that he was 'not putting all his cards on the table' when asked to produce the first page and covering letter?[37] He never did find those cards, and the commission could only conclude in the face of the 'Nile gauge readings' and the sworn testimony of their validity by numerous witnesses that the ministry had acted in good faith. MacDonald was cleared; the case of Willcocks and Kennedy collapsed.

During their investigations it became increasingly clear to the commissioners that Willcocks and Kennedy were out to smear MacDonald. Neither was prepared to charge the ministry with some grand conspiracy; both maintained that MacDonald and only MacDonald was the culprit. The picture of Sir Murdoch MacDonald manufacturing a host of worn postcards with false information in the dead of night and substituting them for the originals may have been Willcocks's fantasy but, if so, it was a bizarre one and certainly not in keeping with MacDonald's personality. How MacDonald could have concocted such extensive—and clumsy—forgeries without the knowledge of others in the ministry defies imagination, as it did for Judge Booth and the commissioners.

He [Willcocks] constantly insists that Sir Murdoch MacDonald, and Sir Murdoch MacDonald only, is guilty, but it is materially impossible that Sir Murdoch MacDonald should have committed these pretended forgeries and frauds without the assistance and connivance of a larger number of officials, high and low, and with the knowledge, almost certainly, of a great many other people. Yet not one single witness comes forward against him or gives him away when called in his favour. If the charges were well founded, how many anonymous letters or offers of assistance would not Sir William Willcocks, to say nothing of the Commissioners, have received? But Sir William has never even hinted that he has received inside information which he cannot use, and it is to be supposed that he would have done this in his books if anything of the kind had occurred.[38]

[37] Ibid. 14.
[38] Ibid. 17.

On 24 June the commission unanimously informed the president of the council of ministers in their interim report that:

After careful consideration of all the evidence we are of the opinion that there had been no falsification or intentional suppression of records nor any fraudulent manipulation of data or gauges by Sir Murdoch MacDonald or by anyone else.[39]

During the hearings and subsequently during the trial of Willcocks for libel and criminal slander, the British establishment in Egypt and at home rallied to support MacDonald. He was, after all, one of them, despite the fact that his education had been practical, learned on the job rather than in Britain's finest schools of engineering. He was popular, charming, a delightful dinner guest. Moreover, MacDonald was not on trial alone; so too was the British administration in Egypt. Outwardly suspicious, inwardly hostile, the Egyptian nationalists and even many moderate Egyptians who had co-operated with the British perceived the Nile duel as Britain on trial. This vulgar dispute was the very manifestation of all that the Egyptians believed, real or imagined, about the perfidy of British rule. If the charges by Willcocks could be substantiated, not only would MacDonald be guilty of a misplaced trust but so too would his countrymen.

The need to clear MacDonald probably influenced the European justices of the consular court in which the libel trial was to be held more than the commissioners, for they were members of that establishment, a small ruling minority in a populous country. The determination to support MacDonald seemed ironically all the more important since many were aware of MacDonald's inattention to record-keeping and sloppy management at the ministry. Such rumours did not encourage any from the British community to question the less than meticulous compilation and maintenance of Nile water measurements. Hurst at the physical department remained discreetly silent. In fact the very savagery of Willcocks's attack convinced cooler but informed heads to keep their own counsel. Indeed, if Willcocks had not been the victim of his own temperament, he might well have won over

[39] 'Report and Opinion of Judge Booth', ibid. 5.

the sympathies of those who regarded MacDonald as too clever by half.

Vindicated by the commission, Sir Murdoch MacDonald sought his own personal revenge. Armed with the final report of the Nile Commission he charged both Willcocks and Kennedy with wilful criminal libel and sedition before the supreme consular court of Egypt in the autumn of 1920. Before the trial actually began in January 1921, Kennedy fled into exile in France, where he died at Saint-Servan-sur-Mer four years later at the age of 51. Cory, who was called to testify later, lamented that 'no act in my life has been more distasteful' than to condemn Sir William Willcocks, whom he greatly admired.[40] Willcocks was found guilty of defamatory libel against MacDonald and sentenced. In consideration of his age, but more likely because no one in the British community wanted to see one of their distinguished countrymen, no matter how difficult, being sent to an Egyptian prison, he was placed on probation for a year, and was allowed to leave Egypt a few months later on condition that he would not repeat his libels elsewhere. Despite the injunction of the court the irrepressible Willcocks could not contain himself for ever, and he used the occasion of presenting a seemingly innocuous paper 'Egyptian Irrigation and Public Health', at the Egyptian Institute on 11 April 1927 to criticize MacDonald and *Nile Control*. Few in the audience were interested in a quarrel which had long outlived its interest.[41] With the exception of this foray into forbidden territory, Sir William Willcocks played no further role in Nile development and had little influence on subsequent Nile projects. He spent the rest of his life in the East, mostly in Egypt in seeming penance, conducting an evangelical mission during which he translated the whole of the New Testament into Egyptian colloquial Arabic and unsuccessfully sought to convert misguided Muslims into true Christians. His death at the age of 80 in Cairo on 28 July 1932 was undoubtedly a relief to himself, the British, and the Egyptians.

MacDonald did not remain long in Cairo to savour his victory. Although completely cleared of all charges by the

[40] Smythe (1920, p. 615).
[41] Willcocks (1927).

commission and vindicated in the courts, his position as adviser to the ministry of public works had been hopelessly compromised by the unseemly duel with Willcocks. He resigned from the Egyptian government a few months after the trial to become the Liberal Member of Parliament for Inverness in 1922, a seat he held until 1950 when he returned as the oldest member of the House of Commons. During these halcyon years he was assiduous in his pursuit of the welfare of the Highlands in public life, where his charisma and eloquence returned him to Parliament through the vicissitudes of changing politics, while amassing a fortune through his highly successful consulting engineering firm MacDonald and MacCorquadale (later Sir Murdoch MacDonald and Partners). In Egypt, however, the post of adviser to the ministry fell into abeyance and was never revived, with disastrous results for the hydrological development of the Nile valley.

Willcocks's scurrilous charges, the abortive six-man committee, the appointment of the Nile projects commission, and the subsequent trial of Willcocks provided continuous encouragement for the conviction of the Egyptian press, the nationalists, and the politicians of the maladministration of Egypt by Britain. The damage which Willcocks had brought upon the work of British officials was out of all proportion to his charges or their refutation. By the time the report of the commission was made public and the results of the Willcocks trial was known, the damage to the British image in Egypt had been done. MacDonald's resignation appeared to the Egyptians as a symbol of the end of British hegemony over Nile planning. Hitherto the British high commissioner had, through the British adviser, the power to direct irrigation projects over most of the Nile basin. Co-operation between the British residency in Cairo and the adviser at the ministry had reached its zenith during the Cromer–Garstin era and might have been emulated by Kennedy and MacDonald but for the war. It was not, and the vacuum for leadership, political as well as technical, seriously compromised the design and construction of a chain of major engineering works over thousands of kilometres of the Nile valley.

Although Sir Murdoch MacDonald wrote *Nile Control* as his defence against Willcocks, it was also a plan, no matter how incomplete, for the development of the Nile basin. Given the publicity accompanying the campaign against MacDonald, it is not surprising that Egyptians flocked to obtain copies of MacDonald's defence. The initial printing was sold out within six months, a rather extraordinary sale for a government report laden with technical data and tables quite unintelligible to the majority of readers, British or Egyptian. A second edition thus followed in 1921. It contained only minor changes of no substantive importance. *Nile Control* reads as if it were prepared in haste, pieced together in a style devoid of elegance, undoubtedly the product of numerous quickly conceived memoranda from the dungeons of the ministry of public works, based on data collected by the irrigation department and computations by Hurst and his colleagues at the physical department. MacDonald designed his defence to mollify his critics in Egypt, but his projects for the regulation of the Nile made less comforting reading for the Egyptians. Nevertheless, the Nile projects commission approved and sanctioned the dams at Sennar and Jabal 'Auliya and the Nag Hammadi barrage. In addition they supported a second regulator on the Blue Nile, presumably at Lake Tana, and the excavation of a Sudd canal in conjunction with a dam and reservoir at Lake Albert.

At this point the unanimity of the commission collapsed. Although approving of MacDonald's projects, the commissioners could not agree on who should derive their benefits, the additional water created by those regulators. In the end the commission failed to resolve its second and its most critical charge, thereby leaving the division of the Nile waters between Egypt and the Sudan in abeyance. The two British commissioners accepted the fundamental argument advanced by the Egyptians to justify their demands for Nile water. Throughout the centuries Egypt had established its claim to the Nile waters by its historic use, from which derived its 'rights'. In 1920 the British commissioners defined those rights in terms of land under cultivation, not in terms of the volume of water used to irrigate them. Thus the historic rights were easily defined as the amount of feddans currently under cultivation in Egypt, 5 400 000 feddans, while the Sudan was awarded the arbitrary figure of 300 000 feddans for the Gezira plus an additional 100 000 feddans for pump schemes. But to allocate water on the basis of land currently under cultivation was to ignore the future. The approval of projects to conserve water and then the refusal to make any attempt to provide principles, let alone proportions, by which the water should be shared was a tragic act of cowardice which crippled Nile development for a decade. To limit the growth of irrigation in the Sudan to 300 000 feddans was to deny the future to that land struggling to embark upon systematic economic development. Lord Allenby foolishly accepted the eagerness of his countrymen on the commission to retreat from any attempt at future allocation and supported their limit on Sudan development, an error he was later deeply to regret.[42]

Without some guide-lines for allocating the spoils, it was unlikely that Britain and Egypt would agree to the construction of regulators, or the future use of water, and Nile hydrology would thus be reduced to the collection of measurements. The cloaking of this timidity in the garb of realism was perhaps the consequence of Britain's declining authority in the Nile valley and the mounting pressures against British administration in Egypt. The Nile duel had demonstrated this situation; but it did not absolve the British commissioners from at least adopting some precepts for the future division of the Nile waters, regardless of inconvenience to their countrymen in Egypt, and regardless too of their manifest lack of interest in the prosperity of the Sudanese. Mr Gebbie and Dr Simpson do not appear to have been fully aware of the consequences of their appeasement, unlike the American, H. T. Cory. He understood exactly what the commission had not done—'the danger of the Sudan losing now a good opportunity of further development in the near future without prejudice to Egypt'.[43]

Cory acknowledged that reliable data were only available for the past twelve or at most twenty years, but thought that this restriction should not inhibit the commission from establishing guide-lines by which future allocations could be made. Indeed, the commissioners had been specifically charged to do so. Moreover, any 'allocation of water in an

---

[42] 'Report on the Second and Third Terms of Reference by the President and Dr. Simpson', by H. T. Cory, in *Nile Projects Commission Report* (1920, pp. 57–8).
[43] Ibid. 59.

equitable manner requires first ascertaining a rule or principle of general application'.[44] Cory sought a principle, not from the specious doctrine of riparian ownership—or, as the Egyptians would argue, 'first in time, first in right'—nor even on the basis of the 'population of the moment', but from the 'great truths' of the holy Qur'an.[45] Quoting from the Qur'an, Cory argued that water was a public trust to be 'administered in the interests of the trust, and accordingly with due regard to the eventual rights of generations yet unborn.'[46] From this principle it logically followed that 'the arable lands unwatered but irrigable belonging to different proprietors, including the "original appropriator", enjoy an equitable right to an adequate share of the unappropriated stream'. Thus, whether maxims of the Qur'an or occidental experience are cited, a river or stream must be considered, not as private property, but as 'a constituent element of the public domain'.[47]

Acting on this principle, Cory first of all accepted the 'vested rights' of Egypt and the Sudan to irrigate 5 400 000 and 400 000 feddans consuming 40 and 1.5 billion m^3 respectively. But Cory went further and proposed that 'the excess water over and above such vested rights should be divided equally between Egypt and the Sudan'. The application of the Cory award to the accepted average annual flow of the Nile of 84 billion m^3 would have resulted in a volume of water for the Sudan of nearly 23 billion m^3, a far cry from the amount of water required to irrigate 400 000 feddans acknowledged by the British commissioners.[48] Cory also made reference to the MacDonald projects, about which there had been no disagreement, and to the Sudd canal. Neither hydrologists nor politicians would quarrel with the construction of these

---

[44] Ibid. 65.   [45] Ibid. 66–8.   [46] Ibid. 67.   [47] Ibid.

[48] Ibid. 77. In his minority report, Cory calculated the Sudan's usage at 1.8 billion m^3 at Khartoum, which was equivalent to 1.5 billion m^3 at Aswan. Since Egyptian water needs were measured at Aswan, consistency should be sought by measuring the Sudan's share at Aswan. The total average annual flow of the Nile has been officially accepted as 84 billion m^3 as measured at Aswan 1900–1959 and confirmed in the Nile Waters Agreement 1959. The Sudan's share of the established flow, according to the Cory minority report, would have been 22.75 billion m^3 (1.5 billion m^3 plus half the additional water—total flow minus the established rights of Egypt and the Sudan or 84 billion m^3 minus 41.5 billion m^3—to equal 22.75 billion m^3 for the Sudan). The Nile Waters Agreement of 1959 in fact allocated only 18.5 billion m^3 to the Sudan.

engineering works, but Cory had no use for Willcocks's grand view of the Sudd as a great reservoir of stored water exposed to 'excessive losses both due to evaporation and plant transpiration'. Garstin had foreseen such losses; MacDonald had reinforced this opinion. Cory concurred: 'The only really effective treatment of the Sudd region is to avoid it altogether. Consequently the programme set forth in *Nile Control* seems the only possible one . . . '.[49]

That Cory's perceptions, let alone his principle, were not employed to their fullest in future negotiations between Britain and Egypt over the distribution of the Nile waters is not surprising. The Cory award was regarded by the Egyptians with open hostility. The reaction of the Sudanese was too inchoate to be observed as public opinion. To the British, Cory's logic was untempered by political realities in the Nile valley; his recommendations constituted an embarrassment. At a time when Britain was seeking to deflect Egyptian intransigence, and in later years, when Britain sought to reach an agreement over the Nile waters with Egypt, any use of the Cory award would be guaranteed to disrupt any negotiations. The British in the Sudan may have begun to view themselves as the stewards for the Sudanese and the trustees of their patrimony, but this comforting justification for British administration in the Sudan was not shared in London, where the negotiators were not prepared to sacrifice Britain's national interests by depriving Egypt of her perceived historic rights to water. The Sudanese took a different view. After their flirtations with Egyptian appeals to the unity of the Nile valley in the years before independence, they were reminded by their British irrigation advisers of the Cory award. To the dismay of the Egyptians, the Sudanese thereafter argued for an amount of water allocated on the basis of Cory's principle of equal shares of any additional water.

[49] Ibid. 70.

5

The Years of Indecision, 1920–1946

> For success in this field the essential factors are competent
> technical direction backed by a consistent policy subject
> neither to political vagaries nor to the transient vicissitudes
> of finance. It is something of an anomaly that these
> conditions which were present in the days when Egypt
> was bankrupt have been lost in times of prosperity.
>
> R. M. MacGregor, 10 December 1945

THE resignation of Sir Murdoch MacDonald in 1921, combined with the political upheavals in Egypt following the war, left the future planning of the Nile in total disarray. MacDonald's position as adviser to the ministry of public works was never again filled, and upon the independence of Egypt in 1922 the British high commissioner in Cairo could no longer play the political and financial role of Cromer, Gorst, or Kitchener. Their successors became bogged down in a swamp of disputations and frustrating negotiations between Britain and Egypt over their own relations and the role each was to play in the Sudan. British power to intervene at the Egyptian ministries was emasculated.

The war had severely strained Anglo-Egyptian relations while at the same time dramatically demonstrating Egypt's importance to Britain's imperial strategy. In 1914 Britain had declared a protectorate over Egypt to ensure its control of Suez and the eastern Mediterranean, gilding the bitter pill with sweet promises to bear the burden of defence and independence for Egypt after victory. Egyptians were mistreated in the name of war. The *fallahin* were conscripted into the Labour Corps; the urban population was forced to cope with inflation, the housing of British troops, and a variety of indignities. These abuses might have been suffered in silence if the British had fulfilled their promise of independence at the end of war. They did not. Despite the advice of Sir Reginald Wingate, British high commissioner, that it should be conciliatory to the demands of the Egyptian nationalists led by Sa'd Zaghlul, the British government refused to abandon the protectorate. Violence erupted; the depth of Egyptian hostility was characterized by the support for the anti-British riots of virtually every class in Egypt—the *fallahin*, the *effendia*, and even the Copts. As a widely popular side-show to the main political event, the unseemly Nile duel between Sir William Willcocks and Sir Murdoch MacDonald continued to play before the Egyptian public to further discredit British administration. In any case the moral basis of British rule was destroyed; the development of the Nile waters was left without the men or the agency to give it direction.

Although the Egyptian revolution had failed to drive the British from Egypt, it had demonstrated that relations between the two could no longer be those of a protectorate. Hoping to discover a way out of the desert of British policy in Egypt, the government sent Lord Milner, the colonial secretary, to Cairo to investigate the political situation in Egypt and to make recommendations for constitutional development. His report, presented in 1921, advocated the end of British administrative control in return for a treaty defining their relations, while at the same time encouraging the Anglo-Egyptian administration in the Sudan to become ever more British. In the Sudan the sentiments of the Milner report may have gratified those British officials seeking more independent action, but they eroded any interest in co-operation with Egypt over Nile development beyond those proposals approved by the Nile projects commission. Indeed, British administrators in the Sudan were most uneasy about the whole question of the Nile waters. They were tired of the wrangling over water issues which the Nile projects commission was supposed to have settled and had not. There was still no agreement as to the principles, let alone the amounts, by which future stored water in the Nile was to be shared. To this end further negotiations would clearly have to be undertaken, but it was not to be in the immediate future. British officials in Khartoum were preoccupied with events in the Sudan and apprehensive of Egyptian intentions; they were thus reluctant to press for a resolution of the Nile waters question when their energies were fully absorbed with untangling the confused financing of the Sennar dam, its construction, and the opening of the Gezira for cultivation.

Thus in 1921 there appeared few reasons to encourage, and many not to insist upon, another British adviser at the ministry. None was appointed, and this absence appeared just a logical step in the administrative withdrawal predicated by the end of the protectorate. On 28 February 1922 the British government reluctantly declared Egypt a sovereign State, but reserved four issues for further negotiation and agreement: security, defence, foreign interests, and the Sudan. The unilateral declaration of independence for Egypt, however, removed at a stroke the powers of the British high commissioner for the political and financial direction of Nile development at a time when the Egyptian irrigation service was left without anyone to direct the planning and execution of a chain of major engineering works embracing thousands of kilometres of the Nile.

This did not mean that the British were unwilling to consider some alternative to the British adviser, or some administrative agency which could perform this function. Indeed, H. T. Cory had recommended an 'adjudication board' in his minority report to the Nile projects commission. He suggested a board of three members, one from the Egyptian ministry of public works, a representative of the Sudan government, and a neutral chairman, selected jointly by the two governments but specifically neither Egyptian, Sudanese, nor English. The board would have powers over all questions and disputes arising out of water rights, the division of water, and the maintenance and operation of conservancy projects, though whether outside Egypt and the Sudan Cory did not elaborate. As with his principles for sharing the Nile waters, nothing come of this proposal, but the idea did not die.

In 1923 C. E. Dupuis, himself a former inspector-general of irrigation for the Sudan and an adviser to the ministry, suggested a 'board of control' to oversee the construction and operation of works for the interest of Egypt and the Sudan. He was specifically concerned about the future supervision of the construction of the Jabal 'Auliya and Sennar dams, but his board as constituted would have had wide powers to settle disputes over the distribution of water. He was politely ignored in both Cairo and Khartoum, and so he recommended upon his retirement from the irrigation service that the Sudan should organize its own department of irrigation. In the aftermath of the assassination of Sir Lee Stack in 1924, British officials in Khartoum sought to act on Dupuis's suggestion as another manifestation of their intention to sever all ties with Egypt. They summarily instructed R. M. MacGregor to set up a department forthwith. MacGregor, like so many other British engineers, had come to the Sudan from India in 1923 as the irrigation adviser, to provide independent advice on irrigation uninfluenced by the view of British engineers in the Egyptian service. Within the year he had established the structure for an organization that would meet the immediate administrative requirements for irrigation in the Sudan.

In fact, by 1925 there was a desperate local need for an administrative unit to manage the irrigation demands of the Gezira scheme. Difficulties had arisen over the flow of water through the distributary canals in the Gezira and over watering at night to reduce loss by the heat of day-time evaporation. W. D. Roberts, then the inspector-general of the Egyptian irrigation service for the Sudan, worked with MacGregor to resolve the former problem, while A. D. Butcher was sent from Cairo to devise successful means for night operations. MacGregor remained head of department as well as irrigation adviser until 1934, and during his tenure the embryonic irrigation department at Wad Medani was totally preoccupied, at first with the operation and expansion of the Gezira and later with the Jabal 'Auliya dam and irrigation in the Gash delta. With few personnel and little direction, the department played no role in Nile development until after the Second World War, when it was called upon to extend its activities to the upper Nile. The only link between the Sudan and the Egyptian irrigation services was MacGregor; in his capacity as irrigation adviser, he was to keep the Sudan government informed of the intentions of the Egyptian irrigation service in the Sudan, but in Khartoum this function was never regarded as a full-time job.[1]

[1] 'The Sudan Irrigation Department', SID Memorandum No. 1, Terms of Service Commission 1950, SAD 495/2/2.

In 1927 the subject of a joint commission for the Nile waters was once again raised by the minister of public works. He proposed a board that in fact would be only a committee within the ministry presided over by the under-secretary. It appears to have been an administrative device within the ministry to preserve control of the Sennar dam by Egypt rather than the Sudan government. Others, however, regarded it as an attempt to recreate the position of adviser to the ministry. A British counter-proposal by P. S. Scrivener, for an advisory board with a controller-general whose powers were reduced to moral persuasion, was stillborn.

In July 1931 the idea of an authority to supervise Nile water development re-emerged on a British initiative following the impetus given to development by the Nile Waters Agreement of 1929. The board was to be advisory, and to concern itself with the larger questions of Nile control and not just with those of Egyptian irrigation. The purpose of this administrative mechanism was to mitigate the inevitable decline of British influence in the ministry by the gradual replacement of British engineers by Egyptians. It, too, never evolved beyond the draft stage, largely for the same reason that any such commission would, if it were worth creating, erode the authority of the minister and thereby of the Egyptian government.

The following year Butcher proposed yet another Nile control board. His motives were similar to those which had spawned the advisory board the previous year. Among the community of British hydrologists in Egypt there was growing concern about the ability of the ministry to mobilize the technological skills required for Nile development in the face of the imminent retirement of British officials. Again, nothing came of this proposal, but the problem of leadership in Nile development remained. Some wanted to resolve the difficulty by simply recreating the post of British adviser to the ministry. Today the proposition appears politically naïve, no matter how technologically sound.

The proposal of this latter, draconian solution prompted numerous efforts to fill the vacuum at Cairo after the signing of the Nile Waters Agreement in 1929 had improved the climate for planning for the Nile basin water needs. In May the Egyptian government appointed Butcher director-general, southern White Nile. His duty was to act as a liaison officer with the irrigation adviser to the Sudan government, MacGregor; they did indeed confer informally on the operation of the Sennar dam, but not about conservancy projects on the upper Nile. The arrival of Sir Stewart Symes, who sought to streamline the administration, and the necessity of balancing the budget in the depths of the Depression resulted in a significant reorganization of the irrigation department. Hitherto the posts of director of irrigation and irrigation adviser had been held simultaneously by MacGregor. They were now separated. The chief engineer became the director, and the irrigation adviser moved to Khartoum where, to the dismay of MacGregor, the position continued to be half-time. This was a mistake. Having ceased to be director of irrigation, MacGregor soon lost contact with Sudan affairs, which in turn diminished any influence he might have had upon Nile development. The informal co-operation between MacGregor and Butcher gradually dwindled, and three years later MacGregor resigned in frustration. At that time an effort was made to revive the position by the appointment of A. N. M. Robertson as a full-time adviser resident in Wad Medani, but the post never regained its former status, and was abolished in 1940. Robertson appears to have had little interest in Nile water planning. Butcher resigned in 1939 and his position as director-general, southern White Nile, lapsed. By 1940 there was 'no machinery through which contact can be made or influence exerted where British or Sudan irrigation interests touch those of Egypt'.[2]

The failure to devise, let alone agree upon, an administrative agency for Nile control to replace the adviser was as much the product of Anglo-Egyptian relations during the inter-war years as a symbol of it. These relations did not improve dramatically after the abolition of the protectorate. After 1922 the Sudan emerged as a serious issue between Britain and Egypt in which water played a central role. Hitherto Egypt had always bowed to British advice concerning the hydrologically strategic lands south of Aswan, but now, as an independent

[2] R. M. MacGregor, 'The Upper Nile Irrigation Projects', 10 Dec. 1945, p. 8, SAD 589/14/48.

State and joint ruler of the condominium, Egyptian opinion about that vast land astride the Nile could no longer be summarily dismissed. British officials had always sought to diminish Egyptian influence in the Sudan. After the Milner report and the abolition of the protectorate they quietly increased their efforts. This was not an easy task. The Sudan government was still dependent upon the Egyptian army to garrison the country. If it were withdrawn, who would pay for an alternative force, presumably Sudanese? The British treasury flatly refused to finance an army for the Sudan. Water was equally important. The hydrological passions of 1920 had not cooled, and in fact they became more intense as work resumed on the Gezira scheme and the development of a Nile valley plan remained in abeyance. The very failure to reach an agreement over the Nile waters increased Egyptian fears that Britain in the Sudan would use its position to disrupt Egypt's historic rights to the water.

Upon the declaration of independence for Egypt, the British government had specifically reserved for further agreement the status of the Sudan—the 'Sudan question'. The Egyptians argued that its sovereign rights in the Sudan should be recognized, and King Fu'ad even proclaimed himself 'king of Egypt and the Sudan' in a draft of the new constitution for Egypt. These words in effect rendered the Sudan an Egyptian possession, a status that the British government refused to accept. Britain threatened force, the Egyptians capitulated, and the constitutional monarchy was proclaimed on 19 April 1923 wih no reference to Egyptian sovereignty in the Sudan. Like the question of the Nile waters, the future of the Sudan remained in abeyance against a rising tide of intransigent Egyptian nationalism.

In January 1924 Sa'd Zaghlul and his Wafd party won an overwhelming victory under the new Egyptian constitution. During his campaign and subsequently in Parliament, Zaghlul had demanded concessions in the Sudan, concessions which even the newly elected Labour party and its prime minister and foreign minister, Ramsay MacDonald, was reluctant to concede, despite MacDonald's personal sympathies with Egyptian aspirations. Any hope by MacDonald of reaching an agreement with Zaghlul dissipated in the summer of 1924 before the anti-British agitation of the White Flag League in Khartoum and more serious demonstrations by the Egyptian army's railway battalion at 'Atbara and the Sudanese cadets of the Khartoum military school in August. The leader of the White Flag League, 'Ali 'Abd al-Latif, was arrested and the demonstrations in 'Atbara and Khartoum were firmly suppressed, but the tension in Egypt and Khartoum did not lessen. Indeed, the fall of MacDonald's Labour government and the return of the Conservatives under Stanley Baldwin as prime minister and Austin Chamberlain as foreign minister strengthened British determination for 'drastic action'. By mid-November the British government had decided to remove the Egyptian army from the Sudan in an attempt to resolve the Sudan Question. A plausible excuse remained to be found for such high-handed and unilateral action. Fate soon provided it.

On 19 November 1924 a group of Egyptian extremists assassinated the governor-general of the Sudan, Sir Lee Stack, in Cairo. 'The months of pent-up frustration in Britain, Egypt, and especially in the Sudan now burst forth with tragic consequences.'[3] An ultimatum was swiftly delivered to Sa'd Zaghlul by Lord Allenby insisting upon an apology, justice for the assassins, a fine of £E500 000, the withdrawal of the Egyptian army from the Sudan, and an increase in the 'area to be irrigated in the Gezira from 300 000 feddans to an unlimited figure as need may arise', agreement with British wishes concerning foreign interests in Egypt, and the suppression of political demonstrations.[4] Zaghlul rejected the ultimatum and resigned, but his successor, Ahmad Ziwar Pasha, faced by British bayonets, agreed to Allenby's demands, protesting, however, about the increase of irrigation in the Gezira.

Deprived of influence in the Sudan and humiliated in Cairo, Egypt's feeling concerning the Nile waters can be gauged by the intense fear with which unlimited irrigation for the Gezira was viewed in Egypt. Foreign reaction to the Gezira clause was equally critical. By and large the major powers could understand the other demands as the price for Stack's assassination; but Allenby's demand for unlimited irrigation

---

[3] Daly (1986, p. 306).   [4] Ibid. 307.

in the Sudan, to compete with Egyptian cotton and threaten the Nile waters, appeared grossly opportunistic, kicking the Egyptians needlessly when they were down. The British foreign office made no secret that it was upset by the Gezira clause. Chamberlain was particularly annoyed. Allenby himself was soon anxious to cover himself in the face of mounting criticism. He proposed an 'impartial commission' to determine the amount of irrigated land permitted to the Sudan after the completion of the Sennar dam, the way in which surplus water would be distributed, and the means by which the Sudan would be held accountable for the commission's recommendations. The commission would be appointed by agreement of the British and Egyptian Governments, and until its report was accepted the Sudan would abide by the 300 000-feddan limit fixed by the Nile projects commission.[5]

Ziwar Pasha demurred. The Egyptians regarded Allenby's proposed commission as an ill-disguised attempt to reassert British control at the ministry of public works. Allenby viewed the commission as a face-saving device for himself as well as for the Egyptians to break the deadlock over Nile waters. He bluntly informed Ziwar that, unless he accepted the proposed commission, the Sudan government would assume complete freedom to determine its limitations of irrigation. Ziwar capitulated on 17 December, being able only to retain a pledge that the president would not be British, according to the suggestion by Cory in his recommendation for an adjudication board. J. J. Canter Cremers, a Dutch engineer, agreed to chair the Nile commission. Several Americans were suggested, but Allenby argued that Americans were not sufficiently distinguishable from Englishmen. Perhaps he had forgotten Cory. R. M. MacGregor, the irrigation adviser to the Sudan government, and 'Abd al-Hamid Pasha Sulayman, the under-secretary at the ministry of public works, represented the Sudan and the Egyptian governments respectively.

The commission began its deliberations in the spring, and from the beginning its success depended upon the close personal relationship between MacGregor and 'Abd al-Hamid. Cremers himself soon became ill and died in June

---

[5] For correspondence during Nov. and Dec. 1924 between Allenby and the Foreign Office concerning this proposed commission, see FO 371/100045–7.

1925, and thereafter discussions lapsed until taken up again informally by MacGregor and 'Abd al-Hamid in February 1926. Since both had virtually identical views, an agreement was amicably and quickly completed, a remarkable event in the history of Nile waters negotiations.

'Abd al-Hamid and MacGregor both worked from the same principle, the sanctity of the historic and established rights of Egypt, by which concurrence on technical matters logically followed. This was an important principle and a fundamental one, upon which Egypt has always based its claims to Nile water. The report was submitted to the two governments in March, the object being to devise a 'practical working arrangement which would respect the needs of established irrigation while permitting such programmes of extension as might be feasible under present conditions and those of the near future, without at the same time compromising in any way the possibilities of the more distant future'.[6] In other words, Egypt's historic and established rights would be recognized while at the same time the future needs of Egypt and the Sudan would be accommodated. Both 'Abd al-Hamid and MacGregor insisted that the question of the Nile waters should be subject to regular review, but that any such review should begin on the accepted principle that the historic rights would be acknowledged first. They had been specifically requested not to attempt an ultimate proportion by which Nile waters might be divided between Egypt and the Sudan. Thus they were required to achieve a division of the Nile waters by manipulation rather than principle. They therefore approached the allocation of water from a different perspective, by fixing the dates by which the Nile flows would be available for each country. Thus Egypt would be entitled to the natural flow of the Nile (except for pump schemes in the Sudan) from 19 January until 15 July. Thereafter, the Gezira canal would draw from the Blue Nile on a sliding scale, permitting the Sennar reservoir to fill by November. This was a floating timetable, not a principle.

By adopting the principle of established rights and then applying what became known as 'working arrangements',

[6] R. M. MacGregor and Abdel Hamid Suleiman (1926), *Nile Commission Report*, para. 21, SAD 500/3/28.

MacGregor and 'Abd al-Hamid avoided the adversarial positions taken up from the start in Anglo-Egyptian water negotiations in the past, and by so doing they were able to avoid the fundamental issue of the shares each country would receive in the future. At least MacGregor and 'Abd al-Hamid refused to employ as a principle the proportion of irrigated feddans cultivated by each country, as had the Nile projects commission. By adopting established rights as a first principle and then using technical adjustments to take account of need, the emotional issues could be ignored so long as the water was available to those who could not understand the necessary arithmetic. By combining the principle of established rights with the working arrangements to manipulate water to meet Egypt's needs during the period from January to July, the Egyptians received what they required without depriving the Sudanese of necessary water. MacDonald had, in effect, proposed the same principle in *Nile Control* when he accepted the fact of Egypt's established rights while he then sought to increase by storage for the period from January to July. His thinking, however, had gone one step further than that of the Nile commission. Like Garstin, he foresaw that the Nile reservoirs could provide water for over-year storage as well as water for the period from January to July. MacGregor and 'Abd al-Hamid had never intended to deal with that concept, seeking instead an easier but transient solution by protecting established rights and promising water for the first half of the year by working arrangements.

The *Report of the Nile Projects Commission* of 1926 was a means to regulate Nile flows, not a plan for Nile development. It might make Nile control possible, but it scrupulously avoided any proposals for regulators or conservancy projects. Thereafter the report was channelled into the larger and more dangerous currents of the rocky Anglo-Egyptian negotiations to resolve the 'reserved' points included in the British declaration of independence for Egypt in 1922. The death of Sa'd Zaghlul in August 1927 removed one of the principal protagonists in the search for a treaty, but the continued political instability in Egypt combined with British interference protracted negotiations characterized by frustration, suspicion, and dreary diplomatic manœuvres. Any hope of acting on the

'Abd al-Hamid–MacGregor report seemed doomed by the changes of government in Egypt, until King Fu'ad dismissed Zaghlul's successor, dissolved Parliament, and appointed a new minority, anti-Wafd government led by Muhammad Mahmud. Mahmud in turn reopened negotiations with a newly elected and sympathetic Labour government in Britain and, unencumbered by Parliament or the Wafd, accepted the Nile projects commission report as a first step towards a more comprehensive agreement on the reserved points. Muhammad Mahmud's conciliatory approach proved a most successful strategy. In 1929 the Nile Waters Agreement was concluded, resulting in a significant political and hydrological victory. Egyptian rights to the waters were preserved, and by the working arrangements Egypt received an overwhelming share of the Nile waters.

The Nile Waters Agreement of 1929 was a reaffirmation of the Nile projects commission report of 1926. It provided for the regulation of the Nile until supplanted by the Nile Waters Agreement of 1959. Like the commission's report, however, it did not refer to Nile development, nor, more importantly, did it provide any mechanism whereby co-ordinated planning for the most effective use of the waters could be designed. The agreement in fact consisted only of an exchange of notes in May 1929 between the British high commissioner in Egypt and the Egyptian government. The Nile report became an integral part of the agreement, while the notes employed the same technique of separating established rights from working arrangements. Egypt insisted that the rates of abstraction of water by the Sudan be subject to periodic review. More important, it was agreed that no works were to be constructed on the Nile or its tributaries or the equatorial lakes, so far as they were under British jurisdiction, which would alter the flows entering Egypt without her prior approval. In order to respect the established irrigation in Egypt and the working pump schemes in the Sudan, the Sudan's need for future water in the Gezira would have to be met by water stored in the reservoir at Sennar according to the working arrangements. After 15 July the Sudan was entitled to take water for the Gezira up to certain maximum daily rates in order to fill the

Sennar reservoir and to flood the area under basin irrigation downstream from Khartoum.[7]

The Nile Waters Agreement was exactly what its creators, R. M. MacGregor and 'Abd al-Hamid, sought to achieve—'a practical working arrangement'. But this arrangement appeared to work solely for the benefit of Egypt. Egypt's established and historic rights were recognized. They increased (in round numbers measured at Aswan) from 40 billion m³ in 1920 to 48 billion by the 1929 agreement. Egypt had the right of review, and thereby control, of any future conservancy works. She could proceed with the construction of the Jabal 'Auliya dam to increase the supply of Timely water. In return, the Sudan could enlarge the Gezira on the basis of her recognized right to 4 billion m³ rather than the 1.5 billion allocated by the Nile projects commission. This paltry and patronizing increase was a far cry from Allenby's 'unlimited irrigation', and a mortgage on the Sudan's future. To accept Egypt's historic rights was to admit to the primacy of Egypt's future needs; Cory had foreseen the danger of accepting this principle.

The agreement did improve the political climate. In fact, both the British and the Egyptians were exhausted by the debate over the Nile waters and were only too glad now to grope toward an arrangement over the reserved points. Neither appeared interested in discussing the future of Nile

[7] The working arrangements may be summarized as follows. From 1 Jan. to 15 July the Sudan was restricted to the use of a definite quantity of water, i.e. the gross contents of the Sennar reservoir, 781 Mm³ at that time plus 141 Mm³, being the allowance for the Gezira canal for 1–18 Jan. and the evaporation losses in the reservoir for the same period. The total credit was thus 922 Mm³. Against this were to be set the losses from the reservoir for the whole period, the discharges into the Gezira Canal, and the compensation water in respect of irrigation by pumps in excess of the areas existing at the time of the agreement. The final volume debited was never to exceed the volume of credit. From 15 to 25 July the reservoir level was to be raised to command the canal, subject always to the establishment of the Roseires–Malakal criterion (the amount of river flow at Roseires plus that at Malakal to average 160 Mm³/d over the preceding 5 days). To 31 July the abstraction of Blue Nile water into the Gezira Canal was to be on a rising scale up to 168 Mm³/sec. From 1 Aug. to 30 Nov. the abstraction into the canal was not to exceed 168 Mm³/sec, and from 1 to 31 Dec. 160 Mm³/sec, subject to certain limitations in low years. Irrigation by pumps from 15 July to 31 Dec. was unrestricted. In assessing the water used on irrigation by pumps from 1 Jan. to 15 July, a rate was to be assumed of 800 Mm³/month per feddan watered in any month. The final filling of the Sennar reservoir was to be according to a definite programme from 27 Oct. to 1 Dec.

waters, quite content that the agreement allowed the working arrangements to take care of the present. The British were absorbed in the Gezira and would be for many years. The Egyptians were pleased to get on with the construction of projects long approved but frustrated by emotions, events, and lack of an agreement. As far as Nile development was concerned, however, the agreement resolved nothing. The future of the Nile waters was not determined. The exchange of notes remained silent as to the real issue, Garstin's fundamental objective, the hydrological evolution of the Nile basin. Nor can one discern any effort to propose a mechanism, any administrative machinery, by which the planned use of the Nile could be most effectively accomplished. It was all very practical but short-sighted. Perhaps in the political climate of the times the Nile Waters Agreement was the best one could expect, but it remains a testament to a lost opportunity, a tragedy.

The limited achievements of the Nile Waters Agreement can be measured by the little subsequent enthusiasm for more cement and stone for conservancy projects. This attitude can be seen in the final completion of projects approved as early as 1914, reaffirmed in *Nile Control* in 1920 but not completed until just before the outbreak of the Second World War. The construction of the Nag Hammadi barrage was actually undertaken before the exchange of notes, but it was entirely within the territorial boundaries of Egypt and completed in 1930. The raising of the Aswan dam, which Willcocks had advocated long before, was finally finished in 1933, increasing the capacity of its reservoir from 2.5 to 5 billion m³. The Jabal 'Auliya dam was not completed until 1937, and the reservoir was not fully filled for another six years. It has been the least successful of Nile valley hydrological projects. Designed to provide Timely water for Egypt, it has been rendered virtually redundant by the construction of the high dam at Aswan but still exacts its very high price of 2.5 billion m³ lost every year by evaporation. There were other efforts within Egypt to conserve water undertaken during the inter-war years, particularly the strengthening of the barrage at Assiut in 1938 and the completion of the new delta barrage in 1940.

Words and paper accompanied the bricks and mortar, but

in each instance the proposals they generated demonstrated only the chaos and distrust surrounding the question of Nile control, the dearth of any comprehensive plan, and the inadequacy of the administrative machinery. The project for a reservoir at Lake Tana, for instance, had been under investigation since the beginning of the century. In 1903 C. E. Dupuis had been sent to Ethiopia by Garstin to determine whether Lake Tana could be an alternative reservoir to Lake Albert. Dupuis concluded that a dam at the outflow from the lake was a simple engineering project, a judgement confirmed by the report of the expedition of G. W. Grabham and R. P. Black in 1920–1.[8] Political instability, the possible inundation of sacred sites, and the opposition of the conservative Ethiopian nobility who wanted no foreign influence obstructed Egyptian and Sudanese designs on Lake Tana water. The Ethiopian advocate for the dam was Ras Tafari Makonnan, later emperor Haile Selassie, but his policies of modernization and centralization were then restricted by his role as regent, the conservatism of the empress Zwaditu, and the xenophobia of the feudal barons, particularly those from Gojjam and Begemdir who dominated the region of the lake. These difficulties did not deter the British, who opened negotiations in November 1922, pressing for an agreement sweetened by generous cash payments and other unspecified rewards for Tafari, made all the more urgent by the construction of the Sennar dam and the proposed expansion of the Gezira. On his part Ras Tafari used the weakness of his position and the hostility of the court to enhance his image as a reformer who needed arms, promoting his own personal ambitions and policies of centralization while demonstrating his suspicions of British intentions in north-east Africa. On 29 November 1923 the negotiations were officially terminated.

Having failed at Addis Ababa, the British sought to invoke Italian assistance in 1925 by supporting an exclusive Italian interest in western Ethiopia in return for the Lake Tana dam concession. This transparent imperialism was soon less successful than the abortive negotiations in 1923, and

---

[8] Dupuis (1904, pp. 209–36); Grabham and Black (1925).

although Tafari made every effort to maintain cordial relations with Britain, he turned for assistance to the one power who had no colonial ambitions in Africa, the USA. In November 1927 he sent his close confidant, Azaj Workneh Martin, to New York to negotiate a draft contract for the Lake Tana dam with the J. G. White Engineering Company for $20 million. The Americans promptly reopened their legation in Addis Ababa. On 2 July 1930 the empress Zawditu died, and eleven months later, on 2 November 1930, Ras Tafari was proclaimed Haile Selassie, the Lion of Judah and Emperor of Ethiopia. The following year he crushed the power of Ras Gugas of Begemdir and Ras Hailu of Gojjam, to assert for the first time the control of the central government over the environs of Lake Tana, enabling him to act as its sovereign. The Lake Tana dam was to be a major component of his programme of modernization. He had already granted the concession to the J. G. White Engineering Company in April 1929, but it remained contingent upon British approval and the amount of the annual subsidy paid to Ethiopia for the water. The Nile Waters Agreement of 1929 suddenly relieved Britain's concern over water for the Gezira, and complicated any proposed arrangement over Lake Tana by recognizing Egypt's right to approve any water conservancy projects south of Aswan. This did not diminish the importance of Lake Tana for Nile control, but since neither the Sudan nor Egypt required additional water immediately there was no longer any incentive to divert funds, in the depths of the world economic depression, for the Lake Tana dam. At a meeting in Addis Ababa in February 1933 called by Haile Selassie and the Americans, the representative of the Sudan government benignly urged the White Company to carry on, while making it clear that neither it nor the Ethiopian government could expect any financial support from the Sudan.[9]

Between 1931 and 1934, White conducted extensive surveys for the Lake Tana dam, on the basis of which a technical agreement was reached between representatives from the Sudan and Egypt in May 1935. Both countries agreed to seek the concurrence of the Ethiopian government to build the dam

[9] See McCann (1981); Marcus (1987, pp. 73–88).

at the outflow from Lake Tana. The benefits in water and the cost of the dam were to be shared by Egypt and the Sudan. In fact the Lake Tana dam agreement was the only Anglo-Egyptian initiative in Nile water development since 1929; but it owed its creation to the work of the Americans, not the ministry of public works, and the unremitting support of the emperor of Ethiopia. Neither the British nor the Egyptians can claim credit for this project to enhance Nile control. Like the other proposals which appeared on paper during this inter-war period, it too suffered from the vicissitudes of Egyptian politics, but it was put to rest by the Italian invasion of Ethiopia in 1936 and the deep suspicions by the emperor of British and Egyptian designs at Lake Tana after the Second World War.

The only tangible outcome of six or seven years of endeavour was the preparation in full detail and proper form of a complete Lake Tsana Reservoir Project, and an agreement between Egypt and the Sudan as to its operations as a joint enterprise. A less tangible, and perhaps more evanescent gain, is to be seen in the fact that a mutually beneficial partnership had been entered into between the two Governments in a field where acute discord had once prevailed.[10]

Other Anglo-Egyptian discussions were not so blessed. In October 1938 the Sudan government sought to obtain an increase in its allotment of water granted under the Nile Waters Agreement, demonstrating how short-term had been the gains acquired for the Sudan in 1929. The Sudan government requested that it be permitted to begin to fill the Sennar reservoir earlier in July than the mandated date of 15 July, in order to increase the volume of water available for pump schemes. It was politely rebuffed. Further discussions were held in 1939 with the intention of increasing the amount of water available for the Gezira by a combination of drawing off more water and raising the Sennar dam by one metre. Egypt never bothered to respond further, and after the outbreak of war the negotiations were never pursued. Perhaps the most dramatic example of the confusion and discord in Nile water planning was the Jonglei Canal. Here in the Sudd virtually every element in Anglo-Egyptian relations over the

[10] MacGregor, 'The Upper Nile Irrigation Projects', p. 5.

Nile waters is to be found—suspicion, secrecy, incompetence, and lack of leadership.

Ever since the resignation of MacDonald in 1921, the able engineers and hydrologists recruited from Britain by the ministry of public works had been devoid of leadership. With no other guide than *Nile Control*, whose data was badly flawed and insufficient, and operating frequently in a hostile physical and political environment, the British scientists of the ministry worked without direction and often in competition. With no grand design to inspire them, they turned inward, becoming obsessed with the collection of data seemingly for no other purpose than the intrinsic merit of the information itself. Men like Dr H. E. Hurst, J. I. Craig, Dr P. Phillips, I. M. Dowson, R. P. Black, W. A. C. Perry, W. D. Roberts, G. Parker, F. Newhouse, and A. D. Butcher thus continued during the inter-war years to amass enormous quantities of measurements, and almost mindlessly devised numerous schemes isolated from any consideration of the Nile basin as a whole. To be fair, one should recognize that they did not perceive it as their responsibility to design a co-ordinated scheme. None of them held the position or power of Sir William Garstin or Sir Murdoch MacDonald. It is curious, however, that none of them, over a quarter of a century, had any conception of how his particular project and parochial study might fit into the larger whole. It is even more surprising that in the numerous reports none sought to create a rational system of Nile development from investigations into a specific conservancy project. They were talented men but of narrow vision. They were terrified of not having sufficient data, but few were able to forge the enormous amount of information they gathered into a rational, coherent, holistic view of the Nile. They were cautious and conservative, suspicious of politicians, often contemptuous of their Egyptian employers. They loathed inefficiency, which was the most frequent rationale for doing nothing. They were devoted to their profession, one singularly lacking in vision. They were honest, incorruptible, sober, and responsible men. They were also dull, rigid, and unimaginative. Reports they could write; dreams they suppressed. Their loyalties were often compromised by being stoutly British in a land where the imperial authority had reigned supreme and lingered far longer after 1922 than most would have thought. They served Egypt well; they should have served the peoples of the Nile valley better.

Harold Edwin Hurst occupied a unique position among this band. He arrived at Cairo in 1906 from a lectureship in physics at Oxford, in the twilight of the imperial period of Cromer and Garstin. Recruited by Sir Henry Lyons, he joined the survey department in October 1906 to begin a long career in the Egyptian service which spanned sixty-two years, from Lord Cromer to President Nasser. He was a modest and mathematical man, a rare combination, whose scientific abilities propelled him from the magnetic survey of Egypt to the director-generalship of the physical department of the ministry of public works in 1915. The physical department was responsible for the preservation, collation, and analysis of data throughout the Nile basin with a view to the construction of the necessary works for Nile control. Here in the physical department lay the power, but also the frustrations, inseparable from any future Nile development. Hurst was primarily a scientist in an alien land, with no desire for personal aggrandizement nor any political instinct. He was quite content to assume the position of scientific servant to the Egyptian politicians, for neither by temperament nor conception of his position in Egypt was he prepared to take the leadership of Nile control. Pressed by his Egyptian employers, he produced his major contribution to Nile development, upon his official retirement in 1946, by the publication of *The Future Conservation of the Nile*. He introduced the innovative concept of century storage, but was more interested in the mathematical probabilities between yield and reservoir capacity which became known as the Hurst phenomenon. Such abstruse abstractions had great practical application but by their very nature were not easily translated into the hydropolitics of the Nile valley. His personality and his interests meant that Hurst never dreamed of following in the footsteps of Garstin or MacDonald—nor would the Egyptians have allowed him to do so. In the end he remained a civil servant, not 'the adviser', and like a well-beloved retainer he was kept on in the Egyptian service long after retirement, without fully understanding the aspirations of those living south of Aswan.

No problem of Nile development exemplifies these characteristics of the British on the Nile more dramatically than the
search for the most effective means of bringing the water from
the equatorial lakes down through the Sudd to the White Nile
and Egypt while conserving the enormous losses incurred in
the swamps. Here was a challenge requiring not just technical
skill but vision, bold ideas forcefully presented, to match the
enormous obstacle of the great swamps of the Nile. In the
decades between 1920 and 1940 the men who went up the Nile
to the Sudd did not lack competence, only confidence. Those
who came before the First World War appear to have had
both. Certainly the advisers at the ministry of public works in
the first decade of the twentieth century regarded the Nile as a
whole, and the Sudd in particular, with far greater insight
than the bright British engineers of the inter-war years.
C. E. Dupuis, although he did not have Garstin's perspicacity,
believed that the difficulties presented by the Sudd were not
insurmountable. He wrote in September 1909:

Without going much into technical detail it may be confidently
asserted that the information collected since the formation of the
Sudan Branch of the Egyptian Irrigation Service has tended to show
that the difficulties of training the river are less, and the advantages
of doing so greater, than they were believed to be when the branch
was founded. . . . The repellent air of gloom and mystery and the
suggestion of prohibitive difficulties surrounding the first reports of
the Sudd Region tend to dissipate with more knowledge.[11]

Thirty-five years later this opinion was shared by
R. M. MacGregor, who lamented: 'there has been no genuine
progress in Nile water planning since Garstin, except of course
the accumulation of gauges.'[12]

The very nature of the Sudd Region appears to have some oppressive
effect on those who for too long have been too close to its detailed
problems, and to make it all the more necessary that direction should
be kept by some superior authority less liable to lose perspective. . . .
The two wars naturally interrupted progress and there were the few
troubled years following the first war. But from about 1922 to 1939 it
seems that the lack of high level control of these studies is all that

[11] Note by Dupuis quoted in MacGregor, 'The Upper Nile Irrigation Projects',
pp. 7–8.
[12] MacGregor to W. N. Allan, director of irrigation, 1 Jan. 1945; SAD 589/14/60.

can account for the meagre progress accomplished. Such projects must be handled in the large, and not only in detail.[13]

The lack of direction from Cairo did not inhibit the British engineers of the Egyptian irrigation service from concocting numerous projects to penetrate the Sudd—quite the opposite. With no administrative control from Cairo, each hydrologist who went up the Nile designed his own Sudd project, for which he then lobbied within the administrative bureaucracy of the irrigation service and the ministry, creating competition and confusion. The advantages and disadvantages of these proposals were discussed, and often strongly attacked and defended, in endless meetings and innumerable memoranda and reports. The more information flooding from the swamps, the greater the demand for yet more data. Soon the volume of technical information became virtually unmanageable and the objective lost in the tide of statistics. It became all too easy to postpone decisions because there was too much known about too little.

Within the ministry, the physical department was responsible for analysing the mass of measurements collected by agents in the field; but Hurst consistently complained that his department had insufficient information regarding the Sudd, or, for that matter, the Nile, as a whole for him to advise implementing the numerous proposals for a Sudd canal. Consequently, the principal task of the irrigation service soon degenerated into collecting rather than deciding what was to be done with the endless flow of numbers. In 1926 alone over 2,600 discharges were measured and some sixty-eight gauges were read daily throughout the Nile basin. No one appears to have questioned the purpose of this massive exercise, which soon became an end in itself; and so it continued from one year to the next. Indeed, the members of the irrigation service, instead of asking why, were content if not pleased to avoid the logical deductions of their efforts. Hurst himself could write with pride in 1927: 'Thus the last twenty years has not been marked by any startling discoveries, but by the collection of accurate numerical information.'[14]

[13] MacGregor, 'The Upper Nile Irrigation Projects', p. 8.
[14] Hurst (1927, p. 441).

The list of proposals for a Sudd canal between 1920 and 1945 includes at least nine separate projects, and more if one considers the variations or the distinct propositions for the Bahr al-Ghazal. In 1913 P. M. Tottenham, then inspector-general, Sudan, Egyptian irrigation service, published his *Report Upon the Upper Nile Projects*, in which he argued that the only way to retrieve water from the Sudd was to reduce the losses in transmission either by remodelling the carrying capacities of the natural channels of the Bahr al-Jabal and the Bahr al-Zaraf by embankments or by diverting the excess flow into an artificial channel.[15] Sir William Willcocks was clearly influenced by Tottenham's report and strongly advocated embankment in the third edition of his *Egyptian Irrigation*, which appeared the same year and became fashionable among the British hydrologists at the ministry of public works during the inter-war years. The alternative, an artificial channel and a diversion canal, the Garstin Cut, was dismissed without study as too expensive and studiously ignored.

W. D. Roberts, inspector-general in the Sudan for the Egyptian irrigation service, argued for the Bor–Zaraf diversion

---

[15] Tottenham (1913); Beshir (1985, p. 139). Dr Amin, director-general of the physical department, and H. G. Bambridge, inspector of irrigation, White Nile inspectorate, identified 11 Jonglei Canal schemes (Amin and Bambridge (1950)): (1) A direct canal from a point on the east bank opposite Rejaf thence along the east bank to the mouth of the River Sobat. (2) A direct canal from Bor to the mouth of the River Sobat. (3) A canal from Bor to the Bahr al-Zaraf at a point 175 km from its mouth and thereafter a remodelling of the natural channel. In addition, the White Nile from the Bahr al-Zaraf to the mouth of the Sobat would be remodelled. (4) A canal from Bor to the mouth of the Sobat River reduced in size at a point opposite km 175 on the Bahr al-Zaraf, where the canal is joined by the Bahr al-Zaraf to utilize its carrying capacity. The White Nile between the confluence of the Bahr al-Zaraf and the mouth of the Sobat would be remodelled. (5) The remodelling of the Bahr al-Jabal from Bor to Lake No and the White Nile to the Sobat. (6) The remodelling of the Bahr al-Jabal from Bor to the Zaraf Cuts and then utilizing the Bahr al-Zaraf to its mouth and the White Nile to the Sobat. (7) The remodelling of the Bahr al-Jabal from Bor to Lake No and the Bahr al-Zaraf from the Zaraf Cuts to its mouth and the White Nile from Lake No to the Sobat. (8) A canal from Mongalla running eastward to the River Veveno, remodelling the channel of the Veveno to its confluence with the River Pibor and thence following the channels of the Pibor and Sobat to the White Nile. (9) A canal to the Veveno–Pibor combined with using the Bahr al-Jabal from Bor to Lake No and the Bahr al-Zaraf from the Zaraf Cuts to its mouth, increasing their carrying capacities by closing the spills and remodelling the White Nile from Lake No to the Sobat. (10) The embankment of the Bahr al-Jabal from Bor to Lake No. (11) A direct canal along the eastern watershed in the clay plain from Jonglei to the mouth of the River Sobat.

canal. Geoffrey Parker, Roberts's successor as inspector-general, and W. A. C. Perry, inspector of irrigation, upper White Nile division of the irrigation service, were the principal advocates for the Veveno–Pibor scheme to bypass the Sudd. Frederick Newhouse, when inspector-general in the 1930s, made no proposal but was satisfied with collecting more data. A. D. Butcher, inspector of irrigation, upper White Nile, worked on a number of schemes to embank the Bahr al-Jabal and the Bahr al-Zaraf until he decided upon the Jonglei diversion project, a modification of W. D. Roberts's Bor–Zaraf diversion canal proposed a decade before. During all this frenetic activity everyone ignored the Garstin Cut, the direct canal from Bor to the mouth of the Sobat River, which Garstin had recommended in 1904. No effort was made even to survey this line, a fact which is all the more surprising when one considers that it is the Garstin Cut which is almost identical with the route of the Jonglei Canal today. The engineers simply dismissed it out of hand since they assumed (without any empirical test) that construction by dredgers would take twenty years to complete, making the canal too costly. They were proved wrong on both counts.

By 1937 the number of projects had been narrowed down from nine to three: the embankment projects, the Veveno–Pibor scheme, and the Sudd diversion canal. The embankment projects appear during this period in numerous forms, but essentially entailed remodelling the existing channel of the Bahr al-Jabal or the Bahr al-Zaraf, or both, by defining the banks of the river to prevent water spilling into the swamps beyond. This proposal was not new and had several variants and as many names. In some the embanking would be done in conjunction with a canal, under the heading of the 'Bor–Bahr al-Zaraf scheme'. In 1936 Butcher revived Garstin's and Willcocks's proposals to remodel the Bahr al-Jabal in his *The Bahr El Jebel Banking Scheme*, published by the ministry of public works. In others only one channel, the Bahr al-Jabal or the Bahr al-Zaraf, would be embanked. In yet another, the Pharaonic project, the Bahr al-Jabal would be embanked only on the west, but this bizarre proposition also entailed extensive work to remodel the Bahr al-Ghazal. The Veveno–Pibor scheme was a single concept of a canal from Bor to the

Veveno River, which would then be remodelled to carry the water around the swamps via Pibor and the Sobat. The Sudd diversion canal was the most simple of them all, which may be why it was not considered. Originally called Garstin's Cut and later the Bor–White Nile project or the Sudd diversion canal, this project entailed the construction of a straight line for a canal through the Upper Nile from Bor to the mouth of the Sobat at its confluence with the White Nile. In 1936 Butcher introduced a variation of the Sudd diversion canal—or, from a different perspective, a modification of W. D. Roberts's Bor–Zaraf diversion canal. Like Roberts, Butcher intended to excavate a canal parallel to the Bahr al-Jabal, but to begin at Jonglei rather than Bor to the south. When the canal met the Bahr al-Zaraf, Butcher intended to continue its construction parallel to the Bahr al-Zaraf, instead of using an embanked river as Roberts had proposed. Thus Butcher proposed digging a canal the length of the upper Nile, like Garstin, but his route was the same as that proposed by Roberts.

Work on the Sudd canal project was first undertaken as early as 1920 by W. A. C. Perry. He proposed to collect hydrological data concerning the Sudd. He argued that the completion of a Sudd canal would enormously benefit Egypt, independently of a dam at Lake Albert, which was considered by some, even in 1920, to be a prerequisite to a Sudd canal. The peculiar link between a Sudd canal and the Lake Albert dam can be found consistently appearing in reports on the Sudd projects, despite the fact that Garstin, Willcocks, and MacGregor had pointed out that dams at the equatorial lakes were of little value without the existence of a passage through the swamps. The excavation of the Jonglei Canal in 1978 began without a dam first having been built at Lake Albert. Construction of such a dam is today politically unlikely, but the proposal has never been abandoned. Perry observed that the water saved from loss in the swamps alone would range from 8 to 40 billion m^3 annually and justify the cost of construction. In 1981 the Permanent Joint Technical Commission for the Nile Waters, responsible for building the Jonglei Canal, advanced the same argument.[16]

[16] PJTC (1981a).

Perry proposed to measure discharges, establish a system of gauges, and to undertake a survey and reconnaissance of the Sudd, for there were no reliable maps, no precise surveys, and little knowledge of the meandering rivers and streams in the swamps. His proposal was quickly approved and £E350 000 appropriated to begin work. Suddenly, in the southern Sudan, Perry was in command of an agency with elaborate facilities at Malakal and a budget far in excess of the total expenditure of the three southern provinces of the Sudan. Houses, power generators, six small steamers, power barges, oil storage tanks, and all the equipment of administration which the envious members of the Sudan political service never obtained until after the Second World War, were hauled up the Nile. Almost without realizing the implications of its arrival at Malakal, the Egyptian irrigation service had set itself up as an autonomous agency on the upper Nile, to the bewilderment of its British rulers.[17]

Perry and his small army of engineers, technicians, and hydrologists worked unobtrusively, and in remarkable isolation from the administrative preoccupations of the district commissioners and the governors, K. C. P. Struvé at Malakal, headquarters of the Upper Nile province, and V. R. Woodland at Mongalla. The former was primarily concerned with reducing expenditure on the tribute patrols among the Nuer. The latter was trying to restrain his district commissioners from a forward course in eastern Mongalla. The measuring and surveying did not overly concern them. Suddenly, the Sudd canal became a reality. Working with the information supplied by Perry, W. D. Roberts presented in May 1925 a proposal known as the Bor–Zaraf Cut, the first of the embankment projects. This scheme entailed the construction of a barrage at Bor to divert water from the Bahr al-Jabal into a canal 70 m wide, extending northward in a direct line 170 km to the Bahr al-Zaraf at Ajwong. From there the Bahr al-Zaraf would be remodelled to carry the water to its confluence with the White Nile, where another barrage would regulate the flow. A modification of this scheme would have the canal follow near to the Bahr al-Jabal to the Bahr

[17] W. A.C. Perry, 'Note on a Proposed Program of Work for the Upper White Nile Division for the Years 1920–27', Sept. 1920, UNP I/9/79.

al-Zaraf, rather than being drawn northward as a straight line
Two other embankment projects were subsequently developed.
One entailed the remodelling of the Bahr al-Jabal from Bor to
Shambe, where a barrage would be constructed to divert
water into a cut eastward to the Bahr al-Zaraf, whose channel
would be improved. A second barrage would be built at the
mouth of the Bahr al-Zaraf, as in the proposed Bor–Zaraf Cut,
to prevent White Nile water backing up into the Sudd when
the Sobat was in flood. Another scheme was the quintessence
of the embankment projects, whereby the banks of the Bahr
al-Jabal would be improved throughout its length to carry the
water now lost in the swamps by spillage.[18]

Support for the embankment projects came not only from
Sir Isma'il Sirry Pasha, the minister of public works, but also
from the British high commissioner, Lord Lloyd. Sirry Pasha
was a great advocate of Nile investigations, but his interest in
Sudd projects was not part of any comprehensive plan for Nile
development. His concern to bypass the swamps of the Nile
was in fact an isolated proposal to acquire additional water for
Egypt, since no plan for the Nile basin existed except for
MacDonald's *Nile Control*, which had been principally designed
to save the Sennar and Jabal 'Auliya dams, referring to the
Lake Tana dam, the Sudd canal, and the Lake Albert dam as
projects for the future. Garstin had done the same. On these
matters the report of the Nile commission of 1926 remained
silent.

With Sirry Pasha's support the Bor–Zaraf Cut was
approved by the Egyptian council of ministers on 19 August
1925 and £E1,100,000 was appropriated. Four dredgers to
begin construction were ordered. The Sudan government,
however, did not officially learn of the project until five months
later, when Roberts forwarded his plan for construction in
December to Sir George Schuster, the financial secretary of
the Sudan Government.[19] The Roberts proposal did not arrive

---

[18] C. A. Willis, governor, Upper Nile province, 'Report on Possible Effects of the
Sudd Project of Irrigation upon the Local Population, 1928', 31 May 1928, SAD 212/
5/50.

[19] W. D. Roberts, inspector-general, Sudan, Egyptian irrigation service, to Sir
George Schuster, financial secretary, 6 Dec. 1925, No. 5.2/3/10860, SAD 589/13/14;
N. Henderson, minister plenipotentiary, to A. Chamberlain, foreign secretary, 23
Aug. 1925, UNP I/9/79.

as a complete surprise to Schuster. The magnitude of the Sudd canal and combined Lake Albert dam project did. He had been deeply involved in the Gezira scheme since his appointment as financial secretary on 1 January 1923, so that he was well informed on questions of Nile waters. He had given an impressive presentation at the residency in Cairo of the position of the Sudan government in regard to its rights and interests in Nile waters. He had emphasized at that time that the Sudan wished to be previously consulted and informed about any Egyptian proposals for conservancy projects south of Aswan. This was a position the Sudan government has consistently maintained and which the ministry of public works frequently ignored.[20] The Sudan government had been neither consulted nor informed during the planning of the Roberts proposal, and reacted swiftly. Within two weeks Khartoum responded officially, demanding to know by what terms Egypt intended to construct works in territories other than its own, namely the Sudan, Uganda, and the Belgian Congo. More importantly, the Sudan government insisted on its right to participate in the planning of such works and on the necessity of its formal approval before any such works could be undertaken.[21] Sirry Pasha responded with a bland excuse that the Roberts report should be regarded as informing the Sudan government of what they wanted to know. Schuster was unconvinced.

If Khartoum was suspicious, C. A. ('Chunky') Willis, governor of the Upper Nile, was furious. Willis had just arrived in Malakal. His snobbish airs and insensitive affectations masked an intuitive intelligence that rightly guessed it was a hazardous proposition to predict the effects of manipulating water. He was manifestly unimpressed with engineers, and wanted to know what would become of the great grazing areas of the Upper Nile when the water flowed instead down a canal to Egypt. He was deeply suspicious of the Egyptian irrigation service, which was under no obligation to tell the governor of the Upper Nile anything. Indeed, he complained that, if he

[20] Sir George Schuster, 'Notes of Conference at the Residency on May 10, 1925', SAD 589/13/14.

[21] Governor-general, Sir Geoffrey Archer, to HM high commissioner, Lord Lloyd, No. 216, 22 Dec. 1925, SAD 589/13/14.

did not invite the British employees of the service to dinner and ply them with whisky, he would have no idea what they were up to. In this way he had learned in December 1925 that they were already laying out beacons for the line of the canal north of Bor. He pointed out that it was strange for the irrigation service to claim they did not know enough about the digging of a canal and yet to send out tenders for its construction. Willis was at Malakal to preside over improving the life of the inhabitants of the Upper Nile, not the *fallahin* of Egypt, and he had no intention of selling out his noble savages to the canal-builders. He wrote in anger to Khartoum: 'I could not permit them to turn a sod without authority from headquarters' and in October 1926 prohibited all employees of the irrigation service from going south of Lake No.[22] In this age of great environmental issues, Chunky Willis, a member of London's best clubs and a man whose love of nature was confined to polo ponies, makes a remarkable if not improbable environmentalist.

Khartoum acted vigorously to Willis's call to arms. Through the British high commissioner, Lord Lloyd, the governor-general demanded and received reassurances from the Egyptian government that the agreement of both the Sudan and British governments would be necessary before actual construction commenced. The Egyptian irrigation service hastily retreated, referring to their proposal as 'preliminary, experimental, and exploratory'. In fact the Bor–Zaraf Cut had proved a considerable embarrassment to the Egyptian government. It helped the British regain the initiative in the discussions concerning the Nile waters at a time when the Nile commission had cleared the way for an agreement and when political affairs in Egypt were more tumultuous than usual, hindering any forward action in the Sudd. Sirry Pasha was replaced at the ministry by Osman Moharram. He had a personal dislike of Roberts and soon contrived to make him the scapegoat for his own project. Roberts was promptly retired from the irrigation service. He was replaced by Geoffrey Parker as inspector-general for the

---

[22] Governor, Upper Nile province (Willis), to civil secretary, H. MacMichael, 4 Oct. 1926, UNP I/9/79.

Sudan. Parker had never been overly impressed with the embankment projects and set out to scrap them.

Nevertheless, the damage had been done. Khartoum was alerted, and accepted the wisdom of Willis's appeal for a study. Major-General Hubert Huddleston, then acting governor-general, wrote to Lord Lloyd: 'Whatever the policy approved by your Lordship in regard to the actual inception of the project, no time should be lost in making a detailed examination into its probable effect on the local population and ascertaining what steps could be taken if any to prevent or provide adequate compensation for any damage to their interests.'[23] Huddleston suggested that such a study be undertaken by W. D. Roberts, the former inspector-general and the proponent of the Bor–Zaraf Cut! Not only did Roberts possess the knowledge of the embankment projects as well as the technical competence, but his abrupt departure from the irrigation service meant that he had no obligations to his previous employers. Indeed, he now had the perfect means by which to justify the proposal for which he had been sacked.

The Egyptians were equally bitter. They had been humiliated over the Sudd canal. Having approved the Bor–Zaraf Cut, appropriated over a million pounds, and sent out tenders for construction, they had been forced to retreat before pressure from the Sudan government and the residency, and to abort the embankment projects. Salt was added to their wounds when they were asked to hand over to Roberts the plans for all the embankment projects, not just the Bor–Zaraf Cut, and were requested to co-operate with him particularly in his investigations of the Lake Albert dam. These demands were deeply resented by the irrigation service, and although the ministry could hardly refuse to give the four Sudd schemes to Roberts, it studiously ignored the invitation for further co-operation.[24] In fact the irrigation service had lost interest in the Lake Albert dam. To the Egyptians the embankment projects in the Sudd were primarily a means of reasserting their control over the Nile water schemes and thereby visibly

[23] Maj.-Gen. H. Huddleston, acting governor-general, to Lord Lloyd, 20 Nov. 1926, UNP I/9/79.
[24] Lord Lloyd to prime minister, 30 Nov. 1927, No. 4911/103; financial secretary, A. Huddleston, 'Interdepartmental Note', 24 Apr. 1929, SAD 589/13/14.

demonstrating Egyptian presence in the Sudan at a time when their army had been ejected before British bayonets and their officials summarily packed off to Cairo. The Bor–Zaraf Cut was the perfect medium to establish the Egyptian flag, construct enormous facilities, and send Egyptian engineers, technicians, and presumably thousands of *sa'idi* labourers to the Sudan. Nothing could have been more repugnant to the British officials.

The Egyptians reasoned that the British could not deny a scheme which British officials had proposed to acquire additional water from January to July; but to them the embankment projects were principally a political ploy to regain their lost presence in the Sudan; they were not part of a comprehensive plan for Nile control. Willis was not the first to question Egyptian motives, but he was the most succinct.

It is of the first importance to know whether the Egyptian Government is starting on the Sudd Project as an integral part of a much larger scheme. As if that be not the case, there is not justification for the disturbance caused to local conditions in the results likely to be obtained. If on the other hand the larger scheme is the true objective, some reason ought to be produced to show that the larger scheme can be carried out and that the political authorities concerned are agreeable.[25]

Willis had numerous objections to the embankment projects, many of which were validated by the more thorough investigations of the Jonglei Investigation Team twenty years later. He feared the impact upon the 273,000 Nilotic inhabitants of the introduction of Egyptian labour; the country would be permeated by large numbers of Arabs and Muslims, and Willis foresaw that the result would be detribalized Dinka and Nuer who, with a smattering of sophistication, would become barrack-room lawyers with an urban conceit and a propensity for litigation. Ironically, in 1928 the Sudan government could not claim to govern the inhabitants of the Upper Nile, but the construction of a canal would surely undermine any efforts of the government to do so. The planned policy of imposing native administration upon the acephalous peoples of the

[25] Willis, 'Possible Effects of the Sudd Project'.

southern Sudan would be made all the more difficult, if not impossible.

Willis's principal objections, however, and one about which he wrote with genuine conviction, was his fear for the way of living of the people of the Upper Nile. The habits and customs of the Nuer and Dinka was for Willis 'the first step towards understanding the main problem under review. The tendency to belittle the importance of local circumstances and to treat the problems on lines better suited to conditions in the north Sudan or in Egypt is likely to lead to a serious confusion of facts in the future.' The central issue was grazing. Like a good environmentalist, Willis pointed out the danger of destroying the present river system and thereby the amount of adequate pasture for the Nilotic cattle.

All the schemes . . . involve certain definite change to existing conditions. The reduction of the low flood to the level of 1922 may disclose new grazing areas on the land exposed between normal low flood and that of 1922 but it is likely that much of this will be bad ground producing only papyrus grass which is not fit for grazing. On the other hand the reduction of the level must inevitably cut off some of the grazing land now regularly flooded. This means a general reduction of grazing available.[26]

Moreover, he expressed a fear reiterated by all who came after to investigate the Sudd canal and its effects on the people and their means of living. 'It is useless to evade the question by contemplating a modification or the abandonment of the scheme at a later stage. Once the principle is accepted and the work seriously commenced, the commitment at the early stages will be far too extensive to permit their cancellation.'[27]

Roberts found himself trapped between his own belief in the Bor–Zaraf Cut and the determination of Willis to protect his people. On the one hand, Roberts sought to placate the governor and his supporters. On the other, he sought to demonstrate the means of ameliorating the hardships imposed on the Nilotes in order to implement the best of the embankment projects—not surprisingly, the Bor–Zaraf Cut. He first 'strongly recommended the Sudan Government to withhold their approval to any work being carried out other

[26] Ibid.   [27] Ibid.

than for purely investigative purposes'. He implied that the
Sudan government should rightly be suspicious of the
ministry and should not depend upon the irrigation service
alone to supply information. Indeed, the Sudan should carry
out independent investigations with a view to defending its
own interests and those of the Sudanese in any future
negotiations. These admonitions were calculated to receive a
warm reception at Khartoum, and they did. The anthropologist
E. E. Evans-Pritchard had been employed to study the Nuer
while the government was preparing to bring those truculent
Nilotes under its aegis by a programme known as Nuer
Settlement. The Sudan government, however, still had to rely
on the irrigation service for its technical information, since it
lacked the men and means to enlarge the activities of its own
irrigation department beyond the operation of the Gezira.
Nevertheless, the dispute precipitated by the Bor–Zaraf Cut
had established the principle that the Sudan must approve
any projects within its territory.

Roberts then turned to the substantive issue, the protection
of the Nilotic regime in the presence of the Bor–Zaraf Cut.
The device to ensure compatibility was the Lake Albert dam.
As inspector-general, Roberts had always been a proponent of
the link between the Sudd canal and the dam at Lake Albert.
Garstin and MacDonald had come to the conclusion that
dams at the outflow of the equatorial lakes were of no
hydrological value without a Sudd canal. No one disputed
that obvious fact. In an effort to disturb the pattern of Nilotic
life as little as possible by the Bor–Zaraf Cut, Roberts carried
the argument for the Lake Albert dam one step further. If the
Lake Albert dam was dependent for its utility upon the Sudd
canal the reverse was equally true—the Sudd canal required
the Lake Albert reservoir in order to maintain the regime of
the swamps and thus the Nilotic way of life.

Now as a result of this inquiry it is evident that its [the Bor–Zaraf
Cut's] use will have to be still further curtailed in order to protect
the Sudan interests. In fact when all the circumstances are taken
into account it is found that the project will be of little practical use,
especially in a year when the natural winter and spring rain supply
for the south falls below the mean. If Egypt were dependent upon
the economy in swamp losses to provide the extra water for the

development of its main agricultural areas, then the restriction in the use of a new channel to protect the Sudan's local interests would be a serious matter. But this is not the case as under no circumstances even if the Sudan's interests were totally ignored could the extra supply derived from economy within the Sudd region meet Egypt's real needs. It is on an improvement in the supply from the south that Egypt has to rely. When this has been achieved by the construction of a Lake Albert reservoir or some other suitable work the supply available during the winter and spring seasons will be far in excess of Egypt's needs for many years. The sudd project will then primarily be required to insure that the extra supply from the south can pass through the sudd regions without undue loss and its use as a means of reducing the swamp losses will become of secondary importance.[28]

Thus the Lake Albert reservoir was necessary not only to provide additional water for Egypt but to protect the Nilotes by increasing the river discharge south of the Sudd, not from it. Then when the extra water was required in the White Nile it could be controlled from the Albert dam at Pachwach in Uganda, diverted from the Bahr al-Jabal by the barrage at Bor into the canal, and then down the embanked Bahr al-Zaraf to the Nile and Egypt without appreciably disturbing the level or flow of water in the swamps. The regime would be left undisturbed, the levels controlled by the Bor barrage to suit local interests. Roberts even asserted that the life of the Nilotes would in fact be improved by a consistent flow of water into their swamp-land, since they would no longer be the victims of high or low floods; the regime of their lives would be stabilized by eliminating the dislocation caused by too much water or too little in any given year. The control of the Nile waters began at Pachwach, not Jonglei.

By placing the Lake Albert dam and the Sudd canal in tandem Roberts in fact vitiated the very reason why Garstin and MacDonald had advocated a passage through the swamps. They did not want to lose the water from the equatorial lakes in the Sudd. Therefore to them the Sudd

---

[28] See W. D. Roberts, 'Report on Irrigation Projects on the Upper Nile and their Effects on Tribal and other Local Interests', Oct. 1928, and all the supporting data, correspondence, and supplements including the written responses from the district commissioners, Upper Nile, in answer to the questionnaire circulated to them by Roberts; see also Willis, 'Possible Effects of the Sudd Project', all in UNP I/9/83, 83, 85, 86.

canal took primacy over the Lake Albert dam. If the dam, however, were built, its chief purpose would be to provide extra water in years of low Nile. They never dreamed that the dam would be used to maintain the water-levels of the Sudd, which they sought to reduce. Roberts's proposal for Sudd regulation was a twist to Garstin's conception, and the idea of a dam at Lake Albert persisted long after the embankment projects had been quietly discarded. In that sense Roberts reaffirmed what had become an article of faith in the irrigation service: the works in the Sudd would have little value without storage at Lake Albert.

The unquestioning acceptance of the need for the Lake Albert dam remains something of a mystery if one accepts the dubious proposition that enquiring minds were at work in Cairo. After Roberts the dam seems to have taken on an aura not normally associated with sceptical hydrologists. In April 1931 a committee of engineers in the ministry recorded this view:

A Dam and Reservoir at Lake Albert are essential for the operation of the Veveno–Pibor Project and *all other diversion schemes* [author's italics] and no such scheme should be sanctioned until the Egyptian Government is assured that the Lake Albert dam can be constructed and operated without delay.[29]

Nor was this belief a momentary aberration. In March 1938 another committee reaffirmed this fundamental principle:

The Committee are of opinion that before embarking on any Sudd Project the Government should be satisfied that the Lake Albert Dam and Reservoir is a feasible proposition, and agreement on all principal points should have been reached with the local authorities.[30]

No one seemed the least concerned, however, whether the Lake Albert dam was a 'feasible proposition' in 1928 or 1938. Roberts, in making his study of the effects of the Sudd canal, had made a reconnaissance to Uganda to look for potential dam sites, but he no longer worked for the Egyptian government. As early as 1901 Sir William Garstin had expressed grave concern that the well-known seismic activity

[29] Quoted in MacGregor, 'The Upper Nile Irrigation Projects', p. 6.
[30] Ibid.

between Lake Albert and Rejaf made this section of the Bahr al-Jabal an unfavourable site for a dam. In fact it was one of the reasons that he had rushed Dupuis to reconnoitre Lake Tana as a possible alternative reservoir, for to store a large volume of water behind a dam located on the great African Rift itself was a serious proposition, not to be lightly dismissed on the assumption that the Lake Albert dam was necessary for any diversion scheme in the Sudd. In 1923 P. M. Tottenham, G. W. Grabham, geological adviser to the Sudan government, and Husayn Sirry Bey, under-secretary at the ministry of public works, had visited Lake Albert and were the first to suggest a dam at Pachwach. From January to July 1932 a preliminary survey of Lake Albert was made by engineers from the irrigation department. They identified four sites, at Tyoki, Pachwach, Panyango, and Mutir, but, after making borings and taking cross-sections, recommended only Mutir, 80 km from Lake Albert. Here the line of the fault from the eastern escarpment crossed the river, but the granite rock foundation was firm.[31] Oddly enough, no consideration in their report was given to earthquakes.

The departure of Roberts and the demise of the project for the Bor–Zaraf Cut in 1926 revived interest in an alternate route to bypass the Sudd: the Veveno–Pibor scheme. This dramatic change of direction was yet another example of the lack of leadership in Nile development. The Veveno–Pibor scheme required an expensive survey, taking four valuable years, when this bizarre proposal might have been discarded on the basis of a little vision accompanied by a quick and cheap reconnaissance. The object of the scheme was defined by its principal advocate, Geoffrey Parker, Roberts's successor as inspector-general for the Sudan.

The provision of an increased supply of water to Egypt during the spring and summer months by storing in Lake Albert the surplus water of the flood season by releasing it for use in Egypt, and diverting that portion of the discharge that the Bahr el-Gebel cannot carry economically, through a canal into the Veveno, Pibor & Sobat rivers and then back into the White Nile: these three rivers offering

[31] H. G. Bambridge, 'Reports on Investigations for a Dam Site at Mutir', Morrice Papers, Rhodes House Library, Oxford.

themselves for the purpose in being practically empty during that season.[32]

The idea was first suggested in 1918 by O. L. Prowde, inspector of irrigation, Upper Nile, when it was thought that, during the extraordinary high flood of 1917–18, water had passed from the Bahr al-Jabal at Bor to the upper reaches of the Pibor River via the Veveno valley. There is no record of Prowde's reasons for believing that this actually took place, but all one had to do was walk through the country during the few weeks of the year it was passable to determine whether this did in fact occur. Upon the retirement of Roberts and his embankment projects, Parker adopted the Veveno–Pibor scheme as his own and, upon succeeding Roberts, diverted all the energies of the irrigation service on the upper Nile to its investigations. In 1927 he decided on a thorough survey of the route, but this required building a road across the Penykuo plain. This wasted a whole year and entailed extraordinary expenditure for the purchase of graders and other road-building equipment, which had to be shipped all the way from the USA to Bor. In December and January 1928–9 two surveying parties finally began work—one between the Bahr al-Jabal and Lyodein Pool on the Veveno and the other on the lower Veveno to Pibor Post. Ground profiles and soil samples were taken along this route in 1929–30 and the next season, 1930–1. The survey was completed by a detailed investigation of a line from Gemeiza near Bor to the Veveno and the Nyanding River. These surveys proved conclusively that there could not have been any water from the Bahr al-Jabal reaching the upper Veveno even in 1918.[33]

In 1929 the Egyptian irrigation service had been reorganized into a department of the Egyptian ministry of public works in order to bring greater co-ordination among all those agencies dealing with the questions of water, its conservation and distribution. In his massive report recommending this reorganization, Dupuis did not deal directly with the upper Nile, being primarily concerned with ministerial reorganization

[32] G. Parker to under-secretary, ministry of public works, quoted in W. A. C. Perry, inspector of irrigation, 'Note on the Veveno–Pibor Scheme', 28 Feb. 1931, SAD 212/5/47.
[33] Parker and Mackintosh (1934).

and Egypt.[34] One of the committees which emerged out of this reorganization, the departmental committee of the Egyptian irrigation department, was specifically charged to examine the Veveno–Pibor alternative and its impact on the Bahr al-Jabal, including estimates of the cost of construction. The committee was headed by Geoffrey Parker. Hurst and Butcher were members. Between 1929 and 1931 the committee held eight official meetings to consider the Veveno scheme. In March 1931 Parker submitted a draft report which was officially published the following year by the ministry under the title *The Veveno–Pibor Scheme*. The report was not promising, and the committee ultimately rejected the project. It came up for review again in 1938, when it was finally discarded.

The surveys had found that a deep canal would have to be cut from the Bahr al-Jabal to the Veveno, while extensive works would have to have been undertaken on the lower Veveno and Pibor at a prohibitive cost of £E7 500 000 for a saving of only 2 billion m³ of water at Malakal. The scheme, of course, assumed the construction of a dam at Lake Albert and possessed the distinct advantage of circumventing not only the Sudd but the Nilotes as well. Despite these advantages, the cost was too great in the depths of the Depression, and the irrigation department returned to consideration of the embankment projects under a new inspector-general, Frederick Newhouse.[35]

The appointment of Newhouse changed the course of upper Nile development once again. He had never been identified with the Veveno–Pibor scheme and so plunged back into the Sudd. His tenure as inspector-general was marked by an obsession with measurements and data, and between 1932 and his retirment in 1937 the volume of statistics greatly increased, although to what purpose is not clear. For instance, Butcher, director-general, southern Nile, Egyptian irrigation

[34] 'The Position and Activities of the State Service of Irrigation in the Egyptian Government with Special Reference to its Relation with other Government Services, and the most Promising Program of Work for Agricultural Development of the Country by Mr. C. E. Dupuis, May 1929', FO 141/510.

[35] See Egyptian Irrigation Service (1932); Newhouse (1939); E. S. Walker, acting inspector of irrigation, upper White Nile division, *Draft Report of the Committee of Public Works Ministry*, 13 Mar. 1931; and W. A. C. Perry, 'Note on the Veveno–Pibor Scheme', SAD 212/6.

department, had devoted eight years of laborious study to the Sudd, published in February 1938 by the ministry under the title *The Sadd Hydraulics*. H. A. W. Morrice, then divisional engineer, projects division of the Sudan irrigation department, described it as a 'masterly exposition of the complicated hydraulics of the Sudd region', yet Butcher himself could come to no conclusion as to the meaning of his material.

The whole course of the Bahr el Gebel from Mongalla to Lake No has now been discussed reach by reach, and though the major problem, the ultimate destination of the lost water, is still not completely solved, a fairly definite conception of the main features of the sadd hydraulics results . . . The vague and amorphous character of the country and the multiplicity of interlacing channels, large and small, will always make impossible an analysis of flow complete in every detail.[36]

Like his predecessors, Newhouse also ignored the Garstin Cut. While his officials carried out extensive surveys in the Sudd, he gave no serious consideration to a 'direct Beresford line from Bor to the Sobat' (the Garstin Cut), and although he suggested that 'it would be advisable, therefore, to survey this line before a final decision on the Bor–White Nile Diversion Canal', inexplicably he took no steps to do so.[37] This omission is all the more surprising since the Garstin Cut would bypass the swamps, making Butcher's herculean efforts to study swamp losses unnecessary, and allowing the time, men, and money to be more productively spent elsewhere. 'The solutions of the problems of the Sudd Region became itself an objective, and attention was diverted not only from the original purpose of making possible the use of Lake Albert as a reservoir, but also from the straight-forward bypass or short-circuit method of conservation.'[38]

Newhouse argued that the Garstin Cut required construction by dredgers working far from the river. Consequently, it was simply assumed that twenty years would be necessary for its construction with the technology and machines then available. This may have been sound reasoning at the beginning of the century, but only a dearth of leadership in Nile planning can

[36] Butcher (1938*d*, p. 38).   [37] Newhouse (1939, p. 66).
[38] MacGregor, 'The Upper Nile Irrigation Projects', p. 7.

account for the failure not to have at least made a survey of the Garstin Cut. In fact, the appearance of the drag-line excavator after the First World War would drastically have lessened the time projected for construction, but again it was simply assumed that the drag-line could not work in the swamps of the upper Nile, an assumption which was not only to be proved wrong but which was another example of failure to experiment, to try heretical ideas, to lead. Loss of direction and discontinuity of effort was the result.

Geoffrey Parker had hoped to overcome the difficulties encountered by the impassable terrain during the Veveno–Pibor surveys by the use of the aerial surveys of the Sudd made in 1929 by the Air Survey Company. The photographs had revealed a large channel on the eastern edge of the swamp at a small Dinka village called Jonglei, about 65 km downstream from Bor. The channel had in fact been known to hydrologists for years as the Gertrude Nile, named by E. S. Grogan, who first discovered it in 1902 during his Cape-to-Cairo trek. In fact, one of the variations of the embankment projects of the 1920s began the canal to the Zaraf at Jonglei rather than Bor. Now the aerial survey seemed to confirm the importance of this channel, renamed the Atem River, which was flowing 250 m wide at Jonglei and actually carrying discharges greater than the Bahr al-Jabal. When the Veveno–Pibor scheme was rejected, Newhouse turned his attention back to the Sudd, the Atem, and Jonglei.

Butcher had already been at work in this area, accumulating data on flow, losses, and the interstices of streams and channels in the Sudd. He revived Roberts's concept of a combination of a canal being used in conjunction with the existing rivers. It was called the Jonglei Canal diversion scheme, the Jonglei Canal scheme, or more simply the Jonglei Canal. As before, the Sudan government was not kept informed of Butcher's investigations, and the Sudan irrigation department only learned of them in December 1936 and then by a casual and private conversation. The Sudan government remained officially ignorant of Butcher's Jonglei Canal scheme for another eighteen months, prompting a sardonic memorandum from Angus Gillan, the civil secretary, to Sir Miles Lampson, the British high commissioner in Cairo, remonstrating that 'the Jonglei Canal was first brought to the attention of the Sudan Irrigation Adviser [A. N. M. Robertson] when he happened to visit the Ministry of Public Works in Cairo on June 19, 1938 at which time he was handed a copy of Butcher's report which had already been released to the press'.[39]

The Jonglei Canal Diversion Scheme[40] and the subsequent press release was the result of an extensive review, unknown to the Sudan authorities, by an advisory technical committee in the ministry, in the spring of 1938, of all Nile projects and particularly the Sudd canal proposals. At this time the Veveno–Pibor scheme was finally laid to rest, and since no survey of the Garstin Cut had been made, it was not considered, leaving one of the embankment projects, Butcher's Jonglei Canal diversion. As in 1925, the Sudan had not been invited to participate in these deliberations, nor was the government even informed they were taking place. It may have been one thing to keep within the bureacratic bosom of the ministry the discussions which led to the reduction of numerous proposals for a Sudd canal from nine to one, but the patronizing attitude towards the interests of the Sudan bordered on insulting indifference. The dearth of communication by the members of Egypt's Britain department with their counterparts in the Sudan, the seemingly conscious effort to exclude Sudan government officials in the planning for a Sudd canal, and the aura of secrecy which became associated with the operations of the irrigation department produced an atmosphere of suspicion, if not downright hostility, which might have been prevented by more candour and co-operation.

Butcher's report proposed the Jonglei Cut, a diversion canal beginning at Jonglei and running parallel to the Bahr al-Jabal for a distance of 200 km to a point on the Zaraf 175 km from its confluence with the White Nile. At this point the discharge from Jonglei would be carried northward, partly by the Bahr al-Zaraf itself and partly by a new canal constructed to the east of the river and parallel to it as far as the White

[39] Civil secretary, J. A. Gillan, to high commissioner, Sir M. Lampson, 5 July 1938, FO 371/46024.
[40] Butcher (1938b).

Nile. By having the river carry a portion of the discharge, a smaller canal would meet the requirements, at a considerable saving in the cost of excavation. Butcher argued that the importance of Jonglei was twofold. First, it could be constructed without the Lake Albert dam and still provide 2 billion m³ of additional water at Malakal at a cost of £E4 000 000 compared with the Veveno–Pibor Scheme, which would have supplied the same amount of water at Malakal but at a cost of £E7 500 000 and the necessity for a dam at Lake Albert. Butcher was the first since Garstin to contemplate a Sudd canal with the Albert dam, but he was careful not to commit himself to this heresy by demonstrating that the construction of the dam, although not necessary for Jonglei, would provide an additional 1.6 billion m³. In his more famous *The Sadd Hydraulics*,[41] published after his report on Jonglei Canal Scheme of 1936, he completely recanted, and emphasized the importance and need for the Lake Albert dam for the completion of the Jonglei Canal.

The second characteristic of Butcher's report is his profound concern about the impact of the canal on the people of the Upper Nile, to which he devoted two full paragraphs! Here Butcher's investigations led him into the swamps; it would appear that he never read the Roberts report, let alone the memoranda of Chunky Willis or, if he did, that he ignored them. He dismissed the effects of Jonglei on the inhabitants by cheerfully admitting that 'the possible damages to local interests' could not be ascertained without 'full discussion with Sudan authorities', who hitherto had been scrupulously excluded from his Sudd studies. His own considered but obviously uninformed opinion was that 'in general, however, it [local damage] may be considered as very small'. He went on to write that 'there will be practically no visible change in the Jebel area'. How he could make such a prediction remains a mystery. He did admit that Jonglei would open new tracts of territory east of the Bahr al-Jabal hitherto closed to the world, and expressed concern as to the economic and administrative problems created by interjecting £5–6 million into an area where the annual individual cash income was less than 50

[41] Butcher (1938*d*).

piastres. In fairness to Butcher, he was a hydrologist charged with investigating Sudd hydraulics, not the Nilotic way of life; but it was irresponsible to relegate their future to a few pious pronouncements that it would all work out satisfactorily in the end.

Butcher's scheme had, however, two serious flaws. One was his failure to come to grips with cross-drainage and creeping flow. Given his years studying Sudd hydraulics, it is surprising that he came to the erroneous conclusion that the slope of the plain was parallel to the north–south line of the canal. Thus the need for east–west drainage across the canal was 'probably of little importance' and could be satisfied by the two cuts to be made between the Bahr al-Zaraf and the canal at kilometres 238 and 261 respectively. This issue, like the environmental one, could not be so easily resolved. The slope of the Nilotic plain is not simply south–north but in fact tilts to the west, so that water coming from the southern highlands and the rainfall on the Nilotic plain 'creeps' in a manner still not fully understood into the heart of the Sudd. In so doing it would come up against any canal which separated the swamp from the plain, presumably flooding the pastures to the east. This problem became central in the Jonglei investigations after the Second World War and remains largely unexplained to this day. Butcher may be pardoned for not dealing with environmental issues he was not charged to examine; he cannot remain above criticism for not dealing with fundamental hydrological ones.[42]

A more serious error was his failure, during his many years on the upper Nile, to measure with greater precision the rate of evaporation. His estimate of gross evaporation in the Sudd of 1,533 mm per year, as against revised calculations a generation later of 2,150 mm, more than accounts for the disparity between inflow at Mongalla and outflow at the White Nile, which he could not explain but which could not be known in 1938.[43] Not only did this mysterious loss of water defy the laws concerning the indestructibility of matter, but it was rationalized by spillage east of Bor on the Penykou plain

[42] See Butcher (1936b) and the correspondence and statistical tables accompanying his report, UNP I/10/84, 85. This was later reprinted as Butcher (1938b).
[43] See Penman (1963); Sutcliffe and Parks (1987).

and to the west into the Bahr al-Ghazal, which probably did not occur and which would not have been necessary to explain the loss of Sudd water if a more realistic rate of evaporation had been applied to the exposed area of the permanent and seasonal swamp.

The reaction to the Jonglei Canal by British officials in the Sudan was instantaneous. John Winder, a member of the Sudan political service for ten years and district commissioner of the Zaraf district in the heart of the canal zone since 1936, raised many of the same criticisms which Willis had done ten years before, but supported by a more thorough understanding of the province and its people than Willis ever possessed. He challenged Butcher on his own ground, hydrology, by citing the fact that the Jonglei Canal would block the *khors* and streams which drain into the Bahr al-Zaraf from the east. At the same time the canal would divert water from the south away from the Gawaar plain, depriving these pastures of moisture. He raised the prospect of the inundation of Zaraf Island and the flooding of the Khor Famyr by back-flow from the Bahr al-Zaraf. He argued that the water from the Atem region would not be able to reach the Bahr al-Jabal.[44] The importance of these criticisms lies not so much in whether Butcher could answer them, but rather in the fact that they aroused a rather somnolent government in Khartoum. In 1928 Roberts had recommended that the Sudan government should begin a programme designed to gather its own information about the Sudd and its people, independently from that of the Egyptian irrigation department. The officials in Khartoum had done nothing. In 1938, however, when faced with the same danger the government could hardly ignore the interests of those people for whom they were the trustees at a time when the senior officials in Khartoum were embarrassingly aware of, and not a little guilty about, their indifference to the southern Sudan.

Winder's letter produced a great stir in Malakal and Khartoum. The Sudan Government had to do something and do it now. Consequently, within a few weeks Winder was on

[44] J. Winder, district commissioner, Upper Nile province, to E. G. Coryton, governor, Upper Nile province, 18 Feb. 1939, UNP I/10/85.

trek with A. E. Griffin, assistant director, Sudan irrigation department, on a preliminary reconnaissance to formulate what questions should be addressed so that the inhabitants of the Upper Nile would not be abandoned by ignorance to the tender mercies of the engineers and the canal-builders. It was the first time that the Sudan irrigation department had been officially involved in Sudd projects.

There were less visible reasons for the Sudan government to inform itself as to conditions on the Upper Nile. In any large bureaucracy accustomed to consuming substantial sums of money, such as the Egyptian irrigation department, there were compelling reasons for building the Jonglei Canal that had little to do with water or the Nilotes. In 1936 the Egyptian irrigation department saw itself running out of projects to propose and concrete to pour in Egypt itself. This was due in part to its own failure to develop a comprehensive programme of Nile control and in part to its preoccupation with parochial projects and narrow investigations, requiring only limited vision but absorbing time and money. The completion of the Jabal 'Auliya dam in 1937 and the increased storage at Aswan had satisfied Egypt's thirst for Timely water for twenty years. If the Lake Tana reservoir were constructed and modest conservancy schemes undertaken in Egypt, the engineers projected (quite mistakenly, to be sure) that Egyptian water needs could be met until 1990. They did not, therefore, foresee any immediate need for water from the Sudd, nor for a Sudd canal, when by 1942 projects within Egypt itself would be few. Rather than retrench, the officials of the ministry of public works began to think of utilizing their established technical competence and financial credits 'on works not urgently necessary', justifying them on the grounds of future use instead of immediate need. The alternative would be to reduce the size of the irrigation department to a care and maintenance basis, and to bring the hydrological development of the Nile basin, however piecemeal, to an inglorious halt. None of this proved true, but in 1938 it was believed, and it was faith in the future more than contemporary facts which could sustain continuous water planning. The Jonglei Canal would satisfy this belief, taking some ten years to complete and employing the energies of an army of officials in the irrigation department.

The impact of Jonglei on the peoples of the Upper Nile was not a serious consideration.[45]

In the late spring of 1939 A. E. Griffin reported his initial findings. He concentrated on Butcher's weakness, already identified by Winder—the problem of cross-drainage, whereby a banked channel or canal running through the eastern swamp would block all lateral spilling on the one hand and the flow of water from east to west on the other. The pattern of cross-drainage was critical in a country where a change in the water-level of a few centimetres would expose or submerge thousands of feddans. These khors are not just drainage streams, however, but 'canals, reservoirs, and drains at various times of the year and provide food and water for the tribes'. Without a means to drain into the swamps, the water from July to December would remain trapped behind the Jonglei Canal unless an expensive system of syphons and gravity drains were constructed under the canal to permit the water to reach the Bahr al-Zaraf and free the land for grazing. Moreover, there were serious doubts whether water released from the canal in the Timely season from January to July would flow eastward when the pattern of drainage was to the north and west. Griffin summed up his brief sojourn in the Upper Nile by repeating Roberts's admonition. 'In view of the limited information given the Public Works Ministry and the Jonglei Scheme Report which at present is the only data available, I consider the opposition shown by the province administration is justified.'[46] The whole tone of Butcher's report was simple, optimistic, and inexpensive. The man on the spot strongly disagreed. The time had come for the Sudan to carry out its own careful, cautious study, independent of the Egyptian irrigation department.

A more persuasive and critical report was submitted in 1940 by John Winder as the storms of war gathered over the Sudan. Like his letter in February 1939, his report in 1940 created concern in Khartoum, for it represented, not the views of an engineer in the irrigation department, but the reasoned opinions of one of the Sudan's rulers. Winder's message was

[45] See Butcher (1936a).
[46] A. E. Griffin, assistant director of irrigation, 'Note on the Jonglei Scheme', 3 May 1939, UNP I/10/85.

written in clear English unconfused by the reams of technical data and the scientific jargon which clutter the reports of hydrologists to exasperate civil secretaries and governors-general. Winder's argument was straightforward. The Egyptian irrigation department simply did not have the information which the Sudan required. Its knowledge was hydrological and statistical, dealing with river flows and discharges. It had little concern and less information about the impact of its schemes in the land beyond the rivers. Winder advocated a different approach. 'Instead of asking the Egyptian Irrigation Service information on points which do not really interest them and on which they do not have the information, get what statistics they have and couple it with our own experience of the country and what we can get from local sources.'[47]

The senior officials in Khartoum concurred so long as Egypt paid for the study. If it had taken twenty years for the irrigation department to collect the hydrological data, the information Winder wanted would take many years and considerable expense. The ministry was wary not so much of the amount of money required but by the sudden resurgence of interest by the Sudan government in matters pertaining to Upper Nile hydrology and its determination to seek information independently from the irrigation department. They had cautiously agreed to discuss financing the Winder programme, when suddenly all negotiations were silenced by the sound of distant trumpets.[48] No serious talks between the Sudan and Egypt about Nile water were held during the Second World War, but the Jonglei Canal was not forgotten.

By the end of 1943 the war had passed beyond the Sudan. The Italians had been defeated in Ethiopia and the Germans in North Africa. The shadows of war remained throughout the Sudan, but the guns were stilled and the thoughts of British officials in the Upper Nile, at Malakal and Khartoum, began to turn to Jonglei. The war had introduced a new spirit into the British trusteeship in the Sudan, marked by a sense that the governance of the Sudanese would never return to the style and

[47] Winder to governor, Upper Nile province, C. A. Armstrong, 13 May 1940; J. Winder, 'Note on Jonglei Scheme', May 1940, UNP I/10/85.
[48] Financial secretary, F. D. Rugman, to civil secretary, J. A. Gillan, 17 July 1940, FO 371/46024.

form of the pre-war years and that the lands beyond Malakal could no longer be neglected. Thus, when C. G. Davies, the governor of the Upper Nile, wrote to the director of the Sudan irrigation department, A. E. Griffin, via the civil secretary, Douglas Newbold, in September 1943 about Jonglei, he did so in the context of the economic development of the Upper Nile province and not just in relation to a water conservancy scheme.

Davies had returned to Malakal in late August fresh from long talks with Newbold and C. H. L. Skeet, governor of Equatoria province, as to the future of the south. Newbold himself had come to the conclusion that new initiatives·had to be made in the southern Sudan, and in February 1944 the governor-general announced to his senior officials a 'new deal' of economic and educational development for the south. Davies's request to begin planning the economic development of the Upper Nile must be viewed in this context. The Nilotes had been pacified, the system of native administration was functioning, and the time had come to find some outlet for the energies of the Nilotes that would lead to the improvement of their material well-being. This could only be accomplished by making an initial investment to obtain expert opinions and scientific data on just how best to develop the economy of the Upper Nile around Jonglei. The Egyptians seemed as determined as ever to build the Sudd canal, and without its own information there would be no way the Sudan could protect its interests or compete with the Egyptians in negotiations over the use or claims on any water conserved by the scheme.[49] Davies was essentially reviving Winder's proposal of 1940, but he also raised the point about the importance of the timing of its construction to the development of the province as a whole, and its role in the sensitive and difficult relations between Egypt and the Sudan as to the distribution of the totality of the Nile waters.

As before, everyone agreed, but in 1944 manpower and materials were short, and Davies was encouraged to begin

[49] A. E. Griffin, director, Sudan irrigation department, 'Note on Technical Procedures for Scrutinizing the Jonglei Canal Scheme in Relation to its Physical Effects in the Sudan', 3 Aug. 1940, SAD 500/13; C. G. Davies, governor, Upper Nile province, to A. E. Griffin, via Sir Douglas Newbold, 4 Sept. 1943, UNP I/9/72.

locally with what he had, additional resources to be mustered by Khartoum as part of the package of economic development envisaged for the southern Sudan. As usual, the Egyptians were ignoring Khartoum and had to be prodded by Huddleston in December 1944 to open consultations. Finally, in March 1945, nearly five years after F. D. Rugman, the financial secretary, had agreed to technical consultations, the Egyptian inspector-general of irrigation now informed Khartoum that Egypt was prepared to begin talks with a view to the consummation of the Jonglei Canal. After five years of silence, the request caught the Sudan government by surprise. Since early in 1944, Newbold had been considering the establishment of an Upper Nile development survey team to undertake the investigations which Griffin and Winder had advocated back in 1939 and 1940. Not having a full team, the financial secretary, J. W. A. Miller, to whom the Egyptian request had been made, did the next best thing and sent H. A. W. Morrice from the Sudan irrigation department to Malakal in May to begin the technical discussions with the Egyptian irrigation department concerning Jonglei; the idea was for Humphrey Morrice to formulate the questions the survey team should tackle.[50]

In 1945 Morrice was the divisional engineer, projects division, of the Sudan irrigation department. He was as brilliant at mathematics as he was at bridge. His passion for books on virtually every subject was matched by his methodical nature, and by a critical mind which he applied to people as well as to numbers. In the same year he had published *The Chasm: The Protest of an Engineer*, the theme of which was the seemingly unbridgeable canyon between practice and theory, or between scientists like himself and those educated in the humanist tradition who dominated government and regarded the former more as the electricians in the house of civilization. In fact he had been educated at Wellington and at Corpus Christi College, Cambridge, was an excellent linguist and a voracious reader in the humanities, and it was the humanists in the Sudan administration whom he most admired. Pleasant

[50] See correspondence on this issue in UNP I/10/85, particularly J. W. A. Miller, financial secretary, to Davies, 10 May 1945; Royal Egyptian ministry of foreign affairs to British foreign office, 29 Aug. 1945, FO 371/46024.

without camaraderie, analytical without introspection, he ranks with Garstin, MacDonald, and Hurst as one of the great innovators of Nile hydrology.

He steamed south to meet H. G. Bambridge, the inspector of irrigation for the White Nile inspectorate of the Egyptian irrigation department and the longest-residing European official of the Upper Nile. Morrice had been deeply influenced by Butcher's *The Sadd Hydraulics*, finding the mathematics elegant and the exposition of the complicated hydrology of the Sudd 'masterly'. To be sure, Butcher had not been overly concerned about the Nilotic people, but neither at the time was Morrice. He was an engineer who had come to discuss with another engineer Butcher's proposal for the Sudd canal. To his surprise Bambridge dismissed Butcher's canal and instead unfolded a different project, as the two sat beneath the tall trees which shade the spacious compound of the Egyptian irrigation department at Malakal.

In that spring of 1945 Butcher's Sudd canal, the Jonglei Canal diversion scheme, had been officially adopted by the ministry of public works. It had been approved by the minister of public works, Isma'il Sirry Pasha, in 1938 and the details of the project had been formally communicated to the Sudan government. All discussions concerning Jonglei had henceforth been predicated on the Butcher proposal. At Malakal Bambridge spoke persuasively of a different project—a straight-line trench from Jonglei to the Sobat, the old Garstin Cut—as a cheaper and more efficient alternative. As early as 1938, when the ministry had all of the Sudd canal projects under review, Bambridge had proposed a direct canal from Jonglei to the Zaraf River as a modification of the Butcher line which ran close to and parallel with the Bahr al-Jabal. The important difference was that the Bambridge canal would be excavated by 'cranker' drag-lines rather than by dredgers. Bambridge had become convinced by the reports of Priestman, Cooke, and Shukry, and by the experience of the Ruston–Bucyrus company, of the superiority and efficiency of drag-lines over dredging machines.[51] It had become an accepted assumption that a Garstin Cut could only be excavated by

[51] H. A. W. Morrice, 'Bambridge Report on the Direct Line', Morrice Papers, Rhodes House Library, Oxford.

dredgers, for it was the only machine that could operate in the Sudd, despite its slowness and the consequent escalation of the cost of construction. Since Garstin, however, the technology had changed dramatically with the advent of the drag-line; and yet no one in the irrigation department had bothered to apply the potential of the drag-line excavator to the construction of the Sudd canal. Butcher had accepted the received wisdom that drag-lines could not be used in flooded areas, yet in 1939 they had been shown to perform successfully in the worst possible conditions. In fact, Butcher himself and Geoffrey Parker had been given detailed information as early as 1932 about the superiority of the drag-line over the dredger. The Monighan drag-line had been employed with great success on the lower Mississippi in conditions not dissimilar to the sudd of the southern Sudan, but, inexplicably, neither Butcher nor Parker made any attempt to test this new technology.[52]

Moreover, the sudd is not a bottomless swamp. It has in fact a firm bed of impervious clay on which drag-lines might rest to excavate a straight, cheap canal. Such a canal would eliminate any danger of flooding the Zaraf Island. The serious problem of cross-drainage would not be resolved, but a straight-line canal would enable engineers to introduce remedial measures more easily than Butcher's combined canal–river scheme. There were other advantages. A direct canal would reduce by half the distance from Bor to Malakal. A straight-line embankment would be ideal for road and rail communications, opening the Upper Nile and dramatically improving links between northern and southern Sudan.[53]

Bambridge had come to the conclusion in 1938, by his own investigations, that the best canal was a straight one. It is difficult to imagine, however, that he was not influenced by subsequent thinking within the ministry in Cairo, for at the end of the war Hurst was completing volume VII of *The Nile Basin, The Future Conservation of the Nile*. In this seminal work Hurst proposed a huge canal from Jonglei to the Sobat, capable of carrying large quantities of water from the

[52] Ruston–Bucyrus Ltd. to A. D. Butcher, director-general, irrigation projects, copy to G. Parker, 17 Sept. 1932, SAD 500/13.

[53] 'Effects of the Jonglei Scheme: Notes on a Visit to Mr. H. G. Bambridge to Discuss the Jonglei Scheme June 19, 1945 by H. A. Morrice', UNP I/9/77.

equatorial lakes, as the linch-pin of his comprehensive plan for century storage in the Nile basin. Bambridge must have known of Hurst's plan and realized that the need for a direct canal would immediately render irrelevant all previous proposals for a Sudd canal. *The Future Conservation of the Nile* had immense ramifications for the Sudan and particularly for the inhabitants of the Upper Nile province. Indeed, even if the Sudan government had not reacted to the latest thinking of the irrigation department which Morrice brought back with him from Malakal in the spring of 1945, the publication of Hurst's proposal for a big canal the following year would have forced its hand.

Like every engineer who has gone to the swamps of the upper Nile, Morrice returned to Khartoum with impressive arguments for yet another cut through the Sudd. The welter of data, the confusion of the recommendations, only solidified opinion, long ago accepted in principle, that a committee be established to investigate the Jonglei scheme with a view to the best development for the peoples of the Upper Nile. More-over, Huddleston was incensed. Throughout the whole history of the Sudd canal the Egyptians had ignored the Sudan government, carrying on their investigations in secrecy and without much consultation, creating in Khartoum only distrust for their proposals, not to mention their motives. Once again, in the autumn of 1945, they ignored the Sudan government when soliciting the views of Uganda and the Belgian Congo concerning the Lake Albert dam. Calculated or not, this insult convinced Huddleston and his advisers that the time had come to find their own team to gather their own information. He wrote angrily to Lord Killearn, the British ambassador in Cairo: 'The Sudan should not be expected to agree beforehand to a final "Blue-print" without preserving the right to ask for modification.'[54] That same month the Jonglei committee was established in order to determine just such modifications, under the chairmanship of the financial secretary, Sir Edington 'Jock' Miller, and including F. D. Kingdon, governor of the Upper Nile, G. F. March, director of agriculture, W. N. Allan, director of irrigation, and

[54] Huddleston to HM high commissioner, Lord Killearn, 17 Nov. 1945, FO 371/46024.

a special irrigation consultant, R. M. MacGregor. The purpose of the committee was to review the reports by the two principal investigators, Humphrey Morrice and John Winder, who, with a team of officers from the veterinary and surveying services and with support from departments of the Sudan government, were to make recommendations to the committee. Its mandate was as wide as its membership. It was to provide reliable information about the effects of the Jonglei scheme on the interests of the Sudan, with specific regard to flooding, grazing, agriculture, fishing, tribal interests, river ports and roads, and to consider possible alternative alignments for the canal. A separate budget was allocated, and the official approval of the Jonglei investigation team was made public by the governor-general on 1 January 1946.[55]

The appointment of the Jonglei Investigation Team and the publication of *The Future Conservation of the Nile* ended the years of indecision. They may have been productive. The engineers of the irrigation department had been assiduous in compiling statistics, the physical department in printing them in manifold volumes. To what purpose the ant-like activity was directed was a question to which no one in the irrigation service or the ministry could have offered more than platitudes. Indeed, progress in the development of the Nile basin came to a halt in 1914. The publication of *Nile Control* had been MacDonald's defence of his stewardship at the ministry, not a plan of action. The Jabal 'Auliya dam and the Gezira scheme were planned and approved before the war. The Lake Tana dam was prepared for execution, not by the irrigation department, but by the American firm of J. G. White Engineering, at the behest of the emperor of Ethiopia. The greatest confusion, dearth of direction, and lack of definition was attached to the Lake Albert dam and the Sudd region conservation project. The site for the dam had not been chosen, and only a preliminary survey made, by 1932. By 1945 the feasibility of building this dam remained in doubt. It remains so to this day. The simplest method of bypassing the Sudd had yet to be examined, while the energies of the irrigation department were absorbed in exhaustive, tangential,

[55] Sir Edington Miller, financial secretary, to legal secretary, 22 Nov. 1945, UNP I/10/85; Jonglei Investigation Team (1954, vol. i, p. iii).

and expensive studies. Despite this misdirected effort, all the vessels, vehicles, and infrastructure based on the huge department compound at Malakal had been ordered in 1906, with major additions of equipment added in 1925.

To be sure, the disappearance of the post of adviser to the ministry of public works was a set-back for Nile planning, for no co-ordinating agency replaced that individual. The inability of the high commissioner to intervene actively in the affairs of the ministry, as Cromer, Gorst, and Kitchener had done, was a demonstrable symbol of Egyptian independence; but no one, British or Egyptian, replaced that imperial influence. But these handicaps cannot account for the lack of continuity and foresight and the ineffectual execution which characterized Sudd studies in the inter-war years. Without leadership, the engineers of the irrigation department responsible for the development of irrigation projects in the upper Nile, Roberts, Parker, and Newhouse, went each their own way, so that in the end all they had to show for a quarter-century of work was a mass of statistics and a dozen worthless proposals. R. M. MacGregor wrote the epitaph for these years of indecision a few short months before his death:

It is difficult to suggest any remedy for this situation or to take a hopeful view of the prospect of advancing these major development projects through any agency now present in the Nile Valley.[56]

---

[56] MacGregor, 'The Upper Nile Irrigation Projects', p. 8.

6

The Equatorial Nile Project

It will be seen that a line drawn through Bor, on the Upper Bahr-el-Gebel, and running due north and south would cut the White Nile at or near the point where the Sobat joins this river (Longitude 31°40′E. of Greenwich). The distance between these two points in a straight line is approximately 340 kilometers. Were it possible to excavate an entirely new channel for the river, following this line, and to bring down its waters by this means from the Upper Nile at Bor, direct to the White Nile, at the Sobat junction, the advantages that would be secured are so great and so obvious as to outweigh almost every objection that could be made to the proposal, short of the fact that further knowledge might prove that its execution was a sheer impossibility—owing to the levels or the conformation of the intervening country.

Sir William Garstin, 1904

In the autumn of 1946 the Egyptian ministry of public works published *The Nile Basin*, volume VII: *The Future Conservation of the Nile* by H. E. Hurst, R. P. Black, and Y. M. Simaika. It was a dramatic event, ending the years of indecision. Hurst himself was fully conscious of its importance. Having just sent the manuscript to the press he wrote to Nimmo Allan, irrigation consultant to the Sudan government, in August. 'Anyway the first thing is to have the engineering and scientific side on a sound basis, and this we think we have done. Of course, the scheme can be modified in detail, but it is useless to devise schemes only for immediate development as has been the practice in the past.'[1] For the first time since the publication of *Nile Control* in 1920, a comprehensive plan for Nile development had been conceived, which included three major innovations in planning. First, *The Future Conservation of*

[1] H. E. Hurst to W. N. Allan, irrigation consultant, Sudan Govt., 27 Aug. 1946, SAD 589/14/1–95.

the Nile was based on half a century of accumulated data, most collected during the inter-war years and published in the first six volumes of *The Nile Basin*. Neither Garstin nor MacDonald had the benefit of this information. Second, Hurst's plan demonstrated the interrelation between the individual projects which had emerged in the form of a variety of separate proposals during the preceding decades. Garstin and MacDonald had regarded the Nile basin from a holistic perspective, but never with such definition. The unique feature of *The Future Conservation of the Nile* was the introduction of the concept of 'century storage'. MacDonald had been the first to propose the storage of Nile water from one year to the next in order to balance low years by high ones. He called this form of conservancy 'over-year storage', but his ideas were vague, and he never explained how they would function. He was much too preoccupied with problems of annual storage in his defence of the Sennar and Jabal 'Auliya dams to think in more far-reaching terms. Consequently, Hurst's century storage not only was new but immediately became the fundamental principle by which all subsequent projects for Nile control have been considered.

Century storage is the logical extension of over-year storage. Hurst combined the theory of probability with an analysis of meteorological phenomena to calculate the capacity of storage required to maintain every year an outflow from the reservoirs equal to the average outflow for 100 years. The longer the period over which that average is to be maintained the more likely it is that an exceptional year, high or low, will be encountered, thereby requiring a reservoir with exceptional capacity to accommodate the exception. The idea of using the equatorial lakes as reservoirs was not new. Sir Samuel Baker had broached just such a proposal in the 1870s, but J. C. Ross was the first specifically to advocate the construction of dams at Lakes Victoria and Albert in 1893.[2] Sir William Willcocks, then the director-general of reservoirs for the public works department, employed this concept in his more comprehensive programme for Nile water development, but did not elaborate on such a prospect because of insufficient data.[3] Garstin, of

[2] Ross (1893).
[3] Willcocks (1894).

course, proposed such regulators in 1904, as did MacDonald in 1920, but Hurst was the first to demonstrate that they could be used for the objective of achieving century storage.

The birth of *The Future Conservation of the Nile* had not been easy. Since the resignation of MacDonald, the irrigation department had been preoccupied with collecting data and rather chaotically proposing individual schemes in lieu of any plan that would relate them one to another. The physical department was absorbed in analysis and computation. Neither perceived the need for, nor was willing to accept, the responsibility for Nile planning, and the initiative for a grand design for Nile control seems to have come from the Egyptian ministers and under-secretaries at the ministry of public works. Husayn Sirry Pasha sought to clarify the relations between the separate projects of the irrigation department in his *Irrigation in Egypt*, but it was a very general exposition, particularly in regard to Upper Nile projects, and without any theoretical principles to give it structure. Its publication did not relieve the pressure upon Hurst and his colleagues to formulate a comprehensive plan from the data assembled, analysed, and published. After the defeat of the German Afrika Korps at El Alamein in 1942, the threat to British control of the Middle East gradually receded, and, conversely, the demands upon the British officials at the physical department for a plan increased. 'Abd al-Kawi Pasha persistently pressed Hurst for a plan, and was duly rewarded with *The Future Conservation of the Nile* in 1946.

Hurst argued that century storage was only possible in the equatorial lakes, where the evaporation is balanced by rainfall but also where any rise in the level of the lakes, confined by their geological configuration, will not greatly increase the area exposed to evaporation. Hurst proposed to convert Lake Albert into a large reservoir in which sufficient water for century storage could be preserved by building the Lake Albert dam at Nimule. The reservoir created could then be supplemented if necessary by a regulator at the outlet from Lake Victoria to provide a more constant discharge and hydroelectric power. The idea of the Lake Albert dam was not new; during the inter-war years it had become an unquestioned assumption at the irrigation department. Hurst, however, conceived of this dam for a new purpose, century storage. He calculated that century storage required a total reserved capacity of 155 billion m³, and thus a very large dam and reservoir. The dam at Lake Albert must therefore be capable of storing at least 140 billion m³, which would mean raising the level of the lake 22 m, from 13 m on the gauge at Butiaba to 35 m. If Lake Victoria were to act in tandem with Lake Albert, then its level could be raised some 2.8 m by a dam to provide a reservoir with a capacity Hurst calculated at some 60 billion m³. Then the Lake Albert reservoir could be smaller, only some 80 billion m³, or a rise on the Butiaba gauge to only 25 m. Either by itself or in conjunction with Lake Victoria, this would be water 'enough for many years to come' so long as a means could be devised to bring it down through the Sudd to the White Nile.[4] Until then the Lake Albert dam had been regarded as a necessity not only to prevent water losses in the Sudd but, according to the Roberts report of 1928, to maintain the regime of the swamps. Hurst now gave a reason for the Lake Albert dam which reduced the previous rationales to insignificance. Century storage, not the regime or losses in the swamps, depended on that big dam at Lake Albert.

Having decided on a big reservoir (see Map 5), Hurst now had to consider the means of transporting a large volume of water through the Sudd. Butcher's canal, the Jonglei Canal diversion scheme, simply would not do. It was totally inadequate for century storage. Butcher's Jonglei Canal could only carry 29 Mm³/d; Hurst required a canal almost twice as large, capable of transporting 55 Mm³/d. So large was the planned reservoir behind the Albert dam, however, the discharge into the Nile below would frequently register flows as high as 100 Mm³/d. The natural flow of the Bahr al-Jabal could accommodate 40 Mm³, and perhaps more by embankment, leaving the Jonglei Canal to carry the rest, 55 Mm³. Such a canal would have to be very different from that of Butcher—but in what way Hurst hesitated to make clear: 'The extra size of channel required to get the water through the Sudd Region, when a low year on the Main Nile makes it

[4] Hurst et al. (1946, p. 5).

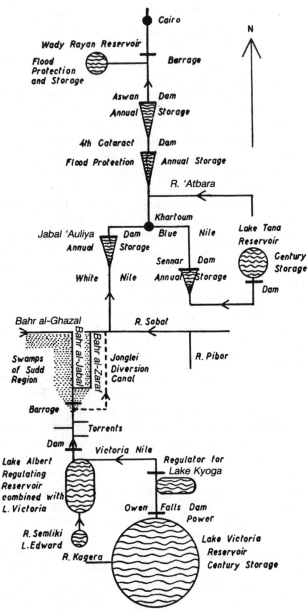

MAP 5. Hurst's plan for century storage
Source: Hurst (1952)

necessary, has not yet been considered.'[5] Hurst vaguely thought of embanking the Bahr al-Jabal to deliver 54 Mm^3/d. This was a direct reference to Butcher's embankment scheme, which had been rejected during the departmental review of Sudd canal projects in 1938.[6] Beyond this suggestion Hurst refused to speculate. All that he required for century storage was a means of carrying 55 Mm^3 through the swamps.

The definition of the Sudd canal, strangely enough, came from the Sudan and not from the irrigation department. When Humphrey Morrice had visited H. G. Bambridge at Malakal in the spring of 1945, the Sudan authorities first learned that some in the ministry were thinking in terms of a direct-line canal from Jonglei to the Sobat. Moreover, they were impressed by Morrice's arguments for a Garstin Cut in his report of the discussions with Bambridge, and instructed the director of the Sudan irrigation department, Nimmo Allan, to sound out the Egyptians. He met with Sabry al-Kurdi Bey, inspector-general, and E. S. Waller, his deputy, in November at the ministry to discuss the line for the Jonglei Canal. They expressed eagerness to begin construction, but it was clear to Allan that there was considerable difference of opinion within the ministry as to the best line for the Jonglei Cut. The influential under-secretary, Naguib Ibrahim Bey, was strongly in favour of adhering as closely as possible to Butcher's route.[7]

Alarmed by these revelations and realizing their own ignorance, British officials in Khartoum speedily formed the Jonglei committee in the autumn of 1945, which in turn appointed Morrice as chairman and John Winder as his deputy to head a Jonglei Investigation Team. They were given a wide charge, and were promised support from the members of the administrative departments of the Sudan government, but in fact between 1946 and 1948 the Jonglei Investigation Team consisted of just Morrice and Winder.

John Winder was the experienced political officer who knew the land and the people of the Upper Nile, just as Humphrey Morrice understood its hydrology. Winder was a Lancashire man, from a family of professional solicitors and engineers in

---

[5] Hurst *et al.* (1946, p. 7).   [6] Butcher (1938*a*).
[7] W. N. Allan, director, Sudan irrigation department, to Sir Edington Miller, financial secretary, 28 Nov. 1945, SAD 589/14/1–95.

Bolton. After a year at Harvard he returned to the more familiar surroundings of Cambridge, after which he soon discovered himself in the Sudan political service on the basis of an offhand remark about the quality of its personnel made by Sir Rennell Rodd and the eagle eye of Sir Harold MacMichael, who was always on the lookout for promising recruits. Judicious and perceptive, Winder was transferred to the upper Nile province in May 1936, first to Gambila and then to Akobo, where he began a long and discriminating association among the Nuer, culminating in his governorship of those Nilotes whom he had done so much to defend against dangers from Jonglei.

The amount of work that two dedicated men can accomplish unencumbered by the administrative trivia of managing a large research team is astonishing; yet it is quite clear that Winder and Morrice could not investigate the whole environment and hydrology of the Sudd. They very sensibly sought to define the problems created by the Sudd canal for the Nilotic inhabitants, their animals, and the wildlife, and to suggest the means of resolving those problems. This had been Morrice's brief when he was sent to Malakal in 1945—to formulate what questions required investigation—when he had been diverted by Bambridge's exposition of a direct canal. Morrice and Winder produced three interim reports in 1946, 1947, and 1948. In the introduction to the *Third Interim Report*, they observed that the preliminary work of identifying the problems was finished.[8] The investigation must now enter a second stage, to seek solutions to the problems they had identified. These researches, however, would require methodical and detailed study far beyond the capabilities of a single hydrologist and a political officer. They proposed an enlarged Jonglei Investigation Team with specialists in hydrology, ecology, anthropology, animal and grassland husbandry, agriculture, and fisheries. The Jonglei committee agreed, and at the end of 1948 established an autonomous research unit with its own experts, facilities, and budget, under the chairmanship of Dr P. P. Howell of the Sudan political service.

[8] H. A. W. Morrice, chairman, Jonglei Investigation Team, to E. V. Rintoul, secretary, Jonglei committee, 5 July 1947; H. A. W. Morrice and J. Winder, *First Second and Third Interim Reports*, Khartoum, 1946, 1947, 1948, respectively, UNP I/10/87.

Morrice and Winder had begun their first survey in the early spring of 1946, on the assumption that Butcher's Jonglei Canal diversion scheme was the Sudd canal proposal officially sanctioned by the ministry of public works, despite what Morrice had learned from Bambridge the previous year about the direct-line canal. They had no other alternative. Hurst was only just completing *The Future Conservation of the Nile*; the draft was sent to the press in late July at the same time that Morrice and Winder submitted their *First Interim Report*. The report made sober reading in Khartoum and was not well received in Cairo. It was primarily concerned with the deleterious effect of the Sudd canal on the living conditions of the people of the upper Nile, but did not suggest opposing the construction of the Jonglei scheme. No one did. Everyone simply assumed that a Sudd canal would be built. The problem was to determine which canal and its operations would do the least damage to the people, and their livelihood, for which the British administration in the Sudan were responsible.

Morrice and Winder came to two important conclusions in 1946. First, if the Jonglei Canal had to be built, the Albert dam and reservoir should be combined with it so that the operations of the reservoir could be conducted to minimize damage to the local environment.[9] This provisional acceptance of the Jonglei Canal was to have lasting ramifications. It established among some officials in Khartoum a fatalistic attitude. However much the Sudan government might complain to Egypt about the damage to the people of the Upper Nile, Egypt needed the water and was determined to get it. To these same officials the excavation of the Jonglei Canal seemed inevitable. Therefore, the Sudan should not seek to block its construction but to seek compensation and remedial measures in return. There was, moreover, a long-term benefit to be gained by adopting an accommodating posture. In November 1945 the Sudan department of irrigation had prepared for the governor-general's council a review of the future water needs of the Sudan, predicting a minimum future requirement of

[9] Morrice and Winder, *First Interim Report*, pt. viii, Nos. 1 and 15, UNP I/10/87 and FO 141/1215; Allan to Hurst, 21 Aug. 1946, SAD 589/14/1-95.

7.5 billion m³.[10] A portion of this water would come from the Sudan's share, 50 per cent, of the additional water conserved from the construction of a dam at Lake Tana, but Nimmo Allan forecast that the Sudan would still require another half-billion m³ from any Jonglei–Albert project.[11] In fact the Sudan needed Jonglei Canal water but had no agreement with Egypt, unlike the case of Lake Tana, to have any claim upon it. If Egypt were going to insist upon the canal, the Sudan might as well benefit rather than lose by obstinate obstructionism. This conviction was strengthened as the researches of the Jonglei Investigation Team in subsequent years sharply escalated fears about the negative effects of the canal upon the inhabitants of the Upper Nile. They had a signed agreement allocating the waters of Lake Tana; they had none for the Equatorial Nile Project.

Second, Morrice and Winder rejected Butcher's Jonglei Canal diversion scheme. It would flood the Zaraf Island and produce back-flooding, it ignored the problem of cross-drainage, and it would seriously damage grazing. They recommended a direct line from Jonglei to the mouth of the Sobat to avoid some of these disadvantages and to reduce others.[12] In this fashion the Jonglei Canal of today was, in fact, the creation of the Sudan government.

Although the *First Interim Report* was a preliminary study and its conclusions provisional, it remains one of the most significant documents in the Jonglei literature. It established the context and tone of virtually all subsequent investigations. It defined the problem: the reduction of losses in the Sudd and the effects of such saving on the living and economy of the peoples of the Upper Nile. It proposed the direct line. It drew attention to the potential damage to the people and their way of living. It defined the future programme of work by members of the investigating team. In effect it was an

---

[10] In 1945 the Sudan was entitled by agreements to 4.4 billion m³. The figure of 7.5 billion m³ forecast in 1945 as the future annual needs of the Sudan was computed by estimating the number of feddans where irrigation was practicable and economical. It envisaged an increase of 2 million feddans, a prediction which by 1948 was woefully inadequate.

[11] Allan, 'Note to Council', 10 Nov. 1945, SAD 589/14/1–95.

[12] Morrice and Winder, *First Interim Report*, pt. viii, Nos. 2, 3, 7, 8, 10, 11; see also W. N. Allan, 'Notes on *First Interim Report*', 21 Aug. 1946, SAD 589/3/12.

embryonic environmental impact report long before those studies were conceived as such. The Jonglei committee unanimously endorsed the report, and forwarded an edited copy in November to the inspector-general of irrigation at the ministry in Cairo. At the same time they instructed Morrice and Winder to return to the Sudd and continue their work 'with the greatest possible energy', incensed by the Egyptian reaction to the *First Interim Report*.

The irrigation department dismissed the conclusions of Morrice and Winder with ill-disguised disdain. Its officials displayed little interest in the authors' sombre warnings of the impact on the Nilotes of the Jonglei scheme, and found the report seriously flawed, since Morrice and Winder had conducted their studies on the assumption that Butcher's canal was the approved project of the ministry.[13] This was grossly unfair. Certainly, officials in Khartoum thought so.

Our first interim report was based on Butcher's proposals. It is for this reason that the Egyptian technicians are reluctant to discuss that report. So its a pity for so long as they have allowed us to pursue a false trail even though the information gathered and in so doing may perhaps be of lasting value. Their proposals [*The Future Conservation of the Nile*] are far more drastic than anything previously suggested and amount to the ruthless development of the upper waters of the Nile on TVA lines with the sole object of extracting from that river the last drop of water for Egypt.[14]

Morrice and Winder were already well into their second year of research when Hurst's *The Future Conservation of the Nile* was made available to them in March 1947. It only seemed to confirm their recommendation for a direct-line canal since Hurst, obviously reflecting the confusion in the ministry, had remained silent as to the canal's structure and alignment. Indeed, he appeared almost indifferent so long as the canal, any canal, would carry 55 million m³. Nimmo Allan had a long conversation with Hurst at his home on the Thames on 29

[13] Public works ministry, 'Comments on the Jonglei Team *First Interim Report*', 21 June 1947, FO 141/1215, UNP I/10/85.
[14] 'Agenda for the Third Meeting of the Jonglei Committee', 9 July 1947, UNP I/10/85. TVA was the Tennessee Valley Authority, a federal corporation of the US government organized in 1933 to develop the Tennessee River valley as a single unit, and a body on which local inhabitants had little influence.

July 1946. 'I explained to Hurst how our investigations had strongly suggested the need to move the line of the Jonglei canal well to the east of the swamp area. I do not think he sees great objection to this, but being primarily a scientist, problems involving construction, and questions such as those of draglines versus dredgers, are not referred to him by the P.W.M. [Public Works Ministry]; indeed, they are really outside his province.'[15] In fact the influence of Hurst, one of the dominant figures at the ministry, was already in decline after forty years in Egypt. He appears to have had after the Second World War even less influence than Butcher before it, and was called upon by the minister only when it suited the latter.

His influence may have been waning, but no one could deny the power of Hurst's plan for the Nile. After its publication in the autumn of 1946 only a hard core of dissidents remained in the ministry to continue to campaign for Butcher's 'very limited ideas', and in February 1947 the Egyptian Government officially adopted in principle the proposals in *The Future Conservation of the Nile* to supersede those of Butcher.[16] Within the year the cluster of *tukuls* called Jonglei was 'seething with Egyptian transport and general equipment for the Direct Line survey'.[17] In Cairo, the adoption of the Hurst plan launched what became known as the Equatorial Nile Project, sometimes referred to as the Victoria–Albert–Jonglei scheme or the Jonglei Canal scheme or simply the Jonglei Canal. Since the Jonglei Canal was only one link in the Equatorial Nile Project, however, it should not be confused with the larger programme. The object of the Equatorial Nile Project was to provide more irrigation water for Egypt, and presumably the Sudan, when the natural supply of the Nile became inadequate. The Project itself was designed to make more water available by reducing losses, storing water, and delivering it when needed, most likely during the Timely period when the Blue Nile flood was exhausted. The way to reduce losses between Lake Albert and

[15] Allan to Miller, 8 Aug. 1946, SAD 589/14/1–95.

[16] Hamid Suliman, under-secretary of state, ministry of public works, 'Memorandum on Nile Basin, Volume VII', 10 Feb. 1947, in Allan to Miller, 2 May 1947, UNP I/10/85.

[17] H. A. W. Morrice, 'Trek Notes (Southern Sudan)', 26 Jan. 1948, Morrice Papers, Rhodes House Library, Oxford.

Khartoum was by means of the Jonglei Canal. By drawing off from the Bahr al-Jabal part of the water that would otherwise drain into the swamps, the Jonglei Canal would diminish the loss in the Sudd and deliver the water to the White Nile at the mouth of the Sobat. The Jonglei Canal by itself could not distribute the flow evenly, however, without a supply of stored water when needed. To accomplish this, Lakes Victoria and Albert were to be converted into reservoirs by dams at their outflows sufficiently large to provide century storage. In order to accommodate such a large volume of water the Jonglei Canal would require a very large capacity, 55 Mm^3/d.[18]

British officials in Khartoum accepted the approval of the Egyptian government for the Equatorial Nile Project with apprehension and not a little bitterness. Morrice and Winder had already demonstrated that the Nilotic people would be endangered by the canal, and that alternate means of livelihood and remedial measures were necessary. Huddleston, the governor-general, might warn Lord Killearn, the British ambassador in Cairo, that it was absolutely essential to have a 'clear understanding with Egypt as to the lines on which the Lake Albert and Jonglei Schemes are to be developed', but the long history of suspicion and distrust between the Sudan government and the Egyptian irrigation department did not justify much optimism that this laudable objective would be achieved.[19] Relationships between individual members of the irrigation department and their counterparts in the Sudan had, on the whole, been friendly, but those of their respective governments were not. The Sudan government had a long list of grievances against the ministry of public works, largely concerned with the working arrangements of the Nile Waters Agreement of 1929. The intention of the working arrangements was for modifications to be made between the respective irrigation authorities to regulate the flow in order to achieve the principles of the agreement. The Sudan government was willing to accept any such modifications upon which the irrigation officials could agree, but the Egyptian government insisted that even minor adjustments were 'amendments' to the Nile Waters Agreement and therefore subject to ratification

[18] Winder (1952).
[19] Huddleston to Killearn, 3 Jan. 1946, FO 371/53371.

by both the British and Egyptian governments. This issue was never satisfactorily resolved, delaying decisions and frustrating their implementation. It was the principle cause for the resignation of Butcher from the ministry in 1939. There were, however, other incidents, characterized more by a lack of propriety than by disagreement on technical matters, that deeply offended British officials in the Sudan. In 1945 survey parties from the irrigation department began extensive investigations for a dam at the fourth cataract in the Sudan without informing any Sudan official. The facilities of the irrigation department were suddenly made 'unavailable' to the Jonglei Investigation Team after the publication of the *First Interim Report.* Numerous official and unofficial requests for information concerning the studies of the irrigation department at Lake Albert were ignored. The seemingly calculated obstructions and contrived insults over the operations of the reservoirs at Sennar, Jabal 'Auliya, and Aswan are too numerous to recount.[20] In all they poisoned the Nile waters discussions which opened at Cairo in June 1947 over the Equatorial Nile Project.

There were two immediate issues in 1947, both of which had potentially grave consequences for the Sudan. First, the Ugandan government urgently needed hydroelectric power but was strongly opposed to the creation of a large reservoir at Lake Albert. Hurst had proposed in *The Future Conservation of the Nile* that the whole of the reservoir capacity necessary for century storage be provided in Lake Albert by raising the level of the lake 22 m to a reading of 35 m on the Butiaba gauge. This would have flooded some 3,500 km² of Uganda around the shores of the lake and along the Albert Nile. Sir John Hall, governor of Uganda, was adamantly opposed. He feared any extension of the Egyptian political presence in East Africa, the Lake Albert dam being the hydrological manifestation of that familiar theme, and did not wish to deprive Uganda's expanding population of its territory.[21] At the same time

---

[20] For a catalogue of complaints see R. J. Smith, director, Sudan irrigation department, to Miller, 22 Jan. 1947, SAD 500/3/8.

[21] Sir John Hall, governor, Uganda, to secretary of state for colonies, 27 Mar. 1946, FO 371/53371; W. N. Allan, 'Notes on the Equatorial Nile Project Dated July 1948', SAD 589/5/1.

Uganda desperately required hydroelectric power which, by making industrialization possible, would help to provide an alternative way of living for the increasing population. In 1904 the Uganda Company had first suggested that Ripon Falls could be a site for hydroelectric power, a proposal strongly supported by Winston Churchill in his book *My African Journey* published in 1907. Uganda, of course, could not at that time use its water-power resources, nor a generation later, according to a study conducted in 1935, but by 1947 Sir Charles Westlake strongly advocated generating hydroelectric power in the vicinity of Owen Falls. The following year the Uganda electricity board was established to supervise Uganda electricity development, and immediately pressed forward with preparatory works.[22]

Governor Hall had retained the services of a well-known consulting engineer, Brigadier C. G. Hawes, who had considerable experience with Indian irrigation, to make a reconnaissance and to represent Uganda as well as Kenya and Tanganyika in the forthcoming negotiations with Egypt. Hawes proposed an alternative scheme which Hurst had only vaguely contemplated. Lake Albert would become a 'balancing reservoir'. The main century storage reservoir would be shifted to Lake Victoria, whose vast area, 67,000 km², would provide huge capacity without drastically raising the level of the lake, yet having sufficient head to generate the power necessary for Uganda's present and future requirements. Hawes submitted his counter-proposal during discussions with Dr Muhammad Amin Bey of the physical department at Entebbe in March 1947. Storage in Lake Victoria would have a maximum rise of 2.8 m, the equivalent of 106 billion m³ of additional water, while Lake Albert would be reduced to a range of 4 m.[23] Essentially, Uganda did not want to inundate its land around the lake for the benefit of Egypt yet wanted hydroelectric power. The Egyptian government sought a reservoir at Lake Albert, or a combination of Lakes Victoria and Albert, with a capacity to ensure century storage.

[22] Westlake *et al.* (1954).
[23] C. G. Hawes, 'Combined Storage in Lake Victoria and Lake Albert', 6 Sept. 1947, Morrice Papers; W. N. Allan, 'Notes on the Victoria–Albert–Jonglei Project', 10 Nov. 1947, SAD 589/3/40.

Second, and for the Sudan a more disturbing development, was the consequent loss of proper flood control in the Sudd by the reduction of the Albert reservoir. If the capacity of the reservoir were diminished to meet Uganda's demands, it would not be able to accommodate years of high water. The sluices of the Albert dam would then have to remain open to disgorge a huge volume of water down the Bahr al-Jabal into the swamps, the greatest flood since Noah. The spectre of another flood the size of the mighty inundations of 1878, 1917, and 1988 was statistically probable, and made more real by the Nile flood of 1946, which was the highest on record in seventy years. The size of the reservoir acceptable to Uganda left the Sudan in danger.

It is difficult to believe that any responsible Civil Engineer would seriously advocate a scheme which did not include proper Flood Protection, unless indeed he was under instructions from his employers to try and get away with it. Control of the Nile means control of the Nile; it does not mean letting the Nile rip when such a course happens to suit the conveniences of Egypt and/or Uganda.[24]

If the Nilotes of the Upper Nile were obliged to change their way of life and adapt to an economy whereby the canal no longer permitted the annual flooding, forcing them to cultivate rain-grown crops or to cultivate, or graze their herds on, land artifically irrigated from the canal, a sudden inundation of flood-waters which the reservoirs could not accommodate and which the Jonglei Canal could not transport would destroy

the new economy which will be imposed on these people. . . . To have the threat of such an inundation perpetually over the heads of the people would be intolerable . . . the ladder of their prosperity might at intervals be knocked from under them and the higher they had climbed the greater must be their fall.[25]

The Sudan had a 'right' to flood protection, and if anyone thought not, the high waters of 1946 'reemphasized strongly

[24] H. A. W. Morrice, 'Notes on Flood Protection', Morrice Papers.
[25] J. Winder, 'Flood Protection for the Sudan', 6 Jan. 1948, UNP I/10/85; W. N. Allan, 'Detailed Comments on the Second Interim Report of the Jonglei Investigation Team By Irrigation Consultant', 10 Nov. 1947, SAD 589/3/47.

the need for the inclusion in Nile development of all possible means for Flood Protection'.[26]

Flood protection was not the only serious problem. The regime of the Sudd is marked by two distinct periods, the 'Timely' from January to July and the 'Untimely' from July to January (aptly named by Newhouse, inspector-general, Sudan, in the 1930s). The Timely period is the dry season of low Nile, during which the Nilotes move their cattle toward the falling rivers of the swamp. Then in the Untimely period the flooding takes place, and the Nilotes retreat before the rising waters to the higher ground, to cultivate and settle their herds in the cattle byres and *luaks*. 'The main object of century storage in the lake is the equalization of the Timely and Untimely flow entering the swamps at Mongalla.'[27] If the Equatorial Nile Project were approved, the Timely and Untimely periods would be reversed, the flow kept low in the Untimely period, normally the months of flooding, and increased in the Timely period, when the water level in the swamp is sharply decreased.

Between Rejaf and Jebelein some 700,000 people and 800,000 Animal Units are in one way or another dependent for their very existence for from four to five months of the year on the flood plain of the river. . . . In some parts of the area the seasonal fluctuations will be reversed, the flood-plain being inundated and therefore inaccessible in the dry or timely period of the year and subject to rainfall only in the untimely period; in others the flood-plains will no longer be inundated by river spill and will be subject to rainfall only, with a probable change in vegetation; in still others, they will be permanently under water throughout the year.[28]

Although obviously related, the Albert dam and the Jonglei Canal were made distinct issues by the Uganda authorities. Uganda needed hydroelectric power and demanded an immediate decision as to the construction of a dam at Owen Falls, the outflow of Lake Victoria. The Jonglei Canal was an

[26] W. N. Allan, 'Note on the Present Nile Waters Positions', 1 June 1948, SAD 590/1/44.

[27] W. N. Allan, 'Combined Storage in Lake Victoria and Lake Albert' (?draft memorandum), SAD 590.

[28] Jonglei Investigation Team (1954, intro. and summary, p. v). 1 animal unit = 1 head of cattle = 8 sheep or goats.

exceedingly complex project which required much further study and must await final approval. To tie the one with the other would delay any prospect of a hydroelectric dam at Owen Falls for many years. Similarly, if Egypt did not meet Uganda's terms for storage in Lakes Victoria and Albert, the Owen Falls dam could be easily enmeshed for years in a web of protracted negotiations. To avoid either of these unpleasant prospects, Uganda made it clear that she would proceed with a small power station immediately, which would operate only on the natural flow of the river so as not to be subject to an Egyptian veto under the terms of the Nile Waters Agreement of 1929. If Uganda were pushed to build such a small dam for power, however, she would be totally uninterested in any scheme for storage, making century storage in the lakes impossible. The Equatorial Nile Project was an immense undertaking. The stakes were high; the negotiations polite but merciless. The principal protagonists were Hamid Sulayman Bey, under-secretary of state for Sudan projects at the ministry of public works, Nimmo Allan, now the irrigation consultant for the Sudan, and Dr E. B. Worthington, the scientific adviser to the East African commission.

The negotiations over the Equatorial Nile Project opened in Cairo on 4 June 1947 at the ministry of public works and lasted four days. During these preliminary discussions Uganda was represented by C. G. Hawes, the hydrological adviser, and Egypt by Dr Muhammad Amin Bey of the physical department. The atmosphere was friendly, but no one was under the illusion that the issues were going to be resolved easily. Hawes bluntly told Muhammad Amin that Uganda could not accept the Egyptian proposals for storage in Lakes Victoria and Albert. Allan put forward the principal points of the *First Interim Report*: the direct-line canal, remedial measures for the people, flood protection, and navigation. He was particularly concerned over the changes in the pattern of grazing occasioned by the loss of the present regime of the Sudd between the Timely and Untimely periods. Taking his brief from Morrice and Winder, he hammered away on the need for further investigations, remedial measures, and alternative livelihoods. He made much of Governor Davies's concept of the canal in 1943 as the basis for the economic development of the Upper Nile, not just a conduit for Egypt's water. 'The carrying out of the whole project [the Jonglei Canal] was to be fitted in with the general development and progress of the Southern Sudan.'[29] Hamid Sulayman Bey, who presided at the discussions, generally agreed with the points Allan had made in his presentation. He was particularly effusive about the direct line for the canal, which the ministry had already adopted, and could hardly object to further study about the impact of the canal on local conditions. The negotiators then adjourned to study the proposals and consult with their respective governments, agreeing to meet in Entebbe the following February. During these discussions Allan became more convinced than ever that the time had come for the Sudan to look out for its own interests. Neither Egypt nor British East Africa was going to do so, and if ever the Sudan government needed to display its quiet autonomy between the two poles of the Condominium, it was over Jonglei.

The birth of the Equatorial Nile project had radically altered Egyptian proposals for the Upper Nile, and the Sudan government had little information or experience with which to confront them, as the Egyptians had spared no pains to point out in their criticisms of the *First Interim Report*.[30] The time had come to seek remedial measures; schemes for alternative livelihoods 'will be an answer to those critics who suggest that the Sudan Government prefers to convert the Upper Nile province into an anthropological museum rather than make any serious attempt to develop it'.[31] Perhaps because he had to bear the burden as the Sudan government's chief negotiator, Allan was the most outspoken of the members of the Jonglei committee to enlarge the Jonglei team. The initial concern by Morrice and Winder about the impact of the canal on the inhabitants had been reinforced in the *Second Interim Report*, and by the ministry's commentary on their first report which implied that the team had overreacted. Allan thought the

[29] W. N. Allan, 'Notes on Technical Discussions in Cairo June 4–7, 1947', 11 June 1947, SAD 590/1; Allan to Miller, 'Victoria–Albert–Jonglei', 11 July 1947, SAD 589/3/31.

[30] 'Comments on the Jonglei Team First Interim Report', note by the public works ministry, in inspector-general irrigation, M. Sabry al-Kurdi Bey, to Sir Edington Miller, financial secretary, 21 June 1947, SAD 589/3/41.

[31] Minutes of the 3rd meeting of the Jonglei committee, 22 July 1947, UNP I/10/85.

ministry's treatment of this very important matter was 'superficial in the extreme and displayed a failure to realize, or at least to admit, the magnitude and reality of the difficult problems which would arise'.[32] He also introduced a new consideration to the Jonglei committee which was to have ever-increasing importance: the need for the team to determine compensation for his use in future negotiations with the Egyptians. Everyone seemed to agree that the Jonglei Investigation Team required a total reorientation.[33] Morrice and Winder could not have agreed more. 'We are now reaching a stage where a knowledge of local geography and economy can by itself take us little further.'[34] Their next report would be their last.

The fourth meeting of the Jonglei committee was held on 17 January 1948, specifically to determine the future of the Jonglei Investigation Team and its composition. Henceforth the team would no longer restrict itself to identifying problems for study but would investigate them with the intention of recommending solutions and remedial measures. An impressive collection of experts was to be assembled, including two senior British irrigation engineers, agriculturalists, veterinarians, and surveyors, all under the chairmanship of Dr Paul Howell, a district commissioner and authority on Nuer law.[35] Nothing appeared too good for the Jonglei team, but the interest in and resources for Jonglei immediately evoked feelings of jealousy from the local administration at Malakal and the heads of departments in Khartoum. The Jonglei Investigation Team was an autonomous unit, a special group with its own budget, equipment, and facilities which answered only to the Jonglei committee, which met infrequently. The governor of the Upper Nile, F. D. Kingdon, complained bitterly that the team got what it wanted, the province administration very little or nothing. At the first meeting of the committee Sir Edington Miller, the financial secretary, had questioned why the information they were seeking could not be obtained from the

[32] W. N. Allan, 'Note on the Victoria–Albert–Jonglei Project', SAD 589/3/43; Morrice and Winder *Second Interim Report.*

[33] Minues of the 3rd meeting of the Jonglei committee, 22 July 1947, UNP I/10/85.

[34] Morrice to Rintoul, 5 July 1947, UNP I/10/85.

[35] Minutes of the 4th meeting of the Jonglei committee, 17 June 1948, UNP I/10/85.

regular departments and local administrators. It was argued that Jonglei was a special case, the issues too important, and the Sudd not sufficiently known by the administrative agencies. Now two department heads on the committee, Dr John J. Smith, director of the department of agriculture and forests, and R. J. Smith, director of the Sudan irrigation department, raised the question once again; but their appeals found little sympathy and were regarded as the captious bleatings of unprogressive bureaucrats. This attitude, however, was soon to become a contentious and, regrettably, an unavoidable issue. Meanwhile the new team was formed and began work at the end of 1948, focusing on problem-solving and acquiring improved statistics on the cattle population, the hydrology of the western Nuer district, and a closer study of the impact of fish, a vital food source for the Nilotes in the dry season. The team was essentially still gathering information, an investigating agency whose activities were leading to, but had not yet reached, the concept of an economic development team for the Upper Nile and the southern Sudan.

While the team members were swatting mosquitoes and contracting malaria in the Sudd, the engineers were engaged in often fractious discussions which culminated in two important conferences, at Entebbe in February 1948 and Cairo in April. The fundamental disagreement between Egypt and the Sudan on the one hand and Uganda on the other was the size of the reservoirs at Lake Victoria and Lake Albert. Egypt wanted the reservoirs to store water for the lean years, century storage. The Sudan sought flood protection. Uganda wanted hydroelectric power. The governor of Uganda declared to the assembled engineers at Entebbe that Uganda faced a land shortage; she could not therefore agree to flood land around Lake Albert. In fact, the land question was a canard. Uganda was quite prepared to accept a reasonable loss of land in return for Egyptian financial assistance for the construction of the Owen Falls dam. Her real concern was that land at the southern end of Lake Albert would be inundated, thereby preventing oil exploration in the Semliki valley.[36] On their part, the Egyptians were prepared to accept a reduced

[36] Allan to Miller, 12 Nov. 1947, SAD 589/3/38.

reservoir at Lake Albert if they could raise Lake Victoria by 3.5 m. The greatest opposition to this proposal came not from Uganda but from the government of Kenya, who would lose the most by flooding in the Kisumu area.[37] Largely through the diplomatic efforts of Dr Worthington, the East African governments had agreed among themselves on 25 November 1947 to accept a rise in Lake Victoria of 3 m above the minimum recorded level. Beyond that they would not go. Hamid Sulayman Bey agreed to accept this limit provided adequate adjustments were made in the level of Lake Albert.[38]

The raising of Lake Albert was another matter. Uganda grudgingly agreed to increase the level of Lake Albert by a meter to 14 m on the Butiaba gauge. This was quite unacceptable to the Egyptian delegation. Not surprisingly, they wanted to obtain as high a level as possible in order to give them the greatest possible flexibility in the control of supply and demand in the Nile basin as a whole in the operation of century storage. Dr Muhammad Amin demonstrated that between 1904 and 1946 conditions in the lakes at a discharge acceptable to the Sudan for flood protection would place the level of the reservoir at 18.3 m on the Butiaba gauge. Dr Amin was persuasive. At a level of 18.3 m, only 740 km^2 of sparsely inhabited land, 240 of which were swamp, would be flooded. Moreover, between 1904 and 1946 the land up to 18.3 m would have been totally flooded in only three years, leaving much of the land available for grazing and temporary cultivation. Allan supported the Egyptians, despite a clash with Hamid Sulayman when the latter asked the secretary to record that Allan was present only in his capacity as adviser to the Egyptian delegation and did not represent the Sudan. This petty incident was quickly smoothed over, made all the more palatable by Allan siding with the Egyptians and arguing for the largest possible reservoir as necessary for flood protection. He hammered away at the same old theme that the Sudan government 'could not encourage the local inhabitants

[37] Ministry of public works, 'The Combination of a Large Reservoir in Lake Victoria with a Small Reservoir in Lake Albert', 25 Jan. 1948, UNP I/10/85.

[38] C. G. Hawes, 'Note by Hydrological Adviser, Uganda', Sept. 1947; Allan to Hawes, 30 Oct. 1947, SAD 589/3/44; W. N. Allan, 'Note on The Equatorial Nile Project dated 1 July 1948', SAD 589/5/1; Morrice diary of the Entebbe conference, 17 Feb. 1948, Morrice Papers.

to change their way of life if we know all the time they are liable to be flooded out at far from frequent intervals'.[39] Nothing was settled, 'the opportunity to shelve the thorny question of Butiaba [the size of the Lake Albert reservoir] was eagerly grasped', and each party left Entebbe to restudy the various proposals and counter-proposals and meet in Cairo in April.[40]

Between February and April each delegation digested the others' proposals and refined their own. Hurst was particularly busy strengthening the Egyptian position. He grafted on to the Egyptian arguments mathematical probabilities on a number of natural phenomena, such as discharges of the Nile itself, arriving at the conclusion that the only safe margin permissible would be 20 m on the Butiaba gauge. Allan again supported the Egyptians. Worthington compromised at 18.5 m, which was a significant concession from the level of 14 m offered at Entebbe. In fact Uganda was not in a strong position. It wanted Egyptian financial help with the dam at Owen Falls. At 18.5 m the Lake Albert reservoir would not inundate a significant portion of Uganda nor interfere with oil exploration in the Semliki valley. That level would accommodate the Sudan. Worthington sought to be flexible. If Egypt and the Sudan agreed to 18.5 m at Butiaba, Uganda would pledge to review the whole project in twenty years from the date of first beginning storage, and would, in the light of experience and data accumulated, adjust the agreed level

---

[39] Morrice Diaries, 17 Feb. 1948, Morrice Papers.
[40] Ibid. For a record of the Entebbe discussions, see W. N. Allan, 'Note on Technical Discussions at Entebbe on 17th February 1948 between Egypt, the Sudan, and Uganda', SAD 589/5; W. N. Allan, 'Note on the Equatorial Nile Project, 1 July 1948', SAD 589/5/13; Allan to Miller, 4 Mar. 1948, UNP I/10/85; H. A. W. Morrice, 'Trek Notes (Southern Sudan)', 15–19 Feb. 1948, Morrice Papers. The delegations to the conference were as follows: *Egypt*: Hamid Sulayman Bey (under-secretary of state, public works ministry, Sudan projects); Muhammad Sabry al-Kurdi Bey (inspector-general, irrigation, Egyptian irrigation department, Sudan); Dr Muhammad Amin Bey (director-general, physical department); Dr Hasan Zaki Bey (inspector-general, upper Egypt); Dr H. E. Hurst (scientific consultant); H. G. Bambridge (inspector, irrigation, Malakal). *Sudan*: W. N. Allan (irrigation consultant); H. A. W. Morrice (chairman, Jonglei Investigation Team). *Uganda*: Dr E. B. Worthington (scientific adviser, East African commission); Sir D. Harris (development commissioner); C. G. Hawes (hydrological adviser); L. S. Potter (financial secretary); Mr Westlake (chairman, Uganda electricity commission); Mr Cosgrove (engineer, Uganda electricity commission).

upward to a maximum of 20. This diplomatic gesture broke the deadlock.[41]

The other matters—the Lake Albert dam, navigation, construction costs, and compensation—were readily settled. The dam would be built at Mutir with a lock for navigation by Egypt, who would be responsible for its maintenance. The Uganda electricity board would be responsible for the construction and maintenance of the dam at Owen Falls, but in accordance with the instructions of an Egyptian technical staff stationed there. Egypt would bear the full cost of the Mutir dam and that portion of the Owen Falls dam required to meet Egyptian needs for storage. The discussions cleared the way for a formal treaty, the Equatorial Nile Agreement, but the Egyptian delegation was not empowered to conclude the negotiations—to the annoyance of the Uganda representatives, who consequently tabled their draft agreement. Since they had hoped to begin construction on the Owen Falls dam as soon as possible, the Ugandans had pressed hard for a formal treaty. When they did not get it, they renewed the threat to build a small power station to operate from the natural flow of the Nile. With little delicacy, they informed the Egyptian delegation that Uganda would thereafter be 'uninterested in any scheme for storage', effectively destroying the Equatorial Nile Project. Negotiations stalled, becoming embroiled in the melancholy saga of Anglo-Egyptian relations. The prime minister of Egypt, Nokrashi Pasha, sought to link the construction of the Owen Falls dam with an agreement with the emperor of Ethiopia, Haile Selassie, to build the Lake Tana dam. Nokrashi argued in July that the Nile should be dealt with as a whole, a sound principle, but then insisted that Egypt and Egypt alone had the constitutional right to negotiate with Ethiopia.[42] Britain could not, of course, countenance such a preposterous claim. She was responsible for Uganda on the one hand and a co-ruler of the Sudan on the other. The following month Britain politely informed the Egyptian foreign minister that Uganda would go ahead with a

[41] Allan, 'Note on the Equatorial Nile Project, 1 July 1948'.
[42] Letter from Nokrashi Pasha, 10 July 1948, quoted in Allan to Miller 9 Aug. 1948, SAD 590/1.

small power station of 90,000 kW based on the natural flow of the river.[43]

Tortuous discussions followed throughout the autumn, characterized by disagreements between Britain and Egypt and between Uganda and the Colonial Office on the one hand and between the Foreign Office and the Sudan government on the other. Uganda sought to disassociate the Owen Falls dam from Lake Tana and a comprehensive Nile waters agreement. Sir John Hall was supported by the Colonial Office. The British foreign secretary, Ernest Bevin, wanted a comprehensive settlement, as did the Sudan, but any hope for negotiations was doomed by the unpopular government in Egypt threatened by riots, the Palestine problem, and King Faruq's bizarre intervention to demand arms in return for talks on the Nile waters.[44] In the meantime Uganda and the Colonial Office had decided to go it alone; but since they wanted Egyptian financial assistance for the dam, they sought to lure the Egyptians to the negotiating table. Uganda would design the Owen Falls dam for a capacity of 150,000 kW, an amount sufficient to give Egypt its desired storage in Lake Victoria, but would only instal turbines to produce 90,000 kW, which could be operated on the natural flow of the river.[45] The important feature of this decision was that, although potential storage was included in the design, Egypt would have no say in its construction or future regulation. It broke Egyptian intransigence.[46] Within a month Dr Muhammad Amin had pledged full co-operation with Uganda, and a readiness to approve £E4 million as Egypt's share of the cost of construction.[47] Thereafter agreement was speedily concluded between Britain, acting on behalf of Uganda, and Egypt in an exchange of notes on 30 May 1949. Egypt agreed to pay £E4.5 million for

[43] Foreign office to Egyptian minister for foreign affairs, 9 Aug. 1948, in Allan to Miller, Aug. 1948, SAD 590/1.

[44] See G. L. Clutton, Africa department, foreign office, to Sir R. Campbell, British ambassador, Egypt, 8 Dec. 1948; Sir R. Campbell to E. Bevin, 14 Jan. 1949, SAD 590/1.

[45] W. N. Allan to Sir Robert Howe, governor-general, 'Record of a Meeting held at the Foreign Office on 17 September 1948', 18 Sept. 1948, SAD 590/2.

[46] E. A. Chapman-Andrews to Ibrahim Dasouki Abaza Pasha, minister for foreign affairs, 19 Jan. 1949, SAD 590/2.

[47] 'Conversation on Nile Waters between Dr Mohammed Amin and W. N. Allan 17 February 1948', SAD 590/2.

raising the dam to increase the level of Lake Victoria to a range of 2–3 m and compensation for flooding. Equally important, the Uganda electricity board, who would build and maintain the dam, 'will regulate the discharges to be passed through the dam on the Instructions of the Egyptian resident engineer' stationed at Owen Falls. This official and his staff have regulated the flow at Owen Falls ever since, even through the most tumultuous years of an independent Uganda. The subsequent exchange of notes on 16 July 1952 and 5 January 1953 dealt with the contracts for the dam and its financing and maintenance respectively.[48] Part of the compensation, £E980 000, was to pay the Uganda electricity board for those occasions when the control of the flow for Egyptian purposes could result in the loss of hydroelectric power to Uganda. Five months after the exchange of notes, in January 1953, C. G. Hawes privately informed Nimmo Allan that Uganda would be willing to consider a level of 20 m on the Butiaba gauge in any future reservoir at Lake Albert.

The Owen Falls dam agreement had a far-reaching impact on the Equatorial Nile Project that few foresaw at its conclusion. Thereafter Uganda lost all interest in the scheme, since she would derive few if any benefits, and although the subsequent civil wars in both the southern Sudan and Uganda have rendered any prospect of its completion remote, any future negotiations as to the construction of the Lake Albert dam and reservoir would have to deal with this problem. As far as the Sudan was concerned, its policy was designed by Allan to reach two objectives: first to guarantee that 'all projects are so designed and developed to ensure at all stages conditions of life which are reasonably satisfactory throughout the regions affected' and second 'to ensure that the water resources of the Nile valley are all developed in the most effective manner possible'.[49] Neither goal was realized. The Owen Falls dam agreement, in effect though not intent, frustrated any hope of an equatorial Nile waters agreement.

[48] Exchange of Notes between the Government of the United Kingdom of Great Britain and Northern Ireland and the Government of Egypt regarding the construction of the Owen Falls Dam in Uganda, Cairo, 30 May 1949/16 July 1952/5 Jan. 1953, SAD 590/5.

[49] Allan, 'Note on the Equatorial Nile Project, 1 July 1948'.

Uganda did not need it, and would not sacrifice land around Lake Albert for no tangible benefits. A more comprehensive Nile waters agreement would founder on the hostile relations between Britain and Egypt so long as Britain remained a riparian power on the Nile.

In the development of the Nile waters the Equatorial Nile Project was the largest and the most important scheme. It would provide century storage, level out the variations between high and low years, and increase the total supply of water available. There was no other project on the Nile which could take its place. Even the high dam at Aswan, in which the ministry displayed no interest at this time, would not produce additional water, only less.[50] When the Equatorial Nile Project was originally proposed by Hurst, it was to be for the benefit of Egypt. By 1948, however, it had become abundantly clear that the Sudan would require additional water over and above that which she would obtain from any settlement concerning the Lake Tana dam.[51] The Sudan would have to claim a share of any water conserved by the Equatorial Nile Project, yet this could only be accomplished by a separate Nile waters agreement between the Sudan and Egypt. Given the history of Anglo-Egyptian negotiations over the Nile waters, such an agreement was hazardous at best, impossible at worst. None of these concerns had surfaced during the discussions over Lakes Victoria and Albert and their dams between 1947 and 1949. The Jonglei Canal was ignored. To be sure, there had been some technical discussions about the line, design, and operation of the canal, but no serious consideration of compensation for loss, damage, and disturbance. Allan argued the obvious:

All past experience shows that a definite figure will have to be agreed upon before the project [the Jonglei Canal] is begun. The great difficulty is to foresee clearly in advance what works will be needed, and thus obtain a firm basis on which to estimate the amount of compensation. The future extent of flooding, loss of grazing, etc. in the Sudd region and along the White Nile cannot be so closely estimated as is possible in the case of the lakes in Uganda.

[50] Hamid Sulaymen Bey to Allan, 21 June 1947, SAD 589/3.
[51] W. N. Allan, 'Note on the Present Nile Waters Position', 1 June 1948, SAD 590/1/44.

It is all the more important that the investigations into future conditions to be expected, and the remedial works which will be required, should be pressed forward with the utmost vigour, so that adequate data for the assessment may be available as soon as possible.[52]

Allan became more insistent that the Jonglei investigations be expanded as the need to calculate compensation loomed ever larger in his mind. 'The Investigation should press on urgently,' he wrote to the Jonglei committee in October 1948, 'for the Sudan Government not only has responsibility for the welfare of the peoples of the White Nile but also to seek adequate compensation from Egypt on their behalf.'[53] Paul Howell was already requesting a substantial increase in staff to carry out a programme of research the magnitude of which would have startled the members of the Jonglei committee three years before. The team was now not only to seek 'methodical solutions of a great variety of problems', but 'to find out how the lives of the Nilotic people will be affected' and how best to assess appropriate compensation for damages.[54]

John Winder was not so sure. Already among some officials in Khartoum 'the newness of things Jonglei is wearing off'. Exasperated, as always, with the Egyptians, bewildered by the complex and mathematical debates among the irrigation engineers, and having only limited supplies of personal energy and time, they were beginning to find Jonglei tiresome. The new financial secretary, A. L. Chick, was a stranger to the mysteries of Nile waters. The civil secretary, Sir James Robertson, was fighting a host of difficult political battles, of immediate importance, with the Sudanese nationalists, and in fact had not been kept well-informed of the issues involved in the Jonglei investigations and the work of the team by the secretary to the committee, E. V. Rintoul. John Winder sighed with resignation: 'Jonglei is a distant problem, and he's got many more on his shoulders.'[55] Humphrey Morrice had

---

[52] Allan, 'Note on the Equatorial Nile Project, 1 July 1948'.

[53] Allan to Rintoul, 26 Oct. 1948, UNP I/10/88.

[54] P. P. Howell, chairman, Jonglei Investigation Team, to Rintoul, 8 Jan. 1948, UNP I/10/88; Winder to Sir J. Robertson, 'The Political Economic Effects of the Jonglei Scheme', 11 Feb. 1949, UNP I/9/83.

[55] 'Notes on Jonglei Affairs', 12 Jan. 1949, UNP I/10/85.

previously described the colonial administrative syndrome that was now surrounding the Jonglei Investigation Team:

> During the last few years I have had the opportunity of seeing them [members of the Sudan Political Service] at work, and have been as much impressed by their intelligence and integrity as dismayed by their attitude towards technical matters. They regard the scientist or the engineer much as the housewife regards the plumber. For them he is a man whom they call in on occasion to put matters right in some magic way of his own, after whch the sooner he makes himself scarce the better. . . . Their capacity for self-deception is unbounded, and I do not delude myself by supposing that I can shake their complacency. They will sit in their chairs, drinking their whisky and quietly fiddling away in unison, while something more important than Rome is burning.[56]

The more Allan was involved in the equatorial Nile project and the role of the Jonglei Canal in it, the less time and energy were devoted to the scheme and its issues by the director of irrigation, R. J. Smith, who had pressing problems in the Gezira. His passion for detail was swamped by the more expansive vistas in the Sudd. Besides, Jonglei was a long way in the future. Bambridge had estimated twenty-five years for the construction of the Equatorial Nile Project. Five years before, in 1944, the governor-general, Sir Hubert Huddleston, had already told the Sudanese that they would be independent in twenty years. Even the minutes of the Jonglei committee were never circulated, and the scheme's visibility vanished as the members of the Jonglei Investigation Team disappeared into the swamps to count cattle. Moreover, there had been some unfortunate contradictions between the *Second Interim Report* and later findings of the team, while a perusal of the correspondence leaves the impression that as much time and energy was absorbed by such mundane affairs as housing, refrigerators, *faluccas*, marriage, wives, and children as was directed to the swamp itself. In the way of the Sudan political service, 'whisky talk' was casting doubts on the availability of men and money for science to find solutions to a problem decades away among a savage people in a bloody swamp. Winder sensed trouble for Jonglei research. He was right.

[56] Morrice (1945, pp. 24–5).

The Jonglei committee held its fifth meeting on 28 February 1949, and with surprising ease approved the Jonglei Canal scheme as part of the Equatorial Nile Project. There was an air of inevitability about the meeting, that events had gone beyond the committee's control, that Egypt had the money and the determination and would ultimately prevail. What remained were remedies, compensation, and the obligations of a trustee who sees the control of his ward being compromised by circumstances. Moreover, by the time these events would occur, the ward would have reached maturity and the trustees' responsibilities would have long ago been discharged. To its credit, the committee did not collapse completely. It insisted on provisions it hoped would cushion the blow to the Nilotic way of life. Discharge at key points would not be allowed to exceed maximum levels; the project would be reviewed at regular intervals during the coming years; conditions concerning excavation and navigation would have to be defined between the Sudan and Egypt. Indeed, there appeared little more for the Jonglei committee to do except determine the amount of compensation for damages. For his discussions with the Egyptians, Allan insisted on knowing what would be lost and how the loss would be remedied. He had to be prepared to present the Egyptians with the cost of compensating the Nilotes in pounds and piastres within three years. That was the new mission of the Jonglei Investigation Team—to calculate a monetary return for a way of life.

On this mandate the inherent and submerged disagreements as to the purpose of Jonglei rose to the surface. A minority of the committee, led by Dr John Smith, argued that Jonglei could only be a benefit, not a loss, the implication being that intensive investigations at great expense and time would not be needed. The Nilotes were a migratory people, he asserted, who might suffer from dislocation but no loss, since their 'cattle would be quite well able to live on rain grown grasses'. He went on to point out that reports from his own department, not from the Jonglei team, had already demonstrated that there was sufficient first-class, rain-grown grass to meet the needs of Nilotic cattle. He pressed his case. Irrigating the Sudd plain artificially with pumps, canals, and regulators was not only expensive but a complex and unnecessary remedy when there was ample rain-grown grazing available on the Nilotic plain. Smith was persuasive, for his simple solution seemed to lighten the weight of the committee's responsibility for the welfare of the Nilotes.[57]

Smith was being somewhat disingenuous. Here, in the issue of rain versus pump irrigation to sustain the Nilotic pastures, emerged the latent rivalry between the traditional departments of the Sudan government and a 'special' task force like the Jonglei Investigation Team. Departmental and often personal interests clashed with the objectives of development teams in such a way that the purpose of the enterprise became obscured and confused, thereby undermining the effective implementation of any development scheme. So it was with Jonglei. In reality, Smith did not want to surrender departmental staff and scarce pumps from well-drilling in Darfur and Kordofan to several years of scientific experimentation in the Sudd under an authority not his own. In this sense, the report of the agriculture department on rain-grown grazing was a screen to protect the department's own priorities, of which Jonglei did not head the list. In a larger sense, it was a symbol of the struggle for control between the departments and the Jonglei Investigation Team, in which policy was determined more by men than ideologies.

Paul Howell and F. D. Corfield, governor of the Upper Nile, fought back. They succeeded in sustaining approval for experiments in artificial irrigation, largely because everyone soon admitted that the agriculture department's report on rain-grown grazing was superficial and limited. Its author, M. N. Harrison, pasture research officer, knew this but failed to dissuade Smith from using it as ammunition against the team's request for his equipment. This dispute over artificial irrigation was but an example of the growing tension between the team and the government departments, but it was a very real issue in its own right. If the Sudd were to be deprived of its natural flood-waters, the pastures of the Nilotes would be dependent upon rainfall. At best rainfall is confined to six months from May to October and is unpredictable; at worst there is none in the alternate six months of the dry season

[57] Minutes of the 5th meeting of the Jonglei committee, 20 Feb. 1949, UNP I/10/88.

when the land becomes parched. Thus it appeared perfectly sensible, as it does today, to draw off water from the Jonglei Canal to irrigate the Nilotic pastures when natural rainfall was insufficient or did not fall where it was needed. Howell felt that Smith had purposely frightened the committee 'by his expensive picture of artificial irrigation' and the somewhat 'factless assumption that the alternate problem has already been solved by the presence of rain-grown grasses in the area'.[58]

The threat to irrigation was not confined to Dr Smith at the agriculture department. In October 1948 Dr Muhammad Amin and H. G. Bambridge published their important paper containing the revised 'working arrangements' for the operation of the Equatorial Nile Project in the light of the negotiations between Britain and Egypt over the reservoirs at Lake Victoria and Lake Albert. In regard to the Jonglei Canal, they envisaged a trough excavated below ground-level to conserve water and prevent flooding. Howell wrote angrily to Rintoul: 'I don't believe the Committee fully realize the Egyptians are deliberately intending to dig the canal under ground level despite extra costs in order to obviate any possibility of gravity irrigation from it. This must not be allowed.'[59] This issue never became a reality since no agreement was ever reached between the British and Egyptian engineers as to the configuration of the canal, but the Jonglei Investigation Team did conclude that irrigation was possible and 'should be done on properly irrigated schemes'.[60]

The decision to continue experiments with irrigation was but a symbolic victory, for neither Howell nor Corfield could overcome the pressure from departments and the financial secretary to abolish the team. During the sixth meeting of the Jonglei committee on 30 June 1949, Howell and Corfield again carried the day on the contentious issue of artificial irrigation, and assumed that the team's proposals for experimental work had been accepted. In fact, they had won a battle but lost the

[58] Howell to Rintoul, 30 Apr. 1949; F. D. Corfield, governor, Upper Nile province, to Rintoul, 11 May 1949, UNP I/10/88.
[59] Howell to Rintoul, 30 Apr. 1949; Amin and Bambridge (1948); J. F. Glennie, 'Notes on the Modified Jonglei Canal Scheme and Overyear Storage Schemes', SAD 500/13/44.
[60] Jonglei Investigation Team (1954, intro. and summary, p. liv).

war. The financial secretary and chairman of the Jonglei committee, A. L. Chick, had actually proposed that the team be disbanded. He had never firmly believed in the Jonglei Investigation Team, and now that any request for money to continue it must go before the Sudanese legislative assembly, where northern interests predominated over southern concerns, he did not want to argue the case for Jonglei in that arena. He suggested that the work of the team be postponed. The committee had agreed at the previous meeting to participate in the Equatorial Nile Project with Egypt and had approved the construction of the Jonglei Canal. Allan himself had indicated that Jonglei 'would undoubtedly have to be constructed sooner or later', but there were other priorities, Owen Falls, and Lake Tana. Jonglei could wait. And so could the members of the committee who wanted to dissolve the team.[61] A decision on Howell's proposal for future work was pointedly ignored, almost in the hope that the team would disappear beneath the Sudd.

Although the team might remain in limbo as to its future during the rains, by the autumn of 1949 a decision about their work plan in the coming dry season could no longer be postponed. At a show-down meeting on 19 December 1949, the team was given specific instructions 'to provide a reasonable estimate of the necessary remedial measures and compensations expressed in terms of money and water'.[62] This task had been decided upon, in fact, the previous February. Now, in December, the Jonglei committee made it plain what 'remedial' and 'compensatory' meant. The attack was led by Chick and John Smith. Chick, who had become the dominant member of the committee and increasingly intolerant of criticism, was adamant against spending large sums of money, currently £E30 000 a year, for devising remedial measures for a project twenty-five years in the future. Smith was more blunt, more bureaucratic. To him the Jonglei Investigation Team had become an autonomous administration, with thirteen divisions, twenty automobiles, two steamers, and

---

[61] Minutes of the 6th meeting of the Jonglei committee, 30 June 1949; Howell to Rintoul, 12 Dec. 1949, UNP I/10/88.

[62] Minutes of the 7th meeting of the Jonglei committee, 19 Dec. 1949, UNP I/10/88.

extensive buildings, for no purpose. He questioned the work of the team itself, sarcastically referring to them as 'four gentlemen writing about fish'. To him, its members automatically assumed there would be damage to the Nilotic way of life without requiring proof of that damage or proof of the value of what was forecast to be damaged. Their whole investigation was thus based on an outrageous assumption which became an end in itself. If practical solutions were required, they should be left to the experts in the departments of irrigation, veterinary services, and agriculture. R. J. Smith at the irrigation department agreed. Buried under a mountain of detail at Wad Medani, he gave little thought to larger questions of policy, regarding Jonglei from a hydrological point of view from which to calculate remedies and compensation.[63] Led by Chick, this faction prevailed. Henceforth the work of the team would be limited, as would the budget and personnel, to three more seasons, in which research would be confined to short-term projects specifically designed to provide Allan with the answers to face the Egyptians with hard figures of cubic meters and pound-notes. Above all, development problems requiring a continuing commitment were to be undertaken by the appropriate departments and not by the team. The civil servants once again had prevailed.[64]

Although the committee did not take the logical step and disband the team, the definition of its role for the next three years could lead to no other conclusion. The committee was obviously losing all interest in Jonglei, and the new members were clearly 'northern-minded and subconsciously ready to grasp at any stick with which to beat the South'.[65] Howell continued to fight to preserve the team, for instance, to carry out long-term research on pump irrigation, but it was a losing struggle with men who had little appreciation for scientific research but a great deal of understanding for administration. They objected to the amount of money expended on the team as a scientific research unit; yet the amount was a pittance in

[63] R. J. Smith to W. N. Williams, 11 July 1949, UNP I/9/80; Morrice Diaries, 26 Mar. 1950, Morrice Papers.

[64] Minutes of the 7th meeting of the Jonglei committee, 19 Dec. 1949, UNP I/10/88.

[65] H. A. W. Morrice, 'Rainfall and its Effects on Irrigation', Morrice Papers.

the Sudan budget, and a small charge to the Sudanese tax-payers for the ongoing study of the most underdeveloped region in their country—a region that would always demand more from the tax-payer than the amount for scientific research to make it productive. But the men in Khartoum came from backgrounds and an education that were devoid not only of exposure to science but, worse, of any appreciation of it. Having little comprehension of basic research, they considered that solutions should arise from the practical work which absorbed the immediate energies of their own departments.

Ironically, the Sudanese themselves, though hardly coming from a scientific tradition, found at independence the need for scientific research, which the British never seemed to appreciate in the Sudan, when the Sudan national research council was established in 1972. Dr E. B. Worthington, the distinguished scientific adviser to the East African commission, saw clearly in 1950 what those in Khartoum did not:

I became impressed with the need for a development plan for the Southern Sudan. By this I mean not a programme with detailed costings, estimates of staff requirements, etc., but a word picture, which might include somewhat imaginary passages here and there, of what we hope the Southern Sudan will look like, economically and socially, some ten or twenty years hence, and by what stages it is desirable that the goal may be reached.[66]

Paul Howell, who had taken a first in the anthropological tripos at Cambridge and later returned to complete a D.Phil., and Frank Corfield, himself educated in the natural sciences at Oxford, tried against overwhelming opposition to convince the committee that accurate information on certain problems could only be resolved by continuing, scientific research programmes. They might as well have been whistling in the wind. The committee insisted that 'any long-term research that might appear in the Team's work should be left to the departments' initiative when the Jonglei Investigation Team's work had been completed'.[67] For the department heads who dominated the Jonglei committee to believe that their

[66] Quoted in R. C. Wakefield, director, Sudan survey department, to Cap. G. W. Ogden, commissioner for development, 29 July 1952, Howell Papers, in possession of Dr P. P. Howell.
[67] Minutes of 8th meeting of the Jonglei committee, 6 July 1950, UNP I/10/88.

overworked and understaffed departments would continue the research of the Jonglei team was so disingenuous as to be dishonest. Corfield tried valiantly to keep the team intact at Malakal to continue long-term research, in a personal and perspicacious appeal to Sir James Robertson, the powerful civil secretary, for research in the southern Sudan:

It therefore appears to me to be absolute folly unless financial considerations are overwhelming to dissolve this team of experts at the very time when they may at last be able to make some useful progress towards their goal, even though the fruits from their labours may not become apparent for some years hence. . . . In say ten years time there may be a considerable change in the political set-up of this country. In spite of their professions to the contrary, would I consider to be asking [sic] too much of the Northern Sudan to pay due regard to the rights and welfare of the Southern Sudan if precious water is at stake. There will be a great temptation for them to adopt very much the same attitude as Egypt first adopted when this project was first put up. What do a few thousand Nilotics matter if we want more water. . . . We therefore have a moral responsibility to develop it as quickly as we can, politically, administratively, and economically before we leave. So even apart from purely Jonglei viewpoint the team are doing most valuable work which I am certain will pay dividends.[68]

These wise words made no impression. Robertson had never shown any interest in Jonglei and remained throughout unconvinced of its utility. During his career in the Sudan he had little association with the southern Sudan or the southern Sudanese and his empathy for their peculiar situation did not extend beyond his administrative integrity. His appointment to the Jonglei committee in July 1951, ostensibly to represent the governor-general, was in fact to guarantee its dissolution. At the eighth meeting of the Jonglei committee on 6 July 1950, the team was directed to ascertain remedial measures and costs. Howell worked doggedly, but by 1951 he was requesting additional time, claiming rather lamely that 'only inexperience prompted us to accept the task with limited time and resources agreed upon'.[69] No further delay was granted;

[68] Corfield to Robertson, 8 July 1949, UNP I/9/80.
[69] Howell to A. L. Chick, chairman of the Jonglei committee, 31 Mar. 1951, UNP I/26/198.

virtually everyone had lost interest in Jonglei. Howell was told to end the team's fieldwork by June 1952 and, upon returning from leave, to complete the final report by 31 December 1953. The team would be disbanded, and any further investigations would be undertaken by the appropriate departments.[70] There was no sympathy from R. J. Smith. 'They will just have to do the best they can. The Jonglei investigation future means the present set of data will have served its purposes.'[71] The Jonglei committee never met again, and the lack of interest by officials and departments was conspicuous in their indifference to the publications of the team. In its own way, this indifference was symbolic of the lack of concern for the southern Sudan that had come to permeate the Sudan government since the inception of the Condominium.

Finally, we [the team] are a bit fed up with all this mystery concerning publication and even more fed up with the criticisms of the uninformed. There is more nonsense talked about Jonglei than any other project in the country and some people seem to think we are sort of a bogus scheme like ground nuts than a straightforward commission investigating a specific problem. Isn't the Irrigation Consultant's word good enough and what about the political section of the Civil Secretary's Office? As for ourselves we remain in the dark. This matter is a comparatively trivial one, but it is symptomatic of a lack of direction. We are told that we must accept decentralization. We run our own affairs entirely and accept our responsibilities but there are some things like publication which must be decided for us.[72]

On their part, officials in Khartoum failed to understand why the report of the team could not be instantly forthcoming. After all, its members had amassed a mountain of information. But the very lack of visible progress towards its publication did nothing to encourage the supporters of the team, while seeming to confirm its critics. Some cynically muttered that the 'Big Report' (Howell was threatening to write 400,000 words) would never be written, despite its composition in the peaceful setting of Christ Church College, Oxford, where

[70] Chick to Howell, 13 July 1951, UNP I/26/198.
[71] R. J. Smith, 'Note on the Jonglei Investigation Team', UNP I/26/198.
[72] Howell to Winder, 16 May 1951, UNP I/9/80; Howell to J. Longe, governor, Upper Nile province, 30 Nov. 1951, UNP I/26/198.

some members spent their leaves writing together.[73] There was strain among the members of the team in the heat and humidity of Malakal, disenchantment at Khartoum. R. J. Smith at the headquarters of the irrigation department in Wad Medani grumbled about Howell 'suffering from examination fever', and the team feeling sorry for itself. 'They also suffer from a sense of loneliness, a combination of realization of the size of the problem of the South, the end of their chapter, and the future without a "a development team"'.[74] In any event, Smith left for Malakal on 9 February 1953 to tell Howell to wind up the report; the Jonglei Investigation Team was finished.

The Equatorial Nile Project and its Effects in the Anglo-Egyptian Sudan. Being the Report of the Jonglei Investigation Team was published in September 1954 in four volumes.[75] Whatever its merits or demerits, the magnitude of the report promptly silenced Howell's critics, but by 1954 most of them had left the Sudan in the transfer of power to the Sudanese. The report may lack the definitive conclusions beloved by the engineers, but it demonstrated the complexities of the way of life in the Upper Nile, its problems, and alternative means of resolving them. Typically, R. J. Smith sought to suppress it 'by claiming that the whole thing should be secret and reduced to typewritten pages'.[76] The report is sometimes difficult to read, uneven in style and lacking in uniformity, but it remains today the most impressive collection of information about the Upper Nile, from which all subsequent researches in any discipline must begin. The first volume is devoted to the hydrology, the economy, and the people and their livelihoods, the second specifically to the effects of the Equatorial Nile Project and possible remedies for damage. The third volume contains the results of special investigations on the Bahr al-Jabal, White Nile, Sobat, and the Machar Marshes. A final volume includes the maps and surveys. There is a separate introduction and summary. Altogether it represents a remarkable achievement

---

[73] Morrice Diaries, 5 June 1952, Morrice Papers.
[74] R. J. Smith, 'Jonglei Investigation Team', 7 Feb. 1953, SAD 500/14/20–2.
[75] An abbreviated version was published in *SNR* 33 (1952) under the title 'A Short Account of the Equatorial Nile Project and Its Effects in the Sudan'.
[76] Morrice Diaries, 26 Sept. 1952, Morrice Papers.

for such a brief period of research, collecting and organizing information about one of the most isolated regions of the world. The reports were written for a cause—the protection of the Nilotic peoples of the Sudd—yet the authors' painstaking adherence to scientific enquiry, in which the complexities of Jonglei are described, holds little interest for those who regard Jonglei as a political rather than a hydrological problem. The Jonglei report was the work of scientists and technicians, not politicians, so its appeal has been limited to those sufficiently interested to read it for what it is—a scientific study. But even as a report of scientific investigations it was not a document designed to promote continuous study of the southern Sudan with a view toward its development, but rather an attempt to resolve particular problems through remedies which have since become obsolete. This, of course, was the task set the team— to find immediate remedies, to calculate compensation—but the Jonglei Investigation Team could have been much more. Rather than the beginning of a scientific investigatory tradition for the southern Sudan, the report has become a historic document about the Upper Nile province in mid-century. Its deficiencies lie not in what it is, but in what it might have become.

While Paul Howell was frantically completing his report, a momentary tremor of anxiety ran through British officialdom that the work of the team might prove a colossal, misdirected waste. In November 1952 the tripartite commission arrived in Khartoum; in December 'Abd al-Azim Isma'il, under-secretary at the ministry of public works, wrote to Chick that Egypt was studying proposals for a higher dam at Aswan. The tripartite commission was the more dangerous of the two because it was the more immediate. As early as 1950 the ministry of public works had begun to question the direct line for the Jonglei Canal. Humphrey Morrice and John Winder had suggested a direct line in their *First Interim Report* in 1946, an idea that was swept up in the enthusiasm produced by Hurst's publication of *The Future Conservation of the Nile* several months later and quickly given approval by the minister. There remained in the ministry, however, a rump of civil servants who insisted that Butcher's canal was less expensive and easier to build. Led by the influential Isma'il Sirry Pasha, who had approved it as the ministerial choice after the review of the various Sudd canal proposals in 1938, they continued to lobby in the ministry to revive Butcher. Allan appears to have been aware of this campaign from its inception, but when the Jonglei Investigation Team was reconstituted in 1948, the advocates of a direct line were in control at the ministry, and Dr Amin and H. G. Bambridge had already carried out their 'modifications' for operating a direct-line Jonglei Canal. This did not silence the supporters of Butcher's scheme. The line of the Sudd canal, in fact, was dependent upon the old issue of dredgers versus drag-lines for its excavation. Butcher had always argued that drag-lines could not operate effectively in the Sudd, despite the investigations and experience of the Ruston–Bucyrus corporation to the contrary. If dredgers were used for excavation, the direct-line canal would take too long to complete and therefore be too costly. By 1952 the Butcher canal-dredger lobby at the ministry had succeeded in casting sufficient doubts on the feasibility of the direct-line canal to necessitate a response. To resolve this debate the ministry of public works appointed in 1952 an international tripartite commission of experts in excavating machinery, composed of members from the Netherlands, the USA and Great Britain. Not surprisingly, they were all 'dredgermen'.

The commission reached Khartoum on 19 November. Its very appearance created alarm among the members of the Jonglei committee and a mild case of consternation within the Jonglei team. If, after all these years of research in the Upper Nile based on the approved direct line, the Egyptians were going unilaterally arbitrarily to opt for the Butcher canal, much of the work of the past six years would be compromised and the remedies, alternative living schemes, and compensation costs made irrelevant. Moreover, the British officials were not reassured by the composition of the commission. The chairman, B. D. H. Tellegen, the managing director of Netherlands Engineering Consultants (NEDECO), had little knowledge of earth-moving equipment except dredgers. Dutch engineers possessed a well-known predilection for dredgers, and Tellegen talked effusively of their operation on the Donzere–Mondrago canal which had a similar profile to the Jonglei Canal. He was regarded suspiciously by Nimmo Allan and R. J. Smith as a 'scout' for the Dutch dredger firms and Dutch international construction companies, for several of which he was a consultant. Schoon, the American representative, was the executive vice-president of the Atlantic Gulf and Pacific Dredging Company, which certainly betrayed his priorities. Humphrey Morrice described him as 'a hard-bitten contractor who merely wanted to get in on the job'.[77] The third member of the triumvirate, J. A. S. Rolfe, a partner in Sir Bruce White, Wolfe, Barry and Partners, consulting engineers, had carried out important harbour works in Bombay using dredgers, but the Sudan irrigation department and the Jonglei team regarded his close ties to Geoffrey Parker as more sinister. Parker was the former inspector-general, Sudan, for the Egyptian irrigation department who had remained in Cairo as a consulting engineer upon his retirement. During his tenure at the ministry he had steadfastly opposed any consideration of the direct line, preferring his bizarre and now discredited Veveno–Pibor scheme. He had had no first-hand experience of the Upper Nile for over twenty years.[78]

The commission spent ten days in the Upper Nile accompanied by a nervous coterie of members from the ministry of public works, among them Sabry al-Kurdi Bey, Dr Amin, and Bambridge, all self-avowed advocates of the direct line. In this brief period they had only time to visit the two ends of the canal at Jonglei and Sobat. They did not venture into the heart of the Upper Nile through which the direct line would pass, and displayed no interest in doing so. They were rather overawed by the Sudd, for none of them had ever experienced anything quite like it. They had never heard of creeping flow and did not fully appreciate the problems of cross-drainage which had been a principal reason for abandoning Butcher's canal. Although their terms of reference did not mention Butcher's alternative scheme to bank the Bahr al-Jabal by dredgers, Bambridge complained that they talked of little else, since it was a project they understood. They came away from Malakal very impressed with the work of the Jonglei

---

[77] Morrice Diaries, 2 Dec. 1952.
[78] 'Note on Conversation on 24th June 1952 between Messrs. J. A. S. Rolfe, G. Parker and W. N. Allan at the Sudan Agency, London', SAD 589/5/25.

team which did nothing to alleviate the suspicions of R. J. Smith.[79]

The report of the triumvirate commission need not have concerned the Sudan authorities, nor did it seriously compromise the work of the Jonglei team as Paul Howell had feared.[80] The members of the commission were in fact unqualified to make a judgement as to the line of the canal, and differed among themselves as to its alignment. This was of no use to Butcher's supporters at the ministry. As everyone had predicted, they dismissed drag-lines for the same reason as Butcher—the country was impassable for drag-lines and impossible for their maintenance—but they made no attempt to assess the arguments for their use. The 'grab' dredger was the unanimous choice of the commission, but this recommendation was of little help without a concurrent suggestion to abandon the direct line. In the end their inadequate report was stillborn and the issue faded from the Upper Nile, Khartoum, and Cairo.[81]

The high dam at Aswan aroused more curiosity and concern at Khartoum than the possible change in the alignment of Jonglei implied by the appearance of the tripartite commission. Any project at Aswan would be made possible only by an agreement between Egypt and an independent Sudan, not Great Britain. The British had never given serious thought to a high dam at Aswan; Hurst's century storage was in part designed to avoid it. The idea for a high dam at Aswan, however, had been around for a long time. General F. H. Rundall had first proposed such a scheme as early as 1876. Willcocks had argued for the project in the 1890s, but after the completion of the Aswan dam in 1902, the proposal for a mighty dam which would essentially provide century storage never received any serious consideration at the ministry.

The Aswan high dam, the *Sadd al-Aali*, was in its contemporary form the creation of Adrian Daninos, a Greek-

[79] R. J. Smith, 'Note to File', 20 Dec. 1952; 'Notes on the Information from "Triumvirate"' 1 Dec. 1952, SAD 500/13; J. F. Glennie, divisional engineer, Sudan irrigation department, to Chick, 31 Dec. 1952, UNP I/10/88.

[80] Howell to Chick, 5 Jan. 1953, UNP I/10/88.

[81] J. A. S. Rolfe to H. A.W. Morrice, 22 Oct. 1953, SAD 589/5/25.

Egyptian engineer, who in 1912 had advocated the electrification of the Aswan dam to promote industry in Egypt. He fell into obscurity between the two wars until 1948 when, in co-operation with an Italian, Luigi Gallioli, he conceived of one grand structure at Aswan to guarantee century storage in a vast reservoir capable of generating enormous quantities of hydroelectric power. On 12 January 1948 he described his proposal in detail to the Egyptian institute, and thereafter he began to haunt the antechambers of the ministry of public works, attempting to promote his project, but receiving little serious attention from British or Egyptian officials. The Equatorial Nile Project was the adopted plan for Nile development, and the authorities wanted nothing to do with Daninos or his dam, preferring the plan of Sir Murdoch MacDonald submitted in 1943 to raise the Aswan dam by 11 m.

In 1952 the political situation in Egypt changed dramatically and in turn changed the attitude toward Daninos's proposal. On 23 July 1952 the secret revolutionary command council within the Egyptian army overthrew the monarchy. Led by Gamal 'Abd al-Nassir (Nasser), the twelve members of the revolutionary council were neither ideologues nor doctrinaire revolutionaries. They had no constituency outside the army, but they were not without fundamental goals—the independence and prosperity of Egypt. To translate these ambitious principles into reality, the free officers desperately needed a spectacular and visible symbol to demonstrate their intentions to the Egyptian people and the world. The high dam at Aswan was that symbol, and within two months it was under active consideration by the revolutionary command council from which there was no turning back. Politically it was a gigantic and daring scheme, a monument to the vision of the revolutionaries. Economically it provided water and power. Most important, and the clinching argument before which all the meticulous research and mathematical propositions by British hydrologists dissolved, the high dam would free Egypt from being the hostage of upstream riparian states by providing for century storage within the boundaries of Egypt. Moreover, the time to complete this massive symbol of a resurgent Egypt was half that required to construct Hurst's

century storage scheme, while providing the necessary hydroelectric potential for industrialization. Whatever the demerits
of the high dam, they were rendered insignificant by these
facts.

Rebuffed by the ministry, Daninos turned to the revolutionary
command council, and in August, a month after the *coup d'état*,
he went directly to two engineers he knew, Samir Hilmy and
Mahmud Yunis, who were free officers and headed the
revolutionary command council's technical office. The Sudan
officials first learned of the high dam in the autumn of 1952
from the members of the ministry who had ignored Daninos's
scheme, and then from officials like Dr Muhammad Amin
who, bending to the winds of change, favoured it. A flurry of
commentary on the project burst forth from the Sudan
irrigation department and its irrigation consultant, upon the
surprising and refreshing request from the new Egyptian
Government for the views of the Sudan. British officials were
astonished and not a little pleased to be asked their reaction
before being presented with an accomplished fact.

The Aswan high dam would do nothing for the Sudan, and
indeed represented a potential loss if it enabled Egypt to store
the flow of waters, thus inundating towns of the Nubian
Sudan like Wadi Halfa. There were many objections: the high
rate of evaporation, siltation, seepage, and scouring. But the
benefits were more 'real, rapid, and immense. They will
include power, flood protection and water—which being at
the point of entry, will be useable as and when required.'[82]
The high dam had four specific functions: to store a large
quantity of flood-water for use in the following low stage; to
give protection against dangerous floods; to store some of the
excess water in high years to increase the supply in low ones;
and to produce large quantities of hydroelectric power.[83] Dr
Amin grandly advanced the proposition that the high dam
would resolve all British concerns about the Jonglei Canal.
'The operation of the Jonglei Canal could, with Aswan to take
up the slack, be arranged as we wished for controlled grazing.
As there would be no need for flood protection or emergency
reserve storage, the more advanced stages of the canal would

[82] R. J. Smith, 'The Greater Aswan Project', 23 Dec. 1952, SAD 500/8.
[83] Hurst *et al.* (1965, p. 79).

not be needed.'[84] H. E. Hurst, evidently accepting the political facts of life, gracefully abandoned his scheme of century storage, in which he had dismissed the large reservoir at Aswan, and now set about calculating the most efficient means of regulating the high dam reservoir for long-term storage.[85] British officials at Khartoum simply recorded these conversations and commented upon them. They could do no more. The signing of the Anglo-Egyptian Agreement in February 1953 effectively terminated the official British presence in the Sudan within three years, and the publication of the report of the Jonglei Investigation Team in 1954 ended British research into the Equatorial Nile Project. Any future discussions about the Equatorial Nile Project and the Jonglei Canal would have to take place between Egypt and an independent Sudan.

These last years of British rule in the Sudan saw one other curious aftermath to the Jonglei investigation—an epitaph of sorts—the southern development investigation team. At the seventh meeting of the Jonglei committee on 19 December 1949, the programme for future research by the Jonglei Investigation Team had been reviewed and specifically limited to short-term studies, of no more than three years, to assess compensation and to determine remedial measures. This decision had precipitated an immediate reaction from Paul Howell, on behalf of the team, and governor Frank Corfield, for the provincial administration. They argued that the decision by the committee should not forbid continuing research necessary for provincial development. Their objections inaugurated debate about the utility of supporting research projects over a long period of time, and, as a corollary, about the more contentious issue of which agency would conduct them. The debate was confused by strong personalities, and by even stronger criticism of the Jonglei Investigation Team that often obscured the concept of research-based development. On the one hand were the department heads determined to protect their interests; on the other were those who supported an interdisciplinary approach by which the Jonglei team would simply continue in a different guise and with a new charge.

[84] R. J. Smith, 'The Greater Aswan Project', 1 Jan. 1953, SAD 500/8.
[85] Hurst et al. (1965).

The controversy bubbled away on the surface of the team's work throughout 1950 and 1951, during which Howell grasped every opportunity to urge that research be organized on a continuing basis.[86] By May 1952 a decision as to development studies in the Upper Nile became all the more pressing since the Jonglei team would be disbanded the following year. On the surface it seemed a simple matter, but underneath the waters were roiled by deep disagreement, not so much whether research should continue but by whom. In March, Howell had proposed that the Jonglei team be retained with a broader charge, to study the problems of development in the whole of the southern Sudan and not just the Upper Nile, a proposition which instantly galvanized the opposition. The work of the team itself had demonstrated the complexity of the problems, which were not going to be properly addressed by short-term studies. Moreover, the political climate in Khartoum was rapidly changing with the rising tide of Sudanese nationalism, in which the role of the southern Sudan became a critical and sensitive issue. Those who, two years before, had seen little return in a continuous research endeavour in the south now agreed that just such a programme appeared the only guide for the development of the southern Sudan, in the faint hope of making the region an economically viable partner with the north. Certainly, there was a growing feeling among those who wished to disband the Jonglei team that by so doing they would also shut the door on future development studies in the south.

To sort out this thicket of personalities, aspirations, and organizational problems created by the indifference of the Jonglei committee, the upper Nile development committee was established in 1952 to make recommendations for the post-Jonglei years. The very fact that such a committee was appointed implied some sort of acknowledgement that development should be pursued, and by May it dutifully suggested that a development plan for the province be prepared. At this point the old disagreements appeared, and the members were sharply divided as to who should carry out the proposed work—a team of experts recruited from outside the Sudan,

---

[86] Howell to Longe, 12 Nov. 1951; G. H. Bacon, director, department of agriculture and forests, to Longe, 20 Nov. 1951, UNP I/26/198.

consulting engineers, or the retention of the Jonglei team, as Howell had proposed. He had been vigorously advocating for months that the team should continue as a 'co-ordinated development team', starting in the Upper Nile but then expanding to include the whole of the southern Sudan. Not surprisingly, Chick regarded the prospect of a revitalized and enlarged empire for Howell with distaste. G. H. Bacon, director of the department of agriculture and forests, wanted any such investigation to be within his domain. Although supporting the idea of development, R. J. Smith considered the only proper authority to organize development research would be a firm of consulting engineers. He had gone so far as to sound out privately Sir Alexander Gibbs and Partners, who were consulting on irrigation projects in the northern Sudan. To his dismay they showed little interest in the Upper Nile, but this did not weaken his determination to oppose the continuation of the Jonglei Investigation Team in any form.[87]

The Upper Nile province development committee agreed with Chick, Bacon, and Smith in the summer of 1952. The Jonglei team was to be disbanded and its functions taken over by the respective departments. Thus, future agricultural development work and pilot schemes would continue under the supervision of the department of agriculture and forests, veterinary research under the aegis of the veterinary services, while the survey needs of both would be co-ordinated by the Sudan survey department. Hydrological considerations would be the province of the irrigation department.[88] This was, of course, the object of the departmental 'States' by dissolving the Jonglei empire, but even R. J. Smith recognized that there had to be some co-ordinating mechanism. It was not easily discovered. R. C. 'Jumbo' Wakefield, the influential head of the Sudan survey department whose brother was a prominent Conservative MP, A. C. Beaton in the civil secretary's office, and Humphrey Morrice from irrigation were strong supporters of the team approach to development problems. They desired, however, better control over any team than that exerted by the Jonglei committee over the Jonglei team, and more precise

[87] R. J. Smith, 'Development in Upper Nile Province and the Future of the Jonglei Investigation Team', 6 May 1952, SAD 500/14/18.

[88] R. J. Smith, 'Jonglei Investigation Team', 7 Feb. 1953, SAD 500/14/20.

terms of reference in order to determine what the team would in fact be investigating. The approval to execute or not would remain with the development committee. J. T. R. Evans, director of veterinary services, and G. H. Bacon at agriculture disagreed, wanting work relevant to their interests to be supervised by their own department. They were strongly supported by Chick.

The controversy remained dormant during the autumn of 1952 and was only revived in January 1953 by Wakefield. He was concerned about the principle at stake, but also about the unco-ordinated requests coming into his office for survey work to be carried out in the southern provinces.[89] Spurred on by Wakefield, Chick reluctantly called a meeting at the financial secretary's office specifically to settle this contentious issue. As before, the representatives of the subsidiary services, irrigation, surveys, and the civil secretariat were strong supporters of the team approach, but those departments which would be primarily involved in any development research, agriculture and veterinary services, were opposed. Wakefield, Beaton, and Morrice argued that a visible team concerned only with southern development would have important political ramifications as well as administrative. It would reassure the southerners, already apprehensive about their future relationships with the northern Sudanese, as to the sincerity of the British about their welfare, so long neglected. Any such team with a dynamic leader would be able to compete with the north in the scramble for scarce resources. The signing of the Anglo-Egyptian Agreement in February, whereby Britain agreed to terminate British administration in the Sudan within three years, made a visible agency established in the south to promote southern interests all the more important in the light of the British departure. As for the opponents, they regarded the re-creation of a team 'as an unnecessary extravagance and in some respects undesirable'.[90]

Despite the arguments of Beaton and Morrice and pleas by Wakefield for an urgent decision, no conclusion was reached, and the matter was left to drift. There was a strong suspicion that the opponents of a team were prepared to delay any

[89] R. C. Wakefield to Ogden, 10 Jan. 1953, Howell Papers.
[90] Bacon, Feb. 1953, Howell Papers.

decision until the present Jonglei team was disbanded and could not 'easily be brought together again'.[91] Chick and Bacon had been particularly outspoken against Howell being involved in any scheme for southern development, and obviously let their personal antipathy obscure the concept of administrative co-ordination. Nevertheless the problem did not go away; it only became more manageable by the retirement of Chick and Bacon in July. By that time the commissioner for development, responding to Wakefield's persistence, drafted a detailed proposal for a southern development team and its terms of reference for consideration by senior heads of departments at a meeting in Khartoum on 22 June 1953. Here the Southern Development Investigation Team was born, amidst an atmosphere of uncertainty as to the political future of the Sudan, particularly the south. John Carmichael had replaced Chick at the finance department, and Allan McCall had taken over Bacon's duties at agriculture. Both were in favour of a development team for the south. J. T. R. Evans of the veterinary services remained sceptical, but he was now a minority, and, although determined not to surrender control of his staff and equipment to the team leader, he could no longer oppose the idea. The Southern Development Investigation Team was duly constituted in the autumn of 1953. Paul Howell returned to Malakal in triumph as its leader.

The team was assembled by Howell at Malakal in March 1954. Most of its members, K. E. Snelson, J. J. Basinski, J. W. Davies, E. A. McLaughlin and J. V. Sutcliffe, had been members of the Jonglei Investigation Team. Their tenure, however, was brief. By May most of them had been transferred or dismissed under the programme of Sudanization designed to replace British officials by Sudanese as part of the planned termination of British administration. Howell himself returned to England at the end of April to supervise the publication of the 'big report' of the Jonglei Investigation Team, leaving behind Snelson, divisional engineer, Sudan irrigation department, to wind up the hasty investigations and prepare a draft report. The team had effectively died, its tombstone the

[91] Wakefield to Ogden, 12 Feb. 1953, Howell Papers.

Natural Resources and Development Potential in the Southern Provinces of the Sudan: A Preliminary Report by the Southern Development Investigation Team 1954. Its conclusions are perhaps obvious. 'Although our knowledge of the resources of the Southern Sudan is far from complete, it seems clear that in the immediate future economic development must necessarily lie in the sphere of crop production, animal industry, and fisheries.'[92] Nevertheless, it is a remarkable document, given the few months available for its preparation, owing much to material compiled by the Jonglei Investigation Team and the energy of Kenneth Snelson, who oversaw its completion by November 1954. Regrettably few Sudanese, northern or southern, have ever read it.

The new government of the Sudan, dominated by northern Sudanese, displayed little interest in the south and less in its economic development. The Southern Development Investigation Team was a British creation and, like the British, had to go. The Sudanese who replaced the British members had no guidance, no competence, and no experience. They did little but draw their salaries until November 1956 when the team was gratefully liquidated, to the bitter disappointment of the southerners. The equipment was sent to Khartoum, and any pretence that the team's retention under another name might be interpreted as a symbol of the Sudan Government's intention to develop the southern provinces was stripped of its hypocrisy by the team's demise.[93]

---

[92] Southern Development Investigation Team (1955, p. i).

[93] O. M. Rann, secretary, Southern Development Investigation Team, to permanent under-secretary, ministry of finance and economics, 23 Aug. 1956, and 'Abd al-Rahim Mirghani for permanent under-secretary of ministry of finance and economics, 12 Sept. 1956, and 'Ali Faki Mustaf for commissioner for development, 7 Nov. 1956, UNP I/26/198.

7
Plans and Dams

If even a 'she camel' is entitled to her share of the water, why not your brothers of the Sudan?

H. T. Cory to the Egyptian committee of engineers, 1920

THE construction of a mighty dam at Aswan was a unilateral decision by the revolutionary government of Egypt in 1952, but even the revolutionary command council could not ignore the reality of the interests of other riparian States. Relations with Uganda had been normalized by the exchange of notes in May 1949 formally agreeing to the construction of the dam and power station at Owen Falls. Britain and Egypt had even revised their agreement of 1935 concerning the Lake Tana dam by the successful completion of the technical discussions in November 1946. The Sudan, however, was the most significant of all the riparian States and, by virtue of her geographical position, the dominant partner with whom Egypt must come to terms if development of the Nile valley was to continue south of Aswan. The Egyptians were well aware of this fact, and at the time of the exchange of notes over the Owen Falls dam agreement, the prime minister of Egypt issued a statement obviously calculated to win Sudanese support for the unity of the Nile valley under the Egyptian monarchy but one which, if taken literally, modified the Nile Waters Agreement by formally obliging Egypt to secure Sudanese permission before undertaking any projects for control of the Nile. Hitherto Egypt had had only to seek the consent of Great Britain.

In accordance with the spirit of the Nile Waters Agreement of 1929 and with our traditional policy which aims at the development and prosperity of the Sudan, the Egyptian Government would welcome the participation of the Sudan in the projects for the control of the Nile which are now under consideration. The participation of the

Sudan in these projects will be the subject of technical discussions between Egypt and the Sudan, the results of which will be embodied in agreements to be concluded in connection with these projects.[1]

Although this pledge was later ignored after the breakdown of negotiations in 1951, in 1949 this affirmation of friendly co-operation was regarded in Khartoum as a refreshing gesture in the convoluted disagreements over Nile waters, and encouraged the Sudan government to renew discussions at Cairo in December 1950 with a view to reaching an agreement to replace the unsatisfactory arrangements of 1929. The Jonglei Canal was not a part of these negotiations. The Sudan government had already agreed to the canal's construction as part of the Equatorial Nile Project, but deferred any technical discussions concerning its excavation until the publication of the report of the Jonglei Investigation Team. The talks in 1950 and 1951 were thus limited to four contentious issues which required agreement if a comprehensive Nile waters treaty were to be forthcoming: negotiations with Ethiopia on the Lake Tana dam project, the raising of the level of the Sennar reservoir, a dam at the fourth cataract, and an increase in the supply of water for the Sudan. The heart of these and subsequent negotiations was the share of Nile waters between Egypt and the Sudan. If agreement on this critical question was lacking, discussions on the other matters would founder. They did. The talks were unfriendly and unproductive. They were broken off early in 1951, and both Egypt and the Sudan began to plan unilaterally for projects to meet their own respective water needs. Separate concerns, not holistic basin development, now dominated Nile water planning.

In 1949 the Sudan government had reviewed its future water requirements, last calculated in 1945, and concluded that it now must find about 11 billion m^3 to irrigate some 2.8 million feddans. After the failure of the Cairo talks, the Sudan consequently began to readjust the working arrangements at the Sennar dam in November 1951 in order to raise the level of the reservoir by 30 cm. The Egyptians, surprisingly, lodged no formal complaint, preferring to curry political favour with the Sudanese nationalists in return for a modest amount of

[1] Quoted in W. N. Allan, 'Nile Waters and the Sudan', pp. 9–10, SAD 590/1.

water. But the Sudan required more water than just 30 cm at Sennar. The intransigence of the Ethiopians over Lake Tana did not augur well for that lake's being a source of new water, so the Sudan government pressed on alone and retained the firm of Sir Alexander Gibb and Partners to undertake a study for a dam and reservoir at Roseires within the Sudan's territorial boundaries.

On their part the Egyptians began to investigate new projects within their own country. In 1951 studies were undertaken in the Wadi Rayan for storage in that depression south of the Fayoum as an alternative to the reservoir at the fourth cataract which would require Sudanese approval and lie outside Egyptian territorial sovereignty. The prospect of utilizing the Wadi Rayan as a reservoir had been around for a long time. It may have been the mysterious Lake Moeris of Herodotus, but in modern times it was first proposed as flood storage by Cope Whitehouse in a lecture before the American Geographical Society in 1882. Despite severe criticism—seepage and salinization into the rich agricultural lands of the Fayoum to the north and improper synchronization of the reservoir with the flow of the Nile—British engineers had carried out detailed investigations in the 1890s. Whatever the results of the Egyptian surveys of the 1950s, the project was abandoned after the announcement of the programme for the high dam in December 1952. While the Egyptians were conducting their research in the Wadi Rayan, the Edfina barrage was completed in 1951 across the mouth of the Rosetta branch of the Nile. Previously the Edfina barrage had been an earthen dam, designed to exclude sea-water and prevent spillage in the Timely period. The new barrage not only was more efficient but conserved an additional billion m^3 which had previously been lost to the Mediterranean.

None of this activity, however, could resolve the Sudan's immediate need for water, and her initiative talks were resumed in 1952 at Cairo which were modestly successful. In an exchange of letters, Egypt agreed to raise the level of the Sennar reservoir by 1 m in return for construction facilities at the fourth cataract. The Sudan also received an additional 200 Mm^3 in the Timely period by raising the level of the Jabal 'Auliya reservoir by 10 cm. These measures might represent a temporary respite for the Sudan but were no substitute for a comprehensive agreement, which became all the more urgent in December 1952, when the new revolutionary government of Egypt announced its intention of building the high dam at Aswan, thereby rendering the fourth cataract dam and Timely water irrelevant. Although the dam would be built within Egypt and therefore be constructed without an agreement with the Sudan, its reservoir would flood the fertile land in Dunqula and inundate the town of Wadi Halfa, the Sudan's gateway to Egypt, which would require the approval of the Sudan government. The prospects for such an agreement did not seem auspicious in 1952 and even less the following year, when Egypt published its Nile development plan. The Nile development plan was prompted by the decision to build the high dam in order to integrate it with the other planned and approved Nile waters projects, Lake Tana and the Equatorial Nile Project; this would provide a net benefit of about 15 billion m^3 of water, of which the Sudan, according to the plan, would receive only 1 billion, and that from Lake Tana—a project which the Ethiopians refused to discuss, let alone approve. The plan was never taken seriously by the Sudan government, who ignored the document as just another example of Egyptian duplicity.

Despite the deadlock between the two governments, informal discussions among Egyptian, British, and Sudanese engineers from their respective irrigation departments continued quietly. In fact these talks had never ceased, an anomaly which characterized the schizophrenic nature of Nile water negotiations. At the personal level the conversations were generally amiable and informative, one engineer to another, but once the discussions involved those more politically orientated they were transformed in the public arena into part of the wider and mutually hostile and emotional relations between Great Britain and Egypt. A series of these informal talks took place in September 1953 in Cairo, during which Nimmo Allan argued the Sudan's case for a fair share of the Nile waters as a whole. The Egyptians reiterated their well-known position that Egypt had no intention of denying the Sudan her 'rightful' share of the Nile waters, but what constituted the Sudan's rightful share remained unclear and undefined. Moreover, the very existence of the Aswan high dam project implied that Egypt intended to retain all additionally conserved water for herself, since she would now have the capacity to store it.

Despite the lack of any progress toward a comprehensive Nile waters settlement, the results of two important Nile studies appeared in 1954 which moved the parties another step towards negotiations. In 1954 the report of the Jonglei Investigation Team was finally completed. Of more immediate importance was the study of the Roseires dam and reservoir concluded by Sir Alexander Gibb and Partners. This report identified Roseires not only as a suitable site but as the only site on the Blue Nile where water could be stored on a large scale within the Sudan, obviating any tiresome dealings with the Ethiopians. The dam was to have a reservoir with a total capacity of 3 billion m^3 for annual storage for the Sudan, a subtraction of Nile water which the Egyptians could not regard with equanimity. At the invitation of the Sudan government, Dr Muhammad Amin, director-general of the physical department, travelled to Khartoum at the end of August and the negotiations were formally opened amidst much fanfare and popping of flash bulbs at 10 o'clock on 1 September at the ministry of irrigation and hydroelectric power.

Knowing that the Sudan needed water and had in place a completed report on the feasibility of the Roseires dam, Dr Amin sought to bargain Egyptian approval for its construction in return for Sudanese acquiescence to the high dam. He also tied Egypt's approval for Roseires to the Jonglei Canal by claiming 3 billion m^3 of the additional water as Egypt's share, one billion from Jonglei, 2 billion from Roseires. No Sudanese minister could agree to such onerous terms. Sayyid Mirghani Hamza, minister for irrigation and hydroelectric power, refused. The Roseires project was one of modest size for which a report by the consultants recommending construction was available. The high dam was an immense undertaking of an unusual kind, about which the Sudan had received little information, and was many years from completion. To make

Roseires conditional on approval for Aswan was absurd; the talks were adjourned on 7 September, the representatives agreeing to meet again at Cairo in November.[2]

In Cairo each side had perfected its position but remained hopelessly distant from the other. Dr Amin insisted on the Sudan's approval for the high dam in return for Roseires, while proposing a paltry maximum of 8 billion m³ as the Sudan's ultimate share of the Nile waters. The Sudan rejected this latter offer as even less conceivable than the proposed bargain of the Roseires dam for Aswan. They demanded 35 billion (out of an agreed total of 84 billion) as the Sudan's share. Amin countered with 9.5 billion. Mirghani Hamza was prepared to compromise at no less than 25 billion. Deadlock.[3]

Two divergent philosophies emerged during the November negotiations. The Sudanese wanted a comprehensive settlement in which the allocation of the Nile waters would be determined before any project was constructed. Then the Sudan would have the right to build such control works as she chose in order to utilize her share most effectively. The Egyptian philosophy predicated that any settlement should be concluded in stages, the all-important matter of each country's share being adjusted as the projects were completed and experience gained in their operation. This gradual approach might clear the way for an agreement on immediate and desperately needed projects, but would require endless negotiations on any future projects which were likely to be contentious and acrimonious.

Nevertheless, both sides needed some agreement to develop their respective water conservancy schemes, and talks continued, despite the lack of any real progress. Discussions at the technical level rambled on into December, in the hope that the more friendly discussions among the engineers might find a common ground by some hydrological legerdemain. They did

[2] Morrice Diaries, 31 Aug. and 1–7 Sept. 1954, Morrice Papers, Rhodes House Library, Oxford.
[3] For a detailed summary of all these negotiations see W. N. Allan, 'Discussions on Nile Waters', 10 May 1955, SAD 500/5/37; Morrice Diaries, 20 Nov.–5 Dec. 1954, Morrice Papers. The 35 billion m³ proposed by the Sudan was calculated on an assessed irrigable area of 4.5 million feddans at 8000 m³/feddan/yr, that rate being the mean used in Egypt. The Sudan actually claimed to have 6.5 million feddans capable of irrigation but 2 million were marginal.

not. Each side recognized that Egypt's established rights to the Nile waters was 48 billion m³ and the Sudan's established share 4 billion, for a total historic use of 52 billion out of the agreed amount of the mean annual flow of the Nile of 84 billion. This left an unused balance of 32 billion. There was nothing magic about these figures; they had been specified in the Nile Waters Agreement of 1929 and its supplements. At this point, however, the Sudan and Egypt parted company. The Sudan representatives argued that any shared proportion must apply to the total Nile flow, 84 billion. Egypt responded with feeling that any basis of sharing should apply to the balance, 32 billion. The Sudanese consistently rejected this contention. Even the technical advisers could not close the gap.[4]

Formal negotiations at the ministerial level were thus opened once again in Cairo in April 1955 at the request of the Sudan, which needed an agreement for Roseires more urgently than Egypt needed one for Aswan. The Egyptian delegation included Sayyid Ahmad Shorbassy, minister of public works, Major Salah Salim, minister for national guidance and the regime's 'expert' on Sudanese affairs, and Colonel Samir Hilmy and his technical advisers. The Sudan delegation was represented by Sayyid Khidir Hamad, minister of irrigation, Sayyid Bashir 'Abd al-Rahim, under-secretary for irrigation, three Sudanese technical advisers, and Humphrey Morrice, the Sudan's irrigation adviser. Major Salim's contribution to the discussion was to reject available land, which the Sudan had in abundance, as a means of determining the proportions of shared water. Colonel Hilmy argued that the amount of each share should be determined by population, which Egypt had in abundance. No progress was made, and the talks were again adjourned after only a day and a half of discussions characterized by their insincerity. The Egyptian representatives agreed to put their position in writing. Time was on their side, and they appeared determined to use it.

In July 1955 a formal written offer was made to the Sudan government in a letter from the Egyptian minister of public works to the Sudanese prime minister Isma'il al-Azhari. The Egyptians argued, rather disingenuously since they were

---

[4] Allan, 'Discussions on Nile Waters'.

prepared to flood much of Sudanese Nubia, that the high dam
was essential for both countries. In order to establish the 'net
benefit' each country should officially assert its historic rights
(presumably 48 billion for Egypt and 4 billion for the Sudan,
although no figures accompanied the Egyptian proposal).
Once the established rights had been subtracted from the total
natural flow of the Nile as measured at Aswan, the 'net
benefit' would be the remainder. Such a proposal assumed
that the Sudan would have to bear an equal portion of the
large losses anticipated from evaporation at Aswan, on the
grounds that she would derive a share. of the 'net benefit'
made possible by the high dam. Under such a proposition the
Sudan would receive approximately 13 billion, a modest
increase on that offered by Dr Amin in November 1954 but
only half the 25 billion which Mirghani Hamza insisted was
the minimum the Sudan would accept.

The Sudan officially responded in November 1955. It
rejected the Egyptian claim that the high dam was a benefit to
both countries. Moreover, the high dam was not the most
efficient means of developing the Nile waters (a reference, of
course, to Hurst's scheme for century storage in contrast to
the big and wasteful dam at Aswan). It was preposterous for
Egypt to expect the Sudan to bear half the burden of
evaporation losses from the Aswan reservoir, from which it
received no benefit and only damage to the Sudanese
inhabitants of Nubia. If established rights were to be
subtracted from the total Nile flow, a position which the
Sudan government could not accept, then they should be
calculated as of 1 January 1955; the agreed figures of 1929
were not acceptable. Moreover, the Sudan government
categorically denied that an independent Sudan would be
bound by the Nile Waters Agreement of 1929, signed by Great
Britain, not the Sudan. Consequently, the Sudan would
proceed unilaterally with the construction of the Roseires
dam, a rather hollow boast but one which the Egyptians took
seriously.[5] They replied promptly and petulantly, withdrawing
their offer of July and invoking the terms of the 1929
agreement. The Sudan again rejected the contention that it

[5] Sayyid Mirghani Hamza to Ahmad Shorbassy, in 'Nile Waters and the Sudan',
SAD 590/1.

was bound by that agreement, and proceeded to draw up its own Nile valley plan. Nasser replied by announcing that Russia had offered to finance the high dam project.[6]

Discussions came immediately to a halt amidst a strident press and radio campaign against the Sudan and the imperialists. Even the informal talks between the two countries' technical advisers, which had hitherto withstood the winds of politics, evaporated. The position of each side had now clarified and hardened. They had nothing to discuss. The Sudan's irrigation authorities were busy pressing ahead with the Roseires dam project, the Nile valley plan, and the Khashm al-Girba scheme; the Egyptians were absorbed by the high dam. In April 1957 A. N. Khosla produced a report in which he reviewed the whole field of Nile water development in the Sudan and proposed the storage and use of water on a scale hitherto not contemplated, but none of his conservancy schemes could proceed without a settlement for sharing the water. The appeal of Egypt and the Sudan to the principles of international law was of little value, for the law was obscure and did not reflect political reality. The Sudan could insist that she was not bound by an agreement she had not signed and press forward alone with her own development schemes. Such a course was highly improbable in fact. The Sudan is a poor country, without the resources to embark upon larger water conservancy projects and irrigation schemes without external assistance. Foreign aid could come from Egypt or other outside sources, but both would require an agreement with Egypt on the utilization of the Nile waters. Moreover, Egypt was the dominant Arab State in the Middle East, and one for which the Sudan was no match in terms of political, economic, or military power. There were many in the Sudan who feared their big neighbour to the north and who did not wish to provoke her into intervening south of Aswan. In Khartoum the parliamentary government left behind by the British when the Sudan became independent on 1 January 1956 had broken down by 1958, while the southern Sudan had been plunged into a protracted civil war, even before independence, by the mutiny of the equatorial corps of the

---

[6] Ministry of Irrigation and Hydroelectric Power (1955).

Sudan army in August 1955. The fighting was sporadic at first, but with the passage of time the southerners became more embittered and intransigent, the fighting steadily escalating to squander men and money which could have been put to better use on development projects. Presumably the approval of the Sudan was necessary for Egypt to proceed with the high dam, but in fact the Sudan could do little to prevent its construction now that Egypt had the financial support from Russia to build it. Both sides had too much to lose by not reaching an agreement, but the Sudan seemed to have more. Once again the Sudan government swallowed its pride and requested that the negotiations be resumed; the Egyptians agreed and discussions begân in December 1957. The Sudanese delegation was led by Sayyid Mirghani Hamza, now deputy prime minister as well as minister of irrigation, who was prepared to go to Cairo but not to accept terms dictated by the Egyptians. For its part, the Egyptian government made his arrival more bearable by calling off its virulent propaganda campaign against the Sudan's water policies and individual Sudanese ministers and officials. In a spirit of brotherhood the press and radio predicted a quick and friendly settlement. This did not prove to be the case. The discussions were complicated and protracted; the issues were still the same—Roseires, the high dam, and particularly the sharing of the Nile waters.

The Egyptian case was now more elaborate and sophisticated. The object was to increase cultivation to keep abreast of an expanding population. Thus the total area irrigated must be enlarged, and the land now cultivated by basin irrigation converted to perennial irrigation to produce two or three crops instead of one per year. But the basins also served as an essential escape for excess water in the years of high flood; therefore, if they were converted to perennial irrigation an equivalent amount of storage capacity must be made available for flood protection in the high dam reservoir. Moreover, the areas in 1957 under basin irrigation totalled over 1 million feddans, and even in present conditions it was not easy to fill them and the Aswan reservoir at the same time.[7] If a reservoir

[7] According to the Egyptians, in order to fill the basins a minimum discharge below Aswan of 640 Mm^3/d for 50 days was required.

was built at Roseires with a capacity of only one billion m³ (the Sudan was planning for a storage of 3 billion m³), it would be impossible in most years to fill both the basins in Egypt and the Aswan reservoir. Therefore no reservoir at Roseires should be filled before storage was available in the high Aswan reservoir.

The Sudan refused to accept this argument. Its representatives disputed the Egyptian figures. They quoted statistics published by the ministry of public works itself to show that the basins could be filled in much less time and at a lower discharge than the Egyptians had asserted. If higher discharges had to be passed down from Aswan, it would not be to fill the basins but to keep the Nile below the barrages at a high level in order to lower the head against them, without which they would give way. The water passed down, of course, was lost, an extravagant and wasteful use of water to keep the Nile barrages from collapse; better to strengthen the barrages than equalize the water pressure on them. In the case of the Roseires reservoir, in low years the working arrangements could be devised so that the basins and the Aswan reservoir could be advanced or, conversely, the filling of the Roseires reservoir could be limited. The Sudan delegation emphatically refused to halt all agricultural development in the Sudan until the completion of the high dam. Nevertheless, the Sudan would agree to the construction of the high dam on three conditions: the Sudan must have a fair share of the Nile waters; she must receive full compensation for all damages in her territory caused by the high dam reservoir; and she must have the right to build any control works which she found necessary to use her share effectively.

The determination of each country's share of the Nile waters was the key to any agreement and consequently the most contentious. The Egyptian representatives argued that the established rights of both countries plus the losses by evaporation in the high dam reservoir should be deducted from the assured annual flow to derive the balance or 'net benefit'. The net benefit should then be divided in proportion to the populations in each country, but also taking into account the climatic differences between the Sudan and Egypt. The Sudan disagreed. It considered that the amount subtracted from the total should include the established rights and those losses in all reservoirs needed to use the shares effectively. The net benefit should then be divided in proportion to the respective areas for agricultural expansion in either country. The Sudan wanted to cultivate over 6.5 million feddans, while Egypt had only about one million feddans for expansion.

Regarding the issue of compensation, Egypt argued that the Sudan would share in the benefits of the high dam because only that project would enable both countries to have in all years assured shares of Nile water. Therefore, both countries should also share in its cost and in the losses and damage it would involve. The Sudan could not accept this view. The high dam would assure Egypt's present and future share of the water whereas the Sudan, being far upstream, would have to construct her own works to utilize her share and bear their damage and costs. She had no intention of paying any part of the cost of compensation; Egypt and Egypt alone should make restitution for the loss of property and provide the people displaced with satisfactory alternate livelihoods. Each side was so far apart both in principle and practice that there was no basis for agreement. The talks were summarily abandoned on 21 January 1958 after six fruitless weeks of negotiations.[8] Rebuffed in Cairo, Mirghani Hamza returned to Khartoum and new elections, determined more than ever not to barter Sudan's claims to the Nile waters for some electoral advantage. At the same time the ministry of irrigation and hydroelectric power unveiled its own master plan for Nile control, the Nile valley plan.

Morrice and Allan's *Report on the Nile Valley Plan* was published in two volumes in Khartoum in June 1958. It is an extraordinary document, the culmination of half a century of Nile studies, combining the sweeping comprehension of Garstin (without, however, his magisterial prose), the hydrological analysis of Hurst (without his caution), and the mathematical skill and the experience of Nile hydrology of Humphrey Morrice and Nimmo Allan respectively.

---

[8] For the evolution of these tortuous negotiations see the detailed summaries at each stage prepared by W. N. Allan, in 'Nile Waters and the Sudan', SAD 590/1; Allan (1958).

It was the first time that a Nile plan—or, for that matter, any other river system—had been devised by computer analysis. The idea of using electronic computation for a comprehensive plan for the Nile valley originated with Humhrey Morrice; in 1955, with the support of Nimmo Allan, Dr E. T. Goodwin of the national physical laboratory at Teddington, and International Business Machines of the UK, Morrice drafted a scheme of hydrological analysis using data from 1905 to 1952, which he first presented in a lecture to the Sudan engineering society and published in the winter of 1956. The prospects were so promising that Morrice, Nimmo Allan, and Kenneth Snelson prepared a program which IBM agreed in March to run on a Type 650 computer, first in Paris and later in London, at their headquarters in Wigmore Street. The computations ran through the summer and autumn, resolving numerous physical and programming difficulties, before they were presented at a conference in Khartoum in January 1957 sponsored by the ministry of irrigation and attended, among others, by Professor J. Th. Thijsse, head of the hydraulics laboratory at Delft, Pierre Danel, managing director of the Société grenobloise d'études et d'applications hydrauliques (SOGREAH), Brigadier C. G. Hawes from Uganda, and Dr M. P. Barnett of the Massachusetts Institute of Technology. In the opinion of the visiting experts 'no more economical and effective approach for the problem of planning the Nile Valley as a whole could have been devised'.[9] By the end of February 1957 the program had been revised in the light of the numerous suggestions arising from the conference, and was put into full operation. Dr Hurst himself praised the use of electronic computing as 'a new venture' which 'introduced a very powerful tool into the study of Nile conservation projects'.[10] Dr Barnett referred to the Nile valley plan as a 'classic study in computer simulation'.[11] Nevertheless, John Bolton of the engineering firm of Bolton, Hennessey and Partners identified the key to Nile control: not to the new technology that was making it possible, but the birth of

[9] Morrice and Allan (1958, i. 66; 1959); Morrice et al. (1959). For a full discussion see Morrice, 'The Effect on Uganda of the Nile Valley Plan', 18 Aug. 1958, Howell Papers, in possession of Dr P. P. Howell.
[10] Hurst et al. (1960, p. 291).   [11] M. P. Barnett, ibid. 294.

independent nation States in the Nile basin, each protecting its national interests:

In the final analysis, politics and people must have the last say. The time had surely come, concluded Mr. Bolton, for a conference of all countries interested in the exploitation of the Nile's potential. . . . Certainly, the time for short-sighted nationalism in the solution of such problems was long past.[12]

In the twilight of empire such an appeal must have seemed patronizing to those who looked to the dawn of a resurgent nationalism. Not surprisingly, Y. M. Simaika, former under-secretary of state and now the technical adviser to the Egyptian ministry of public works, dismissed the plan as 'unacceptable', liable to human error in its regulation to the detriment of Egypt.[13] Humphrey Morrice had no response. He had died prematurely on 31 December 1959. Nimmo Allan chiselled his epitaph on the edifice of the Nile valley plan: 'The whole of the Nile Valley should be treated as a hydrological unity.'[14]

The origins of the Nile valley plan are to be found in Morrice's report, 'The Development of the Main Nile for the Benefit of Egypt and the Sudan', produced for the ministry of irrigation in January 1954.[15] This was an important but not a new contribution to the literature of the Nile. It did not establish any new hydrological principles, and repeated Hurst's case for a series of lesser reservoirs at the sources and on the main Nile rather than a mighty one at Aswan. Its object was to provide as much water for irrigation as the river could possibly supply. Its major contribution was the idea that, if the greatest possible benefits for all users were to be secured, all projects should be so planned that they became component parts of a larger whole. Now the idea to devise a master plan for the Nile basin was not new—Garstin, MacDonald, and Hurst had all presented plans for Nile control based on that principle. But all three were thinking of conserving water primarily for Egypt. Morrice argued the case for all the riparian States, the benefits to whom would best be achieved by a refinement of Hurst's hydrology.

---

[12] J. Bolton, ibid. 308.
[14] W. N. Allan, ibid. 314.
[13] Y. M. Simaika, ibid. 309.
[15] Morrice Papers.

The Morrice report established the principles upon which the Sudan's case for Nile waters had been argued with the Egyptians. It was prepared between 1956 and 1958, as he and Allan submitted mountains of data to the IBM computers to produce the *Report on the Nile Valley Plan*. On the one hand, the report was vintage Hurst, confirming the principles of his scheme for century storage with the equatorial lakes as reservoirs and a large Jonglei Canal to bring down the water. On the other, the Nile valley plan was more comprehensive and much more sophisticated than Hurst's, and included with the aid of the computer many more variables and greater emphasis on hydroelectric power. Additional dams were planned for Lake Kyoga, the upper Blue Nile, at Semna (the third cataract), and the high dam at Aswan to provide century storage. Annual storage would be held in reservoirs built on the Baro River and at Roseires, Sennar, and Khashm al-Girba. Conservation works would be undertaken at Jonglei and the Balas scheme, whereby a tunnel would connect Lake Tana to the upper Balas valley to produce enormous quantities of hydroelectric power. The Nile valley plan was the elaborate evolution of *The Future Conservation of the Nile*.

There were, however, two major innovations. Using the computer, Morrice and Allan could demonstrate from the data between 1905 and 1952 that the amount of water shared between Egypt and the Sudan had no significant effect on planning and the capacities of control works or the methods of regulating them. Thus the question of the proportion of water to be shared by Egypt and the Sudan, the great rock upon which the ship of negotiations had always foundered, and the question of planning for the Nile as a whole could be considered separately. The division of these two issues could produce a major breakthrough in the deadlocked negotiations, but only if the plan were accepted in its totality, since the operation of every single work affected all the others. To consider each piece as it was added to the whole scheme would simply re-join the two issues of sharing and planning.

There were also two glaring deficiencies in the Nile valley plan which the authors did not feed into their primitive computer. When simulating the model for the Nile basin (see Fig. 4), Morrice and Allan derived their calculations on the

THE PLAN

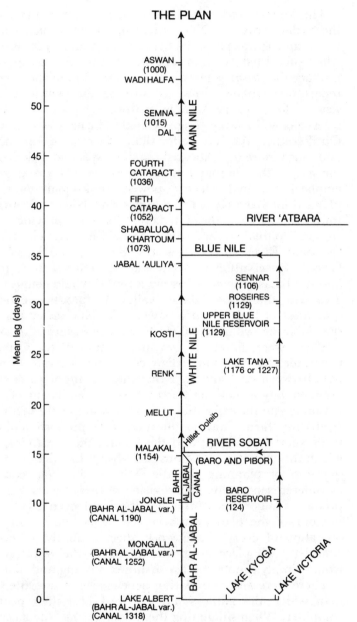

FIG. 4. The Nile valley plan. The figures are given in m³ billion.
Source: Morrice and Allan (1958)

ABSTRACTIONS

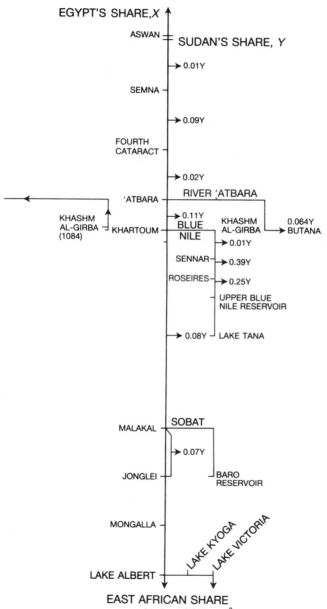

EGYPT'S SHARE, X

ASWAN — SUDAN'S SHARE, Y

→ 0.01Y

SEMNA

→ 0.09Y

FOURTH
CATARACT

→ 0.02Y

'ATBARA — RIVER 'ATBARA

KHASHM
AL-GIRBA — KHARTOUM
(1084)

→ 0.11Y   KHASHM   0.064Y
BLUE   AL-GIRBA → BUTANA
NILE

→ 0.01Y

SENNAR → 0.39Y

ROSEIRES → 0.25Y

UPPER BLUE
NILE RESERVOIR

→ 0.08Y — LAKE TANA

SOBAT

MALAKAL

→ 0.07Y

JONGLEI   BARO
RESERVOIR

MONGALLA

LAKE KYOGA LAKE VICTORIA

LAKE ALBERT

EAST AFRICAN SHARE
assumed to be 1.8 billion m^3

assumption that the previous flows measured from 1905 to
1952 would repeat themselves, an assumption the truth of
which cannot be guaranteed, despite the influence of Hurst
and his belief in periodicity. Structurally conceived by
mathematical formulae, the Nile valley plan did not take into
account the hydropolitics of the Nile valley, nor the economic
requirements which the Nile valley plan demanded from
poverty-stricken lands. It regarded Jonglei strictly as a
hydrological link in the plan, with no consideration of its
environmental impact, proposing not one but two canals, each
designed to carry 45 Mm^3/d, so controlled that between them
they could carry as little as 19 or as many as 89 Mm^3. The
additional water thus saved would, under normal conditions,
amount to about 8 billion m^3. The plan also included both the
Roseires reservoir and the Aswan high dam, the latter,
however, not as large as the Egyptians proposed. Its object
was to let no Nile water reach the Mediterranean Sea. To
achieve this aim, century storage was necessary, and made
possible by a chain of regulators each linked to the other and
managed as a whole. Adopted by the ministry of irrigation as
the Sudan's plan for Nile control, the Nile valley plan was
virtually unknown in the Sudan or Egypt, or outside the world
of the hydrologists and engineers. In the abstract it was an
elegant and efficient use of Nile water, but in the world of
political reality it has been ignored, like the austere but
ultimately sane proposal of Dr Hurst for century storage.
Neither Hurst, a naïve mathematician, nor Humphrey
Morrice, a wizard with figures but a humanist, could have
possibly devised a design for the most effective utilization of
the Nile waters to overcome the destructive power of
nationalism. The Nile valley plan was vehemently rejected by
the Egyptians and therefore ultimately abandoned. Today
it is all but forgotten, to the loss of the peoples of the Nile
valley.[16]

During the summer of 1958 relations between Egypt and
the Sudan reached their nadir, accompanied by a continuous
barrage of propaganda from Cairo about Nile waters, the high
dam, and the unity of the Nile, sprinkled with virulent

---

[16] Morrice and Allan (1958).

personal attacks on the Sudanese prime minister 'Abdallah Khalil and his deputy Mirghani Hamza. When not attacking the Sudanese, the Egyptian government was preoccupied about the final negotiations with the Soviet Union over the finance and construction of the high dam. In the Sudan the government was about to open the first instalment of the Managil scheme, which would require additional water from the Sennar reservoir. The construction of the Managil extension was begun in 1956 by canalization in the western part of the Gezira. Upon its completion Managil was to embrace 800,000 feddans; by July 1958 the first 221,000 had been prepared, and the Sudanese authorities were ready to test the new canals by filling them with water from Sennar. To obtain the water the Sudan irrigation authorities contemplated limiting the flow from the Sennar dam at an earlier date than normal in order to raise the level in the reservoir. The ministry of public works in Cairo had been kept fully informed of these developments and of the Sudan's intentions.

A flurry of diplomatic notes passed between Cairo and Khartoum. The Egyptians charged the Sudan with a breach of the Nile Waters Agreement of 1929 by taking water from the Blue Nile in one of the lowest years on record, to the damage of cultivation in upper Egypt.[17] The Sudan denied having been a party to that agreement, and asserted therefore that she was not bound by it. She argued that her govenment had been negotiating in good faith with Egypt over the Nile waters to no avail, and that she could not be expected to halt her development schemes until such time that an agreement was reached. Egypt had been kept fully informed of the Managil scheme and should not be surprised at the completion of the first instalment. Once again, the only beneficiaries were the employees in the ministry of information in Cairo who managed the campaign to denounce the Sudan government as 'wicked, greedy, and unco-operative'.[18] To ease the tension 'Abdallah Khalil offered to go personally to Cairo to reopen discussions; but he was publicly rebuffed by the Egyptian

[17] In 1958 Egypt exported over 1 million more kantars of cotton (5.4 million) than in the previous year.
[18] *The Times*, 9 Aug. 1958; *Daily Telegraph*, 29 Aug. 1958; 'The Disputed Waters of the Nile', *The Times*, 23 Sept. 1958.

government, which demanded that he first formally recognize the 1929 agreement. This he refused to do.

On the night of 17 November 1958, the Sudan army, under the command of Major-General Ibrahim Abboud, took control of the Sudan government in a bloodless *coup d'état*. Parliamentary democracy came to an end in the Sudan. Few mourned its passing. The mass of Sudanese had regarded the manipulations of the politicians with cynicism. Indeed, it was the prime minister himself who invited the military to take over the government to counter the growing Egyptian influence, not least of which were Egyptian demands in the Nile waters negotiations. The leading Sudanese politicians were pensioned into limbo, and in fact seemed quite willing to hand over the task of governing in which they had failed. Both the two great religious leaders, Sayyid 'Ali al-Mirghani, the spiritual head of the Khatmiyya, and Sayyid 'Abd al-Rahman al-Mahdi, leader of the Ansar, welcomed the army's seizure of power.

General Abboud immediately pledged to settle outstanding disputes with Cairo, and the Nile waters headed the list. In a radio announcement upon the success of his *coup d'état* he dismissed the issues as 'artificial' and created by 'degenerate politicians'. Only a month before, on 23 October, Nikita Khrushchev announced that the Soviet Union would provide a credit of 400 million roubles towards the construction of the first stage of the high dam. If Egypt wanted the high dam, the Sudan wanted Roseires. General Abboud needed to settle outstanding questions with Egypt to gain its support for his regime and to consolidate his somewhat uncertain hold in Khartoum. He and the Egyptians were both suspicious of the agitation in Britain for an international conference to establish a Nile waters authority, an organization in which Great Britain would be a member. The idea for a Nile valley authority had been growing in Britain since the announcement of Egypt's intention to build the high dam and the subsequent failures, despite repeated discussions, of the Sudan and Egypt to reach an agreement over Nile waters. In May 1956 the high dam proposal came under severe criticism in the House of Commons, Conservative and Labour members joining to call for a Nile valley authority to supervise unitary planning and control of the Nile waters. The Egyptians officially condemned the idea, but the issue did not die. Stung by the débâcle over the Suez crisis of 1956, Britain revived the prospect of an international conference for the Nile waters; but neither the Egyptians nor the Sudanese wished to have Britain return as a protagonist to muddy the waters of Nile negotiations.[19]

In March 1959 the Sudan again took the initiative when General Abboud requested that negotiations be reopened. There were new men in Khartoum with a new outlook more favourable to Egypt, but they could not dismiss the old disagreements, at the centre of which was the determination of the proportion of Nile waters to Egypt and the Sudan. Egypt was in a strong position. Virtually assured of Russian support to finance and build the high dam, she was now free of the condition upon which Great Britain and the USA had insisted that she must first seek a settlement on the Nile waters with the Sudan. As for the Sudanese, their needs were more pressing. The first stage of the Managil extension was complete. The second stage was under construction, and the third stage was about ready to begin canalization. All three would need water from the Roseires reservoir, for which the plans were complete but the financing was not. On 19 May 1959 Eugene Black, president of the World Bank, arrived in Khartoum only to make clear what the Sudanese already knew: any financial assistance from the West would be contingent upon a Nile waters agreement with Egypt.

The Egyptians were under more subtle but in many ways greater pressure for a settlement than the government of General Abboud. The Russians were now ready to commit themselves to the construction of the whole project at Aswan, not just the first stage, and although agreement with the Sudan over Nile waters was not a condition for Soviet assistance, the Egyptians could not deliberately flood Sudanese Nubia and Wadi Halfa without an agreement with the Sudan government to do so. More important was the public pressure on President Nasser himself to reach a settlement with the Sudan, pressure which was largely of his own making. Since

[19] *The Times*, 18, 22, 23 May, 1 June 1956; Sir A. P. Herbert, 'Nasser and the Nile', *Daily Telegraph*, 28 May 1957; 'The Sudan Seeks a Free Hand in Nile Debate', *Daily Telegraph*, 7 Oct., 3 Dec. 1958.

the announcement in December 1952 that Egypt intended to build the high dam, Nasser and his regime had made the dam a matter of great national pride, to the point where by 1959 it was inconceivable not to pursue it to completion. Now, with the promise of Russian aid, there were no longer the imperialist scapegoats to blame. The sooner construction was visibly under way, the sooner it would be finished, a personal adornment for President Nasser and a triumphant symbol for the revolution and the regime. Indeed, internal domestic enthusiasm for the dam was so great that to hold up its construction because of failure to reach a settlement with their Sudanese brothers was a situation which would never have been understood by the Egyptian populace. President Nasser had spent years extolling the virtues of the dam; he could not now risk a grievous blow to his personal prestige by failing to sign a piece of paper with the fatherly figure of General Abboud.

Throughout the summer of 1959 there was optimism in Cairo about an agreement. In June Salah Salim wrote with his usual ebullience in *Al Gomhouria* that 'one session between the officials of the two sides would be sufficient to produce a satisfactory settlement'.[20] The Sudanese were more guarded, but the climate of relations between soldiers who ruled in Cairo and at Khartoum was more cordial than that between the politicians. Neither government seemed unduly worried when articles appeared in the official press in Addis Ababa about 'Ethiopia's legitimate and major interests and rights as the greatest supplier of the waters of the Nile', and they remained unruffled when Britain officially informed them, on behalf of their East African territories, that Kenya, Uganda, and Tanganyika would reserve 1.75 billion m^3 of Nile waters for their future irrigation requirements.[21]

---

[20] *The Times*, 3 June 1959.

[21] *Ethiopian Herald*, 10 June 1959. In fact, the report in the *Ethiopian Herald* was based on a reconnaissance and report by the British engineering firm of Bolton, Hennessey, and Partners to the imperial Ethiopian government recommending that the amount of Blue Nile water reserved for Ethiopia be increased from 10% to 20% 'with a view to future bargaining'. G. W. Furlonge to Rt. Hon. Selwyn Lloyd, 3 Aug. 1959, enclosing 'Summary of a Report on Nile Waters dated June 19, 1959, prepared by Bolton, Hennessey and Partners for the Economic and Technical Assistance Board of the Ethiopian Government', Howell Papers.

On 7 October 1959 the Sudanese delegation of ten, led by Major General Talaat Farid, minister of information and culture, arrived in Cairo. He was accompanied by three other ministers from commerce, agriculture, and finance. Khartoum itself had returned to normal after a rather hectic summer in which the regime had been preoccupied by the suppression of an abortive coup in May and the emotive treason trials which followed. Although six army officers who had led the mutiny were sentenced to death, Abboud had wisely commuted the sentences to life imprisonment; but there was no overwhelming enthusiasm for the regime, which could only profit from a successful conclusion to the explosive dispute with Egypt over the Nile waters. Both sides were eager for a settlement; so when the Sudanese arrived in Cairo they exuded goodwill, despite their suspicions of Egyptian good faith and resentment at the vilification heaped upon the Sudan and individual Sudanese by the Egyptian media.

Negotiations opened officially on 10 October, with much fanfare and expressions of friendship. Optimism became buoyant when the Sudanese minister of trade, Brigadier Muhammad Ahmad Irwa, announced on the 14th that Egypt and the Sudan had reached agreement on trade and financial relations. This had been a pesky problem. Early in the year Egypt had suddenly refused to accept Sudanese produce and livestock, bringing trade between the two countries to a virtual halt. These high-handed actions, following Egypt's hostile reception to the testing of the Managil canal and an unnecessary frontier dispute the previous year, had produced much resentment in Khartoum. The withdrawal of the Egyptian troops from the border and the abstraction of water from Sennar for Managil in the summer of 1959 without even an informal Egyptian complaint had done much to placate the Sudanese. Now the conclusion of an agreement on customs, trade, and payments seemed to smooth the way for the more difficult Nile waters negotiations. On the 16th *Al Ahram* could report that the conversations were progressing with 'unrivalled goodwill'.

On 8 November 1959, at the foreign ministry in Cairo Zakariya Moieddin, central minister of the interior, and General Talaat Farid signed an agreement for 'full utilization of the Nile waters' amidst hand-shaking, hugs, and kisses. The Nile Waters Agreement of 1959 was a historic achievement. Not only did it clear the way for the immediate construction of dams at Aswan and Roseires, but it established the principle of the sharing on an equal basis of any additional water obtained by future conservancy schemes. The principle by which the natural flow of the Nile would be shared was the heart of the agreement. To determine the shares of Egypt and the Sudan, the 'net usable amount' must be agreed upon. Since the natural flow of the river varies from one year to the next and is not known before any decision as to the operation of conservancy works needs to be made, the determination of the net usable amount can only be fixed by experience or mathematical probabilities. Barring this method, the only practical and equitable means of defining respective shares is by a percentage of the net usable amount, and not a fixed quantity of water. If the shares are defined as a fixed volume of water allocated to the Sudan, then when the net usable amount is greater, Egypt, not the Sudan, would be the beneficiary by taking or storing the balance. For her part Egypt had always argued that the established or historic rights must be subtracted from the net usable amount and that any division or shares, however calculated, should apply only to the remainder. Even if one admits full respect for established rights, this contention ignored the great differences in the development and the use of Nile waters between Egypt and the Sudan. As a method for allocation between two users of amounts of water which vary from one year to the next, such an arrangement was neither practical nor equitable. The application of an agreed percentage of the total net usable amount would correct these inequities.[22]

Egypt and the Sudan compromised on this critical issue, paving the way for an agreement. In return for the recognition by the Sudan of Egypt's established and historic rights, Egypt would agree to the principle first put forward by H. T. Cory

[22] In the Nile valley plan Morrice and Allan demonstrated that, over a range of sharing from 33⅓ for the Sudan and 66⅔ for Egypt to 22% for the Sudan and 78% for Egypt, the resulting mean net usable amount of water and the mean total loss by evaporation over a long period and with a comprehensive scheme of control would be the same.

that any water beyond or added to the established rights would be shared equally by Egypt and the Sudan. By recognizing established rights the Sudan would abandon its previous insistence on measuring shares from the total amount of the natural flow of the river, and not just that portion left after subtracting the established rights. In return, the Sudan would receive half of the waters above the historic rights, now and in the future. This resolved the problem which the Nile waters commission, by refusing to adopt the Cory award, and the 1929 agreement, which ignored the whole issue of shares above established rights, had not settled. Both parties also agreed to abandon any sharing based on population or irrigable lands, positions to which they had clung tenaciously in previous negotiations, in favour of the principle of a percentage, 50 per cent. This is the lasting and important contribution to the development of the Nile waters of the 1959 agreement. Today there are critics in both Egypt and the Sudan of this principle, but they have yet to devise a better method of reconciling the hydrological and political realities of the Nile valley.

By the terms of the agreement Egypt increased its established rights to 55.5 billion m³, a gain of 7.5 billion. The Sudan received 18.5 billion, a substantial gain of 14.5 billion and much more than Egypt had offered in 1954, 1955, 1957, or 1958. Both countries, however, appeared to have accepted a figure for their established rights considerably below their proposed expansion of irrigated lands.[23] Any additional water which could be conserved or discovered would be divided on an equal basis. Since no additional water was likely to come from Ethiopia, the equatorial Nile project was revived to provide it. Jonglei was its key. In section III of the agreement, the Sudan government specifically reaffirmed the decision made by the Condominium government to approve the excavation of the Jonglei Canal, but for the first time the

[23] These established rights appeared to have been arrived at by compromise at the negotiating table and not by any calculation of need. In the Nile valley plan the Sudan's requirements were fixed between 20.2 and 25.7 billion m³ to irrigate 6.6 million feddans, depending on the intensity of cropping. Egypt required 58 m³ billion to water 7.1 million feddans (Hurst et al. (1931–66, vol. vii)), but Egypt had forecast an expansion to 8.5 million feddans and even 10 million feddans, which would require 70 and 86 billion m³ respectively.

financial terms were agreed upon, each party sharing equally the costs and the additional water. Significantly, no reference was made to the question of compensation or remedial measures for the inhabitants of the canal zone which had so preoccupied the Jonglei committee and the Jonglei Investigation Team.

There were other anomalies in the agreement. The preamble refers to 'full utilization' and 'full control of the river' by Egypt and the Sudan, ignoring the interests of the other riparian States. Great Britain on behalf of her East African territories had formally notified Egypt and the Sudan of the future water requirements of Kenya, Uganda, and Tanganyika, but made no attempt to insert herself into the negotiations, and Whitehall warmly welcomed the accord. Ethiopia simply insisted that all the riparian States should be consulted. The representatives from Egypt and the Sudan paid little attention to the concerns of other riparians, simply agreeing to present them with a united position in any future negotiations. The agreement, of course, specifically provided for the construction of the high dam and compensation to the Sudan for the flooding of its territory, including Wadi Halfa, and the resettlement of the Nubian inhabitants. Oddly enough this last issue proved one of the most contentious. The Sudanese originally requested £E36 million. The Egyptians offered £E9 million. The Sudanese countered, demanding £E20 million. The Egyptians then stood firm at £E10 million. The deadlock was broken by the personal intervention of President Nasser. He suggested splitting the difference and compromising on £E15 million. This dramatic gesture by the acknowledged and admired leader of the Arab world appears to have melted Sudanese resistance, and in their naïvety the generals accepted Nasser's seemingly sensible compromise. It proved to be a disastrous mistake. In agreeing upon a fixed sum of only 40 per cent of what they had initially requested, the Sudanese had not taken into account inflation, the uncertainties involved in the resettlement of 50,000 Nubians, and the high cost of alternative livelihoods. The reaction of the Nubians to the prospect of being removed from their traditional homeland to the alien environment of Khashm al-Girba was violent. The riots were quelled by Abboud's army but seriously damaged the regime's authority, already compromised by the mutinies and treason trials of the previous year. In the end these factors eroded the value of the Egyptian award, and the Sudan had to dig deep into its own meagre treasury to find the funds to complete the resettlement to Khashm al-Girba, which eliminated the small surplus generated by the earlier and more practical decisions to sell the Sudan's cotton crop at the world market price.

Although both sides have subsequently grumbled that their share of established rights was inadequate, it is difficult to believe either could expect more. The advantages to both far outweighed the disadvantages to either. A bitter and contentious issue had been put to rest. President Nasser got his high dam, which he had promised the Egyptians for so long and which he had to deliver in 1959. The Sudan received financial assistance from the World Bank for Roseires. The immediate construction of Nile control projects could now go forward. The hostile atmosphere which had characterized Egyptian–Sudanese relations since 1952 had been replaced by sensible optimism. It brought to an end the polemical bickering which had made nonsense of their protestations of eternal brotherhood. Given the climate of public opinion in both countries, Nasser's concern about the communists in Iraq, and Abboud's predicament, beset with mutinies in the army, neither was in a position to accept failure and each stood to gain politically and personally by success over the Nile waters.

Less spectacular but, for Nile water development, more important was the establishment of the permanent joint technical commission (PJTC), composed of four representatives from each country with a rotating chairman, which would be responsible for the supervision of all the working arrangements as well as for carrying out the necessary hydrological studies for future conservation projects throughout the Nile basin. At long last here was an agency given the authority to plan and to supervise Nile waters development, a goal which had proved so elusive to the British. For the first time since the resignation of Sir Murdoch MacDonald in 1921 there was now a body given the responsibility for directing Nile water projects, despite the fact that the PJTC did not have the authority to commit either government to its proposals or to raise money for them. Nevertheless, it met regularly through the vicissitudes of Egyptian–Sudanese relations, one engineer to another above the scrum of politics; but none of the riparian States have accepted the standing invitation to join such an intimidating array of Egyptian and Sudanese hydrologists. The commission came into being on 17 January 1960 by a special protocol attached to the agreement with the head-quarters of the secretariat at Khartoum. It immediately plunged into 'conducting a vast programme of hydrometeorological studies in the upper reaches of the White Nile in an effort to increase the yield of the river to meet future needs of water and to cope with the increasing demands for agricultural expansion in the two countries'.[24] Released from the inhibitions imposed upon them by the failure of their respective governments to reach agreements, the engineers could now release their hitherto frustrated talents.

After the 1959 agreement Egypt and the Sudan plunged into the construction of their water projects. In 1961 General Abboud announced a seven-year development programme, costing some £S240 million, which included the construction of the Roseires and Khashm al-Gibra dams, the resettlement of the Nubians, and a variety of other development schemes. In June the World Bank formally agreed to loan the Sudan $32.5 million for Roseires, the West German government assisting with a loan of $19 million. Conspicuously absent from the plan was the construction of the Jonglei Canal. It is doubtful whether the Abboud government could have taken on the Jonglei Canal even if there had been no civil war in the southern Sudan. The projects in the north, at Roseires and Khashm-al-Girba, had fully committed the Sudan's economic and human resources, while in the south three important events dramatically changed the context in which the Jonglei Canal of the future would be planned and constructed.

When the Equatorial Nile Project was conceived in 1946 the Jonglei Canal was but one part, although a very important part, of century storage and the chain of dams and reservoirs in the equatorial lakes to make it a reality. This project was designed at a time when the principal riparian territories in

[24] A. M. Ibrahim, 'Co-operation on the Nile: P.J.T.C.—an Example', in *Hydromet* (1968, p. 65); P. P. Howell (1958). 'The Equatorial Nile Project and the Nile Waters Agreement of 1929, Uganda's Case', Howell Papers.

the upper Nile basin were under British administration. Political unity made possible the comprehensive and rational hydrological development of the region, and this fact was still reflected in the Nile valley plan proposed by an independent Sudan. In 1961, 1962, and 1963 respectively the British colonies of Tanganyika, Uganda, and Kenya became independent sovereign States, enormously complicating the development of conservancy projects in the Lake Plateau. The government of Tanganyika (it did not become Tanzania until 1964) was the first to invoke what became known as the Nyerere doctrine: 'Former colonial countries had no role in the formulation and conclusion of treaties done during the colonial era, and therefore they must not be assumed to automatically succeed to those treaties.'[25] On 4 July 1962 the government of Tanganyika addressed identical notes to the governments of Great Britain, Egypt, and the Sudan to inform them that 'the provisions of the 1929 Agreement purporting to apply to the countries "under British administration" are not binding on Tanganyika'.[26] In effect, Tanganyika maintained that the 1929 agreement had lapsed since the country had ceased to be British territory, a position which the Sudan had assumed since independence until signing the 1959 Nile Waters Agreement. On 21 November 1963 Egypt officially (and diplomatically) replied to Tanganyika that, pending further agreement, she regarded the 1929 agreement to be valid and in full force where applicable.[27]

Upon becoming independent Kenya similarly invoked the Nyerere doctrine; and, although the government of Uganda never officially informed the riparian States that it had done the same, it appears to have accomplished the same result by regarding all treaties as obsolete at the termination of British administration. The other riparian States in the upper Nile basin, Burundi, Ruanda, and Zaïre, had not been bound when

[25] Okidi (1980, p. 422). The Nyerere doctrine was not a new idea, and in fact had been proposed, in the context of the Nile Waters Agreement 1929, as early as 1959 by H. A. W. Morrice, the hydrological consultant for the East African territories, Uganda, Kenya, and Tanganyika; see Howell (1959).

[26] Seaton and Maliti (973, pp. 90–1).

[27] Okidi (1980, p. 421). See opinion expressed by H. A. W. Morrice to R. Cranford-Benson (ministry of lands and mineral resources, Tanganyika), 26 June 1959, Howell Papers.

colonies by the 1929 agreement since it was never signed by Belgium, and so they were not obliged to recognize it as independent sovereign States. The Nyerere doctrine legally detroyed the Equatorial Nile Project. Henceforth, any conservancy schemes in the equatorial lakes would have to be negotiated bilaterally or among the riparian States. Consequently, the assumption that the Jonglei Canal and the Lake Albert dam must be regarded in tandem had no legal validity once the British hegemony in the upper Nile had vanished.

Of greater reality in separating the Albert dam from the Jonglei Canal and making it a distinct project was the construction of the high dam at Aswan. Over-year storage, achieved by one massive structure at Aswan, eliminated in one stroke that concept which had plagued British and Egyptian engineers since the occupation of Egypt in 1882, the Timely and Untimely periods of the Nile. Its disappearance from hydrological calculations in Nile development behind the high dam has caused no regrets. Once the *Sadd al-Aali* provided over-year storage in its reservoir, there was no longer any concern about Timely water. There was thus no longer the need for the Lake Albert dam to regulate the regime of the Sudd. This did not mean that the Lake Albert dam and the Equatorial Nile Project could be forgotten; it only meant that they assumed a different mission. Dams at the outlet of the equatorial lakes would now be primarily for conservancy rather than regulation. Indeed, the PJTC had drafted elaborate plans for future conservancy projects throughout the upper Nile basin, of which the Albert dam is a prominent feature; but such plans are no longer tied to the Jonglei Canal which, after all these decades and many studies, has taken on a life of its own, just as the objectives of the Equatorial Nile Project have changed from regulation to storage.

The primary goal of the planners, saving the waters of the lakes, has become, however, ever more tenuous, not through legal constraints nor the construction of the high dam, but through the political realities in the East African States, particularly Uganda. Since becoming independent, Uganda, the pearl of Africa, has experienced tumultuous times. The fall of prime minister Milton Obote, the horrific reign of Idi

Amin, and the recent presidency of Yoweri Museveni have been characterized by insecurity and civil war, all of which have combined to make the construction of a reservoir at Lake Albert unlikely if not impossible. Egypt and the Sudan can hold out little hope in this century of conserving additional water in the equatorial lakes; the need to transport their waters without the enormous losses in the swamps is thereby rendered all the more critical, and the Jonglei Canal consequently ever more important.

After the signing of the 1959 Nile Waters Agreement, the tall shadow of the Ethiopian highlands spread across the plains of the Nile valley. Egypt, and less so the Sudan, had always been wary of their somnolent riparian overlord, whose geographical position could not be denied. Garstin, MacDonald, and Hurst had always included control of Lake Tana in their plains for Nile basin development. Morrice and Allan had included an upper Blue Nile reservoir and the Balas tunnel in their Nile valley plan. The former concerned only Egypt and, parenthetically, the Sudan. The latter was a project for generating hydroelectric power, first suggested by C. E. Dupuis as early as 1906 and then confirmed by R. P. Black in 1921 upon his discovery of the phenomenal hydroelectric potential of a tunnel only a dozen kilometres long down the precipitous drop from Lake Tana to the nearby Balas gorge.[28] Ethiopia had always been the silent partner in these proposals, so silent that the Ethiopians have consistently refused to discuss the Lake Tana dam project, despite the rare accord among Britain, Egypt, and the Sudan that the project should be undertaken as soon as possible. On 6 February 1956, only one month after the independence of the Sudan, the imperial Ethiopian government announced in the official newspaper, the *Ethiopian Herald*, that Ethiopia would reserve for her own use those Nile waters in her territory, 86 per cent of the total Nile flow.[29] This public declaration was followed several months later by official notes to the diplomatic missions in Cairo by which Ethiopia 'reserved its right to utilize the water

[28] Morrice and Allan (1958, i. 12–14); Morrice *et al.* (1959, p. 102); 'Notes on Nile Valley Plan 1958 by Morrice and Allan prepared by John Glennie', enclosed in R. Cranford-Benson to H. A. W. Morrice, 19 June 1959, Howell Papers.
[29] *Ethiopian Herald*, 6 Feb. 1956.

resources of the Nile for the benefit of its people, whatever might be the measure of utilization of such waters sought by riparian States'.[30]

Suddenly in 1958, in the midst of the Nile waters negotiations in Cairo and undoubtedly encouraged by them, the Ethiopians launched a major study of the water resources of the Blue Nile for irrigation and hydroelectric power, in conjunction with their ally the USA and specifically the bureau of reclamation of the department of the interior.[31] Tom Clark of the bureau had conducted a preliminary reconnaissance in 1952, but it was not until August 1957 that the bureau signed a formal contract with the Ethiopian ministry of public works and communication to carry out a massive survey. In fact, as late as 1958 little was known of the Blue Nile from Lake Tana to the Sudanese frontier. The gorge was deep, inaccessible in many places, and poorly mapped. The Portuguese may have traversed parts of the canyon as early as the sixteenth century; few Ethiopians descend into its depths. The American sportsman W. N. McMillan attempted to navigate the river in 1901, but his boats were swamped in the rapids downstream from his departure point. B. H. Jensen, a Swede, tried to come up the river from the Sudan but never got beyond the Azir tributary. Major R. E. Cheesman, the British consul at Debra Markos, tried to make his way through the valley on foot in several expeditions between 1926 and 1929, but even he had to detour upward from the river to cross over spurs of the plateau before descending again to the banks of the Blue Nile. Major J. N. Blansford-Snell made three expeditions in 1964, 1966, and 1969, but his scientific interests were marked by adventure and bravado, and at the time of his first reconnaissance the Americans had completed their massive study.

The Blue Nile plan required five years of intensive research; it is in striking contrast to the more methodical, but plodding, British-inspired studies of the Egyptian irrigation service, and much more comprehensive than volume VIII of *The Nile Basin* dealing with the hydrology of the Blue Nile.[32] With characteristic

---

[30] Whiteman (1964, pp. 1011–12); Ibrahim (1984a, p. 116).
[31] US Department of the Interior (1964).
[32] Hurst *et al.* (1931–66, vol. viii).

conviction the US bureau of reclamation included not just the river but the whole of the Blue Nile basin in its investigations, embracing 'its hydrology, water quality, geology, physiography, mineral resources, sedimentation, land use, ground water and local economy'.[33] A multitude of stream-flow measurements were undertaken during the five-year period, supplemented by aerial surveys and extensive mapping. Although a brief encounter compared with the efforts of the Egyptian irrigation department, in terms of total tonnage the seventeen volumes and appendices of *Land and Water Resources of the Blue Nile Basin: Ethiopia* outweigh the tomes of *The Nile Basin*.

The bureau of reclamation proposed four major dams on the Blue Nile downstream from Lake Tana, at Maradobi, Mabil, Mendala, and on the Sudan–Ethiopian frontier (the border project), with a combined storage of 51 billion m³ equal to the mean annual flow of the Blue Nile, with a hydroelectric capacity three times that of the Aswan high dam. The bureau did not, however, confine itself just to the river. Twenty-nine irrigation and hydroelectric projects were planned on the tributaries throughout the basin; the Finchaa hydroelectric plant, operational since 1972, is the only one to have been completed. Clearly this potential power was far greater than Ethiopia could use in this century or the next, but could be of immense value to its neighbours and traditional enemies, the Sudanese, by the construction of an integrated grid. Of more immediate concern was the effect of the four Blue Nile dams on the natural flow of the Nile and, of course, on irrigation in Egypt and the Sudan. The annual flood of the Blue Nile would be virtually eliminated, the flow into the Sudan becoming constant, and the total quantity of Blue Nile water reduced by 8.5 per cent. If all the projects were completed, which is most unlikely, the amount of land put into cultivation in Ethiopia would be equal to 17 per cent of the current land under irrigation in Egypt and would require 6 billion m³ of Nile water (see Map 6).[34]

Such a prospect, no matter how remote, could not but rekindle ancient Egyptian fears of Ethiopian control of the life-giving waters—a fable, to be sure, but one that is still

[33] See Guariso *et al.* (1987, p. 108).
[34] Ibid. 108–9.

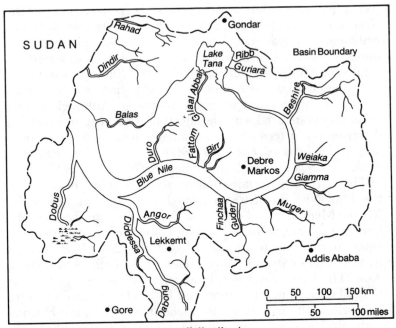

MAP 6. The Blue Nile basin: run-off distribution
Source: Bureau of Reclamation (1964)

believed, and which concrete could make a reality. Here were
the ghosts of Friar Jordanus, Prester John, Jean de Lastic,
Ariosto, James Bruce, and even Sir Samuel Baker emerging
from the mists of the past in the bizarre form of the US bureau
of reclamation, to bestow upon the Ethiopians the plans and
thus the power to control or at least to intervene in Egypt's
historic rights to the Nile waters. If the Egyptians were going
to construct the wasteful and inefficient dam at Aswan to
secure sufficient water in an Egyptian reservoir, they could
hardly be expected to regard with equanimity projects in the
lands of their traditional enemy which would seemingly
deprive them of their national security. This historic paranoia
now came into conflict with the vigorous nationalism of the
riparian States. First the demands of the Sudanese for
additional water, then the Nyerere doctrine, and finally the
Blue Nile basin development plan all loomed as a threat to
Egypt's precious water. And the Ethiopians would not let

them forget. At the United Nations water conference at Mar Del Plata in 1977, Ethiopia reasserted its rights to the waters of the Blue Nile, and in June 1980, at the meeting of the Organization of African Unity (OAU) in Lagos, the Ethiopian representative presumptuously charged Egypt with planning to divert Nile water to Sinai illegally since there was no international agreement as to its disposal. These fears, stoked by misinformed nationalism, have destroyed, and are likely to continue to destroy, any holistic development of the Nile valley for the benefit of all its peoples, not just the Egyptians, the Sudanese, or the Ethiopians.

The recommendations of the US bureau of reclamation are specifically hydrological, and consequently have little to say about the hydropolitics of the Nile valley. Ethiopia has neither the administrative organization nor the capital (borrowed from without or generated from within) to execute the Blue Nile plan. Nevertheless, as a scheme for Nile control it cannot be ignored, and by its very focus on optimum utilization it is congruent with the Nile valley plan and an important contribution to the evolution of the Nile basin. Garstin, MacDonald, and Hurst had all ignored the Blue Nile gorge, for it was one region where the otherwise ubiquitous officials of the Egyptian irrigation department could not carry out measurements. Hurst had always argued that dams in the Blue Nile gorge would be subject to rapid siltation, and consequently they had concentrated on the reservoir at Lake Tana. This project, which appeared possible after the long and tortuous but ultimately successful negotiations among Egypt, Britain, and the Sudan over the Lake Tana dam, were frustrated by Ethiopian suspicions and intransigence, which were a transparent disguise for its own inability to construct conservation and hydroelectric schemes.

Ironically, the Blue Nile plan, if properly managed would not substantially affect the water available to Egypt and the Sudan. Under appropriate working arrangements the amount of water for irrigation throughout the Nile basin could actually be increased; 'even if Ethiopia were simply to pursue its own objective of managing the reservoir to maximize hydropower production, without considering the interest of Egypt and the Sudan, the amount of water available to the downstream riparians would not be substantially affected.'[35] Even if Ethiopia could implement the Blue Nile plan, drawing off 6 billion m³, Egypt and the Sudan would still benefit from the construction of the reservoirs in the Blue Nile, if properly managed, with a maximum loss of only 2.5 billion m³, a trivial amount compared to the total Nile flow and sources of additional water available in the equatorial lakes.

If the projects recommended by the bureau of reclamation were completed, Ethiopia would capture the Nile flood but in return would release 46.9 billion m³—or substantially more than the current mean annual discharge at Roseires—because of a loss of only 3 per cent by evaporation against a loss of over 12 per cent in the Aswan reservoir. This is in essence the Blue Nile plan as it was in the century storage of Hurst and the Nile valley plan of Morrice and Allan—store the water in regions of low evaporation at the Nile sources and thereby gain the additional water to quench the thirst of expanding populations downstream. According to the Blue Nile plan the Sudan, for instance, would receive 2.7 billion m³ more than its present allocation under the 1959 Nile Waters Agreement. Water stored in the four Blue Nile reservoirs and managed in conjunction with a Roseires reservoir freed of debris and heavy siltation could then be released in May to reach Egypt when its water requirement is the highest without sustaining the great loss by evaporation now experienced at Aswan. 'That both the Sudanese and Egyptian allocations could still be higher than their share under the Nile Waters Agreement is simply due to the Aswan reservoir being operated at relatively low levels, thus reducing evaporation losses below the estimates in the treaty.'[36] Egypt, however, would no longer be the beneficiary of additional water in years of high flood, which would then be stored and regulated in the Blue Nile reservoirs, not at Aswan. Moreover, lowering the level of Lake Nasser in order to limit the evaporable loss would concomitantly reduce the hydroelectric power; but in return Egypt would receive additional water for irrigation. Ethiopia could, of course, malevolently withhold water it did not need in a year of low rainfall, to threaten disaster in the

[35] See Guarsio et al. (1987, p. 111).
[36] Ibid. 112.

Nile valley. The Egyptians have historically and deeply feared this threat to their survival, and such an action would be tantamount to an act of war. It was just such a fear, in the jungle of predatory nation States, which motivated the construction of the high dam at Aswan.

While the scientists and engineers of the bureau of reclamation were toiling through and up and down the Blue Nile gorge, nature was capturing the attention of the hydrologists at the equatorial lakes. The most important hydrological event in the Nile basin during the years of African independence after the construction of the Aswan dam was the dramatic but unpredictable rainfall beween 1961 and 1964 on the lake plateau. Since the quantity of rainfall in East Africa has a consistent pattern in this century of an oscillating ten-year cycle, the sudden increase of 20 per cent per year during the early 1960s appears to have been 'a freak produced by two 10-year cycles which happened to have a shift of 5 years', but an anomaly, nevertheless, which evidently has occurred in the past, including its last manifestation in the late nineteenth century.[37] In the later 1960s the rain diminished and the levels of the equatorial lakes retreated slightly, only to rise again in 1980, at the end of another ten-year cycle, almost to the level of 1964. During 1961 and 1964 Lake Victoria alone rose by 2.5 m, producing on its vast surface 170 billion m³ of additional water and doubling the outflow at the Owen Falls dam. Similar rises were recorded in Lake Albert as well as Lakes Tanganyika and Malawi outside the Nile basin. If this phenomenon was the result of the convergence of two cyclical periods of rainfall, it remains speculation as to whether this demonstrable increase will affect the long-term statistical and mathematical probabilities upon which Nile flows are calculated and upon which the Nile waters agreements have been determined.[38]

Around the lakes themselves there was extensive flooding, particularly in the Kavirondo gulf and the port of Kisumu, dislocation of villages and cultivations, and costly repairs and reconstruction works on the disrupted infrastructure. These damages, however, were of less consequence than the disasters

[37] Mörth (1967, p. 6); Piper et al. (1986).
[38] See Kite (1981; 1982).

downstream, particularly in the Sudd. During the years 1961–80 the average annual discharge of the Bahr al-Jabal as it entered the swamps at Mongalla increased from 27 billion m³ (average annual discharge 1905–60) to 50 billion (average annual discharge 1961–80), with an average over seventy-five years of 33 billion. The capacity of the Bahr al-Jabal could simply not contain a discharge of 33 billion, let alone 50 billion, so the flood-waters spilled relentlessly into the Upper Nile, creating massive flooding and increasing the size of the permanent swamp in the Sudd from 2700 km² in 1952 to 16,200 km² in 1980 and more than doubling the flood-plain from 13,100 to 29 800 km².[39] This enormous inundation resulted in the loss of some 120 000 head of livestock and tens of thousands of lives of the Nilotic peoples, to add to the miseries of civil war.

These conditions have only been matched by the stories of the elders about the great flood of 1918, the year which the Nuer call *pi lual*, 'red water', when remembering the tales of great suffering.[40] They were the floods which had haunted Allan and Morrice in 1948 during the negotiations at Entebbe over the equatorial Nile project. In 1961 there was no flood control and, unlike 1918, the waters that came down from the lakes during those three years did not recede to the Bahr al-Jabal and the White Nile but remained at high levels for over two decades.[41] In the Kongor district whole forests perished from the floods, which the Twic Dinka call *awaithar*, leaving behind only the skeletons of dead trees rising from a plain of water. The Zaraf Island virtually disappeared under the waters, the greatest flood since Noah. Old Fanjak town was deserted. The village of Jonglei vanished. Cultivations and pastures were lost. Without food for themselves and their cattle, the people and their livestock died from famine and disease as the waters spread across the Nilotic plain. In East Africa, however, 'none of the countries around the lake [Victoria] found the adjustments they had to make to the rising waters insurmountable'.[42]

---

[39] Sutcliffe and Parks (1987, p. 3).   [40] Howell (1982).
[41] The level of Lake Victoria was reported to have returned in Nov. 1987 to 11.5 m on the Jinja gauge, a level approximately the same as that before the great rains of 1961.   [42] Waterbury (1982, p. 108); Alier (1974).

The increase in the discharge from the lakes produced morphological changes in the Bahr al-Jabal as well as loss of life. In the Aliab valley new spill channels appeared in places where they were hitherto unknown. Sediment transported by the Bahr al-Jabal now carried an estimated half a million m³ of matter a day, drastically altering the bed-level of the river. The hydrological studies conducted by Euroconsult between 1976 and 1978 demonstrated the vulnerability of the channel north of Mongalla to unpredictable fluctuations, making Jonglei as the terminus of the canal hazardous at worst and unreliable at best. The Atem, which was to be a principal feeder for the canal, was heavily silted, and the Bahr al-Jabal between the Atem and Lake Papiu was temporarily blocked by sudd and sediment.[43]

The East African countries did nothing to alleviate the flooding of the southern Sudan, obviously more concerned to ameliorate their own damage, and when their representatives met with the PJTC in October 1961 they studiously ignored the predicament of the rising waters in the Upper Nile. The PJTC generously offered three-quarters of a billion m³ to the East African States for irrigation between 1961 and 1965 to relieve the flood—water which these States could not use and did not need. The immediate decision taken in October was to provide relief for the areas surrounding Lake Victoria by an increase in the outflow through the Owen Falls dam, at the expense of the hapless Nilotes downstream in the southern Sudan.[44] Between 1961 and 1962 the discharge at Owen Falls increased from 20.6 to 38.6 billion m³, and then rose again to 44.8 billion in 1963 to reach the astronomical flow of 50.5 billion in 1964.[45] Allan and Morrice had argued that adequate flood protection for the Sudan was as important as additional water for Egypt. Their successors appear to have forgotten this historic law of the river Nile, as the great floods of 1988 have returned to remind them.

Although the East African Nile waters co-ordinating committee had endorsed the need for a survey of Lake Victoria and its catchment basin as early as 1960, the

[43] Ibrahim (1984b, pp. 23–4).
[44] Ibrahim (1984a, p. 117).
[45] Hydromet (1974, i. 593).

unprecedented rise in the levels of the equatorial lakes made the project all the more imperative. The co-ordinating committee was the idea of Sir Andrew Cohen, governor of Uganda, and the creation of Paul Howell, the former chairman of the Jonglei Investigation Team. Despite approaching independence the colonial governments of Kenya, Uganda, and Tanganyika, as British territories, were bound by the terms of the 1929 Nile Waters Agreement, which gave them no claims to the waters of the equatorial lakes without the prior approval of Egypt. The co-ordinating committee was charged with developing a negotiating position by which to obtain the right of Kenya, Uganda, and Tanganyika to abstract water from the lakes; it was advised by a succession of hydrologists with long experience with the Nile—Brigadier C. G. Hawes, Sir Douglas Harris, and Humphrey Morrice. Independence overwhelmed the status of this committee, its lasting importance being not so much what it accomplished but its role as a model for the co-operation among the East African governments in the hydrometeorological (hydromet) survey first proposed by PJTC in 1960.

In the spirit of unity which accompanied the euphoria of approaching independence, the East African governments, with the guidance of the co-ordinating committee and financial aid from the UN expanded programme of technical assistance (UNEPTA), requested in 1961 a team of three consultants from the World Meteorological Organization (WMO) and the Food and Agricultural Organization (FAO) to make a preliminary survey of the Lake Victoria catchment basin. Their explorations were carried out in January and February 1962, and their report, submitted in 1963, recommended a hydrometeorological survey, not only of Lake Victoria but of Lakes Kyoga and Albert as well. The governments of Kenya, Uganda, and Tanganyika, 'in the spirit of African unity and friendly relations that exist between the East African countries, Sudan, and U.A.R.', the Nyerere doctrine notwithstanding, invited Egypt and the Sudan to participate.[46] In fact, acting on an invitation from the East African Nile waters co-ordinating committee, Egypt had enthusiastically agreed to

[46] Maswanya (1968, p. 21).

join as early as 25 November 1959; the Sudan indicated its willingness the following April.

Indeed, the spirit of unity seemed everywhere promoted, not only by the honeymoon of independence in Africa, but by the establishment of the inter-State committee for the Senegal River basin (Office de Mise en Valeur du Sénégal, OMVS) in July 1963 and of the Niger River basin commission in October. There was also an accord between the riparian countries of Lake Chad, giving birth to the Chad basin commission. Certainly, the agencies and personnel of the UN regarded the hydromet survey as a giant step toward regional co-operation and integrated river basin development. 'The present project is therefore an encouraging example of a rational approach by several governments towards a common problem. . . . Another sign that practical co-operation between African governments is increasing steadily . . .'[47] The hydromet survey was hailed as the very symbol of the OAU; the establishment of a 'strong indigenous scientific and technical base' to lead to 'economic independence and escape the menaces of neo-colonial forces'.[48] Co-operation may have been the spirit of the times; but the translation of the rhetoric of unity into the political agreements to achieve that unity was an illusion. Ethiopia did eventually join the hydromet survey in 1971 and Zaïre in 1977, but only as observers. Observations cost nothing and have led to nothing, despite recent recommendations from the survey for an independent Nile basin agency similar to the regulatory commissions on the Senegal and Niger Rivers. The Ethiopian refusal to discuss a Lake Tana dam agreement, or for that matter any project proposed by Egypt and the Sudan, was more indicative of the realities of future relations than the chimera of co-operation and unity.

Funds for the hydromet study were soon forthcoming from the UNDP special fund, which in turn appointed the World Meteorological Organization (WMO) as the executing agency;

[47] R. M. A. Gardiner, executive secretary of the UN economic commission for Africa, Addis Ababa, *Hydromet* (1968, p. 27).
[48] Inaugural address by H. E. John Babiika, vice-president of the Republic Uganda, *Hydromet* (1968, p. 29); G. Dekker, 'Some Problems Concerning Water Resource Development in Africa', *Hydromet* (1968, pp. 36–9).

the latter submitted a plan of operations in 1966, subsequently agreed upon by all the signatories in May 1967.[49] The technical committee for the hydrometeorological survey of the catchments of Lakes Victoria, Kyoga, and Albert was formed the following year, its headquarters at Entebbe, with the responsibility of organizing and co-ordinating the survey team for five years. The team was to collect and analyse hydrometeorological data in the catchment basins of the lakes to understand more fully the water balance in the upper Nile basin. There were a host of collecting stations (24 hydro-meteorological, 156 rainfall, 67 hydrological, and 14 for measuring lake levels; many others have subsequently been added), aerial and ground surveys, and the training of African staff. The technical committee oversaw the operation from Entebbe, with regional headquarters at Masindi, Kisumu, and Bukoba, at an annual cost of over £2 million.[50]

Once begun, the hydromet survey generated a life of its own, being renewed in 1976 to undertake a follow-up study for three years in an effort to estimate the water balance of the lakes which Hurst had foreshadowed a generation earlier in *The Future Conservation of the Nile*. Collection and analysis continued in January 1976; the intention was to devise a mathematical model for the Nile system as the survey itself expanded to include Lake Albert and the Semliki basin, but also much more. During the meetings of the technical committee in December 1978 the representatives of Egypt and the Sudan from the PJTC 'forwarded a proposal for the establishment of a Nile basin commission to cooperate in the natural planning of conservation, development and allocation of water resources in the basin'.[51] The proposal stopped short of requesting the devolution of political authority from the participating States, but it clearly expanded the scope of the hydromet study both geographically and technically. It did, however, supersede the terms of the 1959 Nile Waters Agreement, by which Egypt and the Sudan regarded the planning and development of the upper reaches of the Nile to

---

[49] The UN allocated $1 837 800, the participating governments $140 600.
[50] Enclosed in J Pascoe, deputy resident representative, UN, to ministry of finance and economics, Khartoum, 15 Feb. 1967, *Hydromet* (1968).
[51] Ibrahim (1984a, p. 119).

be the sole province of the PJTC.[52] Nothing came of this proposal, but the Sudan government continued to press diplomatically, with Egyptian support, for a Nile basin commission, an agency which the other riparians well knew Egypt and the Sudan would dominate by virtue of their historic and technical experience and their political and military power.

Egypt and the Sudan were not, however, completely unsuccessful in their advocacy of a Nile basin commission. By the 1980s they had won over the civil servants of the WMO as the hydromet survey had graduated from being an agency for the collection and analysis of data to an institution charged with planning the 'conservation and development of the water resources of the Upper Nile Basin. Such planning should include investigations of individual water resource policy . . .'. The WMO was now no longer concerned to disguise the intentions of the founders of the hydromet survey behind rhetoric. Rather than confine itself to measuring, digesting, and recommending, the survey should now devise an 'organization for water resource studies for the entire River Nile Basin. Only in this way will it be possible to ensure that future developments will be optimum for the basin as a whole.'[53] These are all tasks which are normally associated with regulatory bodies. Egypt and the Sudan have subsequently continued to argue for a more comprehensive arrangement than the present hydromet survey, an organization that would plan and implement projects on the premiss that such projects would be undertaken as part of the overall development of the Nile basin. That old imperialist, Sir William Garstin, would have approved.

The Egyptian and Sudanese initiatives were not regarded without suspicion by Ethiopia and the East African States. Two years after the signing of the hydromet survey agreements, Tanzania, Ruanda, Burundi, and Uganda sought to establish their own organization on 9 July 1969 to develop the Kagera basin. With the support of the UNDP, the hydromet survey was extended to the Kagera basin in December 1971, and a consortium of Norconsult of Norway and Electrowatt of

[52] A. I. el Moghraby, 'The Jonglei Canal', in Beshir (1948, ii. 39).
[53] Hydromet (1981), quoted in Waterbury (1982, p. 102).

Switzerland was commissioned to undertake a detailed study of the Kagera basin reminiscent of the bureau of reclamation investigations in the Blue Nile basin.[54] In May 1977, the consortium published a thirteen-volume report, the final volume of which summarized a thorough development plan for the Kagera basin which resulted in the 'Rusumu agreement' of 24 August, by which Tanzania, Burundi, and Ruanda created the organization for the management and development of the Kagera River basin, which came into being on 5 February 1978. Uganda joined in May 1981 upon the return to power of Milton Obote. The Kagera basin organization designated the Rusumu Falls as a proposed site for hydroelectric power so badly needed by the member States (see Map 7), but political instability, ideology, and the failure of the regional governments to meet their financial pledges to the organization appear to have postponed this project far into the future.[55]

Meanwhile the Egyptians and the Sudanese continued to press for a Nile basin commission. In March 1981, at a meeting of the irrigation ministers of the basin States in Khartoum, President Numayri personally argued, unsuccessfully, for an accord for the development of the Nile basin as a whole. Three months later the heads of State of Uganda, Zaïre, and the Sudan issued the Badolite declaration on 7 June 1981, calling for an agency to co-ordinate and develop the Nile basin. Their appeal was a far cry from the days of British imperial control, despite the fact that a team from the PJTC was assiduously touring the capitals of the riparian States attempting to arrange at least a meeting, either in Khartoum or Cairo, in September to consider basin-wide planning. The Ethiopians listened with polite interest, but no co-operation was forthcoming.[56] Egypt had hoped to place before this meeting a proposal for a Nile basin organization which would be, not simply a regulatory body, but a development agency with far broader interests

[54] Enclosed in K. Parthasarathy to O. S. Gage, 'Hydrometeorological Survey of the Catchments of Lakes Victoria, Kyoga and Albert, Amendment No. 1', WMO, 6 Dec. 1971.

[55] G. P. Gasarasi, 'A Cooperative Approach to Development (The Organization for the Management and Development of the Kagera River Basin)', in Beshir (1948, ii. 100–32).

[56] Waterbury (1987).

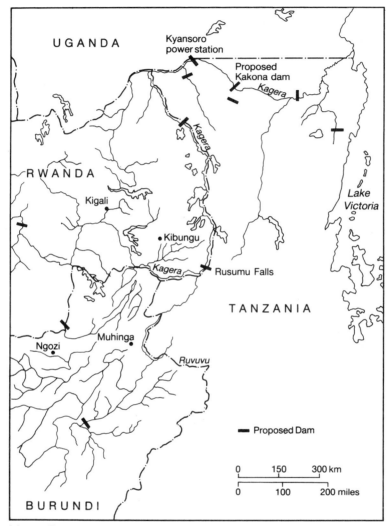

MAP 7. Proposed plans of development in the Kagera basin
Source: Waterbury (1982)

than Nile control. The Ethiopians again failed to respond, and
without them any super-regulatory commission would remain
a chimera. The Egyptians have little to offer the upper
riparian States; in turn they remain suspicious of Egyptian

and Sudanese experience and organization, symbolized by the highly successful work of the PJTC.

While failing to persuade their neighbours to come to the negotiating table, the PJTC had not been idle. Having drafted the plans for the Jonglei Canal, known as Jonglei Phase I, its engineers began to examine more closely projects which had been discussed since Garstin's time, and officially included in the Egyptian master water plan (EMWP) of 1981 to conserve additional water losses in the upper Nile basin besides those in the Sudd.[57] All of these plans are as far into the future as those of the Blue Nile and the Kagera basin, and consequently remain shrouded in an aura of economic and political unreality. Nevertheless, they are taken seriously by the PJTC, relentlessly seeking ways to squeeze additional water from the Nile basin despite the fact that civil strife and political violence in the region have prevented the detailed studies required for their technical execution, let alone the financial, international, social, and environmental implications of any proposed projects. Taken together there are four projects collectively referred to by the PJTC as Jonglei Phase II, or more accurately the Nile master water plan—dams at Lakes Victoria, Kyoga, and Albert, the expansion of the Jonglei Canal, the Machar Marshes scheme, and the Bahr al-Ghazal dams and diversion canals. The Sudd may be the greatest waster of water in the upper Nile basin, evaporating a mean annual loss from 1905 to 1980 of 16.9 billion m^3 but the implementation of Jonglei Phase II could yield as much as an additional 14–20 billion, albeit at great but undetermined cost.[58]

The second phase of Jonglei depended upon additional storage in the equatorial lakes. Every student of the Nile basin water development since Garstin has advocated using the lakes as reservoirs, and although the completion of the Aswan high dam in 1971 momentarily resolved the question of over-year storage and put an end to the historic debate about the need for the Lake Albert dam to regulate the Timely and

[57] Ministry of Irrigation (1981).
[58] The Nile master water plan estimated in 1981 that Jonglei phase II would require a capital cost of £E512 million, but this amount bears no reality to economic and political conditions in 1988. Ministry of Irrigation (1981, main report, p. 74).

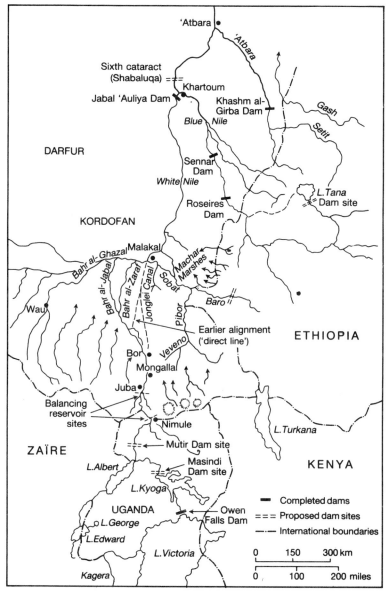

MAP 8. Development projects south of the 'Atbara confluence in the upper Nile basin
Source: Howell et al. (1988)

Untimely flow through the Sudd, the insatiable demand for new water, not merely its regulation, revived interest in making use of the lakes. The great rains of the 1960s made the prospect of storing additional water in the lake all the more appealing. The hydromet survey conveniently provided the PJTC with the data for the proper storage required to produce a constant supply downstream when needed, a condition necessary for the design and construction of dams at the outfalls of the lakes. Lake Victoria would be maintained at a level 2.5 m above the pre-1960 mark of 11.5 m on the Jinja gauge, or at a level comparable to the high-water mark of 1964.[59] The heightening of the Owen Falls dam would be undertaken if the lake should return to its level before 1961— which until recently appeared unlikely. A second dam would be built at Lake Kyoga as a regulator to keep its level constant, with the possibility of using it for additional storage in high-water years. Finally, the much-discussed dam at Lake Albert would be built at Nimule, not Mutir, to create a reservoir with a capacity of some 170 billion m³.[60] These proposals are vintage Hurst with refinements from the Nile valley plan. Egypt may change, but the Nile waters are eternal.

The purpose of constructing storage facilities in the equatorial lakes was not only to provide new water but to make maximum use of it by controlling the discharge at Lake Albert at a constant flow, equalized at 75 Mm³/d, measured at Mongalla. The flow of the Bahr al-Jabal at Mongalla, however, has risen as high as 120 Mm³/d which would result in a proportionate increase in the loss of water in the swamps without the regulators in the lakes to even out the flow by storing the excess—the flood control of Allan and Morrice. The equatorial reservoirs, however, would be of no value if there were no means of conveying this water through the swamps by a canal very different from the Jonglei Canal of

[59] This would be the equivalent of the 3.5 m increase in the level of Lake Victoria proposed by the Egyptian ministry of public works during the negotiations concerning the Equatorial Nile Project, specifically those associated with the Owen Falls dam.

[60] See JEO (1975, pp. 61–2). The maximum rise in the level of Lake Albert would be 35 m on the Butiaba gauge, the same level as that proposed by Dr M. Amin during the Equatorial Nile Project negotiations.

today, with its capacity of only 25 Mm³. The canal envisaged in Jonglei Phase II would require a minimum of 43 million and a maximum of 55 million, equal to the large canal proposed by Hurst for the Equatorial Nile Project. The amount of additional water from storage in the lake and conveyed by an enlarged canal would produce 7.6 billion m³ at Aswan, or an increase of 9 per cent in the total mean annual Nile flow.

Jonglei Phase II conceived of even more extensive conservation measures than just the well-worn plan to top up the equatorial lakes and build a bigger Jonglei Canal. North and east of the Sudd, in the lowlands beneath the Ethiopian escarpment, lie some 6500 km² of swamp, quite separate from the Bahr al-Jabal–White Nile system, known as the Machar Marshes.[61] This forbidding swampland is more isolated and less known than the famous Sudd. No major rivers pass through the labyrinth of lagoons and channels, while the marshes themselves provide little livelihood and remain an obstacle to the passage of man and beast. The authority of the government at Khartoum has hardly ever been exercised in this remote corner of the Sudan, and for the first fifty years of the Condominium the Machar Marshes remained unknown and unexplored. In 1945 the first survey was made by the American air force, but it was not until 1949–50 that a methodical attempt was made to penetrate the marshes by members of the Jonglei Investigation Team, as an adjunct study to their researches concerning the Equatorial Nile Project. The concern of the team was the well-known but unconfirmed fact that the marshes acted as a catchment basin for the Baro River spilling over its banks below Gambila during the flood, the run-off from the Ethiopian torrents from the highlands, and the rainfall of some 800 mm a year. Loss of water by evaporation has never been rigorously measured and would vary with the size of the marsh in any given year, but the absence of any drainage would make these conditions the principal cause of this wastage.

The most obvious loss to the Nile is the large quantity of

---

[61] During heavy flooding in the Machar Marshes from above-average rainfall in Ethiopia in 1946, water from the marshes did spill over into the White Nile to the west.

water which escapes into the Machar Marshes as spillage
from the Baro in flood. Hurst estimated the amount of water
entering the swamp from the Baro as the equivalent of
5 billion m³, but in fact he knew little about the marshes,
devoting only three pages to their hydrology in *The Future
Conservation of the Nile*.[62] Ignorance was compounded by
confusion. In 1946 Hurst had advocated a dam at Gambila
with a reservoir of 4 billion m³ capacity, which would
conserve 3.8 billion of lost spillage.[63] In 1950 he revised
downward the volume of the reservoir at Gambila, for lack of
a proper dam site, a lack which could not be compensated for
by embanking the lower Baro, at high cost given the frequency
of low flooding. 'Unless annual storage can be supplemented
by considerable over-year storage in the Great Lakes, it is not
worth doing as far as Egypt is concerned.'[64] By 1958 Allan and
Morrice in the Nile valley plan had located an ideal site above
Gambila for a dam and reservoir, but were much more
conservative as to the net benefit, estimating a savings of 1.7
billion.[65] The EMWP expected a saving of 4.4 billion.[66] (See
Map 9.)

By storing water in the Gambila dam, wherever it might be
situated, the waters of the Baro could be confined to its
natural channel. An alternative proposal was considered in
1950 but was rejected by Hurst. This bizarre scheme
contemplated embanking the Baro to a point downstream
from Jokau, whence a diversion canal some 400 km long
would be constructed in a north-westerly direction to the
White Nile at Melut. Although longer and much more
expensive than Jonglei, the canal would be entirely within the
territory of the Sudan, rather than in Ethiopia above Gambila,
with all the history of contentious relations over Nile water
development between those two poverty-stricken countries.
Despite the cost and the questionable hydrological benefits,
the PJTC has seriously considered this peculiar project as an
integral part of Jonglei Phase II.

Having impounded the equatorial lakes, traversed the
Sudd, and tamed the Baro, there were only the waters of the

[62] Hurst *et al.* (1931–66, viii. 27).
[63] Ibid. vii. 48.   [64] Ibid. viii. 29.
[65] Morrice and Allan (1958, i. 42). [66] Quoted in Waterbury (1982, p. 71).

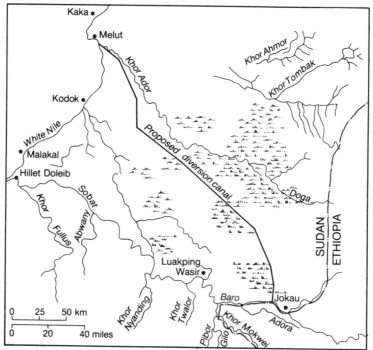

MAP 9. The Machar Marshes: proposed drainage scheme
Source: Waterbury (1982)

Nilotic plain and the ironstone plateau to be captured—the largest basin in the whole of the Nile watershed, with countless rivers flowing through the Sudan from Zaïre and the Central African Republic. Although there are many rivers in the basin of the Bahr al-Ghazal, they disappear into the great swamps west of the Bahr al-Jabal and do not emerge. The officials of the Egyptian irrigation department have measured these tributaries of the Bahr al-Ghazal River for many years, but the region has been the least promising source of new water in the Upper Nile basin. Garstin dismissed the Bahr al-Ghazal as worthless in contributing to Egypt's water needs. 'Under no circumstances can the Bahr al-Ghazal play an important part in the annual Nile flood.'[67] This judgement was premature.

[67] Garstin (1904, p. 113).

The tributaries of the Bahr al-Ghazal generate an estimated aggregate discharge of 13–20 billion m³ a year, all of which is lost in the swamps before a sluggish trickle makes its way to Lake No and ultimately to the White Nile. The solution proposed by the PJTC was to construct a series of small dams and barrages on the tributaries at the edge of the ironstone plateau, and, second, to excavate a canal to bypass the absorbent swamps into which the tributaries disappear (see Map 10). Thus another Jonglei Canal would be built, only longer, 425 km, from the Jur River to the Lol, thence across the Bahr al-'Arab eastward to Lake No. This canal would divert some 7 billion m³ from the major tributaries of the Bahr al-Ghazal; but, as Garstin and Willcocks had long ago observed, Lake No acts as a reservoir, and the blocking effect of the stronger flow of the Bahr al-Jabal could very easily push its water back into the swamps of the Bahr al-Ghazal, where it would be lost as if the tributaries were to follow their natural course. Ever resourceful, the engineers have devised means to correct this anomaly by the construction of a second canal, 225 km in length, which would convey the Bahr al-Ghazal water from Lake No to Melut, where presumably it would join the waters of the Baro flowing down the Machar canal from the south-east.[68]

There is imagination and grandeur in all of these plans and dams but an equal unreality. The land in which all of these conservancy projects are to be built has been racked by civil war for many years. In all the precise calculations by the hydrologists of the PJTC there is little consideration of, and less consultation with, the people who will be most affected by the concrete and construction. Economically, the proposals can only be completed at great cost, supported by dubious financial equations. Unfortunately, these massive projects, on a scale to dwarf those of the Pharaohs, are to be built in one of the most remote regions of the world, devoid of functioning infrastructure and criss-crossed by an incalculable number of natural obstacles. Perhaps these hurdles could be overcome by an international basin agency, mobilizing the combined resources of the riparian States and with the authority to co-

---

[68] *The Nile Master Water Plan*, quoted in Waterbury (1982, pp. 75–7).

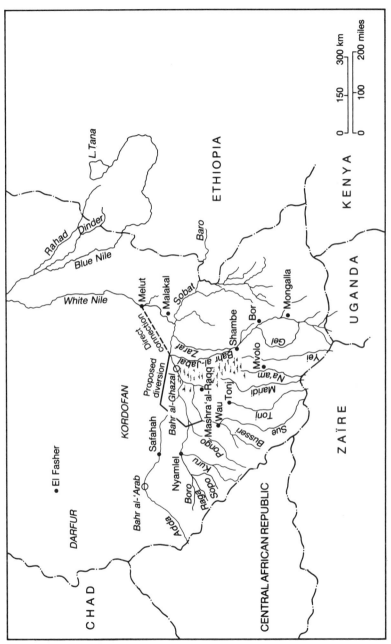

MAP 10. Proposed Bahr al-Ghazal drainage scheme
Source: Waterbury (1982)

ordinate and implement the hydrological works in a manner commensurate with social programmes and sensitive to local concerns, but the British imperial shield has been replaced by narrow nationalism, personal hubris, and ignorance. These are not the building blocks for international co-operation nor the instruments to overcome historic, cultural, and religious animosity. Perhaps the weight of history lies too heavy in the silt of the Nile valley, but man will always need water; and in the end this may drive him to the river to drink with his enemies and return to the tale of the Jonglei Canal.

8
The Revival of Jonglei

Even if there were adequate quantitative data . . . no attempt has been made to weigh in the balance the benefits of conveying much needed water for irrigation downstream against the much less clearly evident advantages and disadvantages of the project to the people of the area through which the canal passes.

Dr P. P. Howell, August 1987

ON the sparkling, sunlit morning of 18 August 1955, No. 2 Company of the Equatorial corps was drawn up on the parade ground at Torit, in preparation for boarding trucks for Juba and proceeding by steamer to Khartoum. The troops were apprehensive, for rumours had been circulating that the transfer to Khartoum was a plot to enslave or murder them. They were all from the southern Sudan, for the most part illiterate veterans who had never served beyond the frontiers of the south and who had settled comfortably at the headquarters of the corps in Torit, with families and farms surrounding the garrison town.

When the command was given to enter the vehicles No. 1 platoon refused to move; and suddenly the whole company rushed the ammunition stores, armed themselves, and then rampaged through the town, killing northern Sudanese and looting shops. News of the mutiny spread like the wind throughout the south, and in the villages and towns of Equatoria northerners were hunted and killed. The official report states that 261 northern Sudanese lost their lives; there were probably more. Although the mutineers had devised a plan to seize Juba and its strategic airport, they failed to co-ordinate their activities; and the rebellion died, the mutineers disappearing into the bush, as élite troops of the camel corps disembarked at Juba airport to re-establish the control of the central government throughout the southern Sudan.

Compared with the scale of violence today, the mid-century southern Sudan disturbances were a minor affair; but no one lounging in the cool of the evening on the verandah of the Grand Hotel in Khartoum or sipping coffee in the *suq* of Omdurman would have predicted that this apparent storm in a teacup would boil ever more vigorously for seventeen years.

Although the transition from British to Sudanese administration in the southern Sudan had been marred by political ineptitude, administrative blunders, and extraordinary insensitivity shown in the virtual exclusion of southerners from positions vacated by the departing British officials, the fundamental cause of the disturbances and subsequent civil war belongs to history. Long accustomed to the paternalistic justice of British administrators, the southern Sudanese had difficulty adjusting to the rough-and-tumble politics of the emerging Sudan. The northerner was still an object of fear and hostility, and although his predatory inclinations of the nineteenth century had been subdued by British rule in the twentieth, the earlier policies of the Sudan government to restrict intercourse between the two Sudans prevented neither the north nor the south from understanding the changes undergone during British governance. The paucity of education and the lack of economic development in the southern Sudan compared with the north during the Condominium only enhanced the suspicion, real or imaginary, that the south would be exploited by northern politicians and profiteers. In fact the rudimentary political consciousness, hastily fostered by British officials in the south after 1947, was regional rather than national, while the presumptuous assumptions of northerners newly arrived in the south did little to fuse together these two disparate regions of the Sudan, instead convincing many southerners that their regional interests were of greater value than the larger association with the Sudan as a whole.

The rebellion stunned the northern Sudanese impatient for independence, but the hitherto more flexible twenty-two southern members of parliament became more unwilling to agree to a declaration of independence which would perpetuate northern control. In order to neutralize these susceptibilities, northern politicians agreed to 'consider' a federal solution for the Sudan, and on the strength of this promise the southern representatives agreed to the declaration of independence for the Sudan on 1 January 1956. Moreover, despite the trials, executions, and deportations in Equatoria, the central government made considerable efforts to regain the confidence of the southern Sudanese, which produced the illusion that they were resigned to the new order of independence in union with the north.

During the two years of parliamentary government from 1956 to 1958, ministers in Khartoum were completely preoccupied with national economic and political problems, characterized by the acrimonious and frustrating negotiations over the Nile waters. The coalition government of the two powerful Islamic sects, the Ansar and the Khatmiyya, was at best the result of political opportunism, personal interest, and sectarian loyalty, all held together by parliamentary manipulation, and ill-adapted to confront the experience and determination of the Egyptians in the negotiations over the Nile waters. Sayyid Mirghani Hamza, tenaciously supported by his civil servants and advisers, Zoghayroun El Zein and Humphrey Morrice, and by the Nile valley plan, would not capitulate to the wish of Dr Muhamad El Amin to inflict upon the Sudan a Nile waters agreement as disadvantageous as that of 1929. The negotiating position of Sayyid Hamza in Cairo, however, was hopelessly compromised by the failure of the northern Sudanese politicians to govern at Khartoum, let alone Juba. His fragile position at the negotiating tables in Cairo became more tenuous when the southern representatives in parliament walked out in protest over the discussions of an Islamic constitution for the Sudan.

On 17 November 1958 Major General Ibrahim Abboud, a gentle pragmatist, took over the Sudan government from the impotent politicians. The change of government did not have any immediate impact in the Upper Nile, for like the parliamentary regime, the new military government of General Abboud was confronted not only by the economic policies of the previous regime but by dissident groups within the army itself. Within a year General Abboud resolved both problems, while clearing the major obstacle to amicable relations with Egypt—an agreement over the Nile waters. In the mean time the economic position of the Sudan had deteriorated, largely because of unrealistic policies regarding the sale of cotton, the principal source of revenue. The Abboud government promptly abandoned these policies, and within six months the ready sale of cotton had given the Sudan's treasury a surplus revenue and dramatically rebuilt the country's foreign reserves. By November 1959 the internecine struggles within the army had failed, and Abboud was now in a position to conclude the most lasting achievement of his regime, the Nile waters agreement.

The Nile waters agreement swept away the obstacles to the construction of the Aswan high dam and the Roseires reservoir, divided the waters, and established the permanent joint technical commission (PJTC), but failed to provide the peace in the southern Sudan without which the engineers might dream but not dig. By 1960 the military regime was unchallengeable, the threat of counter-revolution had disappeared, and the Sudan would have appeared a model of authoritarian, progressive despotism if not for the problem of the southern Sudan. After the dissolution of parliament, the military government sought to quell southern dissent by the bonds of Sudanese nationalism, expressed in Arabic language, Arab culture, and the Arab past fused with the traditions of Sudanese history and the deep emotions of Sudanese Islam. These are strong and dynamic themes in the northern Sudan. They have less relevance among the southern Sudanese, who had frustrated the ambitions of the Mahdi and the efforts of the Khalifa 'Abd Allahi at the end of the nineteenth century to advance Islam up the Nile and in the twentieth century, supported by British imperial policy, formed an African bastion against Islam. Partly in fear of another outburst of discontent, and partly constrained by the moderation imposed upon them by a parliamentary system, the politicians failed to press Arabicization and Islamization among the Africans of the south, who spoke vernacular languages or English and practised their traditional religions or Christianity. The army officers of the military government were under no such restraints. Once the military regime had achieved stability in the north, they were free to obliterate, in the name of unity, the cultural differences between the northern and the southern Sudanese. Arabicization and Islamization were increasingly employed by devoted army officers, who saw no contradiction in binding together the manifold diversities of the Sudan with the cords of Sudanese nationalism. In the south, through which the waters flow, these policies met with violent reaction, which prevented any hydrological development of the upper Nile and led ultimately to the fall of the regime of Ibrahim Abboud.

The southern Sudanese reaction to these political and religious pressures, now combined with the response to economic and educational neglect, was sullen resentment, flight, and finally violence. After the 1955 disturbances, incidents precipitated by the insurgents diminished, and the refugees declined to a trickle until 1960, when the Arab and Islamic policies of the government suddenly produced a flood of fleeing southerners, the politicization of the fragile southern élite, and the establishment in September 1963 of an embryonic guerilla force known as the Anya-Nya, composed mostly of the former soldiers of the Equatorial corps. Their random attacks on isolated police and army posts soon escalated into civil war, affecting much of the southern Sudan. The Sudan army failed to suppress the Anya-Nya, which grew steadily in strength, the magnitude of this failure becoming increasingly apparent to the northern Sudanese themselves, increasingly disillusioned with the regime of General Abboud. By 1962 members of the professions, intelligentsia, trade unions, and the civil service, as well as the powerful religious brotherhoods, had become discontented, and the focus of their discontent became the civil war in the south, over which the generals could not prevail. On 29 October 1964 General Abboud capitulated, and handed over the government as it had been given to him to a transitional civilian government. The new government immediately sought to resolve the 'southern problem', as it was now called, without which there could be no hydrological development of the upper Nile.

The transitional government set out with the genuine intention of ending the conflict in the southern Sudan; but the inexperience and division among the intelligentsia in both the north and the south frustrated negotiations between their representatives at the round table conference which opened on 16 March 1965, only to adjourn thirteen days later without an agreement. Nevertheless, the transitional government pressed ahead with its plans to hold elections despite the continuing conflict in the south—elections which were disputed because of the war, but which returned a government under the leadership of Muhammad Mahjub. He revived the generals' policies of Arabicization and Islamization and sought to crush the rebellion. In June and July the army struck at the southern Sudanese educated élite. The reaction was predictable, and destructive to any hope for peace in the upper Nile basin. The southern intelligentsia fled to Uganda and Zaïre, where they mobilized themselves into political organizations which, although impotent, survived the vicissitudes of war and exile to become acute and active political groups within the Sudan, composed of southerners who had acquired education and sophistication from without. A more immediate threat to the Sudan government in the latter half of the 1960s was the growing strength of the Anya-Nya as it gathered arms from the Sudan army's defeats and deserters, from the Simbas of Zaïre, and from Israel, which had captured arms in abundance in 1967 after her victories in the Middle East war.

Within the Anya-Nya Colonel Joseph Lagu Yacobo, a Madi from Equatoria, former captain in the Sudan army, and a conservative Catholic, managed, by controlling the supply of arms, to emerge as the leading personality, and to organize the disparate units of the guerilla forces into the Anya-Nya National Organization, as a more co-ordinating fighting force under his command. At the same time the Sudan came under military rule for the second time since independence, when a cabal of fourteen officers, under the leadership of Ja'far al-Numayri, staged a bloodless *coup d'état* on 25 May 1969. The officers had long been frustrated by a situation in the Sudan which had left the country dominated by sterile sectarian political parties, with no constitution, a stagnant economy, and the fetid problem of the southern Sudan. Numayri himself was widely respected for his integrity and, despite his radical nationalism, possessed a rustic pragmatism and a willingness to deal with the realities of the southern problem without becoming a captive of revolutionary rhetoric or Arab ideology.

On 9 June 1969 he announced a four-point programme for the south, including an amnesty, social, economic, and cultural assistance, the appointment of a minister of southern affairs, and the training and placement of southerners in responsible administrative positions. He enunciated his belief in the unity of the Sudan, but offered regional self-government for the south.[1]

The southerners greeted Numayri's announcement with caution; but before either side could act upon this gesture for peace, Numayri found his government challenged by the Muslim Brothers on the right, the Communists on the left, and the Ansar lurking in the rear. There were numerous plots to overthrow his regime, culminating in an open clash with the Ansar in March 1970 in which the Imam al-Hadi al-Mahdi was killed; and an even more serious attempt to overthrow the government was staged in July 1971, when dis-affected army officers, supported by the Sudan Communist party, seized power for three days before Numayri's followers in the army were able to recapture control and restore his authority.

The July insurrection profoundly shocked Numayri. Not only did he systematically set out to eliminate the Communist leadership and all visible signs of the party, but he applied renewed interest and determination to resolving the southern problem in the face of a vigorous offensive by the Anya-Nya, whose military and political forces had now been merged by Colonel Lagu into the Southern Sudan Liberation Movement. Southerners were given positions in the army, police, and civil service, while others were enlisted into training schemes. Funds were designated for development projects in the south, and the proposed Federation of Arab Republics with Egypt and Libya, which the southerners had bitterly opposed, was never consummated. These overtures to southern susceptibilities did not go unnoticed. Lagu was anxious for negotiations to end a war which both sides knew neither could win. The erratic Idi Amin in Uganda had begun to restrict the supply of Israeli arms, and Lagu hesitantly suggested negotiations in 1970, repeating his request in June and August 1971. With the

[1] 'Policy Statement on the Southern Question by President Nimeiri, 9 June 1969', in Beshir (1975, pp. 155–7).

assistance of the World Council of Churches, and All Africa Council of Churches, and the emperor of Ethiopia, Haile Selassie, representatives of the Sudan government and the Southern Sudan Liberation Movement met in Addis Ababa on 15 February 1972. The negotiations proceeded on the basis of preliminary discussions held the previous November and innumerable private talks in London, Khartoum, and Addis Ababa. A draft treaty was signed on 27 February 1972, which Numayri promptly declared as a law for the Sudan on 3 March. The Addis Ababa Agreement was ratified on 28 March by Joseph Lagu for the Southern Sudan Liberation Movement and Mansour Khalid, the foreign minister of the Sudan government. Peace had come to the land beyond the rivers.[2]

The Addis Ababa Agreement provided for a considerable degree of autonomy for the southern Sudan, vested in an elected legislature, the people's regional assembly, with powers to maintain public order, to administer the region, and to promote economic, cultural, and social development. A high executive council, with a president appointed by the president of the republic on the recommendation of the people's regional assembly, was charged with the administration of the region and was responsible to the president of the republic and the people's regional assembly. Regional finances were derived from taxation, revenue from commercial and agricultural projects, the national treasury, and a special development budget. The Sudan government retained control over defence, foreign affairs, customs, and overall economic planning— which meant, of course, the hydrological projects in the region.

The agreement itself received international acclaim as an act of statesmanship, prudence, and political realism; President Numayri basked in the universal approval of Arab, African, and Western governments. The implementation of the agreement, however, was not an easy undertaking in a war-torn, isolated land with little infrastructure and services. Roads were

---

[2] The events leading up to the Addis Ababa Agreement are well-known. See Beshir (1975), including 'Draft Organic Law to Organize Regional Self-Government in the Southern Provinces of the Democratic Republic of the Sudan' (the Addis Ababa Agreement on the Problem of the Southern Sudan) (app. B, pp. 158–77).

heavily eroded or mined, telecommunications virtually non-existent, bank facilities primitive, and commerce in the hands of northern merchants, the *jallaba*, who were more concerned with quick profits than with investment. The interim government appointed by Numayri and led by Abel Alier had to grapple with these seemingly insurmountable problems, with only one vintage Humber automobile for official use. That the interim government succeeded is an extraordinary achievement of the Sudan government, of the numerous international relief agencies which rushed to its help, and, of course, the southern Sudanese themselves and their fragile, overworked leadership. Over a million refugees were repatriated to their homes. Over 10 000 members of the Anya-Nya were integrated into the national army, the police, and prison services. A thousand southerners were given senior posts in the civil service.

The first people's regional assembly was elected in November 1973 and met in Juba in February 1974. The regional high executive council under President Abel Alier contained a core of regional ministers who had been members of the interim government, appointed to implement the Addis Ababa Agreement until the elections could take place.[3] Unfortunately, President Numayri appointed Abel Alier before the regional assembly had the opportunity, according to the terms of the Addis Ababa Agreement, to make its recommendations. This was a grave error. Whatever Numayri's intentions to reward Abel Alier for his important role in the Addis Ababa negotiations and his subsequent efforts as interim president to guide the rehabilitation of the south, Abel Alier's appointment as president of the high executive council without the recommendation of the assembly (which would undoubtedly have supported him in any case) established a dangerous precedent for presidential intervention which was ultimately to lead to the destabilization of the political process in the southern region.

As early as 1970 President Numayri announced a five-year plan for economic development for the southern Sudan as part of his overtures to the southerners, including a jute factory at Tonj and programmes for wells, roads, communications,

---

[3] Those ministers retained in the elections were Hilary Paul Logali, Toby Madut, Joseph Oduho, Gama Hasan, Michael Tawili, and Enoch Mading de Garang.

health, and forestry. The escalation of the war by Colonel Lagu prevented the implementation of any of these projects, while those that had started soon stagnated. The regional government, therefore, gave its highest priority to economic development once the immediate problems of refugees and the integration of the Anya-Nya and civil services were accomplished. Old projects were to be rescued and new ones designed to foster economic growth—sugar production at Melut and Mongalla, an electric power plant and canning factory at Juba, and an agricultural and industrial complex at Mongalla. In the midst of all this activity President Numayri signed an agreement on 12 February 1974 to bring the Sudan into 'integration, political and economic, with Egypt'. The way was now clear to revive the Jonglei Canal.

Although Numayri's dramatic realignment with Egypt appears to have been motivated more by political considerations in Khartoum and the prospect of financial assistance from Saudi Arabia and Kuwait than by any desire for the unity of the Nile valley, it was suspected by the southerners as a retreat from the spirit of Addis Ababa, and appeared to many as the first step in a more sinister design to turn the direction of the Sudan away from Africa. This perception was reinforced by the subsequent negotiation of a £S200 million revolving credit from Saudi Arabia for financing the Sudan development corporation, created to implement extensive agricultural projects in the northern Sudan at a time when only £S400 000, out of an allocated 1973/4 development budget for the south of £S7 million, had actually been made available to the high executive council. In the meantime the regional development commission, born from the Addis Ababa Agreement to promote economic development schemes throughout the southern Sudan, languished in Juba without funds.[4] Four months later the Egyptian and Sudanese ministers for irrigation signed an agreement for the joint construction of the Jonglei Canal.

The ink was hardly dry on the Addis Ababa accords when the PJTC came forward in 1974 with a complete proposal for a new and revised Jonglei Canal. During the seventeen years

---

[4] Prunier (1986, pp. 26–7).

of civil war in the southern Sudan, any hope of construction had, of course, been futile, but Jonglei had certainly not been forgotten in Cairo and Khartoum. Three months after Numayri had announced his programme to end the southern conflict, a subcommittee of the PJTC was established in 1969 to devise a project to reduce the losses in the Sudd, and submitted its draft report to the respective ministries of irrigation in December 1971. During the years of civil war in the southern Sudan three significant events made the PJTC rethink Hurst's great canal. The first two of these were the rains of the 1960s and the construction of the Aswan high dam. Both Egypt and the Sudan needed the new water which had fallen on the equatorial lakes, and Egypt now had the necessary capacity behind the high dam at Aswan to eliminate the problem of Timely and Untimely water while providing long-term storage.

The third factor was the technological innovation in canal construction provided by the Bucketwheel. One of the principal reasons why the Lake Albert dam had achieved primacy in British planning for the hydrological development of the upper Nile was the fact that the Jonglei Canal, 280 km long at that time, would require twenty years to excavate with dredgers. Drag-lines would shorten the time required to construct the canal, but even so Jonglei was still regarded as a long-term and consequently expensive project.[5] The introduction of the Bucketwheel changed all these assumptions. It had already proved its capabilities for rapid excavation in the construction of the Chasma–Jhelum link canal between the Indus and Jhelum Rivers in Pakistan.

The Jonglei Canal proposed by the PJTC was an entirely new canal, particularly by comparison with the canal conceived by Hurst. The new Jonglei would not transport a massive flow from the equatorial lakes, diverting only 25 Mm^3/d—a rate of abstraction that would not dramatically change the regime of the Sudd.[6] The project presented by the

[5] The cost of excavation by drag-lines was estimated at £S3/m^3 as against £S.40/m^3 for the Bucketwheel. Interview 18 May 1982, Yahia Abdel Magid.

[6] See JEO (1975, p. 56); PJTC (1981b, p. 2). The original design was to divert 20 Mm^3/d through the canal, which would reduce the flow of the Bahr al-Jabal and the Bahr al-Zaraf by only 5% but effect a reduction in the permanent and seasonal swamps by 29%, from an average total swamp, 1905–80, of 16 900 km^2 to 11 900 km^2,

PJTC was strictly hydrological, a design for a canal excavated in a straight line of 280 km from the Sobat to the village of Jonglei, and capable of delivering at Malakal 4.7 billion m³ annually which, after losses in transmission, would increase the yield as measured at Aswan by 3.8 billion. Since the canal would initially begin at Jonglei, it would there receive the waters of the Atem River, a powerful flow parallel to the Bahr al-Jabal, which would in the context of the proposal be dredged and embanked to improve drainage and navigation and to reduce overspillage, evaporation, and flood damage in the adjacent areas.[7]

The canal itself would vary in width from 28 to 50 m, with wider sections for steamers to pass and a depth of 4–7 m, with a designed flow of 3.5 km/hr to prevent weed growth, and with special equipment at either end to curtail the infestation of the omnipresent water hyacinth. A raised all-season road would be built parallel to the canal, completing the dream of British imperialists long past of a Cape-to-Cairo route, and reducing the distance by water from Malakal to Juba by 300 km. Ferry crossings and a limited number of bridges would be determined at an advanced stage of construction. In accordance with the 1959 Nile Waters Agreement, Egypt and the Sudan would share the cost equally as well as the water benefits of the extra yield. There was only scant reference to the impact of the canal on the Nilotic inhabitants, a serious and insensitive omission, but a matter outside the responsibility of the PJTC. A formal agreement to construct Jonglei was signed by the ministers of irrigation for Egypt and the Sudan on 6 July 1974. The PJTC had already held informal discussions with the Compagnie de Constructions Internationales (CCI) and the Compagnie Française d'Entreprise with a view to concluding a contract for the excavation of the canal. The final contract for the canal was signed on 28 July 1976; under its terms, the cost of the transfer of the Bucketwheel from Pakistan,

or a reduction of only 1000 km² of the average total swamp before the inundations of the 1960s. At a draw-off of 25 Mm³/d, the reduction of swamp would rise to 36% from an average total swamp, 1905–80, of 16 900 km² to 10 800 km². At 25 Mm³/d of natural flow, the average total swamp would be reduced 16% or 2800 km² below the average total swamps, 1905–61, before the great flooding. See Sutcliffe and Parks (1987, p. 156).

[7] El Sammani (1984, p. 15).

excavation costs, and contingencies amounted to £S14 966 310 ($42 953 304), or just over £S3 million, less than the estimate for excavation alone (£S18 million); the high cost (£S2 516 435) of transporting the Bucketwheel from Pakistan to the Sobat was to be absorbed by CCI. Thus the actual cost of excavation from Sobat to Jonglei made possible by the Bucketwheel was £S5.5 million less than projected by the PJTC.[8]

Calculation of the total cost of the Jonglei Canal project (not just the excavation) has always been characterized by confusion, particularly over sources and conversion of hard currencies and over fixed rates of exchange which do not reflect real costs. This state of affairs has been hopelessly complicated by adding the costs of the social and economic development schemes in the canal zone, costs which are virtually impossible to estimate with any accuracy, to the actual cost of excavation, construction of ancillary works, and navigation—which can be computed with some precision. Thus to understand the cost of the Jonglei Canal the construction costs should be separated from those of development. At the time of the Egyptian–Sudanese agreement in 1974, the PJTC estimated construction costs at £S52 million ($149 240 000) while £S18 million ($51 660 000) were allocated for local development projects—a total estimated cost of £S70 million ($200 900 000).[9] (See Map 11.)

In 1980 the PJTC had to revise the costs of construction, a revision precipitated by the proposal to realign the canal and by the discovery that the beds of the Bahr al-Jabal and the Atem between Jonglei and Bor were unstable and liable to change, thus seriously affecting the canal's termination. Thus the line of the canal was shifted eastward to avoid the concentration of population in the Kongor area and extended to Bor, where the river-bed was firm and well defined. After

---

[8] 'Cost Estimates of the Project', in JEO (1975, p. 71); Ministry of Irrigation (1976, doc. 3A, bill of quantities and prices, recapitulation, p. 4). Based upon the performance of the Bucketwheel in Pakistan, the initial estimated cost per m³ was calculated at £S.15, a figure which was based on the price of fuel in 1976 and proved unrealistic after the dramatic rise in the price of petroleum products. In converting Sudanese pounds to dollars for contractual purposes, £S1 = $2.87. This conversion factor determined costs and payments but has no relation to the reality of contemporary conversion rates or economic conditions in the Sudan.

[9] 'Cost Estimates of the Project', p. 71.

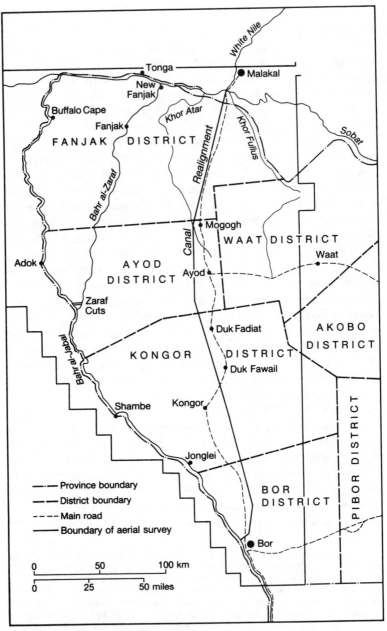

MAP 11. Jonglei Canal realignment
Source: Howell *et al.* (1988)

seventy-six years the Garstin Cut had become a reality, a canal not as straight as Garstin's but nevertheless 360 km long. The PJTC subsequently revised the agreement with CCI, on 13 March 1980, for the excavation of the canal and the construction of navigation works at a total cost of £S43 502 776 ($124 852 967)—or nearly three times the construction costs in 1976 (£S14 966 310) for an extension of 80 km beyond the original terminus at Jonglei. The cost of the eastern alignment and extension to Bor reflected the dramatic rise in the price of fuel in the late 1970s which increased the cost of excavation per cubic metre from £S.15 to £S.40.[10] None of these contractual costs, however, included the Jonglei structures project for canal works, buildings, and infrastructure, such as slipways, a mechanical works regulator, three bridges, twelve ferries, and civil works for the ferry crossings, all estimated at a cost of $60 670 000 plus an additional £S12 010 000 ($34 468 700) in Sudanese currency, or 76 per cent of the total cost of excavation.[11] Although the designs for the bridges and ferries were completed, no contract for their construction has ever been concluded. Assuming that these ancillary structures were necessary for the proper management of the canal, the total cost of construction would rise to some £S77 million or $220 million, perhaps the most realistic price.

The cost of the social and economic development schemes in the canal zone which were to accompany the progress of the Bucketwheel were much more difficult to calculate than the expense of excavation. The development strategy adopted for the canal zone combined research and studies for long-range planning on the one hand with the immediate needs for

[10] Ministry of Irrigation (1980, bill of quantities and prices, recapitulation, p. 22); PJTC (1981b, p. 6).

[11] Euroconsult (1981). The failure to find funding for the Jonglei structures project was the principal reason why no contract was concluded, despite heated disagreements over the canal crossings between the JEO and the PJTC. Anxious to complete the canal, Egypt agreed to provide its half, $30 million, but the Sudan did not have the reserves and so turned again to the EEC for its share, $34 million. The EEC was hesitant to commit yet more funds to the Sudan, which would have meant diverting funds from projects in East Africa. It suggested that the Sudan approach the East African countries to loan the former funds now in return for future contributions to the Sudan by the EEC; but this unwelcome idea died at the outbreak of civil war the following year. Interview, John Mace, EEC representative in Khartoum, 21 June 1982.

community services on the other. By 1982 the cost of commitments in the first category was £S1 000 000 ($2 870 000), a sum provided by the EEC development fund for a comprehensive survey of the environment and ecosystem of the Sudd upon which to formulate Jonglei area planning. The study was conducted by the engineering firm of Babtie, Shaw, and Morton of Glasgow, in co-operation with the environmental consulting company of Mefit Srl. of Rome. The second category, the community projects in the canal zone (arbitrarily defined as a corridor 35 km wide on either side of the canal), was funded by agencies of the UN and the governments of the Netherlands and the USA, totalling some $20 378 000, of which nearly half, $8.9 million, was allocated for the Kongor rural development project. There were, however, separate, individual schemes—*hafirs* at Ayod and Waat, bore wells at Panyagoor, schools at Atar and Khor Fullus—for which an additional $20 665 000 was requested.[12] In all, the capital development programme for the canal zone would require an estimated £S112 million during the 1980s; but funding on this scale was unrealistic in light of the steadily deteriorating Sudanese economy. Thus, although the cost of digging the canal can be determined with a modest degree of accuracy by the contractual arrangements, the vicissitudes of donors, currency fluctuations, domestic economic health, the vagaries of the annual Sudan budget cycle, and the politics of development all conspired to reduce careful calculation to an estimate ranging from $150 million at least to $336 million at most. Undoubtedly the latter figure would be more realistic than the former.[13]

Today these estimates of the cost of Jonglei have little value. The termination of excavation in 1984 after the renewal of civil war by the Sudan Peoples Liberation Army as part of their campaign against the Sudan government will have the effect of dramatically escalating costs whenever the civil war may come to an end. The continued deterioration of the Sudanese economy, the disillusionment of foreign donors, and the political inertia at Khartoum offer little hope of reviving

[12] JEO (1976, table 1, pp. 1–3).
[13] For the problems encountered in calculating costs of research and development projects for Jonglei Phase I see JEO (1918*a*; 1981*b*; 1982).

Jonglei Phase I. When peace returns to the Sudan, the completion of Jonglei will be further complicated by southern hostility to the canal, and by the enormous expense of rebuilding the Bucketwheel and the infrastructure and logistics to support it. Any estimate of the cost of completing the canal under these circumstances would be an act of faith, not of calculation.

Despite these gloomy prospects, any calculation of costs must be weighed against the derived benefits from construction. In 1974 the anticipated economic benefit from the yield of land to be irrigated by an additional 4.7 billion m³ of Jonglei water (3.8 billion at Aswan) would be equivalent to £S56 million, of which half would be the Sudan's share.[14] Four years later, in 1978, the total benefits had been reduced to £S48 million per year, presumably because of devaluation, which still left a healthy difference of £S28 million between the anticipated generated yield against the estimated cost of operation and maintenance of the canal, £S20 million.[15] Even the most optimistic members of the PJTC knew, however, that these projections could not be realistically sustained and in fact were based on the economic equation for cost-benefit analysis used in 1974. Consequently, the PJTC commissioned another economic evaluation in 1979, using 1977 prices, which was reviewed and modified accordingly by both the Sudanese members of the PJTC and the Egyptian planning officers for Egypt's master water plan (EMWP). Their findings were more detailed than descriptive. The calculations of the benefits to costs of Jonglei water were based on the productivity of the Rahad and Kenana schemes and the price systems at the time of the report, modified on the basis of international commodity prices converted into domestic currency and a depreciated Sudanese exchange rate. The most conservative projected rate of return still exceeded 20 per cent so that, even allowing a margin for error of 10 per cent, the Jonglei Canal would recuperate its capital expenditure within ten years. A second projection was made on the economic value of Jonglei, rather than a financial evaluation, whereby an internal rate of return would amount to approximately 23 per cent. A third analysis

---

[14] JEO (1975, p. 86).
[15] PJTC (1981b, p. 15).

took into account the depreciation of Egyptian and Sudanese currency. The analysts could not foresee the drastic devaluation of Egyptian and Sudanese currency a decade later, but at the time, using the 1977 rate of foreign exchange, the return on Jonglei would be slightly over 25 per cent.[16]

All of this analysis was not very helpful in assessing the benefits of Jonglei. Its value cannot be measured solely in feddans at Rahad or hectares at Kenana without taking account of the social costs to those the canal will directly affect in the Upper Nile and their political price for its construction, as much as the financial return on water delivered to the northern Sudan and Egypt. Indeed, the signing of the Egyptian–Sudanese agreement in July 1974 precipitated an attempt by the opposition in the people's regional assembly to overturn the government of Abel Alier and his ministers of the high executive council. Ever since the establishment of the southern regional government, rumours had circulated widely throughout the south concerning the construction of the Jonglei Canal. Unfortunately, neither the central nor the regional government made any efforts to still the rumours, or to educate the inhabitants of the canal zone as to the nature of the scheme, before or after the signing of the July agreement in 1974. Three months later Equatoria, or, more specifically, the regional capital of Juba, exploded into violence over Jonglei.

Before the opponents of Jonglei took to the streets of Juba, the opposition to the canal had been expressed in the southern regional assembly by Joshua Dan Diu from Fanjak and the late Benjamin Bol Akok, the representative from Awiel and the deputy speaker of the assembly, supported by Clement Mboro, Oliver Albino, Stephen Lam, and Simon Morris. They were not motivated solely by their dislike of Jonglei. In fact, they intended to use the agreement to build the canal as a means to unseat the government of Abel Alier, and towards that end they rallied the students from Juba commercial secondary school to protest against the canal. The genesis of the opposition was a clandestine document which originated in Egypt, where it was translated into English by southern students and circulated among students and junior officials in

---

[16] PJTC (1981a); Ministry of Irrigation (1978).

Juba, Malakal, and Bor. This bizarre declaration claimed that some 6000 Egyptian *fallahin*—some of the distributed broadsheets placed the number at two million—would be settled in the canal zone, conjuring up visions of the Arab incursions of the past, the attempts to assimilate southerners after independence, and the imperialism of the present. To add fuel to the fire, environmentalists claimed that the canal would drain the swamps, and that the Sudd would become a parched and barren land devoid of fish and wildlife, the livelihood of the Nilotes destroyed. The normal meteorological processes would be destabilized: there would be no evaporation, no clouds, no rainfall in the Sudan or Ethiopia. The Sudd would become a desert for two million Egyptian *fallahin* to plough.

In the canal zone itself there had been discussion about Jonglei among the chiefs but no organized opposition, since the elders knew nothing of the long and tortuous negotiations between Egypt and the Sudan over the Nile waters, or of the evolution of the many Jonglei schemes. Moreover, their primary concern (and that of the people) was with too *much* water, ever since the floods of the 1960s had destroyed much of their pastureland. Even Abel Alier was not privy to the plans for Nile water development, which were locked in the basement of the Egyptian ministry of public works and since 1959 had become the special domain of the PJTC. The southern leaders had asked no questions about Jonglei. They were completely absorbed with resettling a million refugees, rebuilding the infrastructure of the South, and integrating the Anya-Nya into the Sudan armed forces. They were able to accomplish this by trusting President Numayri, and had no wish to question his decisions regarding national policies during the early years of their experiment in regional autonomy.

Those who opposed the administration of Abel Alier, particularly Benjamin Bol and Joseph Oduho, enlisted other malcontents to use Jonglei as an instrument to discredit the regional government. They appealed to the former members of the Anya-Nya who had not been integrated into the army or been given a job in the swollen bureaucracy. 'The slogan was that the land they fought for was now given up for sale to the Egyptians by those who had now found places in the government.'[17] The reaction was predictable. The opposition to Abel and his government, which was regarded by some as 'Dinkacracy', whipped up the easily mobilized students, who were urged to boycott classes and demonstrate against the government.

The atmosphere in the regional capital was charged with suspicion, uncertainty, and rumour of which Jonglei was the catalyst. Many believed that Jonglei was being used by the government in Khartoum as an excuse to undermine the fledgeling autonomous regional government. Others feared that the Addis Ababa Agreement would not be honoured, and that Jonglei was but a means to round up dissenters and send them to detention camps. None of this was true, but Abel Alier and his ministers were helpless, having no information about the Jonglei Canal other than gossip with which to refute the allegations—which only made the latter seem more plausible. Juba is a long way from Khartoum. When the rumours circulated that Egyptian troops had already arrived in Khartoum to escort the Egyptian *fallahin* to the upper Nile, the students of Juba commercial secondary school staged a demonstration on 17 October, marching through the town to the offices of the high executive council. They were joined by many citizens who had no interest in the canal but saw it as a means to bring down the Dinka-dominated government, which the Equatorians of Juba town had come to regard as almost as much the enemy as the northern Sudanese. The demonstration was blocked by the police; a mêlée ensued which quickly turned into a riot.

The riots were triggered by the attempt of the government to disperse the gathering by force. It had ordered the police to throw tear-gas. There were not enough cannisters [sic] and the police themselves wore no protection against the gas. The crowds answered back with stones and missiles (a commodity Juba has no dearth of). The crowds having tasted its powers over the police repeated the gatherings and marches again the next day. The government then armed the police with firearms instead of batons and gas cannisters (which incidently had run out). The riots were resolved when police actually shot into the crowds and killed two students. The rest of the crowd melted away when the expected Anya-Nya forces did not join them with firearms and grenades which were whispered to be around.[18]

---

[17] H. P. Logali to the author, 12 Oct. 1986.   [18] Ibid.

The government retaliated by declaring a state of emergency on 19 October, introduced a curfew, and arrested some 200 demonstrators including members of the regional assembly. The mercurial Stephen Lam and Simon Morris were apprehended while demonstrating with the crowd; Benjamin Bol and Joseph Oduho were seized the following day, when an incriminating letter was seized by the police in which Bol had indicated that the issue of the canal was simply being used to discredit the government.

Both the regional and central governments reacted to the Juba riots with extraordinary speed. An impressive array of leaders from the Sudan socialist union, accompanied by southern Sudanese students from Khartoum university and engineers from the ministry of irrigation, were flown at once to Juba to explain the facts about the canal to the uninformed and somewhat mystified members of Abel Alier's government —who promptly formed three committees from members of the high executive council and the regional assembly to tour the provinces, particularly the Upper Nile capital, Malakal, and Bor, where there had also been mild demonstrations, to try to dismiss the rampant rumours and emphasize the benefits of the canal to the southern Sudanese. Abel Alier, himself a Bor Dinka, emphatically supported the canal, staking his political fortunes on its construction by issuing a calming statement to the regional assembly which was widely distributed, disclaiming the rumours and declaring that his government was not simply going to accept continuing under-development, backwardness, and poverty. He emphasized the advantages of the canal for the South—mechanized farming, improved communications between Malakal and Juba by river and road, increased pasturage by the draining off of excess water from the 1960s, flood protection for the future, and clean drinking water throughout the year. Whatever happened, he said, the inhabitants of the Upper Nile would not be removed, as the Nubians had been, for the benefit of Egypt, 'and, of course, no Egyptian nationals, soldiers or civilians, will come to settle'.

The Regional Government does not wish and will not associate itself with politics that tend to maintain and perpetuate the present economic status quo in the Region. . . . We are [not] to remain as a sort of human zoo for anthropologists, tourists, environmentalists and adventurers from developed economies of Europe to study us, our origins, our plights, the size of our skulls and shape and length of customary scars on our foreheads. . . . If we have to drive our people to paradise with sticks, we will do so for their own good and the good of those who will come after us.[19]

President Numayri did not leave the task of defusing Jonglei to the regional government alone. Acting again with astonishing alacrity, he established by decree the national council for the development projects of the Jonglei area, charged with 'formulating socio-economic development plans for the Jonglei area and the promotion of studies of the effects of the construction of the canal on the lives and livelihood of the local inhabitants'.[20] Promises were made. The inhabitants of the canal zone were to become the beneficiaries of schools, medical and veterinary care, clean drinking water, agricultural extension services, communications, and jobs, all implemented by the national council which was responsible for Utopia —development projects, procurement of funds, and the designation of which programmes of agriculture, industry, and public works would be undertaken in the canal zone. In fact, the council was an omnibus body with a broad membership, spanning the spectrum of politicians and civil servants, which met irregularly under the chairmanship of Abel Alier himself, the actual work being delegated to the Jonglei executive organ (JEO). The first commissioner of the national council (1974–8), and thereby director of the JEO, was the respected engineer Abdullahi Mohammed Ibrahim, succeeded by Dr Gama Hasan in 1979–80, and by Enoch Mading de Garang in 1980, until his untimely death the following year. He was followed by James Ajith Awuol, another Dinka from Bor.[21]

Almost overnight, what had been a large-scale engineering scheme had blossomed into an ambitious programme for social and economic development in one of the most isolated and neglected regions in the world. In fact, the creation of the national council for Jonglei and its executive organ had its

[19] Alier (1974, pp. 20–1).
[20] 'Presidential Order No. 284, October 1974', in JEO (1975, pp. 93–8).
[21] See JEO (1976b).

precedent in the establishment of the Jonglei Investigation Team in 1946 and its successor, the Southern Development Investigation Team, both led by Paul Howell, who had envisaged the transition to the national council twenty years before. Moreover, the creation of a special agency was a recognition, albeit precipitated by the Juba riots, that neither provincial, regional, nor government agencies could provide the resources for the research, planning, building, and financial challenges posed by the canal; this was a task which only an interdepartmental and interdisciplinary unit, created for a definite purpose, could accomplish. The swift appointment of the national council, along with effective police action and the timely arrest of the leaders of the opposition in the regional assembly, diverted the attention of the southern Sudanese from the Jonglei Canal. The outcry against the scheme diminished, but did not disappear.

The policies for the social and economic development of the canal zone may have required the approval of the national council, but the design and execution of the projects in the Upper Nile were administered by the commissioner and his staff, principally Daniel Deng Yong, the assistant commissioner for planning and economic affairs and Jonathan Jenness, project manager. Daniel Yong, the amiable giant of Jonglei, is a Twic Dinka, seven feet tall, and a former member of the Kongor rural council, trained as an economist at the Universities of Khartoum and Strathclyde. Jonathan Jenness is an American from the State of Maine (whose inhabitants are known for their independence of mind), educated in anthropology at Johns Hopkins and Harvard universities, with many years of experience in Nigeria, Lesotho, and Botswana as a rural development planner for the UN. Together they sought to plan a social and economic revolution in the Upper Nile, to ameliorate by development schemes the dramatic changes which the construction of the Jonglei Canal was obviously going to introduce into the lives of the Nilotes. Such a plan could obviously not be the product of imagination. There was, of course, the report of the Jonglei Investigation Team, but it was concerned with a very different proposal, a large canal with a capacity of 55 Mm^3/d, and with the brief of calculating the cost of compensation and remedial measures rather than costs relating to development and accommodation. Consequently, it seemed that more pilot studies and research were necessary before the JEO could devise a development plan for the canal zone—when the local inhabitants and their politicians had been promised services, not research.

The JEO began its work against seemingly insurmountable obstacles. With headquarters in Khartoum in order to interact with the ministries of the central government and to receive the representatives of the various donor agencies upon whom the social and economic development of the Jonglei Canal zone depended for financial and technical assistance, the JEO appeared to many to be another department of government (which it was not); and, although apparently given sweeping authority by yet another of President Numayri's hastily conceived decrees, the JEO was in fact only a co-ordinating body without the power to coerce. Persuasion and pleading were inadequate means of obtaining the co-operation required among the external agencies and those of the central and regional governments for a programme that demanded financing, research, and planning when the inhabitants of the canal zone had been promised action. Woefully understaffed and plagued by inadequate resources and long and difficult lines of communications, the JEO should be judged by what it *did* accomplish rather than by what it did not.

During the long years of civil war the Nilotic peoples of the upper Nile, particularly the young men, either joined the Anya-Nya or migrated northward from the Sudd, to escape the violence and to seek work in order to recover the wealth they had lost in the floods. They now found themselves in an alien environment in the northern Sudan, and at the bottom of the economic and social hierarchy, only able to find work as menial labourers on building sites in Khartoum or the large irrigation projects at Kashm al-Girba, Roseires, and Managil. Their experience in the north in all its manifestations, subtle and not so subtle, produced an acute awareness of the outside world which was in dramatic contrast to their pastoral life of seasonal migrations in the remote swamp and pasture of the Upper Nile, and a realization of the benefits enjoyed by the northern Sudanese by contrast with their own societies, in which they had great pride and whose traditions they revered.

When peace returned to the southern Sudan in 1972, many of these migrant workers came home to stay. In fact, during the war years there had been a constant migrant flow back and forth between the Upper Nile and the northern Sudan, depending upon an individual's employment, adaptability, and the obligations of family, clan, and lineage. When these migrants did return to the south, either for a few months or for several years, they came equipped with an awareness of a larger world than the ambience of the cattle camp, and with transistor radios and friends who remained behind to retain contact with the world outside the remote domain of the Sudd. It should not have come as a surprise to the Sudan government (although indeed it did) that these angry young men now demanded the services they had previously scorned—schools, dispensaries, veterinary care, and communications. They now expected that the national council for Jonglei and its executive organ should instantly produce these services, with little appreciation for the research from which these services were to emerge.

Moreover, most of these young men, having worked as labourers on building sites, had acquired an intuitive understanding of the dislocation which any construction project entails for the local people and their environment. None of them knew of the tortuous history of Garstin's Cut, but these construction workers could understand that Jonglei meant digging a large canal through their land without their having much say in the matter or knowing how they would be compensated, either by benefits or by the services they were now demanding. The Nilotes of the Upper Nile were no longer gentle savages: they had been educated by war and work, which had made them deeply suspicious of a government committed to despoiling their homelands. Whether migrant labourers, refugees who had fled to Ethiopia, or those who had remained, seeking safety in isolation, they were all suddenly thrown into the political cauldron by the creation of the southern regional government, with its elected regional assembly and the southern ministers of the high executive council. Politics suddenly began to assume a central role in the life of a people with no tradition, knowledge, or experience of the political sphere; and into this unstable atmosphere was thrust the overwhelming prospect of the Jonglei Canal.

The JEO found itself with a mandate from the national council to provide the services promised by the government as part of the canal project, and with a dilemma as to how to carry out such projects without first investing in the research necessary for designing a plan for integrated development—a process which would take years to complete and only prolong the frustrations of the inhabitants. Six years after the establishment of the national council, Majok Ayuen Kur, a Bor Dinka and economist for the JEO, expressed the attitudes of the peoples of the canal zone: 'It was the desire of the Jonglei citizens to see the results of the studies in the form of buildings and works in the fields of health, education, water supply, etc.'[22] Unfortunately, the Sudan did not have the resources to sustain both research and services. In the initial estimated budget for the construction of Jonglei, £S18 million had been designated for 'local development projects', but in fact these funds were allocated for an irrigation canal and network, reclamation, and—as an afterthought—community development.[23] The JEO sought to resolve its dilemma by adopting a dual strategy. On the one hand, it began the planning process and research necessary to determine how best to implement development schemes in the canal zone; on the other, to satisfy the demand for visible schemes, it sought vigorously to enlist foreign administrative and financial assistance. For the first strategy, the JEO received funds for social and ecological research specifically concerned with livestock, range productivity, wildlife, fish, water supply, and soil surveys from the EEC development fund.[24] In an effort to meet the second objective, the need for immediate development schemes, the JEO turned to the UN office of project execution to finance programmes in fisheries and integrated rural development.

Despite its best intentions, the JEO could not produce instant results in either research or services. The technical co-ordination committee established by the JEO had first to define the priorities for the JEO, which then had to negotiate

[24] Yong (1976).   [23] JEO (1975, p. 71).   [22] JEO (1980b).

with foreign governments and the UN, whose own constraints and bureaucracies moved with glacial speed. Research schemes were, of course, more easily inaugurated than development projects, and by December 1976 several had been identified— a 'mathematical model of hydrological simulation of the Nile system in the Sudan' (which one would have thought was within the purview of the PJTC) and soil, swamp, range, wildlife, and livestock surveys, including investigations of the prospects for a buffalo-breeding farm.[25] By 1980 these research efforts had mushroomed into numerous studies, involving both individual investigations by local Sudanese experts, including the JEO's own Jonglei socio-economic research team, and foreign consultants. The most ambitious projects were the two major research reports by Euroconsult and by Mefit–Babtie, a somewhat incongruous alliance of the conservative Glasgow engineering firm of Babtie, Shaw, and Morton with the avant-garde environmental consulting company of Mefit Srl. of Rome. Euroconsult worked with the soil survey administration at Wad Medani to concentrate on a 'soil survey and land suitability classification study'. The Mefit–Babtie project was more comprehensive, embracing virtually every aspect of the ecology of the Upper Nile and culminating in a massive, fourteen-volume report, outweighing even that of the Jonglei Investigation Team published thirty years before.[26]

The programme outlined by Mefit–Babtie was to take four years (not an unduly long time in the prevailing conditions of the upper Nile). The result was a massive report, *Development Studies in the Jonglei Canal Area*, in two parts. The first consisted of a range ecology survey, livestock investigations, and water supply in nine volumes, including one specifically devoted to the impact on the peoples of the canal. The contract was awarded in February 1979 with funds from the EEC and made public in April 1983. In April 1980 a contract was signed for the second part of the report; its scope was solely the swamp ecology, and it was published in four volumes in October 1983, with a separate volume of maps and charts. The study contained an enormous amount of information,

[25] Ibid.   [26] JEO (1982a).

poorly collated, artistically presented, and incomprehensibly organized. It touched on virtually every aspect of the Sudd— livestock, vegetation, wildlife, water supply, limnological and plant studies, invertebrate and fish life, and the advantages and disadvantages of the canal for the environment of the Upper Nile. It appears to have confirmed the impression that Jonglei has been the most studied project in the Third World.

Development Studies in the Jonglei Canal Area recommended livestock development at Ayod, rural development at Fanjak, a water management plan, and yet more feasibility studies in dairy farming and cattle-ranching. There was also to be an ambitious and costly project for water supplies, and a wildlife conservation project with a special study on crocodile utilization, all at a cost of $25,558,000 for a five-year development programme.[27] The outbreak of the civil war in the southern Sudan coincided with the submission of the final report by Mefit–Babtie to the JEO and the national council; and although this was purely coincidental, the report was symbolic of the connection between southern Sudanese discontent and the construction of the Jonglei Canal. Violence in the Upper Nile has made the recommendations of Mefit– Babtie redundant, the proposed projects stillborn. Today, the fourteen volumes with their artistic covers gather dust in Khartoum, while the civil war continues in the southern Sudan and the partners engage in legal confrontation in Europe.

These programmes of research were more cerebral and less painful than construction, but it was public works, not scientific studies, which the people of Jonglei wanted. The JEO could not ignore this fact: 'It is considered essential that Jonglei's population comes to associate the construction of the canal with something in addition to an all-weather road or increased water for areas to the north.'[28] Although the JEO had identified social services as a principal priority, the financial and logistic problems of any project far outstripped those of contractual research. The cost of public services were high anywhere in the Sudan, but even more so in remote

[27] Mefit–Babtie (Apr. 1983, ix. 8). Mefit-Babtie's currency conversion rate was £S1 = $1.04.

[28] JEO (1982b, p. 2).

Jonglei, with its long rainy season and extensive flooding. Moreover, the Upper Nile was not well endowed with such basic ingredients for building as sand and rock, which had to be transported from as far away as Juba, or cement, which had to come from Khartoum, 1600 km to the north. Thus the construction of facilities for community services only began in 1980, six years after the Juba riots, and it was not until July 1981 that a study was commissioned to draft an overall strategy for community services in the canal zone, well after research programmes for the environment and ecology were under way or completed. Obviously, it did not require extensive and expensive research to reach a conclusion about what the Nilotes wanted and needed, and a comprehensive plan for community services in Jonglei was completed in less than a year and presented to the national council in May 1982.[29] A year later the south erupted into civil war, bringing an end not only to the excavation of the canal but to the nascent community services.

While the JEO was groping toward a plan for socio-economic development in Jonglei, it was almost smothered, in the halcyon days following the Addis Ababa Agreement, by support from the international community, led by the formidable Charles la Munière. An anthropologist and director of the UN development programme (UNDP) in the Sudan, he became fascinated, as have so many, by the Nilotes and their homeland. An astute and senior civil servant, he wielded considerable institutional influence, while his personal interest in the Nilotes seemed all the more reasonable given their suffering during the civil war and floods. Jonglei presented a challenge for development in one of the most inaccessible regions in the world, a challenge which la Munière could not refuse. He allocated 25 per cent of the UNDP funds for the Sudan to Jonglei to inaugurate two pilot schemes, the development of Sudd fisheries and a more ambitious project of integrated rural development at Kongor, at a time when the JEO was trying to extract some order and a systematic plan from a plethora of goodwill and disparate offers of humanitarian assistance from a host of wealthy and perhaps guilty donors.

[29] JEO (1981b).

Funds from the UN agencies were drawn from the UNDP, FAO, and the UN capital development fund by la Munière for the Sudd fisheries and Kongor.

The Nile, its tributaries, and its lagoons teem with fish which are a crucial portion of the Nilotic diet at the end of the dry season, when the pastures are reduced, the grain has been exhausted, and the receding waters on the flood-plain make the entrapment of large quantities of fish easy. The objective of the Sudd fisheries programme was to provide technical assistance to catch, process, and transport dried fish south through Juba to Zaïre, where it was in great demand, at profitable prices. The programme was directed by Kristian Fremstad, a fishery expert, with a million-dollar budget over four years from the FAO. Fremsted indicated, however, that the logistic support, equipment, and organization to catch, dry, and market the fish would require at least a ten-year project.[30] There was obviously not going to be any immediate, visible return on this development project, which would in fact affect relatively few inhabitants of the upper Nile, most of whom regarded fishing as a degrading occupation, to be taken up only in the months of hardship at the end of the dry season in May, June, and often July.

The major effort of la Munière was the integrated rural development project at Kongor; but there were ancillary efforts at development which represented humanitarian imperialism and entrepreneurial politics rather than co-ordinated planning. One such scheme was a comprehensive health plan for the Jonglei region, to be administered, not by the JEO, but by the southern regional minister of health under a Dutch project manager. With direct bilateral assistance from the government of the Netherlands, the project was to include a network of public health centres to be constructed over a six-year period; but this commitment, like so many other development initiatives, failed to reach fruition before the outbreak of hostilities in May 1983.

The most significant failure was a substantial mechanized farming project on the Penykou plain east of Bor, initiated in 1976 with funds from the government of the Netherlands. In

---

[30] JEO (1982a). The budget for the Sudd fisheries programme was $834 930 and £129 639.

the euphoria which swept the international community following the Addis Ababa Agreement, Dr Gama Hasan, the regional minister for agriculture, who had studied agronomy in Rome, asked the Dutch to sponsor a feasibility study for large-scale mechanized farming on the Penykou plain. The most influential individual in launching the Penykou plains project was David Bassiouni, who, as director of the regional ministry of agriculture, was the chief civil servant responsible for drafting policy and determining the budget of the regional government for agricultural schemes in the Jonglei area. Bassiouni was a Sudanese whose wife, Mary, was an articulate representative in the regional assembly. He energetically supported Gama Hasan's initiative while the JEO was still trying to determine its own role and devise a plan. An agreement was subsequently signed between the regional government, anxious to assert its autonomy, and the government of the Netherlands to undertake the Penykou project.

The Penykou plains project was administered by the International Land-Use Company of Arnhem (ILACO), with the objective of introducing the mechanized farming project on the plains some 50 km east of Bor, where the forests end. Here the land stretches to infinity, tilting imperceptibly into the shallow valley of the Veveno which had so captivated Geoffrey Parker and the Egyptian irrigation department in the early 1930s as a way of bypassing the Sudd. The idea of utilizing these vast plains with their adequate rainfall was cautiously suggested in the Jonglei Investigation Team's report of 1954, and was seized upon by Gama Hasan with the enthusiastic support of Abel Alier, the vice-president and president of the high executive council.

While the Dutch were carrying out their experiments in mechanized farming on the Penykou plain under the determined direction of Harry Boz of ILACO, John Garang de Mabior, another Bor Dinka, was completing his doctoral dissertation at Iowa State University, to conclude that the intensive development projects in the northern Sudan would exhaust existing water supplies for irrigation by 1984, so that future development would have to be supported by rain-fed agriculture, the most suitable area being the Nilotic plains of the southern Sudan. The presence of the Jonglei Canal would indeed interfere with the traditional way of Nilotic life, but it would also open opportunities for regional development and national integration by developing the Nilotic plain with proper drainage and irrigation, mechanized farming, new forms of land tenure, and the reorganization of the countryside into compact villages. Although he scorned the efforts of ILACO as inappropriate, and likely to end up 'merely containing and managing poverty and misery in the area', he was clearly influenced by the prospects which motivated the planners of ILACO and by his observations of highly mechanized farms in Iowa.[31]

The Penykou project also symbolized political and policy problems which extended beyond the plains. The national council for Jonglei and its executive organ were created in response to the southern reaction to the Jonglei agreement, but this did not inhibit the regional government from concluding bilateral agreements for development projects. Faced with formidable difficulties, and with few resources, the regional government was prepared to accept any and all assistance from sympathetic donors, particularly if the donors were activists rather than planners. Clearly the JEO appreciated the desperation of the high executive council, whose initiatives, however, were often assisted more for humanitarian concerns than for reasons of planned development which the JEO was charged to design. Individual development schemes, negotiated bilaterally with donors by the regional government, not only complicated the task of the JEO but contributed to the growing tension between the national council and its executive and the PJTC.

The PJTC consisted of engineers and hydrologists of international reputation with long experience of Nile waters— not sociologists or environmentalists interested in people and animals. The chairmen of the commission, both Egyptian and Sudanese, were men of remarkable ability who commanded the loyalty of a large staff and the confidence of their governments. The resources at their disposal were substantial, and an awesome amount of data and experience relating to the waters of the Nile available to them. It was no coincidence

[31] Garang de Mabior (1981, p. 227).

that the Penykou plains project was awarded to ILACO, since the latter was a subsidiary of Euroconsult, a principal consultant to the PJTC.[32] So long as the objectives of the PJTC were consonant with the goals of the struggling JEO, with few staff and fewer resources, hydrological needs could be compatible with socio-economic schemes, as they proved to be during negotiations to realign the canal. If not, the struggle between the engineers and the environmentalists was an unfair contest. Much depended upon the personality and sensitivity of the chairman of the PJTC. The most productive years were those from 1974 to 1978, when the PJTC chairman was also the commissioner for development projects in the Jonglei area, in the able person of Abdullahi Mohammed Ibrahim, a hydrologist sympathetic to the objectives of the national council and one who has written with understanding on the environmental impact of the Jonglei Canal on the Upper Nile. Upon Ibrahim's departure in 1978 the positions became separated, with each agency pursuing its own goals under different leadership, often at the expense of the other— the PJTC under Mohammed Amin Mohammedein and Hamad Bahkeit Makki, the JEO led by a succession of commissioners—Dr Gama Hasan, Mading de Garang, and James Ajith Awuol.

The showpiece of the JEO was the integrated rural development project at Kongor. Charles la Munière's support was decisive in launching this proposal, since over $8.9 million was contributed to the project by the UN, half from the UNDP and the remainder from the FAO, the Dutch, and the JEO itself. Kongor was selected since it was a populous area near the canal yet had been relatively isolated, reflecting many of the difficulties experienced by the peoples of the canal zone.

The goal was to provide some of the means and the institutional framework within which the Dinka in the Kongor District of the Jonglei Province can mobilize resources to improve their livestock, agricultural, and fishing economies and develop their educational, health, and social services in order to foster a development process

[32] Dutch international firms have long had a reputation for close co-operation among themselves, with the support of the government of the Netherlands, in competition for foreign contracts. See ch. 6, pp. 236–7.

adapted to the ecological and socio-economic realities of the area, thereby facilitating the process of change and the smooth trans-formation and modernization of economic and social life.[33]

The programme was begun in 1980 and sought to improve livestock, village water supply, and sanitation, to provide a mobile ambulance and health clinics and a co-operative store, and generally to improve communications in road, radio telephone, and air transportation. Kongor and its satellite village of Panyagoor, the headquarters of the project, were to be the visible manifestations of the government's concern to assist the people of Jonglei through the traumatic adjustments made necessary by the presence of the Jonglei Canal. What was learned by the transformation of Kongor could then be applied to the other communities scattered along the path of the canal. The project was planned for ten years and funded up to the end of 1983, when, ironically, it was brought to an abrupt conclusion, with few of its objectives achieved, by the outbreak of civil war.[34]

The Kongor integrated rural development project demon-strated the conscious and unconscious imperialism of the donors, motivated by altruistic humanitarianism in some cases, by personal and professional gain in others. In any event, the allocation of $8.9 million over four years was totally inadequate to achieve the ambitious goals of Kongor in the isolated environment of the upper Nile.

The likely impact of IRD [Kongor Integrated Rural Development Project] under these circumstances will . . . be employment of some local elites and international experts and consultants, and some degree of 'misery management' for the 'target population'. Approximately 40 per cent of UNDP's contribution to Kongor IRD projects, for example, is earmarked to be paid out to foreign experts in the form of salaries, travel, incentive stipends and consultancy fees.[35]

Moreover, in September 1980, of the 139 Sudanese employed in the Kongor project, 69 (or 50 per cent of the work-force) shuttled back and forth between Juba and Khartoum on official duties far removed from the rural realities of Kongor.

[33] JEO/UNDP (1979, p. 3).
[34] JEO (1981b, pp. 19–21).
[35] Garang de Mabior (1981, p. 177); JEO/UNDP (1979).

The one issue which neither the engineers of the PJTC nor the planners of the JEO could ignore, for different reasons, was the realignment of the canal. The decision to undertake the excavation of the Jonglei Canal in 1974 and the subsequent award for its construction to the Compagnie de Constructions Internationales in July 1976 only intensified the efforts of the PJTC to continue its hydrological studies of the Sudd, one of which was the investigation of the Bahr al-Jabal and the River Atem. The study was carried out by Euroconsult of Arnhem, which reported in 1977 that the beds of both rivers were extremely unstable, while south of Bor the river was well defined. The PJTC thus proposed to continue the canal in a straight line to Bor, where a head regulator could be constructed on a firm bottom. Unfortunately, this alignment would pass directly through Kongor, the most densely inhabited region anywhere along the route of the canal, and would cross the limited higher ground upon which were located the only permanent settlements of the Dinka. Several studies commissioned by the JEO, including its own Jonglei socio-economic research team, concluded that the canal would 'separate the high land settlements from the *toic* grazing lands and obstruct free migration westwards as traditionally practised'.[36]

The study by M. O. El Sammani and Dr El Amin in 1977 alerted the JEO to the disruption which would be produced by a straight-line extension of the canal through Kongor to Bor in a densely populated area with some 260 746 inhabitants, cultivating nearly 70 000 feddans, with 450 000 cattle, and the home of the vice-president of the republic and the president of the high executive council of the southern regional government. Consequently, both the JEO and the PJTC invited the Dutch ecologist J. C. Post, of Euroconsult, to identify a realignment of the canal east of the settled areas. With the co-operation of the Jonglei socio-economic research team, two Dutch anthropologists hastily recruited by the Dutch ministry of foreign affairs, and an aerial survey, a preliminary report was completed by January 1978, after rather frenetic investigations, in order to brief the impending conference sponsored by the PJTC to

[36] El Sammani and El Amin (1977, p. 20).

determine a new alignment for Jonglei. The study recommended that the canal be relocated east of the Duk ridge through relatively open land east of the principal villages of Duk Fadiat, Duk Fawail, and Kongor, and then to swing westward back to the Bahr al-Jabal at Bor.[37] This proposal was later confirmed by a more thorough study which the national council approved in September 1979.[38]

The PJTC readily agreed to shift the off-take of the canal from Jonglei to Bor. Since a large amount of the increase in the Bahr al-Jabal flows during the 1960s had disappeared westward into the Aliab valley north of Bor, the PJTC was determined to be able to divert this water down the canal. Moreover, the infestation of papyrus, particularly in the Atem channel between Bor and Jonglei, would involve considerable expense for clearance and embankment. The decisive reason, however, was the discovery by hydrologists from the Delft hydraulic laboratory that the bed of the Atem was noticeably unstable. It was one thing for the PJTC to agree with the national council and the JEO, in a spirit of co-operation, to go to Bor; it was quite another to divert the line of the canal east of the Duk ridge where the sandy soils might require lining the canal to prevent seepage, entailing enormous logistic problems and great expense. Although the official reason has always been that the excavation was already too far advanced to pass east of the Duk ridge, the far eastern alignment would have reduced the interference with the migration routes to the *toic* by 60 per cent, expanded the area available for crop production and grazing by 64 per cent, and relieved the congestion on the high ground.[39] After heated negotiations the PJTC prevailed, as was its custom, and the canal alignment was redrawn from Mogogh, 100 km south of Sobat, to pass west of the ridge and swing round Kongor to Bor. Although an improvement on the direct line from Sobat to Bor, the adopted alignment still required many crossing points in order to get the Nilotes and their animals across the canal. The proposed ferries and bridges—to the lasting resentment

[37] Deng *et al.* (1978).   [38] JEO (1979).

[39] Ibid. Sayyid Bakheit Makki Hamad, head of the Sudanese representatives and deputy dirctor, to the PJTC, May 1982; and F. Lemperiere, chairman and general manager, and S. Agius, deputy general manager, GTMI, 12 Jan. 1987, to the author.

of the inhabitants—would never have been capable of satisfying this requirement.

The debate over realignment and the role which the studies commissioned by the JEO played in the negotiations demonstrated to the sceptics that the JEO was needed more than ever if the interests of the Nilotes of Jonglei were to be represented at all in decisions affecting the canal zone. The JEO now actively maintained an operational office in Bor to co-ordinate the proposed development schemes, a forwarding office at Malakal, and a liaison officer in Juba to establish contacts and communicate with the regional government and the international aid agencies which had offices there. The establishment of the JEO and the expansion of its activities did not, however, have any lasting impact upon the local inhabitants of the canal zone. The JEO had two objectives— to initiate the studies necessary to carry out planned development among the Nilotic peoples, and at the same time to organize and co-ordinate actual development projects in the canal zone. With the assistance of a host of consultants, the JEO partially succeeded in the first but had little success in the second, the few meagre schemes visible after ten years of promises having been destroyed by civil war.

On 13 March 1980, agreement was reached between the ministry of irrigation and CCI to realign the canal according to the wishes of the PJTC, and to extend it 80 km to Bor, the total length being 360 km. The accord stipulated that the revised construction be completed by 13 March 1985 and the excavation of a 2500 m navigation canal above Bor be finished by 13 June 1985, at a total cost of £S43 502 776 ($124 852 967). The completion of the revised agreement, including the substantial increase in cost, was facilitated by a loan from the French government of F150 million (£S10 135 135, or $35 314 059), in addition to a separate guaranteed loan for an additional F30 million (£S2 027 027, or $6 817 547) from two commercial French banks.[40]

[40] Ministry of Irrigation (1976, doc. 3A, p. 4; 1980, p. 22).

9
The Canal-Builders

Whereas the Employer is desirous that certain works should be constructed, viz. a 280 km. (approximately) long canal between River Sobat and Jonglei or thereabouts as determined by the Engineer in the Democratic Republic of the Sudan as further particularized in the Contract and has accepted an offer by the Contractor for the construction and completion of such works . . .

Ministry of Irrigation (1976)

THE Compagnie de Constructions Internationales, SA (CCI) was founded in July 1963 by five French companies, with the aim of undertaking large and high-risk construction projects in foreign countries as well as in France, and with an average annual turnover of some F50 billion.[1] Of the five firms, the leader and dominant partner, by virtue of its capitalization—nearly the total of its four partners—and its experience, was Grands Travaux de Marseille International (GTMI), which subsequently played a central role in the construction of the Jonglei Canal. During the decade after its formation, CCI had built dams in Turkey, Iran, Pakistan, the Ivory Coast, and Mozambique; harbours in Morocco, Saudi Arabia, and Egypt; and railways in Gabon; it had even participated in the glamorous salvage of the great temple at Abu Simbel from the rising waters of the Aswan high dam reservoir. The project, however, which led to Jonglei was the successful completion in 1970 of the Chasma–Jhelum link canal in Pakistan, an irrigation canal 101 km long connecting the Indus and the Jhelum Rivers. By employing a new technology for canal excavation, the 'Roue-pelle', or Bucketwheel, CCI eliminated in one turn of its mighty wheel drag-lines, dredgers, and a

---

[1] The 5 French firms were: Spie–Batignolles, Entreprise Campenon Bernard-Cetra, Société Dragages et Travaux Publics, SGE, and GTMI.

half-century of discussion, memoranda, and reports as to the most efficient means of digging the Jonglei Canal.

In the summer of 1965 and later in 1966, the West Pakistan water and power development authority (WAPDA) approached the Compagnie Française d'Entreprises (CFE) with a view to the construction of the Chasma–Jhelum link canal. Negotiations were successfully concluded in August 1966, and technical discussions followed in Lahore in November. Representatives of the WAPDA visited Germany in November to observe the prototype of the Bucketwheel in operation in the lignite mines near Cologne. There had been considerable competition for the contract, particularly from Italian and American firms using traditional excavating equipment, but R. Plutarque of CFE thought that the machines employed in the German open-pit brown coal-mines could be adapted for more efficient and economical construction of canals than could be achieved by either drag-lines or dredgers. Indeed, it was Plutarque who convinced the sceptics that the principle of the Bucketwheel could be applied to reduce the time and the cost of excavation which had been a major inhibiting factor in the manifold proposals for the Jonglei Canal.

Encouraged by the Pakistanis, Plutarque, on behalf of the CFE, signed a contract with Orenstein and Koppel Tageban und Schiffstechnik of Lübeck on 17 January 1967, to build an excavator on the principle of the Bucketwheel but with a more rapid rate of digging and designed for the dimensions of the canal, the soils to be encountered, and the heat and aridity of Pakistan.[2] On 14 July 1968 the new Bucketwheel was in place in Pakistan. Designed by Dr Raster of Orenstein and Koppel, this Bucketwheel differed from similar machines in Germany in its long boom, independent power system, and broad caterpillar treads, which made it the largest two-crawler mobile excavator in the world, weighing 2,100 tons. Despite heavy sandstorms, swampy ground, and the gravel, loam, and clay soils, the Bucketwheel made several parallel swathes to excavate a ditch with a bed 116 m wide. In all, the Bucketwheel was a great success, spewing out an average of 120 000 m^3 every day, with less maintenance and mechanical

[2] R. Plutarque to the author, 13 Jan. 1987.

failures than predicted. On 29 February 1970 the Chasma–
Jhelum canal was completed seven months ahead of schedule,
an engineering triumph and a financial disaster. The fiscal
difficulties of the WAPDA and the inability to utilize the
Bucketwheel in proposed projects in Sind resulted in the
submerging of the CFE into the conglomerate known as
CCI.[3]

The initiative to use the Bucketwheel for the excavation of
Jonglei came, in fact, not from the French, but from interest
in its technology on the part of the respected Sudanese
hydrologist Yahia Abdel Magid. In 1971 he was minister of
irrigation in the government of Ja'far Numayri, having served
previously as under-secretary of state in the ministry as well as
chairman of the PJTC. He knew of the Bucketwheel's
performance in Pakistan, and had personally visited the
Chasma–Jhelum canal site to observe the machine in 1972,
after the signing of the Addis Ababa Agreement had brought
peace to the southern Sudan and revived the possibility of
Jonglei. On its part CFE was only too anxious to rid itself of
the Bucketwheel, which after its success had lain idle, a white
elephant, incongruously dormant in the sands of Pakistan.
During discussions with Yahia Abdel Magid between 25
October and 5 November 1972, CFE offered to sell the
Bucketwheel to a Sudanese consortium, or to lease it on
favourable terms, with promises of the necessary technical
assistance. Negotiations languished amidst the political
uncertainty in Khartoum following the Addis Ababa Agreement
and the installation of the regional government in Juba.
Meanwhile the principal players in Paris, Cairo, and Khartoum
manœuvred for the possession of Jonglei.

The Egyptians were represented by M. A. Samaha of the
Egyptian ministry of irrigation and later by Barakai Ahmad
Gaber, soon to be minister of irrigation and owner of a large
construction company in Egypt who, not unnaturally, wanted
the canal to be excavated by an Egyptian firm. The prospect
of an Egyptian company digging its way through the upper
Nile raised northern Sudanese suspicions of Egyptian intentions,
and helped to spawn the rumours of Egyptian *fallahin*

---

[3] Rodenberg and Blanc (n.d.).

descending upon the Nilotic plain which led to the Juba riots in October 1974. If the Sudanese did not have the organization or human and material resources to build the canal, better the French than the Egyptians. In January 1974, nearly six months before the signing of the Egyptian–Sudanese agreement to construct Jonglei, P. Voronkoff, representing CFE, and Pierre Blanc of CCI visited the confluence of the Sobat and the White Nile. They were greeted by some forty Shjilluk who, apart from admiring these hairy Frenchmen, did little to facilitate their decision whether to establish a future base camp for the canal at the confluence.[4] Since the completion of the Chasma–Jhelum canal Voronkoff had been searching for a job for the Bucketwheel, and in 1974 he was convinced that the meeting place of the Sobat and the White Nile was its new and natural home. He returned to Paris to campaign ever more energetically for Jonglei among the members of the CCI conglomerate.

Upon Voronkoff's return CCI made a preliminary offer to the Sudanese ministry of irrigation on 24 February for the construction of a canal from Sobat to Jonglei, 260 km, at a cost of £S12 795 000 ($35 186 525). Thereafter negotiations were left to François Lemperiere, chairman and general manager of GTM, who emerged at this time as the principal policy strategist and the driving personality in CCI as far as its involvement in the Jonglei Canal scheme' was concerned. Xavier de Savignac of CCI shuttled back and forth between Paris and Khartoum to carry on the more tedious technical negotiations. Discussions continued in Cairo during the first week of April, led by Yahia Abdel Magid and the veteran civil servant in the ministry of irrigation, Sayyid Zoghayroun El Zein Zoghayroun, whose memory went back to the days of the Condominium and negotiations with the Egyptians leading to the 1959 Nile Waters Agreement. They both, like the under-secretary of state at the ministry, Sayyid El Tayeb Abdel Razek, favoured the French. Barakai Ahmad Gaber and M. A. Samaha again represented the Egyptians. Plutarque, Voronkoff, and de Savignac were there to argue for the Bucketwheel.

[4] Interview with P. Blanc, 12 Jan. 1987.

The Cairo discussions defined the terms for the official negotiations, which were opened six months later on 10 September by a letter of intent to construct the canal from François Lemperiere. Two weeks later, on 23 September, an Egyptian–Sudanese delegation arrived in Paris to complete the final contract. The negotiations did not go smoothly, involving thirty-six hours of continuous talks. For CCI the brunt of these difficult discussions was carried largely by Xavier de Savignac. An engineer trained at the École Spéciale de Travaux Publics, he was a career employee of GTM and intimately involved in these and subsequent negotiations concerning the Jonglei Canal, being the signatory for CCI on both contracts. The policies, however, were the responsibilities of François Lemperiere, representing the board of directors of GTM and the CCI consortium.[5]

There were three major issues preventing agreement in Paris—the terms of the performance bond, revision of the costs of the canal, and guarantees concerning the price of petrol—and a variety of lesser technical problems. Where Lemperiere could make decisions in Paris, however, the Sudanese delegation could not, having to refer the points of difference to Khartoum. Here the French were strongly supported by the quiet but persistent intervention of Yahia Abdel Magid, and within the month a final contract was prepared for signature on 20 Ocober 1974 when suddenly Juba erupted in riots and violence. The Sudan government clearly could not announce the signing of a contract to begin the construction of the Jonglei Canal when the southern Sudanese were demonstrating in the streets of Juba against it. While Abel Alier and his ministers toured the southern provinces calming the populace with promises, President Numayri dramatically created by decree the national council for Jonglei, with the hope of fulfilling those promises. At the same time the ministry of irrigation politely postponed any final signing of the contract by diplomatically handing it over for review to the PJTC, who had been privy to the negotiations but now officially assumed responsibility for negotiations with CCI on behalf of the Egyptian and

[5] Interviews with X. de Savignac, former project director, CCI, and F. Lemperiere, chairman and general manager, GTMI, 12–13 Jan. 1987.

Sudanese governments. It was no coincidence that the commissioner of the JEO, Abdullahi Mohammed Ibrahim, was also the chairman of the PJTC and a close friend of Yahia Abdel Magid at the ministry of irrigation. Together they were able to steer Jonglei past the Scylla of Sudanese politics and the Charybdis of French frustrations.

These were difficult years for CCI, in which the managers never quite knew whether a contract would be signed. The French team of de Savignac, Plutarque, and Voronkoff passed back and forth between Khartoum, Cairo, and Paris, where Lemperiere directed their operations against the discouraging refusal of the French government to guarantee payment to CCI in the event of a forfeiture by the Egyptian and Sudanese governments. The Jonglei Canal was regarded as too great a risk for public guarantees; Lemperiere hastened to convince the members of the consortium and the EEC of the need to cover CCI's liability. During these years the Egyptians began to take a more active part in efforts to reach a successful conclusion to the negotiations, after the Juba riots had ended any illusions that the canal might be built by an Egyptian firm. Sayyid Dr Mohammed Amin Mohammedein, the knowledgeable Egyptian representative on the PJTC who had succeeded Abdullahi Ibrahim as chairman, worked closely with Yahia Abdel Magid during these years to obtain the approval of Presidents Sadat and Numayri for the project. His efforts were continually compromised by Numayri's insecurity, emphasized by another attempted *coup d'état* in September 1975. Again, Yahia Abdel Magid did much to repair the damage, assisted in the spring of 1976 by the French minister of works, M. Gallfy, who promised the Sudan government a credit of F26 million (£S2 million) for the Jonglei project on signing the final contract.[6]

In June 1976 Magid resigned as minister of irrigation, his international stature recognized by his appointment as the secretary-general for the UN water conference to be held at Mar del Plata, Argentina, in 1977. His work, however, was all but completed; his successor, Sayyid Zoghayroun el Zein Zoghayroun, was left to finalize the contract, supported at the

---

[6] X. de Savignac to the author.

JEO by the commissioner, Abdullahi Ibrahim, at the PJTC
by Dr Mohammedein, and at the ministry of irrigation by the
principal civil servants who were in favour not only of Jonglei
but of choosing CCI to construct it.[7] The prospects for a
successful conclusion for CCI after years of discussions
seemed all the better when President Numayri visited Paris at
the end of June, on his return to Khartoum from talks in
Washington. He personally reassured Plutarque that the
contract would be signed.[8] Thirty minutes after his Boeing
707 touched down at Khartoum airport early on the morning
of 2 July 1976, 2000 heavily armed exiles and mercenaries,
secretly returned from Libya under the command of Mohamed
Nur Saad, attacked the airport, military headquarters, and
key government installations in the capital in yet another
attempt to overthrow Numayri and bring back to power Sadiq
al-Mahdi. The president was whisked to safety, and his loyal
troops rallied to put down the coup on the following day after
bloody street fighting. It appeared that the finalization of the
contract, if not abandoned, would again be delayed by
political instability in the Sudan. Surprisingly, despite the
battle raging at that moment in Khartoum, GTM received a
telex in Paris from the ministry of irrigation accepting CCI's
offer. This message was confirmed on the 12th, and the
contract itself was signed by Sayyid Mohamed El Gassem
Osman, under-secretary at the ministry, Plutarque for CCI,
and Voronkoff for CFE at the ministry on 28 July 1976.
Everyone was there except the man who had perhaps done the
most to bring the contract to fruition, Yahia Abdel Magid, then
at the UN in New York: the minister, Sayyid Zoghayroun El
Zein Zoghayroun, Sayyid Mohamed Mohammedein from the
PJTC, de Savignac from GTM, Abdullahi Ibrahim from the
JEO, Kamal Ali from the ministry of finance, and the French
ambassador, Jean-Pierre Campredon. In return for
£S14,966,310 ($42,953,309) CCI had agreed to build the

---

[7] Abdullahi Mohamed Ibrahim, the JEO commissioner, moved from the PJTC to
the ministry of irrigation as deputy minister. Sayyid El Tayeb Abdel Razek remained
a deputy minister; although principally responsible for the Rahad project, he had
always supported CCI. Dr Mohammadein, a known supporter of CCI, succeeded
Abdullahi Ibrahim as PJTC chairman.

[8] President Numayri actually said to Plutarque that 'il a été signé' (R. Plutarque to
the author).

necessary site facilities, transfer the Bucketwheel to the Upper Nile, and excavate an unlined canal 280 km from the Sobat to the vicinity of the former village of Jonglei, its handful of *tukuls* long ago submerged by the great floods.[9]

After six years the idle Bucketwheel had been given a new mission; but the remote and hostile environment of the Upper Nile presented a far more difficult challenge than the sands of Pakistan, within easy reach of port and rail facilities. During the next two years CCI, with the assistance of the engineers from Orenstein and Koppel, refurbished the Bucketwheel and then dismantled it for shipment to the extensive base camp being established at the confluence of the White Nile and Sobat Rivers, where it was to be laboriously reassembled. This complex task was directed by Pierre Blanc, an engineer educated at the École des Arts et Métiers who had spent his career with GTM and who was given the operational responsibility not only for transporting the Bucketwheel from Pakistan but also for its reconstruction and for the design modifications necessary to overcome the peculiar conditions of the Upper Nile. Xavier de Savignac of GTM remained in charge of Jonglei at the Paris office of CCI until 1981, when he was succeeded by H. Vallin. François Lemperiere, later assisted by Spiro Agius, continued to direct overall policy within the consortium from the GTM headquarters in Paris.

Slowly the Bucketwheel arrived, in crates and containers, at Port Sudan between May and June 1977, despite a *coup d'état* in Karachi and difficulties in finding freighters. From Port Sudan the pieces of the Bucketwheel were transported by rail and road to Kosti, where a permanent office had been established to arrange for the steady flow of equipment, fuel, and supplies from the railhead 600 km up the White Nile on specially designed motorized barges, the *Biarritz* and the *Marseille*, to Sobat camp. None of this was easy. There were no cranes at Port Sudan or Kosti capable of handling the huge containers. One for Port Sudan had to be rushed north from

---

[9] Ministry of Irrigation (1976). Information for the above was given by the French and Sudanese participants during interviews between 1982 and 1987; see also Rodenberg and Blanc (n.d.). During these years of negotiations Yahia Abdel Magid became the father of a daughter named Sarah, and, given the French penchant for calling unique machines, usually of spectacular dimensions, after women, the Bucketwheel became affectionately known among the members of the CCI as 'Sarah'.

the Cabora Bassa dam site in Mozambique; two Manitowoc cranes were shipped from Europe to Kosti, where Blanc was engaged in protracted negotiations to obtain a suitable site and authorization to load and unload and to ship CCI materials on their own barges, and not on those of the Sudan department of railways and steamers, which jealously guarded its monopoly of river transport. At the Sobat camp the principal problem was to establish adequate living quarters and food for the men and their families. The confluence consists of a flat alluvial plain of elephant grass, with a single dead tree as a symbolic gravestone. Under the energetic direction of Mme Lucette Vidal, the first arrivals had to live off the land on water-melons, tomatoes, and egg-plant until a more organized commissariat was set up.[10]

Slowly a large camp, complete with living quarters, work-shops, and stores, was erected for the French and Pakistani technicians who began to reassemble the Bucketwheel under Blanc's supervision. Small things were the most frustrating. Numerous pieces were misplaced or lost in transporting the Bucketwheel from Pakistan, particularly the caterpillar treads necessary to move the machine. There were always infuriating shortages of nuts and bolts, several tons of which had to be flown out from Paris. Nevertheless, by June 1978 Blanc and his men were ready to begin operating the Bucketwheel, two years after the signing of the contract in Khartoum. They immediately encountered formidable difficulties which required significant modifications, designed by Blanc, to transform the Bucketwheel into an entirely new machine. The principal problem, which spawned others, was the infamous cotton soil, 'very hard, consolidated, deformable, coherent clay'.[11] This

[10] Interviews with P. Blanc and Mme L. Vidal, 12 Jan, 1987. CCI made an error by not insisting in the initial contract on using its own planes and steamers. Consequently, the Sudan government assumed and demanded that its steamers be used to ship equipment, supplies, and fuel to Sobat, a task for which Sudan railways and steamers had neither the capacity nor the organization. Much heated negotiation subsequently ensued between the ministry of irrigation on the one hand and the ministries of defence and transport on the other. In the end they reached a compromise which allowed CCI to operate its own barges and planes, but only if they were used to transport CCI equipment and personnel, a condition which was rigorously monitored by the officials from the Sudan railways and steamers department.
[11] Rodenberg and Blanc (n.d., p. 6).

soil in the rains turns to viscous mud (hence the sensation of 'walking in cotton'), and in the dry season shrinks to the hardness of concrete. The top layer of cotton soil varies from 0.5 to 1.5 m in depth, below which the clay, although more sandy and calcareous, has a density nearly as great as the cotton soil and a water content not much greater. Moreover, this calcareous clay was extremely abrasive, with a high proportion (45 per cent) of quartz and limestone grains. The Bucketwheel designed for the sands of Pakistan could not eat this cement-like clay.

Six caterpillar diesel engines (increased to eight in 1982) capable of supplying a steady flow of 6000 kW replaced the German engines, which could not provide a sufficient fluctuating flow of current to power the buckets digging into the hard clays. Power, however, was not enough. As the great wheel turned, the adhesive clay caked in the corners of the buckets, clogged the chutes, and lumped like stones on the conveyor bridge, bringing operations to a halt and requiring extensive cleaning, not with soap and water, but with pneumatic hammers. In consultation with the German engineers, who regularly inspected the Bucketwheel during its operations in Jonglei, Pierre Blanc installed in July 1979 new basket-shaped buckets, with chain mats to force out the tenacious clay, and installed specially hardened teeth to bite into the cotton soil. Two ploughs were also arranged at an inclined position right and left of the wheel to push lumps of clay fallen from overfilled buckets back into their path, thereby clearing the path of the excavator. The speed at which debris was passed over the conveyor bridge was also converted to an automatic control related to the output of the Bucketwheel and its forward movement.[12]

During these years of experimentation the results were dismal if not disastrous. In two years of operation the Bucketwheel managed to excavate less than 30 km, and at that rate would have required eighteen years to reach Jonglei. The drag-lines of past proposals could have more than equalled that performance. By July 1980, however, Blanc and his French and Pakistani technicians, by extraordinary effort

---

[12] Interview with P. Blanc.

and ingenuity fuelled by anxiety, had built an entirely new, automated Bucketwheel in one of the most remote regions of Africa, with power, excavating capacity, and the automatic transfer of debris to the east bank for an elevated roadway. The rate of excavation had increased by 53 per cent, while the down-time for cleaning and repair had been drastically reduced. Pierre Blanc had achieved his objectives, and returned to Paris as the technical director of GTMI; the operation of the Bucketwheel was taken over by Guy Charlière, as site director—who was to die in May 1982 from malaria contracted in the Upper Nile.

In the summer of 1980 the Bucketwheel began to move relentlessly through the Upper Nile. It was an awesome machine: its towering bulk, 2300 tons, 70 m wide, and 25 m tall, was dramatically accentuated by the flat Nilotic plain, stretching without relief on either side of the canal to the distant horizon. The wheel itself, 12.5 m in diameter, with its twelve buckets each with a capacity of 3 m^3 revolved about once every minute depending on the soil and climatic conditions, while rotating 180° every five minutes, to excavate between 2500 and 3500 m^3 an hour, digging a canal over 40 m wide at a rate of 1–2 km a week. By May 1981 the Bucketwheel was performing at peak efficiency, excavating an average of 3000 m^3 per hour, or 280 000 m^3 every week, while advancing along the line of the canal at the rate of 300 m a day, or 2 km a week (see Fig. 5).[13]

By 1981 the Bucketwheel had become fully automated so that it could be operated by a crew of only twenty-five French, Pakistani, and Sudanese on three eight-hour shifts, Monday to Friday, with two ten-hour shifts on Saturday and Sunday. The remaining down-time was given over to maintenance. With every 50-m advance the Bucketwheel stopped to refuel. The automation of the Bucketwheel was required, not to save labour costs, but to solve the incredibly difficult problem of keeping this huge machine on grade, excavating neither too

[13] The Bucketwheel was expected to excavate 280,000 m^3 of earth a week, 44–8 weeks of the year—a total annual capacity of between 17 and 18 Mm^3—along a canal of 75–85 km. The canal was divided into 3 sections, each with a differing bottom width depending on flow requirements: the first section, 40 km from the Sobat, was 38 m wide; the intermediate section, 270 km long, was 30 m; and the last section 50 km upstream, was 50 m wide (1982, pp. 5–6).

FIG. 5. The Bucketwheel

little nor too much. The average slope of the Sudd from south to north is 5 cm/km. The requirements set by the PJTC allowed for a margin of error of only 6 cm, 3 cm above grade and 3 cm below, in order for the waters of the equatorial lakes to flow downhill rather than up. There was no possibility that this condition could be met by human manipulation. Blanc, therefore, decided to resolve this dilemma by a laser placed 2 km in advance of the machine, which would automatically activate the hydraulic cables from which the Bucketwheel was suspended to raise or lower it within a second. The extraordinary accuracy was achieved despite the imponderability of the enormous machine's posture.[14]

Automation, however, created problems as well as resolving them. The complex electrical system of the Bucketwheel contained over 3000 circuits which were highly vulnerable to the heat and humidity of the Upper Nile, and prone to frequent collapse on account of overloads produced by the stress of changing soil conditions. There were surprisingly few major breakdowns. In August 1981 a linchpin broke, dropping the conveyor bridge by some 3 m, but no other major fault disrupted work for any significant period. The efficiency and capacity of the Bucketwheel was useless, however, without proper preparation. In fact, the most important aspect of the construction of the canal was clearing a path for the Bucketwheel. This entailed building embankments to prevent flooding in its path, without which the 2300-ton behemoth would sink through the clay to the Umm Ruwaba sandstone in the rainy season, when the Upper Nile was turned into a gigantic quagmire. Consequently, half a dozen bulldozers toiled twenty-four hours a day, under floodlights in darkness, some 20 km in advance of the Bucketwheel to construct two dikes 2 m high on either side of the canal, to prevent creeping flow or flood-water insinuating itself into the track of the Bucketwheel.

This was indeed technology triumphant far beyond the dreams of Garstin when he sent C. E. Dupuis in 1904 to observe the American experience with dredgers, and a triumph reducing to absurdity the sterile debate, during the

---

[14] Interviews with P. Blanc, D. Goumard, deputy project manager 25 Aug. 1982, and B. Kolli, project site manager, 26 Aug. 1982; visits to the site in 1981 and 1982.

inter-war years, over the efficacy of drag-lines versus dredgers. It was one accomplishment for Plutarque's idea, Raster's design, and Blanc's ingenuity to make the Bucketwheel function effectively in the Upper Nile. It was quite another to keep it going. The first, foremost, and everlasting problem was fuel. The Bucketwheel had an insatiable appetite for diesel fuel, consuming 40 000 litres every twenty-four hours. The total amount of fuel required for the Bucketwheel and the ancillary equipment—bulldozers, drag-lines, tankers, trucks, and aeroplanes—equalled about 1000 tons a month. The Sudan government was responsible for supplying the diesel fuel at an agreed price of £S20 ($0.57) per imperial gallon or £S44 ($0.13) per litre, but could not always guarantee delivery at Port Sudan. The price of fuel was obviously a crucial consideration, and had been the subject of prolonged discussions during the contractual negotiations. CCI insisted upon a fixed price, any increase of which would be paid by the Sudan government in any given month that the price rose above the basic unit price.[15] This arrangement was obviously to the advantage of CCI, which could hardly have undertaken the contract otherwise; but it did result in constant concern about the Sudan government's ability to make the necessary fuel available. In fact, construction was halted in February and March 1981 for lack of fuel until CCI arranged for the purchase and transport of petroleum direct from Marseilles.

Having reached Kosti and been transshipped by barge to storage tanks at Sobat camp, the fuel was then transported to the construction site in Klein tanker trucks, each with a capacity of 40 000 l, along the road on the east bank built from the debris from the canal. In the dry season the run from Sobat to the construction site was routine, with tankers leaving daily. In the rains from April to October, the heavily laden tankers, equipped with living quarters, food, and radios, would leave every two or three days, and invariably became mired in the cotton soil, to be extricated by bulldozers. The road itself was regularly patrolled by Toyota trucks to report conditions and necessay repairs. The advanced camps had the

---

[15] The price for automobile and aircraft fuel was £S50 per imperial gallon; £S1 per imperial gallon for lubricating oil, and £S35 for grease. Ministry of Irrigation (1976, p. 25).

capacity to store 1 400 000 l, a little more than a month's supply, in large rubberized balloon storage tanks which could be easily deflated and moved forward to follow the Bucketwheel.

The Bucketwheel dug efficiently on the pathway made clear and dry by the bulldozers; but its excavation cut a trench through the Upper Nile which required a finishing of the banks of the canal which was as important as the preparation. The original design contemplated a profile of 2 : 1, a slope so steep that neither animals nor people could easily reach the water. Pierre Blanc questioned this design during the start-up operations of the Bucketwheel in 1978. He had personally been involved in building canals in France with a 2 : 1 gradient in which several drownings had occurred, when people swimming in the water could not clamber up the concrete slope.[16] The JEO took up this issue with the PJTC, and was principally responsible for insisting on a revision of the gradient to 8 : 1, thus rendering it easy for people, domestic animals, and wildlife to reach the water to drink and, if they were to cross, to ascend the opposite bank. Although the excavated bottom of the canal would vary from 38 to 50 m downstream to upstream, the actual width of the surface would now be more than double the base, more a lake than a canal (see Fig. 6). Since the canal would cut directly across the migratory patterns of Nilotic cattle as well as the herds of wildlife, the slope of the embankment became of paramount importance in the deteriorating relations between the JEO and the PJTC.

The question of crossing the canal aroused much emotion and confusion. The inhabitants of the canal zone were acutely aware of the obstacle the canal presented to the migratory pathways from their wet-season villages to the rich grazing of the *toic* pastures. On the recommendation of Euroconsult, CCI proposed six crossings at places of high traffic—Khor Nyetor, Mogogh, Duk Faiwal, Kongor, Jelle, and Bor. They drafted two designs for bridges, 16 and 8 m respectively above canal-level, and two plans for tunnels underneath.[17] None of

[16] Interview with P. Blanc.

[17] Ministry of Irrigation (1980); 'Works Related to the Jonglei Canal (not included in CCI's contract)' (ministry of irrigation, May 1980), 'Solution 1: Tunnel', GTM No. B-16, 101; 'Solution 2: Tunnel', ibid. 102; 'Solution 3: Bridges', ibid. 103; and 'Solution 4: Bridges', ibid. 104 (Nanterre, GTMI).

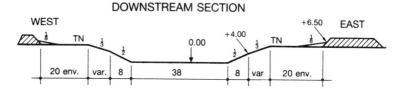

DOWNSTREAM SECTION

INTERMEDIATE SECTION

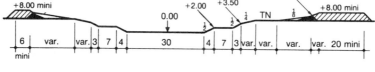

UPSTREAM SECTION

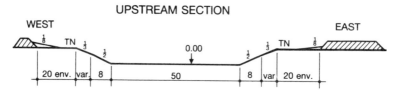

Fig. 6. Cross-sections of the downstream, intermediate, and upstream parts of the Jonglei Canal

these proposals elicited much enthusiasm at the PJTC headquarters in Khartoum. Tunnels were liable to be flooded in the Sudd; bridges were very expensive in that flat plain, into which would have to be brought all the building materials to construct a ramp for an overpass sufficiently elevated for steamers to pass beneath. Under pressure from the JEO and the members of the national council, the PJTC reluctantly agreed to construct four bridges, a dozen ferries, and the appropriate civil engineering works at the astronomical cost of some $92 million, nearly three-quarters of the cost of excavating 360 km of the Jonglei Canal itself.[18]

[18] The cost of each bridge was estimated at £S8 million ($23 million). This figure did not include the cost of ferries.

Although appealing and politically palatable, bridges or tunnels were not the solution. Constructed at great expense to permit the uninhibited passage of Sudan government steamers, the bridges, 10 m wide, could never accommodate the steady flow of tens of thousands of cattle congregating to cross, consuming limited fodder, and exacerbating ancient tensions in the crowded areas at the bridgeheads. The planners' idea of motorized ferries was a fantasy to anyone who had lived in the remote regions of the Sudd. Despite the fact that Euroconsult and CCI designed a ferry to be propelled across the canal by the current, thereby setting it free from dependence upon the vagaries of motor power, the ferries were slow, and could accommodate relatively few cattle and no wildlife.[19] Faced with these inadequacies, the Nilotes devised (and continue to devise) their own means of swimming their cattle across the canal, as the Nuer have done every year on the upper Sobat in flood, provided that the gradient into the water was negotiable for their animals. As for the passage of the wildlife, 'the only known feasible method of overcoming the barrier effect on wildlife migration would be gently sloping embankments now planned for 270 km. of the alignment'.[20] The finishing of the canal, therefore, assumed an importance not normally associated with this aspect of canal construction, and was carried out by two Manitowoc drag-lines, four graders, and bulldozers as reqired, to produce a 1:8 gradient to which most cattle and some wildlife could adapt. Nevertheless, herds of animals swimming the canal would lead to the rapid deterioration of the canal banks, requiring heavy maintenance foreseen in the financial projections for canal operations by the PJTC but not translated into the reality of works in the Upper Nile.

None of the excavations by the Bucketwheel, nor the path cleared by bulldozers, could have been possible without the personnel and the intricate logistic support to sustain an engineering project of these dimensions in a hostile environment. There were 50–60 French expatriates in the canal zone at any one time, some 40 Pakistanis (most of whom had been with the

---

[19] See 'Ferry Alignment and Lay-Out and Cross Section km. 40 thru 309', C-FL-2, and 'Ferry and Guide Boat', C-FL-4, in Euroconsult (1981, vol. i).
[20] Awuol (1982).

Bucketwheel for many years, dating back to the construction of the Chasma–Jhelum canal), and some 1000 Nuer, Shilluk, and Dinka. There were fewer than 50 Sudanese from the north; these did not remain long, disliking the climate and longing for the urban environment of Khartoum and Omdurman. Although the Bucketwheel was excavating at the forward site of the canal, the heart of the operation remained at Sobat camp. Here, at the confluence, CCI built a French village to recreate the family life essential to social stability for a project spanning many years. There were mobile bungalows for 27 French families and bachelors, equipped with domestic conveniences and air-conditioning. There was a pre-school and a school for the children under the supervision of the French ministry of education, and recreational facilities including a swimming-pool, horses, and Club Sobat. Health has always been a fundamental concern of life in the Upper Nile basin, but British experience has been that the plethora of diseases is best controlled by proper housing. The high quality of housing units at Sobat camp resulted in a very high standard of health for the expatriate French families and the Pakistan employees, only two or three requiring medical attention in any week. Sobat camp also administered a hospital with X-ray equipment, a small surgery, and a laboratory, capable of treating up to 50 patients ten hours a day; of these only a third were CCI employees and virtually all Sudanese, the others coming from many miles for treatment. Malaria, of course, was pervasive, commonly blamed by the local inhabitants for virtually any ailment; but flesh wounds incurred in hunting or in disputes, particularly after pay-day and drinking, gastro-intestinal disease, and the most prevalent killer in the southern Sudan, pneumonia, were all common. With the coming of the canal and the opening of the Upper Nile to civilization, venereal disease, hitherto rare among the Nilotes, had reached epidemic proportions.

But Sobat camp functioned efficiently, not because of the decisions made by executives in Paris, but because of the skills and determination of the wives and women of CCI. A combination of foresight, common sense, and tradition initiated a policy whereby the wives of the expatriate personnel worked twenty-seven hours a week, keeping them occupied while their children were in school, allowing them to earn extra income, and providing a trained support staff for the stores, kitchens, and the magnificent gardens surrounding the camp. Such organization was achieved by the skills and determination of women like Mme Lucette Vidal, whose experience in Indonesia and Pakistan was put to a formidable test from the beginnings of Sobat camp in June 1977 to its destruction by the Sudan Peoples Liberation Army on 10 February 1984. She was justifiably proud of the large vegetable gardens, which provided fresh produce for the commissariat, supplemented by a wide range of European and American goods brought by barge and plane.[21]

The Bucketwheel itself, however, did not feed on lettuce, tomatoes, French wines, or Scotch whisky. The objective was to keep the Bucketwheel excavating twenty-four hours a day. Fuel and personnel were critical, the logistic support at Sobat camp was essential; but without a sophisticated maintenance, parts, and repair schedule the complex operation of the Bucketwheel and its necessary infrastructure would fail. The bulk of the parts and machinery were shipped in containers from Marseilles to Port Sudan, where long delays occurred at first, since the Sudan customs service was inadequate for clearing the large amount of supplies passing through Port Sudan for Jonglei. This bottle-neck was relieved by using the Sudanese firm Transintra, whose efficiency was proportional to its influence; but even this innovation could not prevent the usual loss from pilfering if machinery was not readily cleared and transhipped to Kosti. Often charter planes were commissioned to carry immediate and essential loads from France, but even these encountered long delays at customs in Khartoum. In emergencies CCI would send critical parts in the baggage of individual employees shuttling back and forth from France to Khartoum, from where two light aircraft made daily round-trip flights with personnel and parts to

---

[21] Interview with Mme L. Vidal. The French personnel received a credit of £S1000 a month to purchase goods at the Sobat commissariat, which was deducted from their accounts in French francs at the official rate of exchange in France. Most expatriates complained that this sum was insufficient, but the amount required depended upon standard of living. Those French with families had contracts fixed for 10 months, with one and a half months in France and a half month for travel. Bachelors served for 3 months, followed by 15 days in Khartoum.

Sobat camp and the construction site. Despite established procedures and improvisation, the canal-builders had to allow three to six months for the passage of necessary parts from Europe, an intolerable delay which required the stockpiling of a massive inventory of some 50,000 spare parts, computer-catalogued with the need, and lead-time for replacement, carefully calculated. The dynamics of triumphant technology produced by the probability equations of the engineers cut through the land of the Nilotes to achieve the penetration of one of the world's most isolated regions.

Life at the construction site differed from the more comfortable and familial permanency of Sobat camp. The advanced site camp moved every 90 km; the atmosphere at PK141, for instance, was more austere and temporary, the pace of life dictated by the twenty-four hour operation of the Bucketwheel, the advanced fleet of bulldozers preparing the pathway, and the graders and Manitowoc drag-lines finishing the approaches to the canal on either bank.[22] The local store contained some 7000 parts, mainly for maintenance, replacements sent up from Sobat camp to PK141 by plane or truck. Tankers arrived regularly to deposit their loads of fuel into the huge rubber storage balloons. Routine regulated the determined bustle of the camp; relaxation was governed by mutual segregation. The Europeans were housed in self-contained, air-conditioned mobile homes; the Pakistanis and Sudanese in tents, which the Sudanese preferred to their traditional *tukuls* more as a status symbol than for reasons of efficacy. Those Sudanese with families usually lived in the village which sprang up around the construction site to accommodate shops, bars, and camp followers. The *marissa* ladies did a thriving business; venereal disease competed with malaria, wounds, and gastro-intestinal disorders as the most serious illness.[23]

---

[22] The advanced construction sites were PK80, PK141 (Jan. 1982), PK215 (Mar. 1983), and finally PK290. For the final stage of excavation Sobat camp was to be dismantled and rebuilt at Bor.

[23] In the Sudan, *marissa* or beer is traditionally brewed by widows, providing a steady income in their later years. Brewing is a complex process, no less in the Sudan than Bavaria, in which formulae are jealously guarded, and the quality of the product can bring fame and profit to the breweress.

The 600 Sudanese labourers at PK141 were virtually all southern Sudanese—Shilluk, Dinka, and Nuer—from the canal zone. There were only a few dozen northern Sudanese, who kept very much to themselves. In the villages there were, however, numerous *jallaba*, northern Sudanese merchants, some of whom had traded in the southern Sudan for many years. Ostensibly there were no serious labour problems, but the cultural and culinary preferences of each ethnic group produced segregated living and eating arrangements for the Nilotes as well as for the northern Sudanese, the Pakistanis, and the Europeans. Labour disputes were mediated with moderate success by the Sudan government labour office in Malakal, with Shilluk, Dinka, and Nuer representatives. The inevitable brawls precipitated by pay-day, traditional animosities, and *marissa* were the responsibility of the detachment of Sudanese police assigned to guard the camp and keep order in the villages.

Despite having no experience with mechanical devices, the Nilotes were soon performing nearly every function in the camp, from casual labour to operating the Bucketwheel itself. The contract agreement of 1976 had fixed the wages at £S1.10, £S3.85, and £S5.77 per eight-hour day for labourers, drivers, and operators respectively, but with a clause which required the Sudan government to reimburse CCI for the entire increase of any wage adjustment if it exceeded 70 per cent.[24] Although these salaries were far beyond any cash income in the traditional societies of the Upper Nile, the inflation produced by the construction of the canal precipitated a strike by southern Sudanese workers in May 1981—a strike characterized more by spontaneity than by organization but one which successfully readjusted the wages by almost 100 per cent to £S2, £S6–7, and £S10 respectively. A Shilluk, Dinka, and Nuer could now earn in a few weeks a cash equivalent of the annual per capita income in the upper Nile. The burden, of course, fell upon the Sudan government—which was, however, enjoying the unrealistic contractual rate of exchange and could print whatever currency would be necessary to meet the added increase in the local wage for labour.

[24] Ministry of Irrigation (1976, p. 22).

Not all this money was dissipated on beer and women. Although neither the JEO nor CCI have ever enquired as to how their employees spent their money, it appears that a great deal more was saved than the flow of cash and the camp environment would lead one to suppose. The Nilotes wanted cash for cattle, wives, and status. One of the most popular institutions was the company savings bank, in which approximately 20 per cent of the southern Sudanese work-force had accumulated substantial capital (£S1000). The bank also handled remittances to the families of its workers. The principal concern of the southern Sudanese was the uncertainty about their future once the canal was completed. Having acquired skills and moved outside the traditional pattern of living, they were apprehensive as to where they would fit into society upon the completion of the canal. The outbreak of civil war in 1983 has engulfed these individual interests; but the completion of Jonglei without war would have created other development projects, not only in the canal zone, but elsewhere in the upper Nile basin, which would have required the skilled workers from Jonglei.[25]

The most serious labour problem at PK141 was food, or rather its preparation. Originally, CCI provided produce and meat with the intention that each ethnic group would prepare it to its satisfaction—only to discover that a week's ration would be consumed in a few days, forcing the men to purchase dura, the principal foodstuff, from the *jallaba* at extortionate prices. CCI therefore assumed responsibility for operating separate kitchens for southern Sudanese, northern Sudanese, Pakistanis, and Europeans, who, as the expatriate élite, enjoyed a bar and video television with their dining facilities. Separate catering facilities were indeed popular, but created formidable commissariat problems, since the company made a conscious effort to provide the best possible meals for everyone at a modest cost.[26] This was sound economic sense, leaving aside French culinary pride. The men were well fed to their tastes without having to maintain their own households exposed to the extortionate free market dominated by the *jallaba*. As at Sobat camp, health was supervised by a doctor

---

[25] Interview with J. Mohamed, camp manager, PK141, 27 Aug. 1982.
[26] CCI charged each Sudanese worker £S35 per day for food.

in charge of a mobile hospital within the camp site for all CCI personnel, treating some thirty patients a day, while providing a dispensary outside the camp in the charge of the medical assistant, who would see any and all who came for treatment.

At the time the Jonglei contract was amended to include the eastern alignment to Bor, CCI had proposed to build the Jonglei Canal structures including a regulator, a navigation lock, and training works at Bor, in addition to the design for the canal crossing, both bridges and tunnels, pipes for irrigation and cattle watering, and modifications to ameliorate the effects of creeping flow. The construction of these structures would, of course, dramatically increase the cost of the canal, particularly the expensive bridges, but only three—the regulator, navigation lock, and training works—were directly necessary for its completion. The other projects—bridges, pipes, and modifications for creeping flow—were not necessary for the passage of water from Bor to the Sobat, but were important politically and socially to the national council and the JEO. The compromise of realigning the canal around Kongor, but not east of the Duk ridge, may have satisfied the PJTC but did not satisfy either the JEO or the inhabitants of the canal zone. For the JEO the critical consideration, given the unstable beds of the Atem and the Bahr al-Jabal, was the off-take at Bor; for the local inhabitants, it was the numerous structures along the line of the canal, which had little to do with the successful passage of water downstream but were necessary to facilitate crossing the canal, whether by bridges, ferries, or swimming, as well as the drawing off of water from the canal to irrigate crops and grazing land and to provide water for man and his animals during the dry season. Eleven modest proposals put forward by CCI to adjust to these developments received favourable consideration by the PJTC and the ministry of irrigation, but they ultimately agreed to integrate only three of them into the construction of the canal—berthing places for steamers to dock, pass, and exchange passengers and goods, ferries, and the three bridges. None of these three improvements required any abstraction of water from the Jonglei Canal.

Among the eleven proposals was the recommendation by the French engineers of CCI to install pipes, beginning at kilometre 80, to draw off water where it appeared necessary to irrigate crop- or pastureland and to provide drinking water for man and his animals during the dry season.[27] The JEO requested the former minister of irrigation, Yahia Abdel Magid, to conduct a detailed study, which corroborated the on-site experience of the French engineers.[28] Irrigation on the Nilotic plain, particularly east of the canal, where the land becomes desiccated in the dry season, has been a topic of discussion and debate for half a century. A regular supply of water during the dry season would affect the traditional pattern of livelihood for those who remained behind in the permanent villages while the young and the strong followed the cattle to the *toic* and the receding flood-waters. Here, on the desiccated lands, water could possibly provide nutritious pasturage on the intermediate lands; pasturage hitherto lost in the dry season might be resuscitated by Jonglei Canal water.[29]

Similar structures to draw off water were proposed specifically for cattle, not from the point of view of development, but rather to avoid major maintenance on the embankments of the canal at those places where domestic animals would come to drink if water could not be provided on the plains either side of the canal. The arrival of hundreds of thousands of cattle, sheep, and goats to drink at the canal would pulverize the banks; and in fact the canal would not provide adequate watering by comparison with pools flooded artificially on the plain. The same consideration prompted CCI to propose that earthern dikes be constructed every 30 or 50 km across the empty ditch of the uncompleted canal (which grew in length with every passing week of excavation), to create reservoirs of rainwater during the years of canal construction for use in the dry season, to facilitate crossing the canal, and to provide water for the needs of villages and animals along the line of the canal. This was another inexpensive and effective response to local needs, for these dams could be easily constructed, and just as easily removed by a few bulldozers when the canal was ready to transport water. Nothing, however, came of these suggestions.

---

[27] 'Works Related to the Jonglei Canal (not included in CCI's contract)'.
[28] X. de Savignac to the author, 19 Feb. 1988.   [29] Magid (1981).

The proposals for the Jonglei Canal structures had been initiated by Xavier de Savignac, the project director for CCI, during the discussions concerning the realignment, and were pursued after the completion of the amended contract. De Savignac suggested to Bakheit Makki Hamad, the Sudanese representative on the PJTC and at that time its chairman, that 'it will be more economical for the Client, [and] Ministry of Irrigation, to execute them [the Jonglei Canal structures] at the right time and in particular relation with the excavation team and their camps'.[30] Working with the principal consultants, Euroconsult and the Delft Hydraulic Laboratory, CCI made formal proposals for the Jonglei Canal structures, including the works at Bor, essential for the operation and navigation of the canal, as well as for the projects to assist in the development of the canal zone. Between 17 and 19 February 1981 representatives from the PJTC, Euroconsult, and the Delft Hydraulic Laboratory met in Arnhem to discuss the Jonglei Canal structures.[31] As a result of these discussions, the PJTC put out to tender in April 1981 designs for the head regulator, with a navigation lock at Bor only. In the following December the PJTC requested proposals for the excavation and necessary earthworks to open the canal at its tail, either into the White Nile or the Sobat.[32] There were no requests for a tender on the remaining Jonglei structures.

The regulator at Bor was designed to maintain a constant discharge from the Bahr al-Jabal into the Jonglei Canal, despite the seasonally and annually varying water-levels in the river. The structure was to accommodate an average flow of 25 Mm^3/d with a maximum of 30 Mm^3/d, a 33 per cent increase in the volume projected in 1974 (20 Mm^3/d). The regulator itself was a standard ten-sluice gate structure of reinforced concrete, with each opening 4 m wide.[33] The navigation lock, also constructed of reinforced concrete, was to be 27 m wide and 125 m long, capable of accommodating a 'push-tow' steamer with four barges. The lock would have

[30] X de Savignac to the executive member, PJTC, 23 May 1980 (Nanterre, GTMI).

[31] Euroconsult (1981, vol. ii).   [32] PJTC (1982).

[33] 'Regulator, Lay-out, Elevation and Longitudinal Section', in Euroconsult (1981, vol. i); PJTC (1981b, pp. 9–10).

mitred gates, filled and emptied via sluice-gates, with approach harbours designed for the marshalling of waiting vessels.[34]

Although the renewal of civil war in 1983 and the subsequent termination of excavation at kilometre 267 precluded these projects from becoming a reality, the choice of projects for tendering in 1980 and 1981—to the exclusion of more immediate decisions regarding the pipes for the abstraction of water from the canal, which required co-ordinated construction —clearly defined the priorities of the PJTC. Those projects which were not directly concerned with getting water and steamers through the Sudd, despite being identified by Euroconsult and CCI as integral parts of the canal, were not sent out for tender. The reluctance of the PJTC to sanction the draw-off, and its continuing disagreements with the JEO over the crossings, bridges, and ferries, contributed to the growing disenchantement with Jonglei by the southern Sudanese élite and the southern members of the national council—not to mention the inhabitants of the canal zone, who could see the ditch being dug at the rate of 2 km a week through their pastures yet looked in vain for the promises of 1974. This local disillusion with the Jonglei scheme suddenly burst forth at the Bor conference on 10 November 1983, organized by the JEO. Not only did the angry Dinka and Nuer forcefully express their frustration, but articulate criticism of Jonglei was made by members of the Mefit–Babtie team, which had just concluded its voluminous report on the environmental impact of the canal on the ecology and inhabitants and wildlife of the Upper Nile. Both these factors deeply influenced the decision of Colonel John Garang to have the Sudan Peoples Liberation Army shut down the operations of CCI, although he was also concerned by larger questions of the reconstitution of political representation in the Sudan and Khartoum to reflect regional interests and, after Septebmer 1983, the revocation of Numayri's decree imposing the Sharia law of Islam on all citizens of the Sudan.

Three years after CCI had urged an immediate decision on the Jonglei Canal structures, no decision had been taken by the PJTC or the ministry of irrigation other than to tender the

[34] Euroconsult (1981, vol. i).

off-take construction at Sobat, the head regulator, and the navigation lock; meanwhile the excavation of the canal had steadily continued, leaving behind a big ditch and lost opportunities. To the Nilotes of Jonglei the canal had become, not a cause, but a symbol of all the political, religious, economic, and discriminatory grievances against their fellow countrymen in the northern Sudan. Caught in the middle between the bickering of the JEO and the PJTC, the French were particularly bitter about the failure of the two to reach agreement concerning the installation of the pipes to draw off water from the canal, since those pipes, unlike the bridges, could be put in place at minimal expense during the excavation of the canal itself, but would be very costly if installed after its completion.[35] The reluctance of the PJTC to deal with such a modest proposal was all the more perplexing to the administrators of CCI since the reports of British hydrologists of the 1930s, the Jonglei Investigation Team in 1954, the studies of the Egyptian irrigation department concerning the Equatorial Nile Project, and even members of the PJTC all agreed that any abstraction of water for the Nilotic plain would have no significant effect on the total amount of water which would ultimately arrive at Aswan. In their frustration the French embarked, at their own expense (which, owing to their efficiency, proved not to be great), on a project to construct a network of dikes and ditches designed to provide water from the canal, as well as to channel creeping flow east of the canal in the dry season. The PJTC expressed little interest.[36]

Having been rebuffed on ancillary measures to make the Jonglei Canal more effective, the engineers and hydrologists of CCI concentrated on digging the ditch. They were confronted by two problems, one of immediate attention, Khor Atar; the other requiring more deliberate consideration, creeping flow. Khor Atar, sometimes referred to as Khor Chiet, meanders north-west from south and east of Duk Faiwal, crossing the line of the canal just north of Mogogh, 96 km south of the Sobat, and thence proceeding to the White Nile east of the Bahr al-Zaraf. Its flow across the direct line of the Jonglei Canal

[35] Interview with X. de Savignac, 12 Jan. 1987.
[36] X. de Savignac to the author, 19 Feb. 1988.

had long been recognized by the engineers of the Egyptian irrigation department, particularly after the adoption of the Equatorial Nile Project, which required a big canal which would bisect this khor; the problems thereby created were identified by the Jonglei Investigation Team. There had been several proposed solutions, including diverting the khor into the canal or using syphons to pass the water under the canal, all characterized, however, by a lack of information on the size of its catchment basin, depth of khor, flow velocities, and the relationship between the Khor Atar and creeping flow. By 1980 many of these imponderables had been resolved by several years of intensive study of the khor and its hydrology by the French engineers of CCI. The original proposal to construct a syphon was abandoned as prohibitively expensive, as it undoubtedly would have been; and the alternative solution, to pass the flow from Khor Atar into the canal by a diversion canal parallel to Jonglei northward to kilometre 50, where its water could enter the canal at terrain level, was not found to be necessary.[37] The investigations of CCI demonstrated that the flow was significantly less than previously thought but important for the local population. Rather than draw off the water at great expense, the French engineers simply constructed a large dike across the khor to enable the Bucketwheel to pass beyond, after which the dike was demolished.[38] Left standing was the raised roadway which formed the east bank of the canal, behind which a lake of several kilometres in extent, depending on the season, spread across the Nilotic plain, its waters dissipated to the north and into the air.

Having dealt summarily with Khor Atar, the canal-builders had to contend with the mysteries of creeping flow.

Overland or sheet flooding—referred to as 'creeping flow' by the Jonglei Investigation Team and in common use ever since—is characteristic of the rain-fed grasslands of the Jonglei area. It was defined as 'the slow movement of large bodies of water across a plain which slopes very gently and is almost impermeable', impermeable that is after saturation of the soil by rainfall in the wet season. It is a

[37] Euroconsult (1977); 'Works Related to the Jonglei Canal (not included in CCI's contract)'.
[38] X. de Savignac to the author, 19 Feb. 1988.

flood that 'creeps in the sense that it is water advancing over a flat plain without any defined channels'. It can come from afar and appear unannounced by any concurrent precipitation of rainfall in the immediate vicinity. It is not a hydrologically or hydraulically unique phenomenon, for it is no more than a manifestation of run-off in particular topographical circumstances, but it is a frequent, though unpredictable, occurrence in the Jonglei area during the rains, does great damage to crops, and causes discomfort to people and livestock.[39]

But creeping flow may not be all bad. It increases the moisture in the clay soils after the rains to turn the perennial grasses green. When controlled by dikes and embankments, the water could be made available for pasture or crop production in the searing desiccation of the dry season. Indeed, CCI, in conjunction with the Compagnie du Bas Rhône Languedoc, had established successful experimental plots by the canal in part utilizing the water from creeping flow.[40] Creeping flow itself is the product of rain augmented by spill from perennial streams and rivers. Some suggest that creeping flow on the eastern plains could be run-off from the Imatong mountains to the south, but this would only occur in exceptional circumstances, when the capacities of the Pibor, Lotilla, and Veveno Rivers were insufficient to accommodate water from the mountains to the south.

Creeping flow is rarely more than a few centimetres in depth, but its presence may be awesome: P. H. C. Pawson reported from Waat in 1947 a sheet of water 'advancing about 50 km in the space of two weeks over a front of over 30 km with "a definite flow of water about a foot deep and with a current strong enough to make a ripple behind a man's leg when he stood in it"'.[41] Until the construction of the canal, creeping flow would eventually make its way north and north-westward to the Khors Fullus and Nyanding and Khor Atar, and thence into the Sobat and White Nile respectively. Nevertheless, there remains much that is unknown about the genesis, progress, and size of creeping flow as it makes its way

---

[39] Howell *et al.* (1988, p. 479).

[40] This project was only established after 6 years of perplexing negotiations between the CCI, the JEO, and the PJTC, despite the fact that the French government was willing to supply F10 million towards the proposal, to which was added local funding by both the JEO and the PJTC.

[41] Howell *et al.* (1988, p. 480).

across the Nilotic plain. The canal itself acts as a great dike, intercepting the creeping flow passing to the north-west toward the Bahr al-Zaraf and the White Nile, impounding its waters, which in places will stretch eastward for several kilometres across the plain. Although creeping flow never seriously threatened canal construction and did not require sophisticated syphons, as previously thought, to pass the water beneath the canal, the inundation along the east bank has made access to and crossing the canal all the more difficult, while flooding permanent habitations and their adjacent cultivations and thus adding to the growing resentment against the canal which was bitterly expressed at the annual co-ordinating conference sponsored by the JEO at Bor in November 1983. Again, the insensitivity of the PJTC in failing to acknowledge the debilitating effects of creeping flow on the east bank resulted in yet another lost opportunity of winning the approbation of the Nilotes, for it has been estimated that, if properly controlled by a network of dikes, creeping flow could add 500–1,000 km^2 of dry-season grazing on the eastern plains.[42]

While creeping flow did not require any remarkable feats of engineering and was easily prevented from seeping into the path of the Bucketwheel, CCI and Euroconsult proposed that the road embankment be shifted from the east to the west bank at either Duk Faiwal or Kongor, a simple engineering manœuvre accomplished by positioning the gantry to deposit excavated debris in the west bank rather than the east.[43] Since the overwhelming number of inhabitants south of Kongor have their permanent habitations west of the canal, the road along the west bank would greatly facilitate communication among the villages. Unfortunately, the transfer of the road from east to west would require a large and expensive bridge, estimated at £S8 million, in addition to bridges at the head and tail of the canal at Bor and Sobat respectively. The failure of the Sudan government to find funding for this bridge and the others led the representatives of the PJTC to affirm at the JEO Bor conference in November 1983 that the road

---

[42] For a discussion of creeping flow in its many manifestations see ibid. 392, 422; app. 3, pp. 479–82.

[43] F Lemperiere, Sp. Agius, X. de Savignac to the author, 12–14 Jan. 1987.

would remain on the east embankment throughout its entire length. As with creeping flow, this announcement was greeted by much bitter denunciations, and produced deep resentment among the southern Dinka.[44]

And so the frustrated Fench engineers wait in Paris, as they did for Panama and Suez, to return to finish the Big Ditch. Whatever the environmental concerns, the possible ecological disasters, the traumatic changes in Nilotic life, or the hydrological benefits as measured at Aswan, they are determined to return to fulfil their commitments. The financial guarantees of governments and international agencies, and awards for damages by the court of arbitration at The Hague, fade before the Gallic pride of the canal-builders.[45]

[44] Howell *et al.* (1988, pp. 60, 418).
[45] Members of the board of directors, GTMI, to the author, 12–14 Jan. 1987. In 1986 the international court of arbitration at The Hague instructed the Sudan government to reimburse GTMI £S35 million as settlement for work stoppage and loss of the Bucketwheel, under the principle of *force majeure.*

10

Impact and Opportunity

I wish to say that although this [the Jonglei Canal] is a
central government project, the [southern Sudan] Regional
Government supports it and stands for it. If we have to
drive our people to paradise with sticks, we will do so for
their own good and the good of those who come after us.

Abel Alier, 1974

No sooner had the Bucketwheel taken its first bite into the
clay soils of the Upper Nile than a barrage of criticism
concerning the impact of the canal on the ecosystem of the
Sudd was let loose, Originally emanating from the UN
environmental programme headquarters in Nairobi, the hue
and cry of the environmentalists soon appeared in the
European press, particularly in France and Germany. Sometimes thoughtful, often strident, frequently ignorant, a steady
stream of copy poured forth from the media, led by a coalition
of environmental groups in Europe and the USA known as the
environmental liaison centre, with headquarters in Nairobi,
which demanded an immediate moratorium on any construction
work in the canal zone.[1] In 1977 the UN conference on
desertification, held in Nairobi, provided a global forum for
those who denounced the canal as advancing the march of
sand southward from the Sahara while drastically altering the
climate of Sudan's neighbours. The discussions culminated
in a packed meeting, sponsored by the Royal Geographical
Society, in London on 5 October 1982, entitled 'The Impact of
the Jonglei Canal in the Sudan'.[2]

---

[1] See Mann (1977).

[2] The author wishes to acknowledge the generosity of P. Howell, M. Lock, and S.
Cobb for permission to quote from proofs of their edited work, *The Jonglei Canal:
Impact and Opportunity* (Cambridge, 1988), particularly chs. 16–18, dealing directly
with the effects of Jonglei upon the people and animals of the Upper Nile province.

The criticisms of the environmentalists were many, including charges that Jonglei would drastically affect climate, underground water supplies, silt and water quality, and would bring about the destruction of fish and dramatic changes in the life-style of the Nilotic peoples. The spectre of thousands of Egyptian *fallahin* descending upon the Jonglei province still lingers to this day, even after that issue was put to rest following the Juba riots of 1974. The research of the Jonglei Investigation Team in 1946–54 and that of Mefit–Babtie in 1979–83 give little support for many of these criticisms but arouse deep concern for others.

The most bizarre charge was that the Jonglei Canal would turn the Sudd into a Sahara. 'Here is a canal being built in an area that could easily be Africa's next desert.'[3] The environmentalists argued that the reduction in the surface area exposed to evaporation would decrease the amount of moisture entering the atmosphere and consequently result in the decrease in the amount of rainfall. After thorough research the Jonglei Investigation Team had convincingly demonstrated, twenty-five years before the Nairobi conference, that the canal would have no significant effect on precipitation over the Sudd. The research of the Mefit–Babtie team confirmed that conclusion, pointing out that there had been no increase in the rainfall over the Upper Nile between the reports of the Jonglei Investigation Team and the early 1980s, despite the fact that the area of swamp and flood-plain exposed to evapo-transpiratory water loss had increased two-and-a-half times. In fact there is no correlation between rainfall and swamp area in the Sudd.[4] Similarly, the concerns of the environmentalists that groundwater levels would also be drastically reduced by the draw-off from the canal have proved to be unfounded.[5]

Of greater importance to the environment of the canal zone would be the effect of Jonglei on the flooding from the Bahr al-Jabal of the permanent swamp and seasonal flood-plains. Since the canal will reduce the amount of water flowing into the Sudd, not only will the outflow be diminished but the area

[3] Prof. R. Odingo, Nairobi University, environmental liaison centre press conference, Nairobi, Sept. 1977.

[4] Mefit–Babtie (Apr. 1983, viii. 3–4); Howell *et al.* (1988, p. 377).

[5] Mefit–Babtie (Apr. 1983, viii. 5).

of permanent swamp and seasonal flood-plain will decrease, changing the ecology of the Sudd, with a concomitant effect on the human and animal populations. The PJTC has calculated a host of scenarios, based on measured flows from 1905 and controlled by the regulator at Bor, whereby the amount of water being diverted through the canal would vary from 15 to 25 Mm³/d, depending upon the natural flow of the Bahr al-Jabal and the seasons, wet (May–October) or dry (November–April). First, the effect of the canal is understandably greater on the permanent swamp than on the seasonal flood-plain. Second, the reductions in the area of both the permanent and the seasonal swamp are naturally greater when 25 rather than 20 Mm³/d are passed down Jonglei. Thus, at a canal flow of 20 Mm³/d measured against a river flow of seventy-five years (1905–80) the permanent swamp will shrink from 9500 to 6200 km² (35 per cent), the seasonal swamp only from 7400 to 5800 km² (22 per cent); at a canal flow of 25 Mm³/d, the reduction in the permanent swamp will be greater, from 9500 to 5500 km² (43 per cent), the seasonal swamp from 7400 to 5400 (27 per cent).[6] Nevertheless, the predicted net benefit of increased pastures to the peoples of the canal zone, who have been the hapless victims of too much water for the past generation, will range, depending upon canal regulation, between 4500 and 5700 km² (see Table 4).[7]

While the canal will certainly reduce the extent of the permanent and seasonal swamps, it will also change the pattern of vegetation in the lakes and lagoons, just as the appearance of the water hyacinth in the late 1950s and the high flows from the equatorial lakes during the early 1960s dramatically affected the distribution of Sudd vegetation. Since the surface levels in the equatorial lakes, specifically in Lake Victoria, are now, after a quarter of a century, approaching the levels recorded before the great rains, the concomitant decrease in the volume of the Bahr al-Jabal will result in the river spilling further downstream than in the past. Consequently, *Vossia*

---

[6] Sutcliffe and Parks (1982b, table 8.1, p. 46); Howell *et al.* (1988, p. 381).

[7] El Amin and Ezeat (1978); Howell *et al.* (1988, pp. 381–4). The area flooded in 1964 has been estimated at 39 500 km². A canal diversion of 25 Mm³/d would have reduced the maximum flood at that time to 32 100 km² (19%). This reduction in flooded area of 7400 km² would have been substantial.

TABLE 4. *Estimated effects of Jonglei Canal on areas of flooding under three possible natural discharge regimes*

	River returns to pre-1961 discharges (1905–60 data)			River remains at high discharges (1961–80 data)			River returns to mean discharges (1905–80 data)		
	Swamp	Toic	Total	Swamp	Toic	Total	Swamp	Toic	Total
No canal (Area, km²)	6691	6198	12 889	17 858	10 985	28 843	9520	7411	16 931
Canal (20 Mm³/d) (Area, km²)	3528	4611	8139	14 041	9131	23 172	6191	5756	11 947
Decrease	47.3%	25.6%	36.9%	21.4%	16.9%	19.7%	35.0%	22.3%	29.4%
Canal (25 Mm³/d) (Area, km²)	2868	4296	7164	13 113	8688	21 801	5464	5408	10 872
Decrease	57.1%	30.7%	44.4%	26.6%	20.9%	24.4%	42.6%	27.0%	35.8%

Source: Sutcliffe and Parks (1982).

cuspidata (swamp grass) will reclaim sites which it abandoned to *Cyperus papyrus* (papyrus), just as the papyrus belt will retreat. 'A substantial reduction may also be expected in the zone occupied by *Typha* [an aquatic plant]', for it flourishes in shallow water remote from the river, and will retreat with the diminished flow from the great lakes.[8]

Beyond the lakes and lagoons lie the river-flooded grasslands, the *toic*, where *Oryza longistaminata* and *Echinochloa pyramidalis* provide the rich grass fodder for Nilotic livestock during the dry season. These species will undoubtedly decrease in extent as the floods recede, but with their ability to propagate rapidly they should advance toward the river to replace the area now occupied by *Typha*. The retreat of *Oryza* and *Echinochloa* should in turn ultimately open areas of pasture ideally suited to the *Hyparrhenia rufa* grasslands, or even leave space for the beleaguered woodlands. On the basis of experience elsewhere in Africa, the supposition is that *Hyparrhenia* will probably be preceded by *Sporobolus pyramidalis* until *Hyparrhenia* becomes well established. *Hyparrhenia* dominates the intermediate lands and is dependent upon rainfall rather than on fluctuations in the river-level produced either by the season or by the regulation of the canal.[9] The presence of the canal, incomplete to be sure but still stretching for 267 km across the Sudd plain, has resulted in the 'ponding' of creeping flow, in some places backing up behind the canal for 3 km or more. Here the water is too deep for *Hyparrhenia*, and *Oryza* will remain in the inundated enclaves. On the western side of the canal the increased area made available for pasture by the receding waters will experience heavy grazing, and will no longer receive the waters from creeping flow now impounded behind the canal. Beyond, on the higher ground along the Duk ridge and the Zaraf Island, the woodlands struggle to hold their own against man, his procreation, and his annual burnings of the grasslands which scorch defenceless trees, relieved only by the falling water-levels which had previously killed them as surely as the fire-lines at the end of the rains.

The vegetation of the canal zone feeds the cattle which not only sustain the Nilotes, but are the centre of their cultural

---

[8] Howell *et al.* (1988, p. 389); Mefit–Babtie (Apr. 1983, viii. 11).
[9] Mefit–Babtie (Apr. 1983, viii. 16–17); Howell *et al.* (1988, pp. 390–1).

and spiritual life. The return to normality of the equatorial lake levels combined with the draw-off from the Jonglei Canal should reduce the *toic* grazing lands by between 26 and 31 per cent.[10] The months spent in the cattle camps of the *toic* remain the anticipated time of the Nilotic year, when the wet-season villages and *luaks* are left behind for the very old and the very young, and those in the fullness of life follow the cattle to the rich grasslands of the *toic*. Here life in the cattle camps is convivial and compassionate, but as the waters begin to rise with the return of the flood at the end of the dry season, the *toic* is exhausted and the cattle experience a time of stress as debilitating as the confinement during the rains. The rate of mortality increases among the herds, and milk yields begin to fall after the months of heavy lactation in the camps.[11] The reduction of the *toic* will undoubtedly contribute to the stress experienced by cattle at the end of the rains on more limited grazing in a grassland in transition while the swamp becomes pasture. The dilemma for the Nilotic herdsman will be eased if the adaptation from swamp to pasture and from seasonal grassland to intermediate grazing is gradual, thus allowing scope for the unique and enduring adaptability of the Nilotes and their cattle.

In the vicinity of Bor, any fall in the river-levels will turn swamp to grassland, since there is no *toic* in this region. To the north between Kongor and Jonglei, a diminished river-level should expand dry-season grazing as the water-hungry papyrus gives way to pasture. North from Jonglei the edge of the permanent swamp is much less defined, and the *toic* is not only wider than further south but also under-used, so that its reduction would presumably not prove a hardship.

The changes in the area of river-flooded grassland

and hence dry season grazing, although large, still vary considerably over the area and may not be as drastic as has sometimes been feared, particularly if the river stays at its present high level [*which is unlikely, given current lake levels*]. People may have to move further, and they may have to move to different areas (which could result in conflict), but they are unlikely to run out of dry season grazing completely.[12]

[10] Sutcliffe and Parks (1982, p. 46).
[11] Howell *et al.* (1988, p. 292).   [12] Ibid. 400.

Beyond the river-flooded *toic* stretch the rain-flooded grasslands of the intermediate zone which provide quality pasture early in the rains; but by September grazing is limited as the grass becomes long, coarse, and bitter. Burning at the beginning of the dry season allows a fresh succulent growth to spring forth—if there is sufficient soil moisture. Water is thus the essential ingredient for increasing the extent of the *Hyparrhenia* grasslands to replace the reduced *toic*. But the generation of *Hyparrhenia* grass is dependent upon rainfall, or upon creeping flow impounded by dikes, or upon the canal itself, through small-scale abstractions of Jonglei water onto the intermediate lands. The potential to increase the area of grassland pastures by prudent management of water from Jonglei, if it were possible to make it available, far outweighs the reduction of the *toic* which, in turn, should be able to recover pasture from the shrinking permanent swamp. Rather than being an ecological disaster, the canal has the capability of providing the pasturelands for an ever-increasing human and bovine population.

If abstracted water possessed the potential to increase the size of the intermediate grasslands, the canal would also make available the mixed blessings of modernity—improved access by canal and road to the hitherto remote Upper Nile province. By steamer and Landrover would presumably come the veterinarians with vaccines to cure and prevent cattle disease, merchants to trade, entrepreneurs to initiate a market economy by the export of cattle, and officials with the knowledge to improve breeds and thereby enhance the productivity of milk and meat. Modernity would also bring venereal disease, carpet-baggers from the north, corrupt administrators, discrimination, and exploitation. Both the good and the bad would seriously challenge a way of life which, in the fullness of time, would probably have gone with the wind in any case; but the very presence of the canal will certainly add to the erosion of the traditional ways of Nilotic life which was begun by the floods and continued by the debilitating civil war, which shows no sign of abating, and is in fact now being fought in the very heart of the canal zone. Even if there were no war, water available throughout the year from the canal would establish the importance of the permanent village, hitherto abandoned to the young, the old, and the infirm, during the dry season. The possibility of remaining in the same place the year round would challenge not only the migratory life of the Nilotes but the deep cultural and spiritual traditions of the migration, the cattle camp, and the freedom of the pastures in that best of all possible worlds. With all its costs, the canal will ensnare the Nilotic peoples in a larger brave new world which will threaten the old life with no guarantee of improving its quality.

Although cattle are the staple of Nilotic life, fish are an important ingredient in the Nilotic diet, particularly during the lean months at the end of the dry season. The enlarged permanent swamp of the past quarter-century may have inundated pastures on the one hand but has greatly increased the environment for fish on the other. Indeed, some Nuer and Dinka turned entirely to fishing and hippo-hunting upon losing their herds during the great floods. The *Monythany* Dinka, although despised by the cattle-keepers, live in the depths of the permanent swamp where they have become specialized and successful fisher-folk. In the south the papyrus swamps have greatly increased, as has *Typha* further north, in which some fifty species of Nile fish have proliferated in the complex networks of channels broken by intricate shallows and lagoons. During the high-water season numerous species make their way into the shallow waters of the flood-plain, ideal for spawning. Any decrease in the discharge into the Sudd from the equatorial lakes or the Mongalla torrents has already reduced, and will continue to reduce, the number and size of the lagoons as swamp gives way to grassland. Clearly the quantity of fish is so great that the Nilotes need not fear that the fish will disappear; they will simply not be as abundant. 'Thus, as the swamp contracts and reverts to grasslands, some fishing grounds will be lost and others will become seasonal in nature.' To those inhabitants of the Upper Nile who have been forced to fish for survival, 'their best interests would be served by a return to the pre-1961 discharge levels of the Nile coupled with an operational canal' and their return to cattle-keeping.[13]

[13] Howell *et al.* (1988, p. 405–6).

No consideration of the effects of the canal can be complete
without assessing its impact on wildlife. As with domestic
livestock, the canal will change the habitat in which the last
free-roaming herds of African wildlife follow their migration
patterns. Some have been reduced in numbers by the change;
others have thrived. Those species which dwell in the
permanent swamp are hard-pressed by the reduction of the
Sudd. Others who live on the grass and woodlands should
multiply, along with Nilotic cattle. Some, like the tiang and
the reedbuck gazelles, who perform seasonal migrations
across the line of the canal, have to face a formidable barrier.
'Some will swim, others may try to do so and drown', but the
big ditch of an empty, uncompleted canal has produced a new
obstacle.[14] To swim may be possible; but trapped at the
bottom of a waterless canal, disorientated and frightened,
countless tiang have died. Even more destructive is the
ubiquitous raised roadway thrown up by the tailings from the
excavation of the canal along its east bank. Here is the link to
join the disparate Sudans, north and south; the means to
reach Juba from Khartoum in days rather than weeks; the
pathway to modernity for the southern Sudan. The road is a
symbol of the end of the age of animals, it is the single greatest
threat to their survival. They will come to drink at the canal in
the dry season and cross it during their migrations, and they
will be vulnerable to the guns of the inhabitants, to the
automatic weapons of the armed forces, and to the poachers
who, like vultures, will prey upon the victims of contemporary
civilization. Of the large mammals some are threatened, not
only by automatic weapons, but by the reduction of the Sudd
itself. The elephant, reedbuck, tiang, and waterbuck are at
home on the *toic* and in the swamp, and will have to compete
with the concentration of domestic animals for the reduced
seasonal pastures. Those animals who remain throughout the
year in the swamps, the hippopotamus, buffalo, and the Nile
lechwe and sitatunga gazelles, will obviously have to sustain
themselves on a much-reduced permanent swamp.

Other wildlife, however, should be able to adjust more
readily to the presence of the canal. The bushbuck, grey

[14] Ibid. 409; Mefit–Babtie (Apr. 1983, viii. 49–53).

duiker, hartebeest, Mongalla gazelle, giraffe, roan antelope, and zebra are inhabitants of the rain-fed grasslands and woodlands which should expand with the falling waters, and therefore should be little affected by a changing Sudd. To them the canal presents the same obstacle as for domestic cattle, sheep, and goats. A number of these species undertake extensive migrations which cross the path of the canal. This entails climbing the embankment, descending down the gradual slope, swimming across, and climbing out. The migrating animals, such as the giraffe, Mongalla gazelle, roan antelope, zebra and ostrich, may well split into two populations who will remain permanently east and west of the canal, while others like the elephant, reedbuck, and tiang must migrate. The tiang are a special case in that the main population, numbering well over 350 000, must migrate to survive, and will cross the canal between November and January when the female is near the end of her pregnancy.[15] Although the large-herd-forming antelopes of Africa have proved capable of swimming water-courses, the greatest obstacle for the migrating tiang has been, not a full-flowing canal but the unfinished excavation.

Clearly, the reduction of the permanent swamp is going to have an adverse effect on its most famous resident, the shoebill stork (*Balaeniceps rex*), whose numbers are now thought to be about 5500. Other water-birds may have to compete on the edge of the swamp, where they feed on the fish entrapped in pools and shallow waters. With or without the canal there will always be a permanent swamp; this will, however, diminish, so that bird life in the Sudd will remain more dependent upon the regular rise and fall of the river and its seasonal flooding than upon its diminution.

There remains no doubt that the ecological effects of Jonglei will require an adaptation to the changing environment by livestock, fish, and wildlife; but, with some exceptions, the benefits appear to balance the costs. The swamp and *toic* will be reduced, but the *Hyparrhenia* grasslands and the woodlands should expand behind the receding waters. Abstractions from the canal could provide opportunities for the generation of

---

[15] Howell *et al.* (1988, pp. 411–12).

pastures, woodlands, and the expansion of cultivation. The abundance of fish will diminish, but the total fishery potential of the Sudd remains only partially exploited. Migratory wildlife, such as the tiang, are experiencing serious difficulties in crossing the canal, but many wildlife species remain confined in the permanent swamp, the *Hyparrhenia* grasslands, and woodland habitats virtually unaffected by the regime of the canal. Adaptation to a changing and often hostile environment has been a way of life for the fauna of the upper Nile; the new obstacles posed by the Jonglei Canal must similarly be overcome or accepted.

But there are also a quarter of a million people scattered throughout the canal zone. Before the disruptions of the current civil war the majority of the southern Dinka lived in permanent settlements west of the canal. North of Kongor, the Gaawar Nuer villages are scattered on either side, while the Lou Nuer live to the east; but not all migrate west to the *toic*, preferring instead to go north to the Sobat. The slight rise in the land along the Duk ridge makes these habitations possible; this area will expand west of the canal as the size of the permanent and seasonal swamp is reduced and creeping flow from the east is blocked by the canal itself. Moreover, the possibility of improved access and communication afforded by the canal, as well as services, trade, and administration, will undoubtedly concentrate villages along the line of the canal, with the concomitant advantages and disadvantages.[16] The canal will shorten the navigation route from Khartoum to Juba by some 300 km, and will provide a wide range of new economic alternatives to a people dependent upon herding, cultivation, and fishing. At the same time the Nilotes living west of the canal on the Zaraf Island and in the Bahr al-Ghazal will remain as isolated as they are today, in time of war; for even in peace the steamer traffic along the Bahr al-Jabal will become less frequent, if it does not cease altogether, and the river channel will be subject to the accumulation of sudd obstructions. Oil exploration may serve to open this area, as the canal would allow easier access to the heart of the upper Nile lying to the east; but the exploration and exploitation of

[16] Ibid. 415.

oil reserves in the Sudd, like the completion of the canal itself, all depend upon an elusive peace in that war-torn land.

Much of the optimism about the development of the canal zone during the decade of peace in the southern Sudan has been perhaps misplaced, based as it was on the prospect of the numerous benefits to be derived from the raised roadway. The road is only a panacea if it is properly constructed. Roads throughout the Upper Nile have always been notoriously difficult to build. The cotton soil, which turns to cement in the dry season and viscous mud in the wet, is totally unsuited for road construction. Not a stone nor rock nor pebble can be found in the Upper Nile, the nearest road-making material being the ironstone plateau many long and tortuous kilometres to the south in Equatoria. The terrain of the Upper Nile is broken by cracks, hummocks, and holes. The heavy rains relentlessly destroy the construction of the previous dry season, and what remains is soon turned to deep and impassable ruts by the few vehicles who venture along the tracks of the province. Even the expectations generated by the raised roadway are premature. Not only has the PJTC insisted that the road remain on the east bank of the canal, thus rendering it of little use to the populous southern Dinka whose villages are situated on the west bank, but the surface will not be sealed by gravel, asphalt, or cement, so that the clay debris from the canal will be serrated and gutted during the rains by even a few passing cars and trucks, and by migrating cattle and wildlife crossing the canal. Despite slope and camber to facilitate the run-off of rain-water, erosion will be heavy; and without intensive labour, expensive grading equipment, and constant maintenance, as CCI has learned during canal construction, this road will not become the all-weather, northern link to the south, but just another impassable quagmire in the Upper Nile.

A more important and immediate advantage of the canal will be a permanent water supply from the canal for the inhabitants. Although the water quality of the Bahr al-Jabal does not meet the standards of the World Health Organization, people and animals will drink it if they can reach it. The astonishing failure to install off-take pipes between kilometres 40 and 309, as recommended by CCI and the JEO, will result in cattle concentrating along the banks of the canal in order to drink, pulverizing the road and the canal banks, and devouring the limited pasture near the canal instead of watering from pools and *hafirs* fed by pipes and located a sufficient distance away from the line of the road and canal, where grazing is more plentiful. This irresponsible dereliction and the determination to continue the road along the east bank were decisions which have bitterly alienated the inhabitants—decisions known to all, not just the southern élite, and regarded as showing a hostile lack of sensitivity to the needs of the Nilotes, confirming southern Sudan's deeper feelings of neglect and discrimination, set against meagre financial savings.

Flooding along the east bank from creeping flow has already affected the life of the peoples and animals living east of the canal. Although the impounding of water along the 267 km of excavated canal has not reached the extent that many feared, the accumulation of local precipitation and creeping flow is an obstacle to migrating herds of cattle and wildlife. But, as with so many other aspects of the canal, what is perceived as harmful has in fact presented opportunities. The impounded water can be directed and dissipated, as CCI has demonstrated in its pilot scheme, to produce nutritious and palatable grasses in the dry season. The construction of a network of dikes 3–10 km east of the canal would not be very costly, and would open additional grazing and provide drinking water during some months of the dry season.

Uncontrolled, it [the flooding] may also cause damaging inundation of permanent habitations and their adjacent cultivations; indeed, it had already caused considerable hardship in this way before November 1983 when the matter was raised by the JEO's Annual Co-ordinating Conference at Bor. The failure of the PJTC to acknowledge the serious nature of this problem caused much public concern.[17]

While the Nilotes grumbled about the failure of the government to fulfil the promises made in 1974 of socio-economic improvements in the form of schools, dispensaries, and veterinary services, they had experienced only a few of these

[17] Howell *et al.* (1988, p. 422).

services in the past and consequently regarded their appearance in the present with some scepticism. As the Bucketwheel chewed through the cotton soil of the Upper Nile, however, the canal and its impact upon the region suddenly became a reality. The schools, dispensaries, and cattle vaccines may appear in the promised future, but the excavated canal was now, the present. The failure to provide off-take structures and to control creeping flow produced instant resentment; but the presence of the canal was already disrupting the traditional migratory patterns essential for the very survival of Nilotic cattle and wildlife as early as 1982. Cattle had to move through the intermediate lands, at the end and the beginning of the rains, to the *toic* pastures. During this migration most of the people and their animals in the canal zone had to cross the canal.

Not all the Dinka and Nuer need to cross the canal. The Gok Dinka, south and east of Bor, do not have to cross the canal to reach the Bahr al-Jabal. The Twic and the Athoic Dinka north of Bor have their permanent settlements west of the canal, as do the Gaawar Nuer further north. Most Dinka and Nuer, however, must cross the canal twice, some four times, each passage entailing considerable risk for their cattle and demanding much tiresome work for the herdsmen. The number of annual cattle crossings has been estimated at 700 000; sheep and goats 100 000; people 250 000.[18] Clearly, the proposed ferries and bridges are a totally inadequate solution to these daunting statistics; but the failure to find funding for their implementation produced as much resentment as their inadequacy. Cattle can swim, as they do across the Bahr al-Jabal at Bor and across the upper Sobat, but before entering the water hundreds of thousands of hooves will wreak havoc upon the surface of the canal embankment. Goats and sheep are poor swimmers, as are the young, the old, and the infirm human beings who do not remain in the permanent settlements.[19] Indeed, the resourcefulness of the Nilotic cattlemen will probably prove in the end more effective in getting across the canal than any palliatives the government may offer. The Dinka and the Nuer are adroit herdsmen, and

[18] Mefit–Babtie (Apr. 1983, viii. 37–8).
[19] Howell *et al.* (1988, pp. 426–7).

they will undoubtedly exploit new options presented by the canal while seeking means to overcome them. In 1988, five years after the resumption of civil war in the southern Sudan, the peoples of the canal zone have the worst of all possible worlds—a land ravaged by war and an empty canal providing neither water nor benefits. The challenge to their determination and ingenuity has resulted in their digging out the canal embankment and constructing ramps to drive their cattle across to the intermediate lands and the *toic* pastures.

The renewal of civil war in the Sudan in 1983 has brought the return of famine, disease, and death to the peoples of the upper Nile, with effects even more debilitating than the great floods of the 1960s, the seventeen years of civil war from 1955 to 1972, or an incomplete (or, for that matter, a finished) canal. To be sure, the grievances created by the excavation of Jonglei were substantial ingredients in the overflowing stew of discontent among the southern Sudanese, but they were neither cause nor catalyst for the resumption of war against the Sudan government by Colonel John Garang and his followers in the Sudan Peoples Liberation Army. Even if the canal were to produce no benefits, only costs, human and material, the present conflict has been far more destructive to the livelihood of the Nilotic peoples than would be any changes in their way of life to accommodate themselves to an environment altered by the presence of the canal. Few water projects in the world have undergone such scrutiny as Jonglei; and although further research is always needed in the hope of finding more definitive answers, what has already been accomplished can be the basis of realistic conclusions if and when the Jonglei Canal is finally taking water to the northern Sudan and to Egypt. If properly managed, with sensitivity to the concerns of the inhabitants and a reasonable effort to meet their needs, the potential benefits from Jonglei for the Nilotic peoples far outweigh the potential losses occasioned by the changes in their way of life. No longer can the denizens of the Sudd remain in splendid isolation; independence, floods, and civil war have shown that. It appears on balance that in a changing world it is more prudent to have new options (which Jonglei would provide) than to rely on a tradition challenged from without and from within.

Certainly, changing social and economic patterns in the upper Nile and throughout the Sudan before the outbreak of hostilities in 1983 confirm the demands for benefits which the canal could bring to the region, for without its presence the Upper Nile would undoubtedly continue to be ignored in Khartoum. During the first half of this century subsistence gradually gave way to a cash economy. Following the Second World War the appeal of wage-earning opportunities beyond the provincial boundaries in the northern Sudan produced a trickle, then a stream, and finally a flood of migrant labour. New wealth enabled the Dinka and Nuer of the future canal zone to purchase cattle to be used to advantage in the convoluted negotiations attendant upon marriage. New wealth, accompanied by education, produced an élite aware of the larger and more diverse world beyond the Nilotic plain, and consequently no longer tied, culturally or spiritually, to the traditional social system of lineage, clan, and age-set, the cattle camp, or the *luak*. The outward flow of Nilotes to the north sharply accelerated during the civil war and the great floods. This migratory stream was not reduced by the return of peace in 1972 at the signing of the Addis Ababa accords; in fact it became a flood of mostly young men seeking their fortunes, not only as labourers in the development schemes and construction sites in the north, but also in the rapidly growing urban communities of Juba, Bor, and Malakal in the south. Although living outside the traditional environment, most of the migrants had the same objective—to acquire wealth for the purpose of marriage back in the homelands, or to replace cattle lost in war and floods.

Assaulted on all sides by natural and man-made phenomena, the Nilotic social system's most remarkable attribute was its ability to survive in the face of war, floods, the absence of a productive population, and the challenge to the crucial role of kinship by the ability of young men to purchase cattle for marriage or prestige without relying on the collective responsibility of kinfolk as in the past. The current conflict undoubtedly places even greater strain on the old order by its continuous disruption, by political rather than ecological factors, of the traditional social and economic way of life. The Upper Nile has always been a grain-poor province; it has now become a grainless province, whose future prosperity lies more with the possibilities inherent in the Jonglei Canal scheme upon the return of peace than with continued migration to the north or the frantic search for the few employment opportunities in Juba or Malakal. The possibilities of new productive options rest more with the Jonglei Canal after the destruction of war than with any nostalgia for a return to the old moral order of Nilotic life. Some, like Colonel Garang, may advocate a more revolutionary policy of 'transforming' the Nilotic way of life through large-scale mechanized farming and dramatic changes in land tenure.[20] The Dutch have proved the failure of the former; the success of the latter is most unlikely in the human and natural environment of the Upper Nile, where revolutionary transformations are tempered by the implacable conditions of the Sudd. Indeed, this transformation is more likely to come about by the steady erosion—rather than by any dramatic dissolution—of the traditional social system. If the transformation is to come about, the completion and proper implementation of Jonglei and its attendant development projects will create a greater revolution in the Nilotic moral order, already under great strain, than any massive, mechanical agricultural schemes.

Moreover, the two government institutions authorized to develop Jonglei—the PJTC, concerned with the design and construction of the canal and the larger question of Nile control, and the JEO, created to protect the interests of the people and to oversee the development of their resources—are imperfect and competing, if not actually antagonistic, agencies whose collaboration has been characterized more by suspicion and prevarication than by co-operation and candour. Certainly, the regulations of the canal must be based on sensitivity to local concerns as well as on the need to pass the maximum amount of water down to the northern Sudan and Egypt. No amount of sophistry or rhetoric can claim that Jonglei water is part and parcel of Egypt's historic or acquired rights. Those were defined in the 1959 Nile Waters Agreement; and any additional water obtained by Jonglei or any other conservancy schemes is to be divided in equal shares between Egypt and

[20] See Garang de Mabior (1981).

the Sudan, and not on the basis of past usage or future demands of increasing populations. The stipulation in the Nile Waters Agreement of equal shares for the Sudan was intended, implicitly and explicitly, to make water available for all the Sudanese, not just those living in the arid regions of the northern Sudan. The southern Sudanese of the canal zone have an equal claim to the water as a national resource, just as the northern Sudanese have an equal claim to the oil reserves of the Sudd as a national resource. Any such claims, however, will remain but a bone for the dogs of war if the inhabitants of Jonglei are excluded from any decisions concerning the future operations of the canal, and if no real effort is made to listen to and to rectify their legitimate grievances when peace has returned to the southern Sudan.

Thunder on the Nile

Jonglei? Is that the canal that goes nowhere?

Mrs Louise Jack Collins, 1987

RELATIONS between the southern Sudanese and President Ja'far Numayri began to undergo subtle but important changes not long after the euphoria occasioned by the Addis Ababa Agreement dissipated in the face of the political facts of life in the Sudan. The treaty of integration between Egypt and the Sudan of February 1974, and the subsequent inauguration of the Sudan development corporation for the creation of agricultural schemes in the northern Sudan, disturbed the more sophisticated southerners, while the people expressed their disenchantment by the Juba riots in October and grumbled over food shortages and lack of school facilities. Northern lack of interest, if not neglect, was further underlined for the southerners by the appearance of friendly but frequently competitive humanitarian agencies who, with an imperialism untempered by the paternalism of former British administrators, Catholic fathers, and Protestant missionaries, carved out protectorates in which their eagerness to develop and improve was often compromised by their ethnocentrism and arrogance. In Khartoum, the south was conspicuously under-represented in the corridors of power, having only three Cabinet members in charge of minor ministries.

Nevertheless, even these aberrations could not sour the climate of brotherhood and goodwill which prevailed after Addis Ababa. The mass of southerners, and the new political élite and their extended families who, enjoying official appointments and at least the appearance of power, had a vested interest in the new order created at Addis Ababa, all demonstrated their support for President Numayri, the man who had brought peace. There were incidents—demonstrations at Wau and Akobo—provoked by those who had not reaped the expected rewards after Addis Ababa. They were few, however; and during the attempted *coup d'etat* of July 1976 the south stood firmly behind Numayri. Some thought this to be a futile gesture when the president announced his new national policy of reconciliation in July 1977, by which he was willing to pardon Sadiq al-Mahdi for his efforts to overthrow him the previous year. Although Sadiq al-Mahdi agreed to respect the Addis Ababa Agreement, the southern élite remembered with deep concern his pronouncements and writings in the 1960s concerning the 'southern problem', which emphasized more the Arab and Islamic unity of the Sudan than its diversity. To such southerners, national reconciliation meant the re-establishment of the alliance among the northern ruling families to sustain their political dominance.

The elections scheduled in the south for February 1978 only served to focus the growing but so far ill-defined discontent with the regional government of Abel Alier, which was accused of corruption, inefficiency, tribalism and, more specifically, 'Dinkaism'. There were elements of truth in these charges, but they were untempered by any realization (a characteristic frequently found in political campaigns) of the enormous problems of a devastated economy, a dearth of communications, and a lack of qualified manpower and resources. The people appeared to want new faces in Juba, and Abel and his government were soundly defeated. President Numayri picked the Anya-Nya hero, Major-General Joseph Lagu, to form a new government of ministers 'with goodwill'—a government which was determined to enjoy the fruits of political power without professional competence. Corruption in Juba went hand in hand with drought in the countryside, the follies of well-intentioned but poorly conceived development plans combined with increasing criticism of the government in Khartoum. Lagu's political shuffling within the government at the behest of Numayri created political chaos and infighting within the high executive council at precisely the time, April 1979, when the regime of General Idi Amin collapsed in Uganda before the invasion of the Tanzanian army, resulting in a flood of 30,000 refugees into the southern Sudan. Much worse than the influx of refugees was the tidal wave of weaponry from Amin's well-stocked armouries in northern

Uganda, not far from the borders of the Sudan. With every man his own gunfighter, the problems of public order escalated as traditional ethnic animosities, banditry, revenge, and political dissidence all merged into a welter of insecurity which overwhelmed the police and soon challenged the army.

The reaction to Joseph Lagu was soon mobilized, resulting in more political infighting and charges of corruption, in which Lagu himself was personally implicated—all amidst the prevailing economic stagnation and public disorder. The confusion was further exacerbated by President Numayri launching a new proposal in March 1979 for more local government in the west to satisfy growing discontent in Darfur, where the Ansar, followers of Sadiq al-Mahdi, with assistance from the Libyans, were becoming increasingly restless. Once given official sanction, regionalism generated its own dynamics: Numayri's programme for dividing the northern Sudan into three regions had now evolved into a plan for five, in addition to his regressive idea of redividing the autonomous southern region into the three old provinces of the Condominium—the Upper Nile, the Bahr al-Ghazal, and Equatoria. Such a proposal was completely contradictory to the terms of the Addis Ababa Agreement, and although Numayri intervened once again in the elections of 1980 in an attempt to establish a more stable government in Juba, southern confidence in the president had evaporated. The issue of redivision, now combined with the manipulation of the boundaries along the volatile borderlands between Kordofan and the Bahr al-Ghazal and the question of the siting of a refinery for the recently discovered oil in those disputed marcherlands, revived all the latent southern Sudanese fears of the northerners which had been momentarily laid to rest at Addis Ababa.

Redivision, however, was the central issue. On the one hand it destroyed the cherished Addis Ababa Agreement; on the other it appealed to all the small, non-Nilotic, sedentary ethnic groups in the south who feared the power of the Dinka. Redivision also acted as a catalyst for those Dinka, particularly from the Bahr al-Ghazal in distinction to Abel's coterie of Bor Dinka, to join the redivisionists of Equatoria in an opportunism which had become the principal characteristic of southern

Sudanese politics. Following the precedent he had set years before when he had appointed Abel Alier president of the high executive council before receiving the recommendation of the regional assembly, President Numayri intervened once again to dissolve the assembly by decree on 5 October 1981; he relieved Abel Alier and his ministers of their duties, which he assigned to a provisional council presided over by Major-General Gasmallah Abdallah Rassas, an energetic Muslim southerner from Wau. Since Abel and his Cabinet had vociferously opposed redivision in the south, their summary dismissal demonstrated to the south the ease with which southerners could be manipulated and divided by decree. When Numayri reshuffled his ministers on 24 November 1981, there was no southern minister. Even to the most committed redivisionists in Equatoria, the relegation of the south to yet another pawn on Numayri's political chess-board could not have been more obvious.

The issue of redivision could not be made to disappear by sacking its opponents and appointing a caretaker government under the neutral Rassas. The council itself was divided; so too were the people. Riots between anti- and pro-divisionists broke out in Juba; but to many on either side such discontent concealed other political goals. Behind the apparent concern with the constitutional issue of the president's authority unilaterally to abrogate the Addis Ababa Agreement were the resentments of Equatorians who chafed at Dinkacracy as well as of those Nilotes who were suspicious of the dominant position of the Bor Dinka. In the 'unity' group there were those who had been sworn opponents of Joseph Lagu and his corrupt administration, more flagrant than their own. To confuse the issue President Numayri, in one of his characteristic reversals, announced on 22 February 1982 that there would be no redivision in the south. The redivisionists felt betrayed; the Ansar and Muslim brothers in the north were astonished, since Numayri's decision to abandon redivision in the south was accompanied by his determination to pursue it in the north.

This political turmoil, administrative confusion, and insecurity created in the southern Sudan an atmosphere of frustration and hostility. Numayri turned increasingly to the State security service for support in the midst of the political chaos of his own making, promoting its chief, General Omer Mohammed Al-Tayyib, to be first vice-president in 1982; but to the southerners 'the South remained virtually as it was when the war ended ten years ago'.[1] The elections held in June 1982, presumably to resolve the redivisionist issue, only produced chaos instead of clarity as each amorphous group, the unionists and redivisionists, shattered into particularist segments more concerned with personal alliances than party loyalities, personal gains than public principles. Unable to rally around any standard the southern Sudanese settled for a compromise, Joseph Tambura, an amiable man and a member of one of the great aristocratic families of the Azande, but one with neither the power nor the responsibility necessary for restoring political sense or order to the southern Sudan.

In the midst of the political confusion in the south, President Numayri signed his third charter of integration with Egypt on 12 October 1982.[2] This pact was a transparent effort upon the part of Numayri to bolster his deteriorating economic position. In January 1982 the International Monetary Fund had insisted that Numayri devalue the artificially inflated Sudanese pound. He refused, and the IMF suspended payments on the Sudan's stand-by line of credit. Numayri needed Egyptian economic support, but the integration charter of 1982 included military clauses as well, which enabled the Egyptians to send military advisers unobtrusively to the Sudan. The presence of the Egyptian military in Khartoum provoked a profoundly hostile reaction in the south. It emphasized the idea of Egyptian imperialism which was symbolized by the Jonglei Canal. The preposterous rumour that Egyptian *fallahin* were about to descend upon the canal zone still persisted; it was given credence by the Arab press, and later used by the Sudan People's Liberation Movement as one of its grievances.[3] Since 1976 the canal had become a reality, but the success of the Bucketwheel,

---

[1] *The Economist*, 29 May 1982; Prunier (1986, pp. 27–49).
[2] The previous 2 treaties were in 1970, the more substantive agreement in 1974.
[3] See 'The Middle East', *Asharq al-Awsat* (Beirut), 1 Feb. 1981; Sudan People's Liberation Movement (1983, ch. 5, p. 10).

relentlessly eating its way through the Upper Nile despite the vagaries of southern politics and the forsaken promises of schools, dispensaries, and veterinary services, only dramatized the absence of the more tangible benefits which the Nilotes had been led to believe the canal would bring to their impoverished lives. As the political situation in Khartoum and Juba deteriorated, so the Jonglei Canal emerged as a symbol of frustration and failure.

Ten years after the Addis Ababa Agreement President Numayri toured the south in December 1982. His reception was very different from his earlier visits. He was jeered and stoned in Rumbek—whereupon he ordered the immediate arrest of the anti-redivisionist demonstrators, including that indomitable southern patriot Joseph Oduho, along with members of the regional assembly, Ambrose Ring and Justin Yak, as well as teachers and students at the Rumbek secondary school who were held responsible for the hostile reception. More curious, and indicative of the collapse of confidence between Numayri and the southerners, was the arrest of Dhol Achuil and Matthew Ubor. Achuil was an articulate lawyer and former commissioner of Lakes province. Ubor was an economist and speaker of the regional assembly. They were both redivisionists and supported James Tambura. Yet when they criticized the government before southern students at Khartoum University in February 1983, they were arrested.

Given the discontent with Numayri, the political chaos over redivision, economic neglect, and the presence of large quantities of automatic weapons, it is surprising that violence did not erupt long before the mutiny of the 105th battalion of the Sudan army garrisoned at Bor. Ironically, the detonator of their demonstration was the same as that which had led to the mutiny of the southern soldiers of the Egyptian army against the orders of Emin Pasha in 1887 and the troops of the Equatorial corps in 1955. The 105th battalion consisted of former members of the Anya-Nya integrated into the Sudan army after the Addis Ababa Agreement. Like their predecessors they had settled in Bor, intermarried, and, to supplement their income, had farms in the surrounding countryside where they led a pastoral life while soldiering. The orders of

President Numayri to reassign these garrisons to stations in the north meant removing the members of the 105th battalion to the alien environment of northern Sudan, away from their families and surrounded by rumours of being sent to Iraq to fight in the war against Iran, a conflict which they regarded as not their war.

In January 1983 the garrison at Bor demonstrated, and there were several casualties. Peace was restored, but the mutineers remained unpunished and unrepentant. A commission of inquiry, presided over by Dhol Achuil, investigated the incident and was critical of the insensitivity of the northern officers. The following month Dhol Achuil was arrested in Khartoum after speaking to southern students. During the ensuing months the garrison continued to smoulder. There were numerous attempts at mediation, including efforts by Abel Alier himself, with no demonstrable results. Finally, in May 1983, President Numayri sent Colonel John Garang, director of research at the headquarters of the Sudan army in Khartoum, to reason with the recalcitrant garrison and, it was hoped, to restore order.

Colonel Garang was no ordinary officer. Born in Wangkulei on 23 June 1945 in the Upper Nile province and educated at a mission school at Wau and Magambia secondary school in Tanganyika, he left Africa for Grinnell College in Iowa on a scholarship, where he gained a BA degree in economics. Upon returning to the Sudan he joined the Anya-Nya, despite the reservation of Joseph Lagu that he was over-educated—which he undoubtedly was. He served with the Anya-Nya from 1971 to 1972, and after the signing of the Addis Ababa Agreement he was commissioned as a captain in the Sudan army in the 104th and later the 105th battalion. Here he worked assiduously to promote the welfare of his men, organizing literacy classes and self-help schemes. As part of his military training he attended the US infantry school at Fort Benning, Georgia, in 1974. He returned to the USA in 1977 and obtained an M.Sc. degree in agricultural economics in 1980 and a Ph.D. the following year from Iowa State University.

Garang's dissertation was about the Jonglei Canal. His thesis echoed the aspirations of the national council and the JEO; but because intensive development projects in the northern Sudan would exhaust existing water supplies for irrigation by 1984, he argued that future development must be supported by rain-fed agriculture, the most suitable region for this being the Nilotic plain. Consequently, if Jonglei were developed merely as a conduit for water to irrigate Egypt and the Sudan, it would disrupt the traditional way of living of the Nilotic peoples with no compensating advantages. If properly designed, managed, and financed, the canal had the potential to create opportunities for regional development and national integration far beyond the localized schemes of integrated rural development, like Kongor, which Garang dismissed as 'marginal improvement'. His objections were not to the canal itself but to the limited strategies for development formulated by the national council and the JEO. In effect, he anticipated the criticisms levelled at Jonglei during the conference at Bor in November 1983—that the socio-economic schemes had been a failure and that the basic technologies of the UNDP and ILACO for modernization were inappropriate and would 'likely end up merely containing and managing poverty and misery in the area'.[4] He identified four basic necessities for preventing poverty and misery—modern drainage and irrigation works, mechanized farming, new forms of land tenure, and the reorganization of the countryside into compact villages. Whereas the JEO had based its development strategies on the improvement of traditional livelihoods, John Garang was advocating a more sweeping revolution—without identifying where the resources would be found to accomplish it. Presumably, the human and material capital would come from the restructuring of Sudanese political power under a federal system, in which the disparate regions of the Sudan would have a greater say in the distribution of the nation's resources. Whether a federal system would be able to mobilize or dissipate these resources remains to be seen.

Upon returning to the Sudan from Ames, Iowa, Colonel Garang was made director of research at the headquarters of the Sudan army in Khartoum, where he observed the corruption within Numayri's inner circle and watched with dismay the latter's unilateral decrees to undo the Addis Ababa

[4] Garang de Mabior (1981, p. 227).

Agreement. Although his dissatisfaction with President Numayri was shared privately, it was publicly challenged when he was sent to Bor to confront the mutineers of the 105th battalion. Here, among his relatives, his farm, and his former soldiers, he received the supplications from the men to lead them. For two days he agonized over his loyalty to President Numayri, before defecting on 16 May 1983 at the head of the mutineers. His defection was a catalyst for southerners from other garrisons in the Upper Nile and the Bahr al-Ghazal to drift into the bush with their weapons to join him. Even in Equatoria, where there was no love for the Nilotes, soldiers from Torit, Kapoeta, and some from western Equatoria sought out Garang, who had taken up sanctuary just over the border in Ethiopia. By the summer of 1983 more than 2500 men had deserted from the army in the southern Sudan, soon to be joined by an indeterminate number of police, prison warders, and gamekeepers, all with their arms.

The reaction in Khartoum was dismay among the civilians and the decree of 5 June by President Numayri redividing the south into three autonomous regions, making a mockery of consultation and fools of those southerners who still believed in or benefited from his leadership. The Addis Ababa Agreement was now officially dissolved; it had been effectively dead since 5 October 1981, when Numayri had summarily dismissed the regional government of Abel Alier, but its formal demise only appeared to give legitimacy to Garang's call to arms. This conclusion seemed fully confirmed two months later, when Numayri announced, again by decree, on 8 September that the Sharia laws of Islam would replace the Sudan civil and penal codes as the law of the land. This eclectic decision was motivated by Numayri's political manœuvres in the northern Sudan to secure support for his regime; but there was no other issue guaranteed to mobilize southerners of every ethnic group against the government. 'The symbolic impact of the decision was much greater than its practical consequences', since the laws were never rigorously applied to the Muslims or non-Muslims of the southern Sudan.[5]

Throughout the summer of 1983 the flow of recruits into the

<hr>

[5] Prunier (1986, p. 59).

bush steadily increased, from schoolboys to that old political
warhorse Joseph Oduho and the former foreign minister
Mansour Khalid, who came to offer their services to the
political arm of the organization, the Sudan People's Liberation
Movement (SPLM). During that summer Garang was absorbed
with two principal problems. The first was the difficult task of
welding his forces, soon swollen to some 4000 veterans, into a
cohesive guerilla army, the Sudan People's Liberation Army
(SPLA), with its training camps located in the safety of the
Baro salient of Ethiopia, which protrudes onto the Nilotic
plain below the Ethiopian escarpment. The second and more
immediate threat came from Garang's chief rival, known as
Anya-Nya II, led by one of the former Anya-Nya leaders who
had never accepted the Addis Ababa Agreement, Gabriel
Gaitut, a Nuer from Akobo trained in Israel who had survived
during the years of peace more on banditry than on principles.
His men, mostly Nuer while Garang's were mostly Dinka,
numbered considerably fewer than those of the SPLA, but
throughout that summer Garang and Gaitut carried on an
acrimonious dialogue at the headquarters of the SPLA at
Bilpam, west of Gambila, in Ethiopian territory. The debate,
in effect, was a contest for leadership of the movement.
Garang argued that the SPLA represented all the Sudanese
people, not just the southerners, seeking to overthrow the
present regime, particularly President Numayri, and the
establishment of a democratically elected federal government
to rule over a united Sudan. Gaitut, whose political horizons
were much narrower than Garang's, demanded a separate,
southern independent state. After the promulgation of the
September laws Gaitut, in frustration at Garang's intransigence,
departed from Bilpam in a huff with several hundred followers
to the Zaraf Island, where he sulked at his failure to win over
Garang's troops. By November, however, he had realized the
futility of his isolation and returned to the fold of the SPLA,
where he sought by stealth to achieve what he had failed to
accomplish in open debate. His inept attempts to subvert
individual officers and men of the SPLA only forced a final
confrontation, where he was killed in a shoot-out between the
SPLA and his Anya-Nya II in February 1984.

Upon Gaitut's departure for the Zaraf Island in November,

John Garang had turned to the task of revolution. During the late summer and early autumn the SPLA had overrun isolated police posts and small army garrisons, culminating in the destruction of Maluel Gahoth on 17 November. More important was Garang's determination to strike at the two successful development projects in the southern Sudan, in order to embarrass the government and deprive it of the potential gains from the multinational corporations, Chevron Overseas Petroleum, which had discovered oil, and the Compagnie de Constructions Internationales, which had discovered water. Garang's decision to terminate the excavation of the Jonglei Canal coincided with and was confirmed by the Bor conference of 10 November 1983. This meeting was convened at Bor by the JEO, and consisted of the planners and the PJTC from Khartoum, administrators of the international aid agencies, members of the Mefit–Babtie research team, politicians, and the local people from the canal zone, their elders, and their representatives. Members of the SPLA/SPLM were also there. It was a tempestuous occasion, in which the grievances against the canal were vehemently expressed; these were soon to reappear in the warnings by the SPLM to CCI to cease its operations in the canal zone. Six days later the SPLA seized nine CCI employees, seven French and two Pakistanis (released unharmed three days later at Panganyoor), with a warning to CCI that continued excavation would result in further action by the SPLA. It was no coincidence that this incident was timed to precede President Numayri's forthcoming visit to Paris, as an additional embarrassment to his government. The Bucketwheel came to an ungainly halt.[6]

On 30 November Joseph Oduho wrote to the Egyptian ambassador to Kenya, giving specific reasons for Garang's decision to have the SPLA terminate the construction of the canal. The abrogation of the Addis Ababa Agreement was the cause of the resumption of the civil war, but the stoppage of work on the canal was the result of the failure to honour promises to the southern Sudanese, of which the installation of pipes for drinking and irrigation water led the list. 'Work on

---

[6] Collins (1985, p. 145).

the canal must remain stopped', Oduho wrote, until these and other grievances—the failure to build schools, dispensaries, and bridges—were satisfied, 'otherwise no work need take place till our control of the Sudan is complete'.[7] On 7 December Oduho prepared a second letter to Chevron, the Total Oil Company, and CCI demanding that the French cease operations immediately, assuring the company that the SPLA/SPLM 'had no grudges' and had no intentions to renegotiate agreements to replace CCI.

Although we are aware that your firm was only hired to excavate the canal, you will however realise that there are parts of the agreement that deal with the welfare of the people whose life would be affected by the canal as well as the wildlife of this region of our country.

As far as Garang was concerned these issues had not been resolved by the PJTC, the JEO, or the Sudan government.

In the meantime agricultural projects, hospitals, towns and model villages that were to be carried out in the canal zone will only remain in the text of the agreement never to be executed after you have completed your works on the canal. You can therefore see our determination to see to it that the work on the canal stops.[8]

The Bucketwheel had reached kilometre 267 before it turned its last cubic metre of cotton soil, having excavated 65.5 Mm^3 in five years. The construction of Jonglei was ahead of schedule, and its completion by 13 March 1985 assured. The unfilled canal cutting across the Nilotic plain was a dramatic symbol of the changes rapidly overtaking the peoples of the canal zone, whose herds, as well as wildlife, were already having to cope with the presence of a big ditch without water whose steep banks at the level of the canal presented a major obstacle. Moreover, the fragile structures which marked the beginnings of the Kongor integrated rural development project, the frustrated efforts to promote fishing in the remote regions of the permanent swamps, and the failure of mechanized farming at Penykou all seemed a

---

[7] J. Oduho, chairman of the political and foreign affairs committee of the Sudan People's Liberation Movement, to the Egyptian ambassador to Kenya, 30 Nov. 1983, published in *Horn of Africa*, 8/1 (1985), pp. 53–5.

[8] J. Oduho to Chevron, Total, and CCI companies, 7 Dec. 1983, ibid. 52–3.

pathetic attempt at fulfilment—if not a betrayal—of the promises made by Abel Alier, in his ringing speech before the regional assembly in November 1974, 'to drive our people to paradise' by the economic and social development of the canal zone. The Jonglei Canal was no longer a daring engineering project in the hydrological development of the Nile valley but the symbol of all the frustration and resentment produced by the failure of the national council, the JEO, and the PJTC to match the skill of the canal-builders. No one was more aware of this than Garang, the student of Jonglei and native of the region, who perceived that to terminate construction of the canal would not only embarrass the Sudan government but would be popular among the people upon whom he was dependent for the local support and the success of the SPLM in the upper Nile.

Following the abduction of the French and Pakistani employees of CCI a week after the Bor conference, most of the French and Pakistani engineers and technicians were withdrawn to Sobat camp; wives and children were quietly returned to France. At Sobat the French began to dismantle the camp with the intention of relocating it at Bor, a project which had been previously scheduled by CCI but which could now be done more easily while the Bucketwheel was shut down. Reinforcements from the Sudan army appeared to support the platoon assigned to protect the installation. The French had no further warnings, for unfortunately the letter from Joseph Oduho was too little and too late. In a BBC interview during the first week of February 1984, Benjamin Bol Akok, the representative of the SPLM in Britain, indicated that a letter had been written to CCI in December, and the Oduho letter was subsequently sent by Bol to CCI via the French embassy in London. It reached the Khartoum office of CCI on 14 February, four days after the SPLA had attacked the Sobat camp, driven off the defenders, and destroyed much of the facility, on Friday 10 February. The previous evening an ominous silence had settled over the camp.

We [Mme Vidal, M. Ben, M. Reynaud, and Peter Clarke] were eating on the verandah. There wasn't any noise. There was a silence to which we were not accustomed . . . and the dog too, she was

worried. So when we finished eating we took the dog, and we walked
Peter [Clarke] to his bungalow and then returned. But it was all so
strange because [there was] nobody, nothing, not a noise, just an
agonizing silence. And suddenly around a quarter to four [in the
morning], I heard a loud 'Boom'! I got up and put on a *jallabia* and
began to make coffee. You could hear the mortars firing in both
directions. A bullet went through the bungalow; the rebels were in the
garden and the government troops were behind it [the bungalow].
Bullets were going through in all directions banging on the saucepans.
We were caught in a crossfire. I was thinking. 'When the day comes,
they will stop.' But no! They kept on shooting until 9 [a.m.].[9]

The SPLA had in fact infiltrated themselves between the
Sudanese guards stationed on the perimeter and the installation
itself, so that the stores and living quarters were caught in a
cross-fire which cut down Peter Clarke, the Australian bush
pilot, near his plane on the exposed runway. The SPLA took
six hostages indiscriminately, two French, a Scot, a Kenyan
Englishman and his pregnant German wife, though they
specifically sought the camp doctor without success. Having
routed the Sudanese guards, the SPLA did not remain long.
One drank coffee with Mme Vidal; others 'liberated' the bar
and told the French to leave immediately, for they would
return that night. Then they disappeared as silently as they
had come.

Upon their departure pandemonium broke over the camp,
and there was a general rush for the barge, the *Biarritz*, under
the command of Captain Eugene Chevrolleau, which had
fortuitously arrived at the Sobat camp from Bor at about eight
o'clock to see the smoke rising from the burning stores and
commissariat before docking to take on the camp personnel as
the SPLA retired with their hostages.[10] Most reached the
barge with only the clothes on their backs; others had the
presence of mind to return for a dog, the cash-box, spare
parts. By midday the *Biarritz* was steaming for Malakal,
where Chevron, at the request of CCI, had hastily mobilized
its fleet of aircraft to fly out the evacuees. CCI immediately
announced the termination of all work on the canal, leaving
behind the ruins of Sobat camp to join the lone dead tree at

[9] Interview with Mme L. Vidal, 12 Jan. 1987.
[10] Interview with Mme C.-L. Chevrolleau, 12 Jan. 1987.

the landmark of the confluence between the Sobat and the White Nile.[11]

In Paris the canal-builders remain determined to finish what they have begun. When peace will return to the southern Sudan no one can predict, but that does not appear to have diminished the resolve of the leaders of GTM to complete the Jonglei Canal. 'We are canal-builders, and we will complete what we have begun whatever the cost.'[12] On 20 August 1986 Orenstein and Koppel, at the request of CCI, estimated the cost of a new Bucketwheel at $8,216,654.[13] The total cost of reviving Jonglei, including the Bucketwheel, barges, bulldozers, planes, and domestic facilities, was calculated at $48 million.

Today, a big ditch stretches from the Sobat 267 km to the Bucketwheel, which squats silent and forlorn, towering into the sky above the Nilotic plain like a great ship upon a sea of Sudd, now covered with rust by the heat and humidity of the sun and rains of the Upper Nile, the victim of a long, bloody, and debilitating war. Behind the dying body of the Bucketwheel, the very symbol of triumphant technology in this century, lies a big ditch—where half a ditch is worth less than no ditch at all.

[11] These events have been reconstructed from the testimony of CCI employees at the Sobat camp during the attack by the SPLA, and of members of the SPLA who participated in the assault. I have flown many thousands of miles with Peter Clarke who, although a taciturn man, would in the boredom of flight regale me with stories of his flying days in the Solomon Islands. The incident was widely reported in the world press. See J. de Linares, 'Soudan: Nouvel enlèvement de techniciens français', *Le Matin*, 13 Feb. 1984. Upon the appeal by GTM and the European diplomatic community in Addis Ababa, Ursula Morson, who was 8 months pregnant and required medical treatment, was released with her 18-month old son, Lloyd, into the custody of the ambassador of the Federal Republic of Germany in Addis Ababa on 13 Mar. 1984 and flown to her home in Nairobi: *Ethiopian Herald*, 13 and 14 Mar. 1984. The remaining hostages, Yves Parisse and Michel Dupire from France, Ian Bain from Britain, and Gwyn Morson from Kenya, were less fortunate. The SPLA demanded a ransom from GTM of F10 million, a radio, and a large quantity of clothing and boots. The negotiations were difficult and protracted as the French government, under pressure from GTM, mobilized an intensive diplomatic campaign, including the assistance of a dozen African countries, directed at the government of Ethiopia. After nearly a year in confinement, during which they were well treated, all 4 were released on 29 Jan. 1985 for 'humanitarian reasons' and in return for 'compensations' to the SPLA.

[12] F. Lemperiere to the author, 13 Jan. 1987.

[13] Orenstein and Koppel to CCI (M. Vallin), 20 Aug. 1986 (Nanterre, GTMI). The price was quoted as FF194 000 plus DM 17 195 062, at a rate of exchange of FF6.8 or DM2.1 to the dollar.

Three months after the destruction of Sobat camp, the annual
rains failed in Ethiopia. The drought resulted in the lowest
Nile flood of this century and the death from famine and
disease, despite massive international aid, of over a million
Ethiopians and an unknown number of Sudanese. The
Egyptians would have suffered commensurately, as they had
done in the past, if it had not been for the reservoir behind the
Aswan high dam. But even the Sadd al-Aali has not proved
adequate to withstand a decade of less than average rainfall in
the Ethiopian highlands. From 1977 there has been a
precipitous decrease in the volume of Nile water, 86 per cent
of which comes from the Ethiopian plateau. From 1870 to
1987, 117 years, the average annual flow of the Nile as
measured at Aswan was 88 billion m³. This generous volume
is distorted by the high flows from 1870 to 1899. A more
accurate reading, and one which was accepted by both the
Egyptians and the Sudanese in the 1959 Nile Waters
Agreement, is an average mean annual flow from 1899 to 1959
of 84 billion m³. During the twentieth century the Nile flows
fluctuated from 120 billion m³ in 1916 to 42 billion in 1984.
During the past decade, 1977–87, however, the average mean
annual flow of the Nile has been recorded at 72 billion m³; but
what is more disturbing is the plunge from 1984 to 1987, when
the Nile flows declined by 28 per cent from 72 billion to
52 billion m³.

The Egyptian response has been one of surprise and
anguish. Given all the data, the statistical analyses, the
application of probability theory to models of best and worst
scenarios, no one could have predicted this steady decline in
Nile flows over the past decade. Hurst's random periodicities
were the result of half a century of sustained Nile studies from
a data base which was flawed, to be sure, in past centuries but
which has been very precise from 1870 to the present. Nothing
in Hurst's probability models contemplated Nile flows like
those recorded in 1984 (42 billion m³), 1985 (64 billion), 1986
(56 billion), and 1987 (45 billion). This was neither God's
doing nor that of the Ethiopians.

These flows would have threatened the Pharaohs; still less
can they accommodate an Egyptian population expanding
today at an annual rate of 3.4 per cent—an additional 1.7

million Egyptians to consume the water, along with the 52 million people who now inhabit the Nile valley in Egypt. Although accurate measurements are improbable given the number of variables, the crops of Egypt required some 54 billion m³ annually during 1984–7. Moreover, the irrigation upon which this cultivation depends is now almost a century old, and some works date back to the days of Muhammad 'Ali, the father of modern Egypt, in the early decades of the nineteenth century. These systems waste water, and although the Egyptians have opened areas with the highest state of the art in irrigation technology, they are too few and too capital-intensive to have any significant impact on Egypt's water balance. The antiquated irrigation system by which basin irrigation is still practised and the canals and barrages built in this century are profligate wasters of water, creating a conveyance loss by evaporation in the canals and basins of probably another 10 billion m³.

Egyptian households require 3.5 billion m³, while industry consumes another 3 billion. Navigation and barrage protection probably need another 3 billion.[14] Thus the mean average annual total demand, including domestic and industrial use, navigation and barrage protection, irrigation, and evaporation loss during these years of little rainfall in Ethiopia has been approximately 74 billion m³. Thirteen billion have probably been reclaimed through re-used drainage and available ground-water, leaving the Egyptians, during these years of drought, to find 61 billion m³ to quench their thirst and to grow their crops for cash and consumption. The prospect of finding sufficient water is not good, unless one looks southward from the Sadd al-Aali 2000 miles to the lakes of equatorial Africa.

Left with a demand for 61 billion m³, Egypt must today examine what will come down the river and what remains in the great reservoir at Aswan. As of August 1987 the level of Lake Nasser was 17 billion m³ above dead storage, to which can be added 45 billion m³, the 1987 annual flow as measured at

[14] Barrage protection is the necessity of maintaining the head or pressure on the barrages to avoid the danger of collapse. This was a contentious issue during the negotiations over Egypt's water requirements leading to the 1959 Nile Waters Agreement.

Aswan, to provide a water balance for Egypt of 62 billion m³. From this munificent sum must be extracted 13 billion, lost by evaporation in Lake Nasser. Thus in the dry winter of 1988 Egypt had available for her needs some 49 billion m³ for crop needs, conveyance loss, household and industrial use, navigation and barrage protection, above the dead storage limit, when the decision had to be made to sacrifice water for crops or hydroelectric power.[15]

Egypt appeared to be on the brink. With water demands of nearly 61 billion m³ and an available supply of only 49 billion, the Egyptian water deficit in 1988 amounted to 12 billion m³ or 19 per cent less than demand. This was a new and perplexing situation for the Egyptians. The high dam was constructed to relieve Egypt of the tyranny of drought and famine. The euphoria over the completion of the Sadd al-Aali did not take into consideration the acts of man, nor the seeming change of atmospheric patterns producing a 'periodicity' which even Hurst had not contemplated. Whether these patterns are random or irreversible remains unclear, but they have certainly introduced a new dimension in Nile hydrology to revive the ancient fears of the Pharaohs, pashas, proconsuls, and today's elected rulers of Egypt. These fears have emphasized as never before the need for new water from the south, in the equatorial lakes, where there is water despite the return of Lakes Victoria and Albert to more normal levels— water, however, which cannot be tapped by Egypt without Jonglei.

Yet the debate continues. To many scientists, the Nile drought of this decade is the manifestation of significant atmospheric and environmental changes reminiscent of dinosaurian disasters, many millennia in the past and irreversible. Others argue that the low Nile flows may only be the fabled biblical seven years of famine. The only certainty appears to be that neither protagonist has made a convincing

---

[15] 'Dead storage' is a term used by hydrologists to determine the amount of water that must be retained in a reservoir to maintain its integrity. In the case of Lake Nasser this amount was 30 billion m³. If the lake-level falls below 30 billion m³, the turbines at Aswan (which produce 40% of Egypt's hydroelectric power) will be in danger of admitting air bubbles which would implode and destroy them. See I. Murray (1987); Evans (1987); also pers. comm. from T. E. Evans, director, Sir M. MacDonald and Partners Ltd., Cambridge.

case, for in August 1988 Ethiopia and the Sudan experienced the greatest rainfall and the most extensive flooding in this century, and far greater than any recorded in the nineteenth century. Until the completion of the Aswan dam in 1902 the Egyptians feared flood as much as drought. Now they welcome the waters to fill their depleted reservoir and provide water for produce and power. Meanwhile the Sudanese have lost their homes and land to the life-giving waters.

Appendix

Agreement
between
the Republic of the Sudan
and
the United Arab Republic
for the Full Utilization of the Nile Waters

As the River Nile needs projects for its full control and for increasing its yield for the full utilization of its waters by the Republic of the Sudan and the United Arab Republic on technical working arrangements other than those now applied:

And as these works require for their execution and administration, full agreement and co-operation between the two Republics in order to regulate their benefits and utilize the Nile waters in a manner which secures the present and future requirements of the two countries:

And as the Nile Waters Agreement concluded in 1929 provided only for the partial use of the Nile Waters and did not extend to include a complete control of the River waters, the two Republics have agreed on the following:–

First:

THE PRESENT ACQUIRED RIGHTS

1. That the amount of the Nile waters used by the United Arab Republic until this Agreement is signed shall be her acquired right before obtaining the benefits of the Nile Control Projects and the projects which will increase its yield and which projects are referred to in this Agreement. The total of this acquired right is 48 Milliards of cubic meters per year as measured at Aswan.

2. That the amount of the waters used at present by the Republic of Sudan shall be her acquired right before obtaining the benefits of the projects referred to above. The total amount of this acquired right is 4 Milliards of cubic meters per year as measured at Aswan.

Second:

AGREEMENT OF THEIR BENEFITS BETWEEN THE TWO REPUBLICS

1. In order to regulate the River waters and control their flow into the sea, the two Republics agree that the United Arab Republic constructs the Sudd el Aali at Aswan as the first link of a series of projects on the Nile for over-year storage.

2. In order to enable the Sudan to utilise its share of the water, the two Republics agree that the Republic of Sudan shall construct the Roseires Dam on the Blue Nile and any other works which the Republic of the Sudan considers essential for the utilization of its share.

3. The net benefit from the Sudd el Aali Reservoir shall be calculated on the basis of the average natural River yield of water at Aswan in the years of this century, which is estimated at about 84 Milliards of cubic meters per year. The acquired rights of the two Republics referred to in Article 'First' as measured at Aswan, and the average of losses of over-year storage of the Sudd el Aali Reservoir shall be deducted from this yield, and the balance shall be the net benefit which shall be divided between the two Republics.

4. The net benefit from the Sudd el Aali Reservoir mentioned in the previous item shall be divided between the two Republics at the ratio of 14½ for the Sudan and 7½ for the United Arab Republic so long as the average river yield remains in future within the limits of the average yield referred to in the previous paragraph. This means that, if the average yield remains the same as the average of the previous years of this century which is estimated at 84 Milliards, and if the losses of over-year storage remain equal to the present estimate of 10 Milliards, the net benefit of the Sudd el Aali Reservoir shall be 22 Milliards of which the share of the Republic of the Sudan shall be 14½ Milliards, and the share of the United Arab Republic shall be 7½ Milliards. By adding these shares to their acquired rights, the total share from the net yield of the Nile after the full operation of the Sudd el Aali Reservoir shall be 18½ Milliards for the Republic of the Sudan and 55½ Milliards for the United Arab Republic. But if the average yield increases, the resulting net benefit from this increase shall be divided between the two Republics, in equal shares.

5. As the net benefit from the Sudd el Aali (referred to in item 3 Article Second) is calculated on the basis of the average natural yield of the river at Aswan in the years of this century after the deduction therefrom of the acquired rights of the two Republics and the average losses of over-year storage at the Sudd el Aali Reservoir, it is agreed that this net benefit shall be the subject of revision by the two parties at reasonable intervals to be agreed upon after starting the full operation of the Sudd el Aali Reservoir.

6. The United Arab Republic agrees to pay to the Sudan Republic 15 Million Egyptian Pounds as full compensation for the damage resulting to the Sudanese existing properties as a result of the storage in the Sudd el Aali Reservoir up to a reduced level of 182 meters (survey datum). The payment of this compensation shall be effected in accordance with the annexed agreement between the two parties.

7. The Republic of the Sudan undertakes to arrange before July 1963, the final transfer of the population of Halfa and all other Sudanese inhabitants whose lands shall be submerged by the stored water.

8. It is understood that when the Sudd el Aali is fully operated for over-year storage, the United Arab Republic will not require storing any water at Gebel Aulia Dam. And the two contracting parties will, in due course, discuss all matters related to this renunciation.

Third:

PROJECTS FOR THE UTILIZATION OF LOST WATERS IN THE NILE BASIN

In view of the fact that at present, considerable volumes of the Nile Basin Waters are lost in the swamps of Bahr El Jebel, Bahr El Zeraf, Bahr el Ghazal and the Sobat River, and as it is essential that efforts should be exerted in order to prevent these losses and to increase the yield of the River for use in agricultural expansion in the Republics, the two Republics agree to the following:

1. The Republic of the Sudan in agreement with the United Arab Republic shall construct projects for the increase of the River yield by preventing losses of waters of the Nile Basin, the swamps of Bahr El Jebel, Bahr el Zeraf, Bahr el Ghazal and its tributaries, the Sobat River and its tributaries and the White Nile Basin. The net yield of these projects shall be divided equally between

the two Republics and each of them shall also contribute equally to the costs.

The Republic of the Sudan shall finance the above-mentioned projects out of its own funds and the United Arab Republic shall pay its share in the costs in the same ratio of 50% allotted for her in the yield of these projects.

2. If the United Arab Republic, on account of the progress in its planned agricultural expansion, should find it necessary to start on any of the increase of the Nile yield projects, referred to in the previous paragraph, after its approval by the two Governments and at a time when the Sudan Republic does not need such project, the United Arab Republic shall notify the Sudan Republic of the time convenient for the former to start the execution of the project. And each of the two Republics shall, within two years after such notification, present a date-phased programme for the utilisation of its share of the waters saved by the project, and each of the said programmes shall bind the two parties. The United Arab Republic shall at the expiry of the two years, start the execution of the projects, at its own expense. And when the Republic of Sudan is ready to utilise its share according to the agreed programme, it shall pay to the United Arab Republic a share of all the expenses in the same ratio as the Sudan's share in benefit is to the total benefit of the project; provided that the share of either Republic shall not exceed one half of the total benefit of the project.

Fourth:

TECHNICAL CO-OPERATION BETWEEN THE TWO REPUBLICS

1. In order to ensure the technical co-operation between the Governments of the two Republics, to continue the research and study necessary for the Nile control projects and the increase of its yield and to continue the hydrological survey of its upper reaches, the two Republics agree that immediately after the signing of this Agreement a Permanent Joint Technical Commission shall be formed of an equal number of members from both parties; and its functions shall be:-

    (a) The drawing of the basis outlines of projects for the increase of the Nile yield, and for the supervision of the studies necessary for the finalising of projects, before presentation of the same to the Governments of the two Republics for approval.

(b) The supervision of the execution of the projects approved by the Governments.

(c) The drawing up of the working arrangements for any works to be constructed on the Nile, within the boundaries of the Sudan, and also for those to be constructed outside the boundaries of the Sudan, by agreement with the authorities concerned in the countries in which such works are constructed.

(d) The supervision of the application of all the working arrangements mentioned in (c) above in connection with works constructed within the boundaries of Sudan and also in connection with the Sudd el Aali Reservoir and Aswan Dam, through official engineers delegated for the purpose by the two Republics; and the supervision of the working of the Upper Nile projects, as provided in the agreements concluded with the countries in which such projects are constructed.

(e) As it is probable that a series of low years may occur and a succession of low levels in the Sudd el Aali Reservoir may result to such an extent as not to permit in any one year the drawing of the full requirements of the two Republics, the Technical Commission is charged with the task of devising a fair arrangement for the two Republics to follow. And the recommendations of the Commission shall be presented to the two Governments for approval.

2. In order to enable the Commission to exercise the functions enumerated in the above item, and in order to ensure the continuation of the Nile gauging and to keep observations on all its upper reaches, these duties shall be carried out under the technical supervision of the Commission by the engineers of the Sudan Republic, and the engineers of the United Arab Republic in the Sudan and in the United Arab Republic and in Uganda.

3. The two Governments shall form the Joint Technical Commission, by a joint decree, and shall provide it with its necessary funds from their budgets. The Commission may, according to the requirements of work, hold its meetings in Cairo or in Khartoum. The Commission shall, subject to the approval of the two Governments, lay down regulations for the organization of its meetings and its technical, administrative and financial activities.

Fifth:

GENERAL PROVISIONS

1.   If it becomes necessary to hold any negotiations concerning the Nile waters, with any riparian state, outside the boundaries of the two Republics, the Governments of the Sudan Republic and the United Arab Republic shall agree on a unified view after the subject is studied by the said Technical Commission. The said unified view shall be the basis of any negotiations by the Commission with the said states.

If the negotiations result in an agreement to construct any works on the river, outside the boundaries of the two Republics, the Joint Technical Commission shall, after consulting the authorities in the Governments of the States concerned, draw all the technical execution details and the working and maintenance arrangements. And the Commission shall, after the sanction of the same by the Governments concerned, supervise the carrying out of the said technical agreements.

2.   As the riparian states, other than the two Republics, claim a share in the Nile waters, the two Republics have agreed that they shall jointly consider and reach one unified view regarding the said claims. And if the said consideration results in the acceptance of allotting an amount of the Nile water to one or the other of the said states, the accepted amount shall be deducted from the shares of the two Republics in equal parts, as calculated at Aswan.

The Technical Commission mentioned in this agreement shall make the necessary arrangements with the states concerned, in order to ensure that their water consumption shall not exceed the amounts agreed upon.

Sixth:

TRANSITIONAL PERIOD BEFORE BENEFITING FROM THE
COMPLETE EL AALI RESERVOIR

As the benefiting of the two Republics from their appointed shares in the net benefit of the Sudd el Aali Reservoir shall not start before the construction and the full utilization of the Reservoir the two parties shall agree on their agricultural expansion programmes, in the transitional period from now up to the completion of the Sudd el Aali, without prejudice to their present water requirements.

Seventh:

This Agreement shall come into force after its sanction by the two contracting parties provided that either party shall notify the other party of the date of its sanction, through the diplomatic channels.

Eighth:

Annex (1) and Annex (2, A and B) attached to this Agreement shall be considered as an integral part of this Agreement.

Written in Cairo in two Arabic original copies this 7th day of Gumada El Ouda 1379, the 8th day of November 1959.

For the Republic of Sudan For the United Arab Republic
(*signed*)   (*signed*)

Lewa
MOHAMED TALAAT FARID ZAKARIA MOHIE EL DIN

Annex (1)
A SPECIAL PROVISION FOR THE WATER LOAN REQUIRED BY THE UNITED ARAB REPUBLIC

The Republic of the Sudan agrees in principle to give a water loan from the Sudan's share in the Sudd el Aali waters, to the United Arab Republic, in order to enable the latter to proceed with her planned programmes for Agricultural Expansion.

The request of the United Arab Republic for this loan shall be made after it revises its programmes within five years from the date of the signing of this agreement. And if the revision by United Arab Republic reveals her need for this loan, the Republic of Sudan shall give it out of its own share a loan not exceeding one and a half Milliards, provided that the utilization of this loan shall cease in November, 1977.

Annex (2 A)

To:

The Head of the Delegation of the Republic of Sudan.

With reference to Article (Second) paragraph 6 of the Agreement signed this day concerning the full utilization of the River Nile

Waters, compensation amounting to 15 Million Egyptian Pounds in sterling or in a third currency agreed upon by the two parties, and calculated on the basis of a fixed rate of $2.87156 to the Egyptian Pound, shall be paid by the Government of the United Arab Republic, as agreed upon, in instalments in the following manner:

£3 million on the first of January, 1960
£4 million on the first of January, 1961
£4 million on the first of January, 1962
£4 million on the first of January, 1963

I shall be grateful if you confirm your agreement to the above. With highest consideration.

> Head of the United Arab Republic Delegation
> (*signed*) Zakaria Mohie El Din

Annex (2 B)

To:
The Head of United Arab Republic Delegation.

I have the honour to acknowledge receipt of your letter dated today and stipulating the following:

'With reference to Article (Second) paragraph 6 of this agreement signed this day for the full utilization of the River Nile waters— compensation amounting to 15 million Egyptian Pounds in sterling or in a third currency agreed upon by the two parties and calculated on the basis of a fixed rate of $2.87156 dollars to the Egyptian Pound, shall be paid by the Government of United Arab Republic as agreed upon in instalments in the following manner:

£3 million as at 1st January, 1960
£4 million as at 1st January, 1961
£4 million as at 1st January, 1962
£4 million as at 1st January, 1963

I shall be grateful if you confirm your agreement to the above.'

I have the honour to confirm the agreement of the Government of the Republic of Sudan to the contents of the said letter.

With highest consideration.

> Head of the Delegation of the Republic of Sudan
> (Lewa)
> (*signed*) Mohamed Talaat Farid

Select Bibliography

The documentation concerning Jonglei is immense, and this Bibliography includes only those works which are particularly relevant to this book. Three repositories deserve special mention: the National Records Office, Khartoum, under the supervision of the historian and Sudan government archivist Muhammad Ahmad Ibrahim Abu Salim; the Public Records Office, London, notably the papers of the British Foreign Office (FO 371) and the Consular Files (FO 141); and the Sudan Archive, Durham University (SAD). All three contain, in public and private papers, extensive collections of information about the Nile waters and Jonglei which reflect the importance attached to the water and its control by both the imperialists and the inhabitants of the Nile Valley.

Abdulla, Ismael H. (1971). 'The 1959 Nile Waters Agreement in Sudanese–Egyptian Relations', *Middle East Journal*, 7.

Agius, S. (1982). 'Le Canal de Jonglei au Soudan', *La Revue Travaux*, 3/8.

Alier, Abel (1974). 'Statement to the People's Regional Assembly on the Proposed Jonglei Canal.' JEO, 1. Khartoum.

Allan, W. N. (1958). 'Decisions over Nile Waters', *The Economist*, 25 Jan.

Amin, Mohammed Bey, and Bambridge, H. G. (1950). *The Modified Jonglei Canal and Over-Year Storage Schemes*. Cairo.

Arthur, Sir George (1920). *The Life of Lord Kitchener*. 3 vols., London.

Associated Consultants (1981). *Small-Scale Abstraction of Water From Jonglei Canal*. 2 vols., Khartoum.

—— (1982). *Pipe Offtakes and Associated Structures*. Khartoum.

Awuol, James Ajith (1982). 'The Role of the Executive Organ, National Council for the Development of the Jonglei Area', in paper presented at The Impact of the Jonglei Canal in the Sudan Conference, Royal Geographical Society, London.

Badr, G. M. (1959). 'The Nile Waters Question: Background and Recent Development', *Revue Égyptienne de Droit International*, 15.

Bell, B. (1970). 'The Oldest Records of the Nile Flood', *Geo. J.*, 136.

Beshir, Mahdi E. (1987). 'On the History of Planning for the Jonglei Canal', *International Journal of Water Resources Development*, 3.

Beshir, Mohamed E. Mahdi (1979). *The Jonglei Canal Project*. Uppsala.

—— (1985). *The Jonglei Canal and the Upper Nile Swamps*. Wad Medani.

Beshir, Mohamed Omer (1968). *The Southern Sudan: Background to Conflict*. London.

—— (1974). 'The Jonglei Scheme—What Is It? What Is It For?' University of Khartoum.

—— (1975). *The Southern Sudan: From Conflict to Peace*. Khartoum.

—— (ed.) (1984). *The Nile Valley Countries: Continuity and Change*. 2 vols., Khartoum.

Brooks, C. E. P., and Mirrlees, S. T. A. (1932). 'Atmospheric Circulation over Central Africa', Geophysical Memoirs, 55, London: British Meteorological Office.

Broun, A. F. (1905). 'Some Notes on the "Sudd"—Formation of the Upper Nile', *Journal of the Linnean Society (Botany)*, 37.

Bureau of Reclamation, US Department of the Interior (1964). *Land and Water Resources of the Blue Nile Basin: Ethiopia*. 14 vols. and 5 apps., Washington, DC.

Butcher, A. D. (1936a). *The Future of the Sudd Region*. Cairo.

—— (1936b). *The Jonglei Canal Scheme*. Cairo.

—— (1936c). *Upper Nile Projects: The Jonglei Canal Scheme*. Cairo.

—— (1938a). *The Bahr El Jebel Banking Scheme*. Cairo.

—— (1938b). *The Jonglei Canal Diversion Scheme*. Cairo.

—— (1938c). *The Jonglei Canal Project*. Cairo.

—— (1938d). *The Sadd Hydraulics*. Cairo.

—— (1938e). *The Veveno–Pibor Scheme*. Cairo.

—— (1939). *Zeraf Hydraulics*. Cairo.

Cecil, Lady Gwendolen. (1929–32). *Life of Robert, Marquis of Salisbury*. 4 vols., London.

Chavanne, J. (1883). *Afrikas Ströme und Flüsse*. Vienna.

Chélu, A. (1891). *Le Nil, le Soudan, l'Égypte*. Paris.

—— (1910). *Le Nil et son Bassin*. Paris.

Chirol, Sir Valentine (1920). *The Egyptian Problem*. London.

Cobb, Stephen, *et al.* (1982). 'Ecological Studies of the Jonglei Area', in *The Impact of the Jonglei Canal in the Sudan*. London.

Collins, Robert O. (1972). *Land Beyond the Rivers: The Southern Sudan 1898–1918*. New Haven, Conn.

—— (1983). *Shadows in the Grass: Britain in the Southern Sudan 1918–1956*. New Haven, Conn.

—— (1985). 'The Big Ditch: The Jonglei Canal Scheme', in Daly (1985).

—— (1987). 'The Jonglei Canal: The Past and the Present of a Future', 6th Trevelyan Lecture, University of Durham.

Cory, H. T. (1920). 'Report on Second and Third Terms of Reference', in Nile Projects Commission (1920).

Craig, J. I. (1910). 'England—Abyssinia—The South Atlantic: A Meteorological Triangle', *Quarterly Journal of the Royal Meteorological Society*, 36.

Daly, G. (1984). 'In Search of the "New" Nuer: an Anthropological Study of New Fangak [a Nuer town] and its Hinterland'. Interim Report, Department of Sociology, Trinity College, Dublin.

Daly, M. W. (ed.) (1985). *Modernization in the Sudan: Essays in Honor of Richard Hill*. New York.

—— (1986). *Empire on the Nile: The Anglo-Egyptian Sudan, 1898-1945*. New York.

Deng, P. L., Van den Hoek, B., and Zanen, S. (1978). 'Interim Report on the Easter Realignment of the Jonglei Canal'. Bor: JEO and Ministry of Foreign Affairs, Netherlands.

Drar, N. (1951). 'The Problem of the Sudd in Relation to Stabilizing and Smothering Plants', *Botaniska Notiser*, 1.

Dupuis, C. E. (1904). 'A Report upon Lake Tana and the Rivers of the Eastern Sudan', in Garstin (1904).

Earthscan (1978). 'The Jonglei Canal', Briefing Document No. 8, London: International Institute for Environment and Development.

Economist, The (1982). 'Re-inventing the Water-Wheel', 22–8 May.

Egyptian Irrigation Service in the Sudan (1947). 'General Comments on the Jonglei Investigation Team's First Interim Report of June 1946'. Khartoum.

Egyptian Ministry of Irrigation (1980). 'Jonglei Canal Project, Phase I and II: Water Cost Study'. Cairo.

Egyptian Ministry of Public Works (1947). 'The Combination of a Large Reservoir in Lake Albert'. Cairo.

—— (1948). 'Nile Control: Agreed Conclusions of Technical Discussions on 17th and 18th February 1948' under 'Egypt, Sudan and Uganda', in *Annual Reports of the Egyptian Irrigation Department*. Cairo.

—— (1981). *Water Master Plan*. 17 vols., UNDP/EGY/73/024, Cairo.

El Amin, M., and Ezeat, Nasser (1978). 'Jonglei Canal Water Benefit (Offtake at Bor)'. PJTC, Khartoum.

El Beshir, Mehdi (1981). 'The Jonglei Canal', Ph.D. thesis, University of Khartoum.

El Hassen, M. A. K., Fadul, H. M., Ali, M. A., and El Tom, O. A. (1978). *Exploratory Soil Survey and Land Suitability Classification of*

Jonglei Projects Area, Southern Region. Soil Survey Report No. 90. Khartoum.

El Hemry, I. I., and Eagleson, P. S. (1980). *Water Balance Estimates of the Machar Marshes.* Report No. 260, Boston, Mass.

El Moghrabi, A. I. (1984). 'The Jonglei Canal', in Beshir (1984, vol. ii).

El Sammani, Mohamed Osman (1978). 'The Existing Services in Kongor and Bor Districts', Report No. 6, JEO, Khartoum.

—— (1984*a*). *Jonglei Canal: Dynamics of Planned Change in the Twic Area.* Khartoum.

—— (1984*b*). 'Socio-Economic Research and the Approach to Change in the Jonglei Canal Area', in Beshir (1984, vol. ii).

—— (1985). 'The Jonglei Canal: An Evolution of the Project Model'. Paper presented at conference on north–south relations since the Addis Ababa Agreement, 6–9 Mar. Khartoum.

—— and Deng, P. L. (1978). 'The Seasonal Migration of the People and their Livestock in Kongor and Bor Districts'. Report No. 10, JEO, Khartoum.

—— and El Amin, Farouk Mohamed (1977). 'The Impact of the Extension of Jonglei Canal on the Area from Kongor to Bor'. Report No. 3, JEO, Khartoum.

—— and Hassan, A. (1978). 'Agriculture in the Dinka and Nuer Land (Jonglei Province)'. Report No. 10, JEO, Khartoum.

Eshman, Robert (1983). 'The Jonglei Canal: A Ditch Too Big?', *Environment*, 25.

Euroconsult (1976–9). 'Jonglei Structures, Phase One: Interim Report'. 3 Nos., Arnhem.

—— (1977). 'Summary of Available Data on Khor Chiet Diversion of Khor Chiet into the Canal; Preliminary Study of a Solution Type Canal'. Jonglei Canal Project, Report No. 1, Arnhem.

—— (1977–8). 'Jonglei Canal Project, Phase One: Progress Report'. 3 Nos., Arnhem.

—— (1978). 'Jonglei Environmental Aspects'. Arnhem.

—— (1981). 'Jonglei Structures Project, Phase One: Progress Report No. 4'. 2 vols., Arnhem.

Evans, T. E. (1987). Letter to *The Times*, 14 Nov.

Fabunni, L. A. (1960). *The Sudan in Anglo-Egyptian Relations: A Case Study in Power Politics.* London.

Farmer, G. (1981). 'Regionalisation and Study of an Alleged Change in the Rainfall Climatology of East Africa'. Ph.D. thesis, University of Sheffield.

Garang, Mading de (1980). 'Address to Meeting for Co-ordination of JEO Works Plans for 1981'. JEO, Khartoum.

Garang de Mabior, John (1981). 'Identifying, Selecting and Implementing Rural Development Strategies for Socio-Economic Development in the Jonglei Projects Area, Southern Region, Sudan'. Ph.D. thesis, Iowa State University, Ames, Ia.

Garretson, A. H. (1960). 'The Nile River System', *Proceedings of the American Society of International Law*, 54.

—— (1967). 'The Nile Basin', in A. H. Garretson, R. D. Hayton, and C. J. Olmstead (eds.), *The Law of International Drainage Basins*. New York.

Garstin, Sir W. (1899*a*). 'Note on the Soudan', *Egypt* No. 5. London.

—— (1899*b*). 'Report on the Sudan', *Parliamentary Accounts and Papers 1899*, 112.

—— (1901*a*). 'Irrigation Projects on the Upper Nile', *Egypt* No. 2. London.

—— (1901*b*). 'Report as to Irrigation Projects on the Upper Nile, etc.', *Parliamentary Accounts and Papers 1901*, 91.

—— (ed.) (1904). *Report upon the Basin of the Upper Nile*. London: HMSO.

—— (1909). 'Fifty Years of Nile Exploration, and Some Results', *Geo. J.*, 33.

Gasarasi, C. P. (1981). 'The "Pooling of Resources" Approach to Development in a Regional Integration Grouping: The Organization for the Management and Development of the Kagera River Basin'. Paper presented at the Conference on the Nile basin, (Sudanese) Institute of African and Asian Studies, Khartoum.

Gibbon, E. (1946). *The Decline and Fall of the Roman Empire*. 3 vols., New York.

Gleichen, Count von (ed.) (1905). *The Anglo-Egyptian Sudan—A Compendium Prepared by Officers of the Sudan Government*. London.

Glennie, J. F. (1957). 'The Equatorial Nile Project', *SNR*, 38.

Godana, Bonaya Adhi (1985). *Africa's Shared Water Resources*. London.

Grabham, G. W., and Black, R. P. (1925). *Report of the Mission to Lake Tana 1920–21*. Cairo.

GTM (Grands Travaux de Marseille) (1980–5). *Annual Reports*.

Guariso, Giorgio, *et al.* (1987). 'Implications of Ethiopian Water Development for Egypt and Sudan', *Water Resources Development*, 3.

Hady, M. Samaha Abdel (1979). 'The Egyptian Water Master Plan', *Water Supply and Management*, 3.

Hoedreböe, Kjell (n.d.). 'Cattle and Flies: A Study of the Cattle Keeping in Equatoria Province, Southern Sudan, 1850–1950', University of Bergen.

Hoek, Bert van den, *et al.* (1978). 'Social Anthropological Aspects of

420   BIBLIOGRAPHY

the Jonglei Development Projects in South Sudan', Fieldwork
Report, Instituut voor Culturele Antropologie en Sociologie der
Niet-Westerse Volken, Rijksuniversiteit Leiden.

Hope, C. W. (1902). 'The Sudd of the Upper Nile: Its Botany Compared with That of Similar Obstructions in Bengal and American
Waters', *Annals of Botany*, 16.

Hopkins, A. G. (1986). 'The Victorians and Africans: A Recon-
sideration of the Egyptian Occupation of Egypt, 1882', *JAH*, 27/2.

Horn of Africa (1985). 8/1.

Hosni, M. (1967). 'Legal Problems of the Development of the River
Nile', Ph.D. thesis, University of New York.

Howell, Paul P. (1953). 'The Equatorial Nile Project and its Effects
in the Sudan', *Geo. J.*, 119.

—— (1959). 'The Ultimate Requirements of Irrigation Water from
the Nile Basin in the East African Territories'. Howell papers.

—— (1982). 'The Equatorial Nile Project and the Jonglei Canal',
paper presented at The Impact of the Jonglei Canal in the Sudan
Conference, Royal Geographical Society, London

—— (1983). 'The Impact of the Jonglei Canal in the Sudan', *Geo. J.*,
149.

—— (n.d.). 'The Equatorial Nile Project and the Nile Waters Agreement of 1929: Uganda's Case'. Howell papers.

—— Lock, M., and Cobb, S. (1988). *The Jonglei Canal: Impact and
Opportunity*. Cambridge.

Hurst, H. E. (1925, 1927). *Report on Lake Plateau Basin of the Nile*, vols.
i and ii. Cairo.

—— (1927). 'Progress in the Study of the Hydrology of the Nile in
the Last Twenty Years', *Geo. J.*, 70.

—— (1952). *The Nile*. London.

—— Black, R. P., and Simaika, Y. M. (1965). *Long-Term Storage: An
Experimental Study*. London.

—— *et al.* (1931–66). *The Nile Basin*. 10 vols. with supplements.
Vols. i–ix, Cairo; MPW. Vol. x, Cairo: Ministry of Irrigation.
This series includes the famous vol. vii, *The Future Conservation of
the Nile* (1946).

—— *et al.* (1960). 'Discussion on Planning for the Ultimate Hydraulic
Development of the Nile Valley', *Proc. Inst. Civ. Engrs.*, v. 16
(July).

Hussein Sirry Pasha (1935). *Irrigation Policy*. Cairo.

—— (1937). *Irrigation in Egypt*. Cairo.

Hydromet (1968): *Hydrometeorological Survey of the Catchments of Lakes
Victoria, Kyoga and Albert*. Entebbe.

—— (1974): *Hydrometeorological Survey of the Catchments of Lakes Victoria,
Kyoga and Albert*. 4 vols., RAF/66/025, Geneva.

—— (1981): *Hydrometeorological Survey of the Catchments of Lakes Victoria, Kyoga, and Mobutu Sese Seku: Project Findings and Recommendations.* RAF/73/001. Geneva.

Ibrahim, Abdullah Mohammed (1974). 'Reply to Points Raised by Opponents to Jonglei Canal Project', Jonglei Commission Public Relations Files, Khartoum.

—— (1975). 'The Jonglei Development Project—1975', *Sudan International*, 1.

—— (1977). 'In Defense of the Jonglei Canal Project', speech at the American University, Cairo (Dec.).

—— (1984a). 'Development of the Nile River System', in Beshir (1984, vol. i).

—— (1984b). 'The Environmental Impact of the Jonglei Canal in the Sudan in Beshir', (1984, vol. ii).

—— and El Nur, Mohammed El Amin M. (1976). 'Bahr el Jebel Discharge Losses as a Result of the Jonglei Canal', PJTC, Khartoum.

—— and Nur, M. A. (1981). 'Increase of Nile Yield by Utilization of Lost Waters in Machar Marshes and Lost Waters in Ghazal Swamps', PJTC, Khartoum.

ILACO (International Land-Use Company) (1981). *Penykou Plain Development Project.* 2 vols., Arnhem.

—— and Kingdom of the Netherlands (1979). 'Kongor Integrated Rural Development Project: Project Plan'. Arnhem.

Jal, G. G. (1987). 'The History of the Jikany Nuer Before 1920', Ph.D. thesis, University of London.

Jenness, Jonathan (1982). 'Planning for Development of Landuse in the Jonglei', paper presented at The Impact of the Jonglei Canal in the Sudan Conference, Royal Geographical Society, London.

JEO (Executive Organ for Development Projects in the Jonglei Area) (1975). 'The Jonglei Project: Phase One'. Khartoum.

—— (1976a). 'The Jonglei Canal'. Khartoum.

—— (1976b). 'Regulations of the National Council for the Development Projects in the Jonglei Area'. Khartoum.

—— (1976c). 'A Request for the Funding of Development Projects in the Jonglei Area'. Khartoum.

—— (1979). 'Comparative Socio-Economic Benefits of the Eastern Alignment and the Direct Jonglei Canal Line'. Khartoum.

—— (1980a). 'Jonglei Canal: A Development Project in the Sudan'. Khartoum.

—— (1980b). 'Report on Meeting for Coordination of Jonglei Executive Organ Work Plans, 1981, Khartoum, 27–29 Oct. 1980'. Khartoum.

—— (1981a). 'Programmes of the Executive Organ of the National Council for the Development in the Jonglei Canal Area'. Khartoum.

—— (1981b). 'Progress Report: April 1, 1979 to August 31, 1981', Khartoum.

—— (1982a). 'A Brief Note on the Progress in the Development Programme of the Executive Organ of the National Council for the Development in the Jonglei Area'. Khartoum.

—— (1982b). 'A Comprehensive Plan for the Development of Community Services in the Jonglei Canal Area, the Sudan', Draft 0136 S, Khartoum.

—— (1983–5). 'Meeting for Coordination of Jonglei Executive Organ Work Plans, 1984', Bor.

—— and UNDP (United Nations Development Programme) (1979). 'Integrated Rural Development in the Kongor District'. SUD/78/016, Khartoum.

Johnson, D. H. (1988). 'Adaptations to Floods in the Jonglei Area: A Historical Analysis', in D. H. Johnson and D. Anderson (eds.), *The Ecology of Survival*. London.

Johnston, Sir H. H. (1906). *The Nile Quest*. London.

Jonglei Investigation Team (1950a). 'First Three Interim Reports'. London and Khartoum.

—— (1950b). '1949 Annual Progress Report'. London and Khartoum.

—— (1954). *The Equatorial Nile Project and its Effects in The Anglo-Egyptian Sudan*. 4 vols.

Kamal, A. M. (1982). 'The Design and Construction of the Jonglei Project', in paper presented at The Impact of the Jonglei Canal in the Sudan Conference, Royal Geographical Society, London.

Kamel, Ghaleb Pasha (1951). 'Le Mikyas au Nilomètre de l'Île de Rodah', *Mémoires de l'Institut d'Égypte* (Cairo).

Keller, H., and Kalfe, Baudouin (1966). *The Nile Waters Question in View of the Nile Agreement, 1959*. Basle.

Kendall, R. L. (1969). 'An Ecological History of the Lake Victoria Basin', *Ecological Monographs*, 39.

Khalid, M. (1966). *Le Régime international des eaux du Nil*. Paris.

Kirwan, L. P. (1957). 'Rome Beyond the Southern Egyptian Frontier', *Geo J.*, 123.

Kite, G. W. (1981). 'Recent Changes in Level of Lake Victoria', *Hydrological Sciences Journal*, 26.

—— (1982). 'Analysis of Lake Victoria Levels', *Hydrological Sciences Journal*, 27.

Klemens, V. (1974). 'The Hurst Phenomenon: A Puzzle?', *Water Resources Research*, 10.

Klöden, G. von (1856). *Das Stromsystem des oberen Nil*. Berlin.

Lako, George Tombe (1985). 'The Impact of the Jonglei Scheme on the Economy of the Dinka', *African Affairs*, 84.

Langer, William L. (1956). *The Diplomacy of Imperialism, 1850–1902*. New York.

Lawry, Steven (1982). 'The Jonglei Canal and the Endogenous Change: A New Framework for Policy Analysis', in paper presented at The Impact of the Jonglei Canal in the Sudan Conference, Royal Geographical Society, London.

Lombardini, Elia (1984). 'Saggio idrologico sul Nilo', *Memorie del R. Istituto Lombardo*, x (Milan).

——(1865). *Essai sur l'hydrographie du Nil*. Milan.

Lyall, Sir Alfred (1905). *The Life of the Marquis of Dufferin and Ava*. 2 vols., London.

Lyons, Capt H. G. (1906). *The Physiography of the River Nile and its Basin*. Cairo.

McCann, James (1981). 'Ethiopia, Britain and Negotiations for the Lake Tana Dam, 1922–35', *IJAHS*, 14.

McDonald, Sir Murdoch (1920). *Nile Control*. 2 vols. (2nd edn., 1921). Cairo.

MacGregor, R. M., and Suleiman, Abdel Hamid (1926). *The Nile Commission Report*. Cairo.

Magid, Yahia Abdel (1975a). 'Control and Use of Nile Water in Sudan', Ministry of Irrigation and Hydroelectric Power. Khartoum.

——(1975b). 'Problems Encountered in Integrated River Basin Development: The Case of the Nile Basin', in *Proceedings of the UN Conference on Interbasin Development*. Budapest.

——(1982). 'The Conservation Projects of the Nile and Irrigation Development in the Sudan'. Paper presented at Royal Geographic Society Conference, London.

——(1984). 'Integrated River Basin Development: A Challenge to the Nile Basin Countries', in Beshir (1984, vol. i).

Maitland, Alexander (1971). *Speke*. London.

Mann, O. (1977). 'The Jonglei Canal: Environmental and Social Aspects'. Environment Liaison Centre. Nairobi.

Marcus, H. G. (1987). *Haile Sellassie I: The Formative Years, 1892–1936*. Berkeley, Calif.

Maswanya, Hon. S. A., Minister for Home Affairs, Tanzania (1968). Hydrometeorological speech, 27 Feb. 1967, in *Hydromet* (1968).

Matronne, M. E. de (1897). 'Hydrographie des oberen Nil-Beckens', *Zeitschrift den Gesellschaft für Erdkunde*, 5.

Mefit–Babtie Srl. (1980). 'First Interim Report: Range Ecology Survey, Livestock Investigation and Water Supply'. Glasgow, Khartoum, and Rome.

——(Apr. 1983). *Development Studies in the Jonglei Canal Area: Final Report*. 10 vols., Glasgow, Khartoum, and Rome. (Vol. i, *Summary*;

ii, *Background*; iii, *Vegetation Studies*; iv, *Livestock Studies*; v, *Wildlife Studies*; vi, *Water Supply*; vii, *Interactions Within the Jonglei System*; viii, *Effects of the Canal*; ix, *Recommendations*; x, *Maps*.)

—— (Oct. 1983). *Development Studies in the Jonglei Canal Area: Final Report*. 4 vols., Glasgow, Khartoum, and Rome. (Vol. i, *Introduction, Summary, Conclusions*; ii, *Limnological and Plant Studies*; iii, *Invertebrate and Fish Studies*; iv, *Fisheries Socio-Economic and Technical Studies*.)

Migahid, A. M. (1952). *Further Observations on the Flow and Loss of Water in the Sudd Swamps of the Upper Nile*, Cairo.

Ministry of Irrigation and Hydroelectric Power (Sudan) (1955). *The Nile Waters Question: The Case for the Sudan, the Case for Egypt, and the Sudan's Reply*. Khartoum.

—— (1975). *Control and Use of the Nile Waters in the Sudan*. Khartoum.

—— (1976). *Jonglei Canal Project*. (Agreement between the Ministry of Irrigation and Hydro-electric Energy and CCI/CFE, 28 July.) Nanterre.

—— (1978). Vol. i of *The Main Report: Blue Nile Water Study*, vol. i: *Phase 1A: Availability and Use of Blue Nile Water*. Khartoum.

—— (1980). *Jonglei Canal Project: Eastern Alignment to Bor*. (Agreement between Ministry of Irrigation and CCI/CFE.) Nanterre.

—— (1981). *The Nile Master Water Plan*. 17 vols., UNDP/EGY/73/ 024, Cairo.

Moghraby, A. I., and El Sammani, M. O. (1985). 'On the Environmental and Socio-Economic Impact of the Jonglei Canal Project', *Environmental Conservation*, 12.

Mohammedein, M. A. (1982). 'The Objective of the Jonglei Canal Project', in paper presented at The Impact of the Jonglei Canal in the Sudan Conference, Royal Geographical Society, London.

Morrice, H. A. W. (1945). *The Chasm: The Protest of an Engineer*. London.

—— (1957). 'Electronics Applied to Water Storage on the Nile', *The Times*, 22 Mar.

—— and Allan, William Nimmo (1958). *Report on the Nile Valley Plan*. 2 vols.

—— and—— (1959). 'Planning for the Ultimate Hydraulic Development of the Nile Valley', *Proc. Inst. Civ. Engrs.*, No. 6372, vol. xiv.

—— *et al.* (1959). 'Discussion on Planning for the Ultimate Hydraulic Development of the Nile Valley', *Proc. Inst. Civ. Engrs.*, 14.

Mörth, H. T. (1967). 'Investigation into the Meteorological Aspects of the Variations in the Level of Lake Victoria'. Meteorological Department, East African Common Services Organization, Nairobi.

Müller, Fritz F. (1959). *Deutschland–Zanzibar–Ostafrica*. East Berlin.

Muller, Mike (1978). 'The Jonglei Canal', Earthscan Press Briefing Document No. 8. London.

—— (1977). 'The Next Great Canal: A Vast New Nile Project Will Soon Save Water and Change Life Styles', *Atlas World Press Review*, 25.

Murray, I. (1987). 'The Mighty Cradle of Civilization Is Drying Up', *The Times*, 5 Nov.

Newhouse, F. (1929). *The Problem of the Upper Nile*. Cairo.

—— (1939). *The Training of the Upper Nile*. London.

Nile Projects Commission (1920). *Report of the Nile Projects Commission*. Cairo.

—— (1955). *The Nile Waters Question*. Khartoum.

Okidi, Charles O. (1980). 'International Laws and the Lake Victoria and Nile Basins', *Indian Journal of International Law*, 20.

Parker, Geoffrey, and Mackintosh, W. D. (1934). 'The Veveno–Pibor Canal Project Survey', *Geo. J.*, 84.

Payne, W. J. A. (1979). 'Economic and Social Aspects of the Various Alignment Proposals for the Jonglei Canal', UNDP, Khartoum.

Penman, H. L. (1963). *Vegetation and Hydrology*. Technical Commission 53. Farnham, UK.

Peters, Karl (1891). *Die deutsche Amin-Pascha Expedition*. Munich.

Piper, B. S., Plinston, D. T., and Sutcliffe, J. V. (1986). 'The Water Balance of Lake Victoria', *Hydrological Sciences Journal*, 31.

PJTC (Permanent Joint Technical Commission for Nile Waters) (1959). 'Agreement Between the Republic of the Sudan and the United Arab Republic for the Full Utilization of the Nile Waters', 8 Nov. (see Appendix above.)

—— (1981a) 'The Jonglei Canal Project: An Economic Evaluation'. Khartoum.

—— (1981b). *Jonglei Project: Project Evaluation*. Khartoum.

—— (1982). *Jonglei Project Evaluation, Text and Drawings*. Khartoum.

Platenkamp, Jos D. M. (1978). *The Jonglei Canal: Its Impact on an Integrated System in the Southern Sudan*. Publication No. 26, Instituut voor Culturele Antropologie en Sociologie der Niet-Westerse Volken, Rijksuniversiteit Leiden.

Proceedings of the Royal Geographical Society. These contain a multitude of references to the Nile and upper Nile, particularly in the nineteenth century, when the Society was directly involved in the search for the source (Baker, Brun Rollet, Du Chaillu, Chaille Long, d'Escayne de Hauture, Gessi, Gordon, Speke and Grant, Petherick, Schweinfurth, Thibaut, Tinné). The references are too numerous to include in this Bibliography; but the enquiring reader should consult the excellent *General Index to the Proceedings of the Royal Geographical Society*.

Prunier, Gerard (1986). *From Peace to War in the Southern Sudan 1972–1984*. Occasional Paper No. 3, Department of Sociology and Social Anthropology, University of Hull.

Rijks, D. A. (1969). 'Evaporation From a Papyrus Swamp', *Quarterly Journal of the Royal Meteorological Society*, 95.

Roberts, W. D. (1928). *Irrigation Projects in the Upper Nile and their Effects on Tribal and Local Interests*. Cairo.

Robinson, Ronald, Gallagher, John, and Denny, Alice (1981). *Africa and the Victorians*. 2nd edn., New York.

Rodenberg, Joachin F., and Blanc, Pierre (1982). 'A Bucket Wheel Excavator for Canal Building on Two Continents'. Lübeck and Nanterre.

Ross, J. C. (1893). 'Irrigation and Agriculture in Egypt', *Scottish Geographical Magazine*, 9.

Rzoska, J. (1974). 'The Upper Nile Swamps: A Tropical Wetland Study', *Freshwater Biology*, 4.

—— (ed.) (1976). *The Nile: Biology of an Ancient River*. The Hague.

Sagheyroon, S. E. (1966). 'Proposed Projects for Utilization of the Sudan Share of Nile Water', *Sudan Engineering Society Journal*, 11.

Sanderson, G. N. (1965). *England, Europe, and the Upper Nile, 1882–1899*. Edinburgh.

Sayed, H. E. (1982). 'Irrigation for the Sudan and Utilisation of the Increased Nile Yield', paper presented at Impact of the Jonglei Canal in the Sudan Conference, Royal Geographical Society, London.

—— *et al.* (1982). 'The Construction of the Jonglei Canal', paper presented at Impact of the Jonglei Canal in the Sudan Conference, Royal Geographical Society, London.

Seaton, E. E., and Maliti, S. T. (1973). *Tanzania Threat Practice*. Nairobi.

Seed, N. Tagvi (1984). 'Jonglei Canal and the Treaty of Aquatic Weeds', in Beshir (1984, vol. i).

Shahin, Mamdouh (1985). *Hydrology of the Nile Basin*. New York.

Smythe, William E. (1920). 'The Struggle for the Nile', *American Review of Reviews*, 62.

South Dakota State University (1978). *Remote Sensing Studies of the Jonglei Canal Area*. Brookings, S. Dak.

Southern Development Investigation Team (1955). *Natural Resources and Development Potential in the Southern Provinces of the Sudan: A Preliminary Report by the Southern Development Investigation Team, 1954*. London.

Stanley, Sir H. M. (1878). *In Darkest Africa*. London.

Stewart, Cosmo (1927). 'Sudd Cutting', *Blackwood's Magazine*, 221.

Sudan Meteorological Department (1973). 'Rainfall Averages 1941–1970'. Khartoum.

Sudan Monthly Record (Feb.–Mar. 1952). 'The Equatorial Nile Project'.

Sudan Peoples Liberation Movement (1983). 'Manifesto', 31 July.

Sutcliffe, J. V. (1957). 'The Hydrology of the Sudd Region of the Upper Nile'. Ph.D. thesis, Cambridge.

—— (1974). 'A Hydrological Study of the Southern Sudd Region of the Upper Nile', *Hydrological Sciences*, 19.

—— and Parks, Y. P. (1982*a*). 'An Assessment of the Effect of the Jonglei Canal on Areas of Seasonal Flooding', paper presented at The Impact of the Jonglei Canal in the Sudan Conference, Royal Geographical Society, London.

—— and —— (1982*b*). 'A Hydrological Estimate of the Effects of the Jonglei Canal on Areas of Flooding'. Institute of Hydrology, Wallingford, UK, for FAO.

—— and —— (1987). 'Hydrological Modelling of the Sudd and Jonglei Canal', *Hydrological Sciences Journal*, 32/2.

Tahir, Abdullahi A., and El Sammani, Mohamed Osman (1978). 'Environmental and Socio-economic Impact of the Jonglei Canal Project'. JEO, Khartoum.

Tignor, Robert L. (1977). 'Nationalism, Economic Planning and Development Projects in Interior Egypt', *IJAHS*, 10/2.

Times, The (1958). 'The Disputed Waters of the Nile', 23 Sept.

Tottenham, P. M. (1913). *Report on the Upper Nile Project*. Cairo.

Tvedt, Terje (1981). 'The Jonglei Canal: A Case Study in Water Planning'. Proposal for a Ph.D. thesis, University of Bergen.

University of Juba (1986). *The Role of the Southern Sudanese People in the Building of the Modern Sudan*. Juba.

US Department of the Interior (1962). 'Sudan: Official Standard Names Approved by the United States Board on Geographic Names', *Gazetteer No. 68*, Washington, DC.

—— (1964). *Land and Water Resources of the Blue Nile Basin: Ethiopia*. 17 vols., Washington, DC.

Ventre, Pasha (1894). 'Hydrologie du bassin du Nil', *Bulletin de la Société de Géographie*.

Waterbury, John (1979). *Hydropolitics of the Nile Valley*. Syracuse, NY.

—— (1982). 'Riverains and Lacustrines: Towards International Co-operation in the Nile Basin', Discussion Paper No. 7, Research Program in Development Studies, Princeton University, Princeton, NJ.

—— (1984). 'The Near-Term Challenge of Managing Water Resources in the Nile Basin', M. O. Beshir (ed.). *The Nile Valley Countries: Continuity and Change*, vol. i. Khartoum.

—— (1987). 'Legal and Institutional Arrangements for Managing Water Resources in the Nile Basin', *International Journal of Water Resources Development*, 3/2.

Watt, D. C. (1968). 'The High Dam at Aswan and the Politics of Control', in N. Rubin and W. M. Warren (eds.) *Dams in Africa*.

Weaver, R. (ed.) (1937). *The Dictionary of National Biography: 1922–1930*. London.

Wells, Rick (1982). 'Sudan's Giant Furrow Will Have Far-reaching Effects', *Financial Times*, 5 Oct.

Westlake, C. R., Mountain, R. W., and Paton, T. A. L. (1954). 'Owen Falls, Uganda, Hydro-electric Development', *Proc. Inst. Civ. Engrs.*, 3 (pt. 1).

Whittington, D., and Haynes, K. E. (1985). 'Nile Water for Whom? Emerging Conflicts in Water Allocation for Agricultural Expansion in Egypt and Sudan', in P. Beaumont and K. McLaughlin (eds.), *Agricultural Development in the Middle East*. London.

Willcocks, Sir William (1894). *Perennial Irrigation and Flood Protection for Egypt*. Cairo.

—— (1908). *The Nile in 1904*. London.

—— (1913). *Egyptian Irrigation*. 2nd edn., 2 vols., London.

—— (1919). *The Nile Projects*. Cairo.

Williams, C. R. (1986). *Wheels and Paddles in the Sudan, 1923–1946*. Edinburgh.

Winder, J. (1952). 'The Equatorial Nile Project', *SNR*, 33/1.

—— (n.d.). 'Unpublished Reports on the Jonglei Scheme', Durham: SAD.

WMO (World Meteorological Organization) (1967). Third draft of the 'Plan of Operation'. Khartoum.

—— (1971). Amendment No. 1 to the 'Plan of Operation'. Khartoum.

—— (1977). 'Hydrologic Model of the Upper Nile Basin.' 7 vols. Prepared by Snowy Mountains Engineering Corporation, Geneva.

—— (1980). 'Lake Victoria Levels, 1950–1980'. Unpublished report. Entebbe.

Woolf, Leonard (1968). *Empire and Commerce in Africa*. New York.

Worall, N. (1978). 'Jonglei Canal', *Financial Times*, 12 Apr.

Worthington, E. B. (1929). 'The Life of Lake Albert and Lake Kioga', *Geo. J.*, 74.

—— (1972). 'The Nile Catchment', in M. T. Farvar and J. P. Milton (eds.), *The Careless Technology*. New York.

Wright, J. W. (1949). 'The White Nile Flood Plain and the Effect of Proposed Control Schemes', *Geo. J.*, 114.

—— (1950). 'The White Nile and the Sobat', *SNR*, 32.

Yong, Daniel D. (1976). 'The Development Aspect of Jonglei Scheme in the Sudan'. Paper presented at seminar on socio-economic studies in Jonglei area, Cairo, 12–15 Jan. Khartoum: JEO.

—— (1982). 'A Brief Note on the Progress in the Development Programme of the Executive Organ of the National Council for the Development in the Jonglei Area'. Khartoum: JEO.

Index